A Handbook of
Christian Theologians

A Handbook of
Christian Theologians

*Edited by Dean G. Peerman
and Martin E. Marty*

Abingdon
Nashville

A HANDBOOK OF CHRISTIAN THEOLOGIANS

Copyright © 1965 assigned to Abingdon

ISBN-0-687-16566-0

PREVIOUSLY PUBLISHED AS ISBN 0-529-01988-4
BY THE WORLD PUBLISHING COMPANY.

Library of Congress catalog card number: 65-18010

MANUFACTURED BY THE PARTHENON PRESS AT
NASHVILLE, TENNESSEE, UNITED STATES OF AMERICA

CONTENTS

6 Contents

A Handbook of
Christian Theologians

INTRODUCTION

A Handbook of Christian Theologians is a companion volume to *A Handbook of Christian Theology.* The earlier handbook, published in 1958, provided readers with 101 brief definitions of theological terms as used in present-day religious writing. *Theology* is a term which refers to words and ideas about God and the world. These words and ideas do not make their way in disincarnate fashion but are developed and discussed by individuals called theologians. In each generation those who form words and ideas about God and the world give a distinctive shape and pattern to these words and ideas. No one can profess to have a rounded view of theology without looking squarely at theologians. Twenty-six authors propose to do just that in the present book.

As inheritors of a pattern and a procedure, we are grateful for the achievement of the earlier handbook. At the same time, we confess to a certain uneasiness as we apply the term "Christian" to a group of men who happen to belong to the non-Roman-Catholic half of the Christian world. With the exception of the Russian Orthodox thinker Nicolai Berdyaev, all the theologians discussed herein could be classified as Protestant. The absence of Roman Catholic thinkers is not the only limitation imposed by the brevity of this work. We have concentrated first on the giants who gave a new language to theology in the nineteenth century. The second part of the book deals with a number of thinkers who refined that tradition. In the third section we turn to the main line of theological thought of the past three decades.

Such an outline finds us neglecting much liberal theology of the second through the fourth decades of our century. In particular we have had to slight philosophical theology. Readers who are familiar with this form of inquiry will note the absence of chapters on William Ernest Hocking, Edgar S. Brightman, William R. Inge, Henry Nelson Wieman, and numbers of others whose stature is comparable to that of many of the twenty-six who are included. We apologize for not being able to include in one volume all those we would have liked to include (particularly do we regret the omission, owing to an unfortunate concatenation of circumstances, of a scheduled essay on the great nineteenth-century theologian Ernst Troeltsch); nevertheless we justify this handbook on the grounds that the twenty-six theologians dealt with represent types of theologizing which have evoked much curiosity throughout the Christian world. Perhaps in a future volume it will be possible to enlarge the number of prominent thinkers to be given handbook-sized attention.

The earlier handbook listed its 101 theological concepts in alphabetical order. Such an arrangement is not feasible here. The present volume has a plot—one which tries to do some justice to three general ways of talking about God and the world. While no convenient labels adequately describe these three ways, we shall try to characterize them.

Each of the three sections begins with one or two theologians who have employed the category "religion." That is, they began their enterprise by giving due notice to human experience of the spiritual or the divine. Any history of theology in the past two centuries must begin with Friedrich Schleiermacher. He came upon the scene at the end of the Enlightenment, after men had long been speaking about laws of nature and nature's God. Suddenly, with Schleiermacher, all the categories of Christian thought were reinvested with meaning. In the United States, Horace Bushnell, working independently, came to beknown as "the American Schleiermacher"; he shared Schleiermacher's interests and his somewhat romantic view of human response.

In the early twentieth century Rudolf Otto, a devotee of Schleiermacher, traded upon the newer interests in world religions and concentrated on "the holy" as a basis for theology.

More recently, the Swedish theologian Anders Nygren has made a motif-study of religion the basis of his work. The second cluster of thinkers in each of the three sections come at the data of theology from a different viewpoint. They breathe the historicizing spirit of the past century and a half. The giant who stands at the head of this line is Albrecht Ritschl. In the Ritschlian lineage historians such as Adolf von Harnack stressed the empirical side of the record of faith. The Ritschlians were also well known for their accent on the ethics of Jesus and on the concept of the Kingdom of God. Albert Schweitzer used the tools of history against historicism, but he too accented the ethic of the Kingdom. A half-century earlier, in England, F. D. Maurice worked out a Kingdom-concept which shared many of the Ritschlian ethical interests. William Temple is a twentieth-century representative of this line. In America, Social Gospel advocate Walter Rauschenbusch blended historical and ethical interests. Canadian-born D. C. Macintosh was noted for his attempt to locate theology in empirics, psychology, and history.

In the twentieth century, pure-form Ritschlianism has been out of fashion. The painstaking methods of biblical and historical inquiry have lived on, however, in men like Gustaf Aulén, who insists that his systematic theology is not normative but descriptive. They are also recognizable in the notable tradition of biblical theology, upheld herein by the British New Testament scholar C. H. Dodd and the Continental exegete Oscar Cullmann.

The third line begins with Søren Kierkegaard, who is often regarded as the father of modern existentialism. He and those who share his attitude are less interested in propositions about faith than in the study of existence and of the encounter between God and man. The remarkable British Congregationalist P. T. Forsyth introduced the concern for this encounter into Anglo-American theology. The highly individualistic Russian exile Nicolai Berdyaev refined this way of doing theology. On the Continent, Karl Heim employed existentialist methods to relate Christian faith to the scientific order.

The last eight thinkers dealt with in this volume have all been influenced by existentialist thought, though they are at variance with each other in many ways. The brothers Niebuhr, for example, share much of the Ritschlian interest in ethics and history. Karl Barth, Emil Brunner, Friedrich Gogarten, Rudolf Bultmann, and Dietrich Bonhoeffer are among the theological giants of the past four decades in Germany and Switzerland. In a variety of disciplines they have tried to relate the Word as witnessed in the early Christian documents to man as he is today. Paul Tillich began with many of these Continental interests, but in recent decades in America he has come to be known chiefly for his concern with correlating theology and philosophy.

If these men could be easily labeled or classified, there would be need not for a handbook of theologians but only for a guidebook to theological types. But however individual and personal the approaches of the twenty-six theologians may be, the broad classifications centering on the motifs of "experience," "empirics," and "existence" should help guide the reader.

We are deeply indebted to Marvin Halverson and Arthur A. Cohen, the editors of the earlier handbook, who began the work on this one. To them goes the credit for the original conception, the selection of most of the subjects and authors, and editorial supervision and correspondence over a period of years. They and we have in each case sought to select an author whose name has been associated with the subject. Some of the authors have studied under the theologians whose lives and works they discuss; others have written extensively about them elsewhere. While the writers are generally sympathetic with the work of these masters, they are noted theologians in their own right; we have encouraged them to be critical.

The transition in editorship unavoidably occasioned some delay in the publication of this book. Whoever has pursued two dozen theologians around the world through their academic schedules, their researches, their sabbaticals, will understand that a work of this kind cannot be produced overnight. We mention this in order to explain that some of the essays were prepared earlier than others; hence not all the authors were able to refer to materials produced during the past year or so. Many of the authors provided extensive bibliographies. Recognizing the limitations of space in a handbook, we have had to do away with these. Instead we have selected one work by and one work about each theologian, with the hope that readers who are making a first acquaintance with the subjects of these chapters will find their appetites whetted for further association with them (extensive bibliographies are easily available elsewhere on almost all twenty-six). The authors of the chapters should not be defaulted for the absence of comprehensive reading lists; the brief suggestion comes from the editors.

We thank Messrs. Halverson and Cohen, the twenty-six authors, and Cecelia Gaul and Joanne Younggren for their assistance in bringing this manuscript to fruition.

Dean G. Peerman
Martin E. Marty

I
The Nineteenth—century Traditions

FRIEDRICH SCHLEIERMACHER

Richard R. Niebuhr

Religiously speaking, we must concede the nineteenth century to Schleiermacher. No other judgment is possible when one takes account of the development of Protestant thought in the extraordinary epoch that embraces the French Revolution and Immanuel Kant at its beginning and the First World War and Ernst Troeltsch and Adolf von Harnack at its conclusion. The great human struggle of these times in the West took on, for Protestantism, the form of an effort to establish once again the Reformation's steady and clear sense for the true roots of personal faith and religious community, in the aftermath of the critical destruction of rationalistic orthodoxy and the cooling of the tepid ardor of deism. But the endeavor's success depended upon the ability of its leaders not only to recognize the symptoms of atrophy in their inherited systems but to use creatively the most profound ideas that had taken possession of the Enlightenment and that were pulsing in the social, political, and intellectual ferment of Europe and America.

Among the most important of these: the idea of history as a story of events with a content whose human meaning could be divined through critical and imaginative reconstruction and so appropriated as an enrichment of the present; the idea of reason as an operation or deed of the human spirit, capable of disciplined employment as the instrument of liberation from man's "self-incurred tutelage" but also freighted with the pathos and finitude of that spirit; the idea of the individual endowed with inalienable rights and a self-consciousness competent to range through all of human experience and reduce it to the order of the moral and aesthetic judgments of the mind; the idea of science as the pursuit of universal truth through which universal community arises; and the idea of religion as an inborn personal sense for the true and the eternal, drawing its vitality from a source much earlier in human nature than the speculations of metaphysical philosophers and officially sanctioned systems of theology. Schleiermacher by no means carried all or even one of these ideas to the highest stage that the century was to achieve, but he lived more actively among them than any other man of his profession and gave them the added impetus of his own genius through his books, teaching, and personal engagement in the history of Germany, so that the theologians of the 1960's have still to reckon with him above all others as the progenitor of the spirit of modern religious understanding. Kierkegaard is the only other who can approach him on this score, but due to his wider interests, deeper sympathy for the church catholic, and superior systematic powers—along with the fact that Kierkegaard became an influence only after 1918—Schleiermacher for better or worse continues to bear this responsibility.

Schleiermacher's popular reputation as philosopher of religion and theologian lives chiefly in and through two books: *On Religion, Speeches to Its Cultured Despisers,* a product of his youth; and *The Christian Faith,* the dogmatic theology that is his magnum opus. However, both of these works emerged so naturally out of his personal history and the intellectual modes and problems of the times that the outlines of Schleiermacher's biography belong indispensably to any introduction to his intellectual achievements. The chronological beginning of such an introduction is 1768, when Friedrich Daniel Ernst Schleiermacher was born into the family of a Prussian army chaplain stationed in Breslau. Although the father was a Reformed clergyman, he wished for his children a Moravian nurture, and so it was that Friedrich was imbued from his earliest years with the one form of eighteenth-century Protestantism that preserved and cultivated the religion of the heart, namely, pietism. Schleiermacher liked to think that he always remained a Moravian in sentiment, and later on his letters to his sister, who had entered one of the community's "sister homes," show his continued affection and respect for the way of the Herrnhutters. But he himself was forced to break both from them and temporarily from his family when he found that his teachers carefully screened from their charges every breath of the new intellectual life of Europe. He departed for the university at Halle with the despairing consent of his father and very little money. There he lived with his uncle, read Kant, listened to lectures on theology in the Protestant orthodox tradition and took his examinations for ordination without particular enthusiasm. Schleiermacher's real entrance into consciousness of self and world appears to have begun after his university days, when he took the position of tutor in the family of Count Dohna and on its East Prussian estate encountered for the first time the mixture of intimate family relationships with lively and intelligent sociality for which his nature had a hitherto unrealized affinity.

Beginning in 1796, Schleiermacher came fully into his youthful powers in response to the stimulus of Berlin's philosophical and literary romanticism, fused with a fashionable social life that centered for him and his friends in the home of Henrietta Herz, wife of a wealthy Jewish physician. In addition to discharging his duties as preacher to the Charité hospital, he worked intensively in his own philosophical studies and rapidly emerged as a leading personality in the aforementioned salons and as a man with a great capacity for friendship. Friedrich Schlegel, with whom he shared his rooms, acted as his tutor in the Romantic spirit and taunted him for his literary unproductivity until, having reached the age of twenty-nine with nothing to show for his promise of originality, Schleiermacher pledged to do something and wrote the *Speeches* on religion. He was the only clergyman among his circle, and it was thoroughly characteristic of him that he used this occasion to issue both a critique of his friends' world view and an apology for his own identity and vocation as a preacher by expounding the mood and themes of Romanticism—especially the idea of individuality—in such a way as to argue that the life uninformed by the cultivation of personal religion and religious community is artificially sterile and out of joint with universal being. The book's instant acclaim emboldened the author to publish in the following year (1800) *The Soliloquies,* a species of literary confession written in the ethical-heroic and often too sentiment-ful style of Fichte. Its theme was a continuation of that of the *Speeches,* the idea of the individual as an underivable and unrepeatable self, a unique microcosmic statement of the macrocosm and "compendium of humanity." True human freedom, he philosophized, is to recognize and develop one's identity in the only real world, the "eternal community of spirits."

The *Speeches* brought Schleiermacher to the threshold of his public career, but Schlegel was responsible for another stage in his growth that proved finally to be of still greater significance, when he proposed that they translate and edit the dialogues of Plato. Even though Schlegel soon lost interest in the project, Schleiermacher persevered in what was to him a labor of love. All the other minds that had worked upon his—Spinoza, Leibniz, Kant—now found their true interpreter and critic in the literary and philosophic master of dialogue. As Wilhelm Dilthey wrote of him, Schleiermacher was a "Plato-kindred spirit," and thereafter his reflection was stamped with two Platonic ideas: that of the highest good as the life-giving and organizing principle of human action, and that of reason as the unending historical dialogue of mind with mind.

The Berlin years dissolved in melancholy. Schleiermacher had fallen in love with Eleonore Grunow, the wife of another minister. With the Romantics, he advocated the moral justification of divorce, but Eleonore, although unhappily married, was prevented both by her conscience and her fear of wounding her family from taking such a step, and Schleiermacher had finally for her sake and on account of the uneasiness of his church superiors to resign his post and become a provincial pastor. To his sister, Charlotte, he had written in 1801 that he would gladly sacrifice his prospects of national renown for marriage. "Except in domestic life, all that we enjoy and all that we attempt, is but vain illusion." His despondency was correspondingly great in 1802 upon his leaving Berlin. However, the personal tragedy weakened his ties with Romanticism, while the isolation of his parish gave him time for writing a critical examination of ethical theory, published under the title *Kritik der bisherigen Sittenlehre*, as well as for the continuation of his translation of Plato. This period of two years was the beginning of his final maturation and of his career as systematic philosopher and theologian.

When he was called to the university at Halle in 1804, he resolved to give his life to the university and the church. He lectured on philosophical ethics, hermeneutics, or the discipline

of interpretation, dogmatic theology, Paul's Letter to the Galatians, and began work on his book *Brief Outline of the Study of
Theology,* a descriptive, critical account of the interrelations of
the several theological sciences. The best insight that we have
into the state of his religious and theological principles at this
time comes from a small publication titled *Christmas Eve (Die
Weihnachtsfeier),* which he cast in the form of a dialogue among
a group of friends and family members gathered together to exchange gifts and converse about the meaning of the nativity. In
some respects, and especially because of its highly stylized
form, the book recalls the *Speeches* and the *Soliloquies;* it is
also, like the other two, transparently autobiographical, reflecting the circumstances of the life of Schleiermacher and of several of his friends. But its content presages his later dogmatic
theology, *The Christian Faith,* particularly in his effort to deal
with the growing skepticism concerning the historicity of Jesus
and with the characterization of Christian faith as rooted in a
feeling or a mood that seizes the individual from without and
transforms all the elements of his inner being and outer world
into the component moments of "a universal pulsing of joy."
Such a joy, the father of the family group declares, cannot originate in the divided consciousness of the fallen and corrupted individual; hence "we look for one point . . . from which this
impartation went forth, although we know that it must go forth
again from each individual as self-active. . . . That one, however, who is seen as the point of origin of the church . . . that
one must already be born as man-in-himself, as the God-man."

At Halle, Schleiermacher had also been appointed preacher
to the university, and as Napoleon invaded the German lands
he started to develop a style of "political" preaching, illustrated
in his second book of sermons (1808). In the second edition of
the *Speeches,* prepared during this time, he warned that Napoleon meant to extinguish both Protestantism and the German spirit. In fact, the French army did capture the city, close
the university, and occupy Schleiermacher's house. Without a
salary, he and his sister held on as long as their means allowed,
refusing another appointment, until there was no more hope for
a reopening of classes. He then returned to Berlin and his
friends. There King Friedrich Wilhelm III made him a preacher

to Trinity Church in 1809, a pulpit that was occupied conjointly by a Reformed and a Lutheran minister. Schleiermacher regarded the terms of Prussia's peace with France as dishonorable, and he intensified his preaching against the background of the political disquiet and national confusion of those days. Dilthey attributes to him an effectiveness equal to Fichte's in arousing the spirit of freedom in the citizens of Berlin. Schleiermacher even joined the patriots who sought to promote war. He also supported from the pulpit and otherwise the liberal social and political reforms advocated by Baron von Stein—reforms which Prussia greatly needed, since it still existed on a feudal level far below England and France. Schleiermacher did not regard these activities as incidental or injurious to his vocation because of his conviction—set out most carefully in his ethics —that the individual must participate fully in the several spheres of public life in order that a healthy balance may be struck and preserved between them for the good of both the national entity and the individual citizen. After the retreat of Napoleon from Russia and the liberation of Prussia, along with many other liberal leaders Schleiermacher fell into official disfavor and was accused of antiroyal sentiments; but he continued to speak and act in accordance with his conscience on all issues that came within his competence. During the second decade of the century, church politics figured increasingly among these, and Schleiermacher's position propelled him into the debate and polemics attendant upon the efforts to reform the organization of the Protestant church and concomitantly to unify its Reformed and Lutheran branches. Here again he felt obliged to oppose the king when the latter tried to reform the liturgy without heeding the principle of church representation in the matter. The church union, however, was finally accomplished and Schleiermacher was able to preach the sermon at the celebration of the event on Palm Sunday, 1822.

In 1809 Schleiermacher at the age of forty married the young widow of a close friend. When two years later he was called to a chair of theology at the University of Berlin—he himself had been active in founding the university as a member of the state's department of education—the scope of his life and work was defined. His letters to his wife and children show him as a devoted and gentle patriarch. His labors in the academic arena speak for themselves. While continuing to hold his pulpit, he assumed an ever enlarging responsibility as professor, lecturing on each division of theological studies save the Old Testament, and on dialectics, history of philosophy, psychology, and political science, as well as hermeneutics and philosophical ethics. His colleague in the neighboring faculty of philosophy was Hegel, and there can be little doubt that the ethics upon which Schleiermacher worked intensely year after year constituted his own critique of this greatest of German idealists, although we find no mention of Hegel by name in the notes from these lectures. Of all these undertakings only the dogmatic theology issued in a book, whose full title is *The Christian Faith, Presented in Its Inner Connections according to the Fundamentals of the Evangelical Church.* It appeared in two parts, in 1821 and 1822, and again in revised form in 1830. He had hoped to prepare his dialectic (his critical analysis of human self-consciousness) for the press also, but only the introduction was completed before his death in 1834. Friends and pupils compiled his notes and literary remains, so that in addition to individual critical editions of his most important works we today have thirty-two volumes of his essays, addresses, sermons, articles and lecture notes, plus several collections of his letters, of which that edited by Dilthey and translated by Frederica Rowan is the most extensive. "The art of making time do," Schleiermacher once wrote to his friend Frau Herz, "is, after all, a great art; nay, I might almost say, the most important one in this world next after the art of loving, for upon this depend all others."

To his contemporaries, Schleiermacher's principal métier appeared to be society and friendship, earnest conversation, lecture and sermon. It was his habit to speak almost extemporaneously or from the briefest notes, and his congregation in Trinity Church was crowded with "Moravians, Jews, baptised and unbaptised, young philosophers and philologists, elegant ladies" and many others. But his *Brief Outline on the Study of Theology,* notes on dialectics and on ethics, and, above all, *The Christian Faith* exhibit systematic powers unequaled in the history of Protestant theology. In fact, Schleiermacher steadfastly took care to inform each side of his daily life with the corrective of his experience in the other. He could not countenance a sharp division between the personal and the scientific and had no use for the still-prevalent image of the scholar as a solitary archivist or seer. It is moral man who perceives, reasons, and strives to know; the real world is humanity, and into such a world it is that we are born and attain to consciousness. Self-consciousness arises in response to the words and gestures of others. Indeed, thinking is but inner speaking, as speech is the outerside of thought and the organ of the commonalty of reason.

Schleiermacher used the teaching-learning situation, that is, the dialogue, as the paradigm of man's rational activity, thereby emphasizing that insofar as all communication occurs within a particular historical language, be it classical or modern, all thinking and knowing has its genesis likewise in a given time and place as response to the uttered judgments and analyses of other historical selves. To the extent, then, that an individual's judgments are made possible by the public speech within which he thinks, each deed of reasoning reflects and is conditioned by the history of the language; to the extent that each such judgment represents a criticism and reformulation of the statements of the other, it constitutes a new moment both in the history of the self and of his culture. Our reasoning, therefore, even the highest and most abstract, takes its departure from no absolute beginnings or wholly self-evident first principles but from the history of other minds. Schleiermacher alluded to the experiential basis of this principle in the *Soliloquies*, where he wrote that he could not appropriate anything new, except in the company of friends and colleagues. The detailed import of the principle is spelled out in his philosophical ethics and in his dialectics, in which he presents a full-scale analysis of human consciousness and selfhood in the polarities of spirit and nature, mind and body, self and object, individual and community. Practically, these convictions led Schleiermacher to conceive of the university as a federation of faculties or sciences rooted in the history of a people and its language and to define its function as the critical preservation and extension of the knowledge contained potentially in that history. On his terms it is manifestly impossible to assign to any single discipline the position of queen of the sciences; rather, the natural and the human studies (*Geisteswissenschaften*) require each other collectively and severally as equally active partners in the unending dialectic of reason.

Over against his more thoroughly idealistic contemporaries, therefore, Schleiermacher had to reject the notion of an intuition of the absolute or of the appearance in human consciousness of pure, undifferentiated reason. Thinking is the deed of a naturally and historically individuated subject; the ground of all being cannot be an object. He was more than willing to ascribe to philosophy the title of the highest knowledge, for he regarded philosophizing as the natural and most original business of the human understanding, but the plurality of historical languages and the still incomplete state of the empirical sciences testify that it also is perpetually becoming itself and is never whole. Only when all historical information has been gathered in, when the natural basis of human consciousness is known in the totality of its relations to the cosmos, and when the inner individuality of all selves is fully revealed and understood, will the highest knowledge assume its true and final form and philosophy be perfected.

This doctrine of the sciences made it entirely natural for Schleiermacher to conceive of the university as the proper place for the study of theology. While he could not tolerate the pretensions of speculation to independence of or priority to historical life, neither could he have accepted the cogency of objections to the dialogue of philosophy and theology. In a most revealing letter to Friedrich Heinrich Jacobi, he made use of his favorite image of polarity to depict the relations of the heart and the head, of faith and reason: "Understanding and feeling [the organ of piety] in me . . . remain distinct, but they touch each other and form a galvanic pile. To me it seems that the innermost life of the spirit consists in the galvanic action thus produced in the feeling of the understanding and the understanding of the feeling, during which, however, the two poles always remain deflected from each other." Therefore, he wrote, his philosophy and dogmatics were "firmly determined not to contradict each other, but for this very reason, neither pretends to be complete; and as long as I have been able to think they have always been more or less attuning themselves to each other and drawing nearer to each other."

Despite the incredible busyness of his life, Schleiermacher was throughout really governed by that one galvanic principle to which he referred in his letter to Jacobi—the interaction of pulpit and contemporary intellectual culture, first in Berlin among the Romantics, then in Halle, and once more in the capital. The theological formulation of the problem with which he wrestled can be simply stated: what is the nature of the creature, man, whose existence is determined both by God and the world? Schleiermacher sought an answer that would do justice to his conviction that the two poles of religious self-consciousness and understanding energize the total field of man's life without destroying each other. The supposition that these two foci of human existence can be isolated from each other and considered apart was as little tenable to his disposition as the old Orthodox division of reality into a supernatural and a natural world, incorporating parallel structures of being that miraculously impinge only from time to time, according to the inscrutable will of their maker. So long as this kind of division lies as a presupposition of thought, the intellectual life of Christendom will find itself caught in the hopeless shuttlecocking of rationalism to biblicism and naturalism to supernaturalism and back.

One age bears the penalty of the misdeeds of another, but seldom knows how to redeem itself, except by the perpetration of a new misdemeanour. By the utter subversion of the letter of the Scriptures all historical continuity was dissolved and it is as great madness to destroy such continuity in religious matters as in political matters. *That* had therefore, to be re-established; but as Tieck has admirably expressed it, in attempting to screw the thing back we shall only be destroying the historical continuity in the opposite direction.

Consequently, Schleiermacher addressed himself to the inquiry after that in human nature from which the sense of destiny, absolute dependence, and election arises—in a word, religious identity—and then to the exposition of the growth and conformation of this consciousness in the polarity of self and world. By abandoning the natural-supernatural dichotomy, he was returning to the prescholastic idea of man and the world that we find in the church fathers and the biblical milieu, in which the operations of nature and grace and the natural and theological virtues cannot be neatly segregated and labeled, and man is conceived to be not yet fully human and in possession of his "nature" until his genesis and destiny in the divine economy are fully understood and appropriated.

> . . . I have placed myself on the footing to demand of others that they shall prove to me where is the ultimate limit of nature. When, therefore, my Christian feeling is conscious of a divine spirit indwelling in me, which is distinct from my reason, I will never give up seeking for this spirit in the deepest depths of the soul's nature; and when my Christian feeling becomes conscious of a Son of God, who differs from us in another way than merely being better than the best of us, I will never cease to search for the genesis of this Son of God in the deepest depths of nature, and to say to myself, that I shall most likely learn to understand the second Adam just as soon as the first Adam or Adams, whose coming into existence I must also admit without being able to understand.

But Schleiermacher, of course, could not simply repristinate the earlier theology; he had to think this idea afresh in the language and concepts of the epoch.

This he set out to do for his *Speeches* on religion in order to show his Romantic friends the culture-affirming character of piety and the integral place of religious self-consciousness in the full development of the human spirit. Two of the points that he insisted on here and always thereafter are of the greatest moment for the whole of his religious and theological view. One of them is that the deeply personal locus and ramifying nature of piety make religion impossible except in community. Religiously we are no less dependent for the birth of self-consciousness upon the stimulus and response of personal encounter than we are intellectually, and, as Schleiermacher's life encompassed broader responsibilities for the church, he came to see that likewise the religious consciousness requires a tradition, a common and public medium, a cultus, that the individual may both teach and learn, just as the university or science needs a common vocabulary and knowledge of its history. While he was intensely and perennially involved in the analysis of the ethical meaning of personal individuality, he had no patience for the anti-institutional individualism that issued in superiority or indifference rather than reform. This grasp of the meaning of community for historical development, for the moral life of the individual, and of the meaning of the individual as the historical source of life, criticism, and progress for the community enabled Schleiermacher to hand on to Protestantism a renewed understanding of the church and a means of transcending the alternative of viewing faith as a purely private, personal affair or as adhesion to a time-sanctioned, unalterable institutional form. In effect, he recovered for Protestantism something of Augustine's vision of men living in commonweals according to the agreement of their loves for the good. But Schleiermacher accented the equality of all citizens of the city of God (he himself regarded the distinction between clergy and laity as functional only), and always insisted that the common life of the church must proceed afresh from each of its members. The Christian consciousness is not implanted in the community by any man or office but by the Spirit, and the task of the minister is to address and elicit that Spirit in each of its members.

Religion, then, is not the creation of ecclesiastical institutions and dogma; rather, it is their creator. It emerges out of a prior community and is rooted in a dimension of self-consciousness that cannot be expunged from the nature that is fully human. Here we have the second of the points that is first made in the *Speeches*, and it constitutes the best-known element in Schleiermacher's work. Religion or piety is an original form of self-consciousness that is not to be identified either with doing and morality or with knowing and science. In the *Speeches* Schleiermacher gives to it the name of feeling and again of intuition (*Anschauung*). Later, in the *Christmas Eve*, he speaks of the Christian feeling and mood, in his philosophical ethics of feeling as a subjective knowing; in the dialectics it is the representation of the transcendent ground of being, and in *The Christian Faith* he defines religion as an immediate self-consciousness and a feeling of absolute dependence.

Despite these changes and additions in Schleiermacher's terminology, the general intention of his language and ideas is relatively clear. First of all, he firmly disavowed the reduction of religion to moral sanctions or its identification with good works. Again, religion is not the fruit of assent to dogma, nor is it dependent for its actualization upon theological systems. Nor is its truth to be found in the purer concepts of speculative philosophy. To the Romantics he explained the content of feeling as harmony with the All; piety is "a sense and taste for the infinite," an awareness that the infinite is immediately present in the finite self and that the self is a unique statement of the universal concourse of being. The religious moment is not one of mystical absorption and loss of identity, but a moment in which identity is received and affirmed, while the kinship of self with all other being is intuited through an immediacy with the All that almost suspends the distance between subject and object. Consequently, religious experience is the sensitizing nerve of consciousness, the eye of the self upon the world of humanity. "What is finest and tenderest in history . . . can only be comprehended in the feeling of a religious disposition." Religious feeling is really the expression of that which is most original in the self, the welling up of being or life in the form of an historical existence that is at once related to all being and inwardly individuated. When this inner sense is raised to the level of thought and discourse it has already been partially dissipated, but its energy and quality pervade all that the pious individual is and does.

As he worked further into his philosophy, ethics, and systematic theology, Schleiermacher tried to introduce more precise distinctions among the grades of feeling and to give a fuller account of the way in which it becomes ingredient in the specifically Christian consciousness and of its theological significance. In his dialectics and ethics he makes clear that he means by feeling not a "faculty" but a quality of self-consciousness. Its content is the inner individuality of the self that cannot be derived from membership in a species, people, or community. As feeling selves we are enveloped in an awareness of the peculiar and inexplicable givenness of our existence in our world for which no object of perception and thought or of will and activ-

ity can furnish an explanation. It is the "original expression of
an immediate existential relationship," the form of self-consciousness that is anterior to all subject-object relations and is
in fact the source of the special affective content that distinguishes the doing and thinking of one self from another. No
single moment of temporal activity or consciousness—including
even the consciousness of the self as an object or a "me" over
against the "I"—can adequately symbolize or exhaust the content of feeling, for the fundament of feeling is really the life-
unity of the individual and the source of the imagination that
synthesizes the elements of thought and volition into organic
wholes.

Hence the difference between authentic and ephemeral art
depends upon the degree to which the artistic representation
embodies a will to create that has been thoroughly mediated by
the permanent feeling of the artist. And insofar as all historical
acts and thoughts are meditated or spontaneous expressions of
such feeling (or mood), life itself is art and interpretation, the
setting forth of self and the critical, intuitive reconstruction of
the inner individuality of others. When considered at its utmost
inner reach, such feeling bespeaks the radical unfreedom of the
self, its "absolute dependence," and the "whence" of this immediate existential relationship and givenness of self-consciousness, Schleiermacher writes in the most famous paragraph of
The Christian Faith (§4), is what we mean by "God."

God is therefore not an object of knowledge in the ordinary
sense of the term, for an object in the knowing relationship is
by definition a being that enters into consciousness and differentiates it, calling forth a particular response, and no response
or series of responses of intellect and will can suffice to express
the God-relationship. Consequently, Schleiermacher found no
profit in the efforts to demonstrate the existence of God, for
concepts—which are the only fruit of demonstration—are later
products of the dialectical skill of the mind and at best symbolically evocative of that which is earliest in the self's history.
Schleiermacher quite naturally hesitated to speak of a knowledge of God or of feeling as cognitive; God is "known" only in
the sense that there is a certain analogy between knowing and
feeling. That is to say, as in knowing, the subject is determined

by the object, submits himself to the object, as it were, in an attempt to reconstitute the object ideally in himself, so through
feeling the subject-self likewise is aware of being determined.
But it is a determination or placing of the self as such, and,
furthermore, of the self in the totality of its relations to and in
the world. "What we call feeling here is the immediate presence
of the whole, undivided personal existence, both sensible as
well as spiritual, the unity of the person and its sensible and
spiritual world." And such feeling arises, as we have already
seen, not in the isolated man but in the participant of the world
of humanity. It is called forth by the gestures and religious addresses of others, and, more generally, by the whole style of
their personal bearing, and it takes on the historical character
of the particular community in which the individual is nurtured.
Thus the Christian faith can be simply defined as that feeling or
consciousness whose entire content refers to Jesus Christ as its
mediator. Schleiermacher's dogmatic theology is in fact a description of the content of this consciousness, exemplifying his
contention that theology is not a species of theoretical knowledge but the statement in the most precise, dialectical language
available of the personal consciousness that the Christian community shares in.

There could be no question in Schleiermacher's mind about
the propriety of calling Christianity a religion among other religions. By virtue of his analysis of the nature of human existence, he must necessarily have ranged Christianity alongside all
the other manifestations of the human phenomenon and comprehended it under the general rubric of immediate self-consciousness and feeling. Nor could he have defended it, on his
terms, as attesting to its own uniqueness through its infallible
dogma and correct doctrine. Those who discover the distinctiveness or superiority of Christian faith here intellectualize
and scholasticize its genius and so misplace it. All that really
marks it off from other religions is to be found in the specific
structure and quality of its consciousness, as it appears in the
person of Jesus Christ, in his individuality and life and in the
communication of the same to others.

Continuing in the tradition of the Reformation, Schleiermacher understands the church's origin and mission to be in

preaching, the proclamation of the word. But the word proclaimed is not understood as doctrine to which the proper response is assent. The word is vessel of life. The church is the
historical community deriving from Jesus' own self-impartation
in parable, discourse, and deed, and the life of the church is
the appropriation of that impartation and the re-enactment of
its communication through the preaching and hearing, sacrament and communion, that form the Christian consciousness
into the mind of Christ and the people into his body. The work
of Christ is "person-forming," and the Christian church is the
people who know themselves as persons through him. The essential type of Schleiermacher's theology is the ancient idea of
the divine economy, in which the redeemer is presented as the
last Adam, the Son of Man, the recapitulator and perfecter of
the race. Christ appears in history with a sinless humanity, a
humanity uninterruptedly and fully indwelt by God—by which
Schleiermacher means that Christ's total consciousness of world
and self was wholly dominated and regulated (not extinguished)
by his God-consciousness. He was further marked by a fully
developed consciousness of man, by a sympathy, that brings
community into being about himself. In relation to him and in
dependence upon him, the human consciousness belonging to
historical, adamic manhood experiences the pain of its own
dividedness and inconstancy, the guilt of its suppression of the
feeling of absolute dependence, and the confusion in its resulting disorderly consciousness of self and world. But this awareness of sin is at the same time also an awareness of the potency
of Christ's God-consciousness and of its already begun creative
work in the self.

Thus the Christian is one whose consciousness is historically
mediated by Jesus Christ and structured by the antithesis of sin
and grace. He is caught up in a tide of pain and joy. Schleiermacher does not actually give much attention to these affective
states in his dogmatics, although the whole conception of feeling
and religious self-consciousness is rife with possibilities for an
extensive phenomenology of the Christian "mood." The reader
must turn back to the earlier *Christmas Eve* and to the occasional references in the letters for hints of his mind on this aspect of the subject. Quite characteristically, and in keeping with

his view of sin as a state of inchoateness and imperfection of consciousness, he designates the pain of Christian faith as melancholy rather than remorse, "a holy sadness"; "I always picture to myself Christian piety . . . as excitatory of pain. But it is the sweet pain of melancholy so well calculated to soothe other pains. Surely, if there was any good in Saul's soul, it must have been an *adagio* that exorcized the evil." However, joy is the term he most frequently gives to the disposition created by faith, and it, in turn, is best interpreted by Schleiermacher's commitment to the belief in providence. This is the dominant theme in his treatment of the doctrine of God: the divine determination of all things, God's *eudokia*, "good pleasure." Much of the subsequent interpretation of Schleiermacher's theology has been so preoccupied with his startling use of human feeling that it has forgotten the consistency with which he defined it as a God-determined feeling that becomes actual "only as consciousness of His eternal power." Hence Christianly potentiated feeling leads away from all speculation about the separate operations of justice, mercy, and love in the Godhead, and their reconciliation. The divine love is simply the inclusive name that faith gives to the totality of the content of the God-consciousness as it arises through the work upon us of Christ's person, and so all the distinctions between real and possible, freedom and necessity, that are derived from historical judgments are inapplicable to the being of God, who is present in the consciousness imparted by the Redeemer in one way only, as choosing and ordaining what is and comes to be.

As a theologian Schleiermacher belongs unmistakably to the tradition of Augustine and Calvin, and if one judges him only from the dogmatic point of view, his handling of the divine government and of Jesus Christ as the mediator of the true consciousness of God is enough to establish him as the most powerful systematic mind in this line since the Reformation. He gave to the Augustinian-Reformed spirit a fresh embodiment that has enabled it to live on in modern times. Undoubtedly, however, his greatest achievement is his articulation of the self-consciousness and the God-consciousness that relate to feeling. In doing so, Schleiermacher sought and gained for faith and

theology an independence of speculative philosophy and scho-
lastically inclined theology and rationalism. With his idea of
human nature and individuality, in effect he laid down a religious world view that culminates in Christian faith. Here again,
by teaching that the consciousness of self and world remains
confused and intermittent until it is clarified and ordered by
the God-consciousness mediated through Christ's person, he
points directly back to the ideal of Augustine, who pictured the
remembering, thinking, willing soul as fully self-conscious only
when it remembers, thinks, and wills its creator; and to that of
John Calvin whose *Institutes of the Christian Religion* begins
with the declaration that the sum of human wisdom consists of
two parts—the knowledge of God and of man.

Theology since Schleiermacher, in turn, points back to him
in its development of a number of themes. Among them is the
search for the human ground of the experience of and knowledge of God, the religious a priori—not a term Schleiermacher
used—as carried out by Ernst Troeltsch and Rudolf Otto, although 'the former is much more faithful to Schleiermacher's
meaning than the latter. More generally, however, the whole
quest of the nineteenth-century theologians for the moral, personal, or existential heart of the movement of faith, as exemplified in Coleridge, Albrecht Ritschl, and Wilhelm Herrmann,
is to be identified with Schleiermacher's idea of theology and
religion. Troeltsch's essays on the historical nature of the Christian faith and community, together with his effort to analyze
their relations to culture, are also inspired significantly by the
insight into the character of religion and Christianity that Schleiermacher emphasized from his *Speeches* and *Brief Outline of
the Study of Theology* to *The Christian Faith*. The present-day
concern for Christocentric theology has its origin in Schleiermacher also, though his Christocentrism is certainly not that
of the objectivist species of neo-orthodoxy espoused by the
school of Karl Barth. Nevertheless, *The Christian Faith* first
demonstrated the need of recognizing that the mind of the
church is wholly determined by the mediator of its faith; the
person and work of Christ inform not just Christology but the
whole scope of theology. And, finally, we have to thank Schleiermacher for establishing high on the list of virtues indispensa-

ble to honest theology the resolution to maintain Christian thought in the painful but necessary dialogue with the faculties of the university and their secular sciences—the most valuable trait of Protestant liberalism in the last century and this.

Bibliography

Friedrich Schleiermacher, *The Christian Faith*, H. R. Mackintosh and J. S. Stewart, eds., N. Y., Harper, 1963, 2 vols. (Harper Torchbooks).

Richard R. Niebuhr, *Schleiermacher on Christ and Religion*, N. Y., Scribner's, 1964.

HORACE BUSHNELL

Sydney E. Ahlstrom

Horace Bushnell (1802–76) was the most creative and interesting theologian to emerge from the New England Puritan tradition during the nineteenth century. Like the great eighteenth-century claimant to that distinction, Jonathan Edwards, he spent his entire active career in the local pastorate, devoting much attention to the problems of conducting a viable parish ministry. Like Edwards, too, he broadened his range of concern to include many of the oldest and deepest issues of Christian theology, but he did so by concentrating on certain of the most critical problems rather than by a systematic discussion of Christian dogmatics. Also like his great New England predecessor he took with great seriousness the apologetic task of justifying God's ways to his fellow men and made his total *opus* as classic a theological expression of romanticism as Edwards had of the Enlightenment. He eminently deserves the titles given him: the "American Schleiermacher" and "father of American religious liberalism." Such designations, however, are only a partial indication of his claim to remembrance and they veil many factors which have sustained or actually widened interest in his thought for over a century.

Bushnell's insights into the nature of language, communication, symbolism, community, and nationhood have almost limitless applicability. Christian thinkers of all persuasions have continued to draw upon his views of the family, conversion, congregational life, religious nurture, spiritual growth, and the nature of dogma. Americans from North and South may in time come to appreciate his profound understanding of the Civil War, just as historians, literary critics, sociologists, and philosophers are becoming aware of his penetrating and fruitful analysis of the social dimensions of human thought and institutional life. Man in community is the persistent theme of his most enduring thought; the contextuality and interpenetration of all

things, in history and nature, was a constant preoccupation. Out
of these interests grew another lasting contribution: his lifelong
and ever intensifying meditations on the meaning of love, forgiveness, sacrifice, and reconciliation. In the last analysis it may
be that Bushnell's undoubted relation to the rise of liberal theology in the American churches is a relatively minor and tran-
sient aspect of his significance. Be that as it may, Bushnell is
most certainly to be remembered for what he thought and wrote
rather than for what he did in his fairly uneventful life as a
pastor. "My figure in this world," he once wrote, "has not been
great, but I have had a great experience." After a brief account
of his career, therefore, we will here be concerned with the writings that grew out of that experience.

Horace Bushnell was born in the village of Bantam, two
miles from Litchfield hill in Connecticut, the first child of En-
sign Bushnell, a farmer and a Methodist, and Dotha (Bishop)
Bushnell, a gentle and pious Episcopalian. "My mother's loving instinct was from God," he said in his characteristic way,
"and God was in love to me first therefore; which love was
deeper than hers, and more protracted." Three years later the
family moved westward to a farm in New Preston, Connecticut.
As he delightfully described it a half century later, it was an
"Age of Homespun" wherein the internal economy of a household could be calculated by observing the sheep in the pasture,
and when on winter mornings children went to school warmed
by wool shorn from sheep individually remembered. In these
isolated rural surroundings he experienced the meaning of a
covenanted New England community under about as favorable
circumstances as persisted anywhere in the early nineteenth century. Even the old Puritan Sabbath—beginning at sundown on
Saturday—was observed in the more pious homes. In the local
Congregational church he "owned the covenant" in 1821, and
he recalled the sturdy piety of that congregation with gratitude.
"If the minister speaks in his great-coat and mittens, if the
howling blasts of winter blow in across the assembly fresh
streams of ventilation that move the hair upon their heads, they
are none the less content if only he gives them good strong exercise. Under their hard . . . stolid faces, great thoughts are
brewing and these keep them warm." Not surprisingly young

Bushnell left for Yale College two years later with plans to enter the ministry.

During his college years his faith deteriorated and these plans changed. After being graduated in 1827, he taught school for a time, served as associate editor of the New York *Journal of Commerce,* then returned to Yale to study law, serving meanwhile as a tutor in the college. In 1831, however, just when almost ready for admission to the bar, his religious doubts were dissolved during a revival in the college; he experienced a deep renewal of Christian commitment. A friend remembered a confession that anticipates the theologian: "My heart wants the Father; my heart wants the Son; my heart wants the Holy Ghost." The student of law transferred thereafter to the university's theological department, which was then looked upon as being unusually progressive in tendency, with the eminent Nathaniel William Taylor as its head and dominant personality. Taylor was a metaphysician in the tradition of eighteenth-century Scottish common sense philosophy; and the "New Haven Theology" was under fire from the more conservative bastions of New England orthodoxy for its modifications of the old views of Jonathan Edwards on God's glory, original sin, and man's utter dependence on divine grace. Taylor made man's freedom a cornerstone of his rationale for revivalism in a democratic ethos.

Bushnell was actually to occupy much of the new ground Taylor had broken, but he did not admire the eighteenth-century rationalism that still prevailed at Yale. Insofar as the characteristic temper of his developing thought was owed to other thinkers (and he was not prodigal with admissions on such matters) it was rather to Samuel Taylor Coleridge, whose *Aids to Reflection* brought him to see "a whole other world . . . a range of realities in a higher tier. . . ." In due course, too, he, like so many dissatisfied American religious thinkers, would be stirred by Friedrich Schleiermacher's discussion of the Trinity which Professor Moses Stuart of Andover Seminary published in the *Bibliotheca Sacra* in 1835. Bushnell was to express nevertheless a kind of romanticism that was indigenous to America; and he naturally imbibed much during these and subsequent years from the Transcendentalist ferment beginning to be felt in Boston and soon to be dominated by the figure of Ralph Waldo Emerson. Even his undeniable romanticism, however, would largely be excogitated by himself in solitary meditation. As a biographer remarked, "He published first and read later."

In 1833, having been licensed to preach, he accepted a call from the North Church in Hartford, which in 1824 had been formed by seceders from the revivalistic First Church, with merchants and retailers the dominant element in the congregation. Bushnell was its third minister. (Later in the same year he married Mary Apthorp of New Haven.) At the time he admitted to certain doubts about the significance of infant baptism, but his congregation had confidence in his seriousness and dedication. During his long ministry he healed the contention within his parish between "New Haven" and "Old School" factions, and by a determined effort to comprehend opposing views won the loyalty and deep regard of his congregation. They remained steadfast even when he was being vigorously attacked for his alleged departures in doctrine. In 1852 when moves were being made to bring him to trial for his views, North Church withdrew from the local consociation so as to preclude an ecclesiastical process. The hostility of most of his fellow ministers in and around Hartford did not therewith abate, but with the passing years he played an active and farsighted role in many civic affairs, and his memory has been substantially honored by a grateful city.

Bushnell's first major publication and the one which has probably had the most sustained influence was on *Christian Nurture* (1847; revised edition, 1861). The original lectures as well as the book revealed his continuing concern with the meaning of baptism. They documented a fundamental shift in his own thinking, and in the longer perspective they mark a turning point in Congregational church history. *Christian Nurture* is a thoroughgoing, indeed a classic critique of views which were intrinsic to Puritanism and heavily accentuated by the Great Awakening. Bushnell returns to an older conception of baptism and nurture. He stressed the churchlike quality and genuinely redemptive role of the family and, inversely, another theme that would concern him increasingly, the familylike qual-

ity of the true Christian congregation. Attacking the notion of
the Christian life oriented on brimstone, conversion, and re-
vivals, he insisted that a child of Christian parents should never
know himself as being otherwise than Christian. Though fairly
conservative in doctrinal framework, though widely acclaimed
in antirevivalistic circles, even by Professor Charles Hodge of
Princeton Seminary, and though consonant with other critiques
of latter-day Puritanism, the book ran counter to the main-
stream of American evangelical Protestantism and marked its
author for the time being as a dangerous innovator. In time,
however, the negative animus of the work faded from view; it
came to be appreciated as an important commentary on the
practical and familial significance of infant baptism and a path-
breaking inquiry into the nature of character formation, sub-
conscious influences, and the social dimensions of life and
learning. As reinterpreted by persons of more naturalistic bent,
his work became a pioneer expression of "progressive education" and a veritable bible of the Christian education
movement. Bushnell's own interpretation was perhaps more
"familial" than sacramental; and the book illustrates his persistent effort to make the church's message meaningful to people
who were becoming increasingly removed from their traditional Christian moorings. He was determined to strike a respondent chord in the sentiments—and the sentimentality—of
an urban middle class which was almost invulnerable to older
revivalistic techniques. "If Bushnell could not appeal to his public as Christians," writes one biographer, "he knew they would
listen as parents." In a striking way both Bushnell's circumstance and his response anticipated the impact of another century's social change on the Protestantism of America's urban
middle classes.

God in Christ (1849) is Bushnell's central work. It consists
of a Dissertation on Language and three discourses: on the
Atonement, the Divinity of Christ, and the problems of "Dogma
and Spirit" in the reviving of religion. These addresses were delivered in 1848 at the Harvard Divinity School, at Yale College as the Concio ad Clerum to the assembled ministers of
Connecticut, and at Andover Seminary. They announced themes
which were to remain at the foreground of his own thought,

and brought Bushnell into the center of New England's theological discussion, provoking a storm of controversy. One old participant in those conflicts wrote in 1902 that "it is impossible for those who have come upon the stage of public life within the last thirty years to realize the intense excitement and tremulous apprehension caused by these charges of heresy against so prominent a character."

The lectures which precipitated Bushnell's temporary ostracism were preceded by deep spiritual crisis and a specific experience of widened mystical vision, to which the writings of Madame Guyon and Fénelon made a vital contribution. In his wife's words, the year 1848 became "the central point in [his] life. . . . He had reached one of those headlands where new discoveries open to sight." When criticism arose over these discoveries, he defended and amplified each of his positions in *Christ in Theology, Being the Answer of the Author, before the Hartford Central Association of Ministers* (1851). His treatises on *The Vicarious Sacrifice* (1866) and *Forgiveness and Law* (1874) provided still more complete statements of his view of Christ's atoning work, a profounder general understanding of reconciliation, and a deepening conception of God's sacrificial love. In this cluster of works one confronts the heart of Bushnell's theological message.

At the head of these productions stand the writings on language which had been maturing at least since a lecture on "Revelation" given at Andover in 1839. This theme was rightly judged by his daughter to be "the key to Horace Bushnell." He expounds the implications to be drawn from the organic character of the family, the state, and above all, the church. He delineates the social nature of language, and therefore its many-layered, metaphoric structure, its evocative function, its symbolic value. Poetry, to him, is the norm of language and "religion has a natural and profound alliance with poetry." Theological terms and doctrinal creeds, therefore, become lifeless and artificial counters or rationalistic prisons of the spirit if their form and history and atmosphere are not entered into and appropriated. Even when we proceed in this way of "participation," we cannot assume the adequacy or completeness of what we say. When we venture beyond the merely physical in our discourse, even the law of contradiction does not apply. "Accordingly we never come so near to a truly well rounded view of any truth, as when it is offered paradoxically; that is, under contradictions; that is, under two or more dictions, which, taken as dictions, are contrary to one another." How this could relate to a matter such as the atonement, he made clear: "It would not be as wild a breach of philosophy itself, to undertake a dogmatic statement of the contents of a tragedy, as to attempt giving in the same manner the equivalents of the life and death of Jesus Christ." Here is indicated the problem Bushnell created for his stricter, less imaginative brethren in the ministry: it was not so much that he was heterodox as that he made heresy a very elusive thing. As for creeds, "one seldom need have any difficulty in accepting as many as are offered him." Bushnell might even have seen *some* value in the diction of his archcritic, Bennet Tyler, who "writes about the human spirit as if it were a machine under the laws of mechanics."

Yet Bushnell was not an apostle of intellectual license; there was drive and purpose behind his own diction and intuitive methods. On the divinity of Christ, the trinity, revelation, conversion, the atonement, and on the comprehensive questions of nature and the supernatural (to be discussed below) Bushnell was moved by a single conviction: that the depths and riches of the Christian faith, so powerful and certain a reality in his own life, were being lost to his own generation and, *a fortiori*, to future generations because the entire world was entering "a new age of doubt." He saw it engulfing the churches at home and the mission fields abroad. Yet to him Christ was

the Grand Chief Miracle of the world . . . a Saviour come to bring salvation. Mankind can rely on no stock powers in human nature; men are not going to mend themselves; neither history or evolution will avail. Nothing short of a salvation brought down from out of nature and above, in his divine person, can be any sufficient remedy. This most certainly is what is given us for gospel, and this we are firmly to hold and boldly publish.

Bushnell's Christology, accordingly, did not accent the human, historical Jesus, but dwelt upon the divine Christ with such insistence as to stir up legitimate cries of docetism and

Patripassianism. Neither did Bushnell "naturalize" the church. It was to him not simply a human historical organization but a new society "called the kingdom of heaven, . . . the Society of Life, the Embodied Word . . . the body of Christ, the fullness of him that filleth all in all." His instrumental view of the trinity likewise had man's experience of the Godhead as its point of departure. And in 1848 he professed an inability to speak of the divine nature, except that God is one and that he manifests himself to men as Father, Son, and Spirit. This was a modified Sabellianism. But his later thought moved toward the Athanasian position developed at the Council of Nicaea.

Bushnell had no desire to alter or blunt the offense of the kerygma; he did not seek to remove the scandal of the cross; he was willing "that we maintain our ground in what are called offenses against reason." But he did not want needless scandal or the wrong offense; he would not maintain offenses "against immutable morality." In a general way this brought him into conflict with the inelastic, propositional, "rationalistic" Calvinistic-Puritan dogmatic structures which to his mind had incarcerated the religious spirit in New England. He wished to make theology experientially relevant and morally powerful; and the atonement inexorably became the focus of his concern. Especially in need of revision, he thought, were those doctrines which explained the atoning work of Christ as a legal or penal "satisfaction" of God's wrath. This "theory" he could not countenance even if he had to assert that what "the Master's words have been plainly teaching for eighteen hundred years" was not discovered until the true insight came to him on a "particular day of accident" six months before the publication of his final treatise!

Bushnell's "moral theory" of the atonement took its rise from his persistent pondering of man's own experience of love, and a deep conviction, expressed in *Forgiveness and Law,* that "a grand analogy, or almost identity subsists between our moral nature and that of God." In his lecture of 1848 he had insisted that Christian preaching must include or comprehend both historic views of the atonement: (1) the *subjective* view that Christ's work was to change the lives of men, to "redeem us from all iniquity"—that "God was in Christ, reconciling the world unto himself"; and (2) the *objective* view that Christ "died for us" as a propitiatory sacrifice that we might be accounted righteous before God. His own emphasis, however, is "subjective," with the stress falling on the way Christ's work upheld the "sanctity of the Law" and on the danger of preaching forgiveness without demanding reformation of character. In *The Vicarious Sacrifice* he further expounds this conception of love as being "essentially vicarious in its own nature." Christ's sacrifice, therefore, is universally comprehensible, not a forensic mystery or a governmental transaction: it is God's healing work.

Finally, shortly before his death, Bushnell moves explicitly toward a traditional position by underlining the "Godward" element in the atonement, though he still employs his analogical moral argument. This last phase of Bushnell's thinking was preceded by a genuine reappropriation of Jonathan Edwards, perhaps especially a radical distinction between natural virtue and "true virtue" which he could not have accepted when he was writing *Christian Nurture*. There also came over Bushnell in these later years an awareness of tragedy that stood in sharp contrast to the evolutionary optimism of his age. "Christianity is a mighty salvation, because it is a tragic salvation . . . in an essentially tragic universe . . . with a fall and an overspreading curse at the beginning, and a cross in the middle, and a glory and shame at the end. . . ." True forgiveness, he now insists, is not a simple cleaning of the slate; it involves suffering for and with the offender quite regardless of his merit or comeliness. True forgiveness is impossible unless the wronged party take on himself the experiences of the malefactor. In like manner God himself, by his great sacrifice, is propitiated and inclined to mercy.

Nature and the Supernatural (1858) is the most comprehensive and wide-sweeping of Bushnell's major treatises; it deals with nothing less than the one "system of God." In this one system "nature" is seen as that realm of being which is governed or determined by law; the "supernatural" as that which is *not* in the train of cause and effect but which acts upon the chain from without and out of its own agency. These realms are seen as consubstantial or interpenetrated so that man and all living things, and how much more one knows not, partake of or participate in the supernatural and are in this way divine. The whole realm of spirit or freedom, in other words, was conceived of as supernatural, or transcendental in an Emersonian sense. On this foundation Bushnell then expounds his views of sin, miracle, incarnation, revelation, and Christ's divinity, all along vigorously defending these Christian views from skeptical attack. In this work as in no other the full scope, though by no means the full power, of his "romantic orthodoxy" is made manifest, as is the preponderant place that the apologetical task takes in his thinking.

As in all of his works one may note in this one an oscillation between liberal and conservative positions. A kind of incompleteness in the work also suggests that he had bitten off more than he could chew. Neither his historical nor philosophical preparations had been extensive enough to enable him to carry out a sufficiently penetrating work. His understanding of science and its method, moreover, was too limited to permit a fulfillment of his chosen apologetical task. The book's shortcomings explain why John Fiske, long before he became a famous evolutionary philosopher, saw in Bushnell what he took to be the hopelessly antiscientific bent of all Christian theology. Misunderstanding science and miscalculating the power and permanence of the rising philosophies of social and religious Darwinism, Bushnell probably overestimated the need for radical theological restatement. During most of his life his fears of popular skepticism overrode his own fundamental conservatism.

There were extremely liberal theological implications in much that Bushnell wrote, especially in his views on the essence and purpose of dogma and on nature and the supernatural. On public affairs, however, and in social philosophy he was a moderate conservative, suspicious of popular democracy and an admirer of the great Whig, Daniel Webster. Convinced that the wealth, health, and social excellencies of New England were the fruits of the Anglo-Saxon genius and Puritan piety, he was not sympathetic with the new, predominantly Irish and Roman Catholic immigrants who were moving into the New England cities and factory towns during his lifetime. He was very active during the 1840's in forming a Protestant League and Christian Alliance to combat the Roman Church, and the chief public result of his trip to Europe in 1845–46 was an outspoken open letter to the Pope, denouncing his despotism. His strategy in these efforts was to create a united Protestant front. He hoped that the various denominations would submerge their distinctive tenets and combine against the mutual enemy. His aims, thus, were practical rather than ecumenical in the modern sense. He believed that "most of what we call division in the Church of God is only distribution." The creed-based Evangelical Alliance did not interest him. It is a fact, moreover, that Bushnell's antidoctrinal liberalism did provide a rationale for the emerging type of common-denominator Protestantism that replaced the Puritan tradition in New England during the later nineteenth century.

Given these fears and this orientation, it goes without saying that in the great agitation over the "church question," which during these same years preoccupied leading theologians on the Continent, in Great Britain, and in America, Bushnell felt none of the "catholic" tendencies of the Oxford or Mercersburg movements. Though deeply imbued with romanticism in the general sense of that many-sided term, Bushnell, like so many thinkers of Puritan background, including Emerson, was relatively untouched by the historical interest usually associated with the impulse. Neo-medievalism held no charms for him, nor did the contemporary renewal of interest in the Reformation and the early church. Anglicanism at times seemed almost as menacing as Rome.

In the great sectional controversy that was racking the country throughout his adult years Bushnell was, of course, morally opposed to slavery and he criticized both the compromises of 1820 and of 1850; but he was not an abolitionist. Though he attacked the Kansas-Nebraska Bill and applauded antislavery victories in Kansas as a turning point in American history, he discountenanced most forms of antislavery activity. He was convinced that northern population growth would combine with other natural pressures to extirpate slavery in God's good time. In 1860 he did not like the "provoking uppishness" of the Republican Party but was gratified to see an "honest man" replace an "inveterate huckster" at the helm. Lincoln, he said in February, 1861, "may turn out one of the best and even ablest Presidents we have had." News of the Emancipator's assassination left him grief-stricken.

The awesome experience of a nation in arms had meanwhile added depths to Bushnell's understanding of sacrifice and expiation, a fact one may observe in his wartime sermons and in his two last treatises on the atonement. He was also led by this total experience to a profound application of his organic view of the state as a holy commonwealth. The Civil War he saw as a veritable *Volkskrieg* in whose antecedent iniquities both North and South were implicated and by which both were chastised. From it emerged a *nation* where before there had been only a group of states "kenneled under the constitution." The country's great tragedy had at least opened the possibilities for national rebirth and rededication; it had been "good" in the way Good Friday was good.

In all that he thought and wrote Bushnell was to a degree victimized by the increasingly superficial nurture and tastes of his Victorian audience; like Mark Twain he had to yield to the sentimental preferences of a "fastidious people." Caught between the regnant tradition of Congregational revivalism and the social amenities of the Episcopal parishes, he was during most of his career a kind of anticipatory prototype of the twentieth-century minister to suburbia. Notwithstanding these shortcomings and obstacles, Bushnell singlemindedly devoted his mature life to the exposition and deepening of an experience, insight, and vision which had been given him. In his later years he transcended both his times and his milieu. He produced a well-nigh classic theological literature which is justifiably compared with that of Albrecht Ritschl and, even more, Frederick D. Maurice. Bushnell made an enduring contribution to American educational theory, intellectual history, and, above all, to American theology and church life.

Bibliography

Horace Bushnell, *Christian Nurture,* New Haven, Yale, 1948.

Barbara M. Cross, *Horace Bushnell, Minister to a Changing America,* Chicago, Univ. of Chicago, 1958.

ALBRECHT RITSCHL

A. Durwood Foster

Through the last quarter of the nineteenth century the most prominent figure in German and in all Protestant theology was Albrecht Ritschl of Göttingen. A generation later, as H. R. Mackintosh observed, he was "behind a passing cloud."[1] The cloud was less simple oblivion than misrepresentation and misguided secondhand opinion; whether it really is passing remains to be seen. But in any case, the thrust of Ritschl's work has so basically coincided with the modern theological task as to identify his importance with the possibility and destiny of modern Christianity in general. Not even Schleiermacher, whom Ritschl acknowledged as "theological lawgiver" especially in this respect,[2] can be said to have compassed with such self-conscious intensity *both* poles of the modern theological problem: on the one hand man's existence shaped by the conditions of modernity, and on the other, the biblically grounded Gospel. Ritschl drew angry fire from modernists who would relinquish the Bible as well as from biblicists who would reject modernity. His polemical sharpness also antagonized many whose intentions did not sharply differ from his own. But all who follow the path of mediating theology in the larger sense stand greatly in his debt. Through one of the most crucial periods in the intellectual history of Christendom he was the theologian's theologian, who worked more effectively than anyone else to save the openness, the honesty, and the relevance of Christian thought. Among those who seek a responsible theology today, his successors include the emphasizers of biblical church dogmatics as well as the emphasizers of correlation with contemporary existence. And while neither Barthians nor Tillichians have been duly mindful of his services, this very fact indicates that the present

[1] *Types of Modern Theology* (London, Nisbet, 1937), p. 141 n.
[2] *A Critical History of the Christian Doctrine of Justification and Reconciliation* (Edinburgh, Edmonston & Douglas, 1872), p. 442.

49

day has not settled its account with him. It suggests that when and if modern theology should take another look, it might still find in Ritschl essential aid.

I

The son of a distinguished Lutheran preacher and bishop, Ritschl was born in Berlin in 1822. He grew up in Stettin amid a dedicated engagement with the affairs of the church. In the home were established significant insights into the deeper meaning of Christian spirituality and the "Reformation life-ideal." Fellowship with God in spite of confessed sin, unshakable trust in the divine providence, humility, patience, and prayer within the supporting communion of the church, cheerful striving in one's moral vocation—these were the indelible features of a *way of life* which the theologian later confirmed through wide-ranging historical study and for which he sought systematic intellectual formulation. But Ritschl remembered that such formulation is preceded by the nurturing objectivity of the church, that feeling and will have place with knowledge, and that abstract and traditional conceptions must appeal to practical need and experience.

Already committed to theology, in 1839 Ritschl entered university life with a "speculative urgency to grasp the highest."[3] But though he dug deeply in historical, biblical, and systematic subjects, neither at Bonn, Halle, or Heidelberg was he able to gain a "right understanding" of what had become and was to remain central for him: the Christian idea of reconciliation. At Tübingen he found some temporary satisfaction in the Hegelian standpoint and published his first work (*Das Evangelium Marcions und das kanonische Evangelium des Lukas*, Tübingen, 1846) as a disciple of F. C. Baur. However, the agreement with Tübingen was revoked as Ritschl independently reworked the sources for his own lecturing in New Testament and historical theology, begun at Bonn in 1846. In an 1851 article on the state of Synoptic Gospel criticism, he reversed his earlier position on Luke and declared against Baur for the priority of

[3] O. Ritschl, article on Ritschl, in *Realencyklopädie für protestantische Theologie und Kirche*, 3d ed., Vol. 17, p. 22.

Mark.[4] The break became definite with the second edition, in 1856, of his important monograph on the rise of the old Catholic Church, where Ritschl argues that the history of the early church is not a logical synthesis of primitive Jewish and Gentile Christianity (*Die Entstehung der altkatholischen Kirche,* Bonn, 1st ed., 1850). On the contrary, the New Testament canon, for all its variety, is grounded in the unified apostolic witness to Jesus as the Christ; the Judaizers condition this mainly as a rejected countermovement, and the Hellenic world, in mediating the transition to ecclesiastical forms, dilutes and obscures the original substance, as is seen particularly by comparing Paul with the subapostolic writers.

Desirous of greater academic freedom, Ritschl decided to leave Bonn in 1864 for Göttingen. There he taught for his remaining twenty-five years, declining invitations to Strassburg and (four times!) to Berlin. While he continued to lecture in New Testament, attention was henceforth given largely to systematic theology. At the height of his powers everything converged upon his lifelong focal interest in the doctrine of justification and reconciliation, wherein he saw the pivotal Christian teaching for which everything else was either presupposition or consequence. Following some solid preliminary articles, he began in 1870 the publication of his magnum opus, *The Christian Doctrine of Justification and Reconciliation.* The first volume (translated by J. S. Black, Edinburgh, 1872) dealt with the history of the doctrine. The second volume, on "the biblical matter of the doctrine," regrettably never translated, was a pioneering effort at critical biblical theology, presented at a time when the field was divided between fundamentalist biblicism and the scholarly quest for "pure" history. The third volume, appearing concurrently in 1874, gave the "positive development of the doctrine." Its English translation, marred by some unfortunate renderings, was completed in 1900.

The climax of Ritschl's career was the publication of his great work. It was primarily through it that he began to exert a wide and radical influence. Though always deprecating party spirit, he now encouraged the alliance of motives which began

[4] "Ueber den gegenwärtigen Stand der Kritik der synoptischen Evangelien," reprinted in *Gesammelte Aufsätze* (Freiburg, 1893), pp. 1 ff.

to characterize a school. Included were such ascending figures as Wilhelm Herrmann, Julius Kaftan, Adolf Harnack, and many others. This development, and the extension of Ritschl's influence not only in Germany but throughout the Protestant world, was reciprocally conditioned by the rise of an organized and vociferous opposition. Resultant controversy affected revisions of the main work, as well as several of his later small pieces such as *Theologie und Metaphysik* (Bonn, 1881). However, the continued pursuit of historical interests bore further fruit in a massive account of Pietism, *Geschichte des Pietismus* (Bonn, 3 vols., 1880–86), and his concern for religious education showed itself in a Gymnasium text, *Instruction in the Christian Religion* (Bonn, 1875; translated by Alice Mead Swing, 1901). Although the latter proved too condensed for its original purpose, it is the only fully outlined systematic statement of Ritschl's thought ever provided.

Death came to Ritschl in 1889, after a lifetime of vigorous health had been interrupted by a heart attack in the preceding autumn. Suffering through the last months, Ritschl, according to his son and biographer, manifested the same patience and humble trust as when deprived of his beloved wife some twenty years earlier. Though he devoted his life to the vocation of academic theology, the root substance of that theology was a practical faith which the man sincerely believed and lived.

II

"In reference to method," wrote Ritschl with better insight than many of his interpreters, "[Schleiermacher] is my predecessor."[5] The agreement goes beyond formal procedure to theological motive and to the positive conception of the Christian faith, though in the latter there are also crucial differences. Like Schleiermacher, Ritschl accepts the theological task as that of reconceiving faith with the modern world responsibly in purview. The pledge of this reconceiving is taking with inward seriousness the questions arising in principle from the age, in particular from natural science, biblical research, comparative religion, and philosophy. In expounding the finality of the Christian revelation, Ritschl deals trenchantly with everything

[5] *Theologie und Metaphysik* (Bonn, Marcus, 1881), p. 54.

from Enlightenment ethical criticism to "Life of Jesus" historicism and the possibility of personal beings elsewhere in the
universe. Thus Otto Ritschl's remark that the apologetical tendency is "entirely foreign" to his father holds true only so far as
apologetics is limited to the explicit arrangements of conversing
with unbelief.[6] The remark is misleading if the best defense for
faith is at bottom its systematic correlation with modern intelligence.

Correlation implies independence and interdependence.
Christianity must be exhibited as discrete from scientific knowledge and the cultural functions, yet as humanly imperative.
Though heteronomy must be avoided, man's needs nevertheless
are shown to correspond with the Christian answer. The former
requirement—that man shall be free—is not for Ritschl a mere
concession to Kant and modernity; it is an innermost element of
the Gospel. Sincerity about this gives genuine integrity to his
synthesis, however anthropocentric some may hold it to be. In
creation, in redemption, and in the world's final goal, God intends man's spontaneity as a moral and spiritual person. Christianity, as indispensable means and form, accords with the end
and self-fulfillment of humanity itself. This is the basic intention of the Ritschlian "proof of the necessity" of Christianity.
Thus, while maintaining "as the foundation-principle of the
Evangelical Church that Christian doctrine is to be obtained
from the Bible alone,"[7] Ritschl can also censure J. C. K. von
Hofmann for knowing "nothing except Biblical theology" and
for refusing to seek a "necessary concatenation between revelation and the necessary idea of God, and the necessary view of
the world and human history."[8]

However, Ritschl is well aware that faith cannot be logically
coerced. Following Spener he appeals to the motto that "whoever
willeth to do the will of God will know the truth of Christ's doctrine."[9] He concedes that "the proof is nothing but a demonstra-

[6] *Albrecht Ritschls Leben,* 2 vols. (Freiburg, Mohr, 1892–96), Vol.
II, p. 167.

[7] "Instruction in the Christian Religion," in A. T. Swing, *The Theology of Albrecht Ritschl* (London, Longmans, Green, 1901), p. 172.

[8] *A Critical History,* p. 540.

[9] Cf. John vii: 17; *The Christian Doctrine of Justification and Reconciliation,* translation edited by H. R. Mackintosh and A. B. Macauley,
2d ed. (Edinburgh, Clark, 1902), pp. 8, 24–25.

tion of the harmony of the ideas which are bound up together in the Christian view of the world and the Christian view of the self. The man who altogether rejects this system of ideas will find their proof meaningless too."[10] The conditions of the proof include, then, both a deciding and a participating subjectivity reminiscent on the one hand of Kierkegaard and on the other of Schleiermacher. But for Ritschl the dialectic of individual subjectivity is assimilated into a kind of historicized Kantian practical reason. He reasons, that is, in terms of universal moral ends informed by the categorical imperative, yet he knows that such ends are historically conditioned and that their universality must be asserted teleologically rather than typically or statically. The moral and spiritual goal of all history appears concretely through a given historical community and can be fully known and validated only within the living faith of that community. But the fact that the Gospel can be confirmed only through commitment to it does not diminish the role of reason in the understanding, outworking, and communication of faith. In principle the Christian revelation pertains to every man's destiny, since it clarifies and fulfills that toward which moral and religious experience are universally reaching. Moreover, faith implies a world view alongside which no fully coherent or adequate alternative is possible. The disjunction of the practical and the pure reason is therefore only provisionally and not finally possible. For, as Ritschl points out with respect to the moral proof of God, either the account of things must stop short of the whole, which betrays the aim of philosophical theory, or it must embrace the subjective moral exigencies which are an ineradicable part of the whole.[11] Faith, its primacy presupposed, proves itself through meeting practical personal concern and therewith through its power to illuminate the whole.

It may seem surprising that faith's relevance for a view of the whole is maintained along with a severe restriction upon the use of metaphysics in theology. The contemporary neo-Kantian skepticism which, in von Hartmann's phrase, turned theory of knowledge into "theory of ignorance," does not lead Ritschl to dispense entirely with metaphysics. He insists that theological

[10] *The Christian Doctrine of Justification and Reconciliation*, p. 530.
[11] *Ibid.*, Chap. IV, especially pp. 223–25.

science is obligated to clarify metaphysically its epistemological assumptions, and he attempts this in his own case by affiliation with his Göttingen colleague Hermann Lotze.[12] Yet for two related reasons Ritschl speaks out against substantive intrusions of metaphysics. First, faith has its own source and security quite apart from metaphysical props. It is wrong, therefore, to articulate the faith as though it had to be prefaced and buttressed by "natural theology"—a procedure which the Reformers succeeded in interrupting only temporarily. Here as elsewhere Ritschl says that the Reformation must continue. In the second place, perhaps an even more decisive ground for the stricture against metaphysics is the specific character of the biblical God. Ritschl argues that metaphysics, in Aristotle and traditionally, investigates being merely as being. But the radically personal God of the Bible cannot be subordinated to a theory of being in general or being itself. Thus the *analogia entis* is repudiated, not in favor of sheer transcendence but for the sake of the decisive analogy of the Divine Fatherhood apprehended by faith through Christ.

While acknowledging the difficulties of defining religion as such, Ritschl makes use, as Schleiermacher had, of a regulative concept of religion. This serves to clarify the relation of faith to philosophy, science, and morals; it aids in the discrimination of what is essential within the heterogeneous totality of the received tradition; and it provides for a critical and consummating relation of Christianity to the other religions. Ritschl's concept diverges from that of his predecessor in centering upon the rectification and ultimate guarantee of personal worth. The content of religious concern is fully clarified in the Christian affirmation of the individual person as God's child and image, exceeding in value the whole world. This corresponds to Ritschl's personalistic theism, the lack of which he regards as Schleiermacher's crippling defect. Also involved is concern for personal eternal life, or the dominion of personal values in relation to God, as against any kind of mystical absorption. The Christian hope for what may lie beyond earthly death is not analyzed by Ritschl, though he clearly rejects the notion of the indefinite temporal survival of a detached soul. He continually attacks that relig-

[12] Cf. *ibid.*, pp. 19–20; *Theologie und Metaphysik, passim.*

iosity which would contract man's eternally significant being into an inward detachable substance. On the contrary, integral to every person is the context of responsibility and community. The essential self cannot be divorced from moral life in history, and here too eternal life must manifest its primary import.

The other main component of Ritschl's regulative concept of religion is the determination that all strictly religious knowledge is comprised of independent value-judgments. Unlike theoretical knowledge, the affirmations of faith root in immediate personal concern. They belong properly to the subjective and not to the objective consciousness, to the practical rather than to the pure reason. As one would say today, they are radically "existential," with no admixture of merely intellectual cognition or information. Thus Ritschl opposes the Reformation idea of faith as trust (*fiducia*) to the Thomist notion that an independently determinable intellectual content must be assented to as an integral part of faith in addition to trust. His assertion is not that faith is intellectually formless but that it is *"in intellectu tanquam in subjecto."*[13] That is, the intrinsic intellectual structure of faith is inseparable from the subjective movement of feeling and will which faith essentially is. The "faith which is believed" is indefeasibly conformable to the "faith which believes" as trusting response to the God revealed in Christ. Decision for Christ thereby stipulates no preamble of metaphysics, dogma, or historiography.

However, faith *is* conditioned by the human situation. It presupposes the ultimate practical concern which is independent of special theoretical acquirements and peculiar emotional temperament. It is not the needs merely of an elite which Christ answers, but the universal personal question of our final meaning and being. This question, in turn, is posed by the two intermingling factors of finitude and sin. Man experiences the limitations of natural and social life—smallness, weakness, death—as threats to the life of the spirit. But guilty alienation from God compounds and gives sting to these limitations by cutting off the hope of overcoming them. Thus the resolution of the human predicament must deal with the problem of guilt as well

[13] *The Christian Doctrine of Justification and Reconciliation*, p. 105.

as the problem of finitude. It must include justification as an integral element in the securing of one's ultimate personal meaning and worth.

In the order of being, though not in the order of knowing, this construction of the human situation implies more fundamental premises regarding God's nature and purpose as well as the nature and end of man. Partly these have to do with the personality of God, which Ritschl not only affirms on a biblical basis but also defends rationally. Strauss and others (including thinkers as far back as Plotinus) have objected that personality would mean inadmissible dividedness in the Absolute. But, says Ritschl, this is the case only if the Absolute be conceived as empty space. Now on the one hand the merely negative concept of undividedness does nothing to explain our world as a unified and yet developing manifold. On the other hand personality is the best analogy we have for representing dynamic diversity within unity, especially with respect to spiritual and moral purpose. Unless the Absolute is personal there is no hope for fulfillment of the religious concern for ultimate personal meaning; nor, certainly, is there any basis for responsibility, sin, and guilt. As for the dividedness and multiplicity of finite personalities, neither of course can be carried over to God. But why should either be? God's personal will is the ground and embracing unity of the creation, history and end of finite but genuinely free moral and spiritual persons. There is still a structural over-againstness of man and God, but this depends upon the creative act of God. It is God's eternal purpose that man's moral and spiritual history should occur and should be consummated in Christ. This is the goodness of creation.

Of equal moment with the rejection of an impersonal Absolute is Ritschl's critique of the ethical premises determining the traditional concept of God. He observes that in classical orthodoxy as well as in its Socinian antithesis the original relation of God to man has been controlled largely by notions of merely impartial justice or equity. On the one hand the assertion of the transcendent and arbitrary divine majesty has implied toward the created order an essential indifference, the logical consequences of which have been exposed by Duns Scotus. This implicit indifference entirely justifies the argument of Socinus that

God might as well forgive sins freely. On the other hand there has been juxtaposed with the idea of indifference that of the divine moral government of the world. But the understanding of this latter element has been shaped not so much by the Bible as by the model of the Greek city-state whose tyrant impartially guards the laws and administers punishments and rewards. Again with respect to this model, Socinus is right that the idea of forgiveness cannot be combined with that of justice. The trouble, Ritschl argues, is that orthodox theology has never given methodical centrality to the specifically Christian norm. From Augustine onwards, Christ and the Gospel have been subjoined to a frame of reference erected on other grounds. Schleiermacher, once again, has pointed out the right direction by defining Christianity as the religion in which everything is related to the redemption wrought by Jesus. But Schleiermacher has not heeded well enough his own insight, and in particular he has not been aware of the decisive importance of the Old Testament as the special context of Jesus' person and work. Thus while Schleiermacher has understood the necessity of construing creation and redemption in close interdependency, his *Glaubenslehre* does not, in Ritschl's judgment, represent either the one or the other with sufficient fidelity to the biblical revelation.

With the whole Bible as background, "the content of the Divine will is to be deduced from the revealed reciprocal relations between Christ and God, and from no other principle."[14] There results from this a view quite opposed to that of indifferent majesty or impartial justice, for God must now be understood radically as the Father. From the beginning—that is, essentially and from eternity—our world and history are grounded in the purposing righteous love whose reality Christ fully discloses. The divine aseity and justice do not stand over against this disclosure; they too are known through and determined by it. God in himself is God for man and with man in Jesus Christ. But for Ritschl the purpose which is revealed through the Bible and climactically in Christ is more than merely a soteriological one. As given in the notion of covenant

[14] *Ibid.*, p. 237.

and supremely in that of the kingdom of God, it aims at a universal community whose form is personal freedom and whose content is righteous love. Within the embracing goal of the kingdom everyone has an individual moral vocation which ideally includes the development of autonomous personality in dedicated service to the whole. Ritschl holds that only by being committed to the will of God in Christ—that is, to the good will for the whole—can true liberty be attained.

In the doctrine of providence faith affirms, without being able to demonstrate even for itself, that the entire world order subserves God's kingdom. How, then, is providence related to the history which has occurred before and apart from Christ, and how is it related to sin and evil? Ritschl wrestles with these problems but concedes the impossibility of fully solving them. He rejects twofold predestination and chides Augustine, Luther (in respect of *De servo arbitrio*), and Calvin for "unwarranted overstepping of theological competency."[15] Consciousness of election in Christ does not imply that some individuals were passed over and others picked out from an array of neutral prehistorical souls. The unevenness of personal destiny, rooting as it does in natural and historical contingency, may presumably have been presupposed by the end of an uncoerced moral and spiritual development of mankind. In any case, no life where love and moral value have been experienced is devoid of eternal significance. Yet Ritschl is far from claiming that any nice balance can be struck between a partly known divine plan and the actual course of history. At least non-Christian history does not stand under the condemnation of God. The heathen are not threatened with eternal punishment. It is as though Ritschl would have us think that sufficient unto them is the meaning they have.

Sin can be partly understood as conditioned by finitude, in particular by ignorance. But since it roots in moral freedom it cannot be wholly explained in any way. In this connection Ritschl regards the traditional doctrine of original sin as worse than useless. For by exaggerating the powers of Adam, it renders the first sin more inexplicable; and by referring subse-

[15] *Ibid.,* p. 126.

quent sins back to the first, it obscures present responsibility for them. Furthermore, the doctrine tends to swamp the field of necessary moral discriminations with a blanket description that cannot be taken seriously in practical life. The premises of education as well as normal moral intercourse refute it. The function of the doctrine has been to overthrow human merit and thus register the need for redemption. But its use for that purpose is "just as appropriate as it would be to use a boulder to kill a gnat."[16] Nevertheless, man's guilty alienation from God does pose a felt need that becomes the more drastic as the sinner compares himself with Christ. Also of fundamental importance are the socio-historical structures which Ritschl groups under the "kingdom of sin, . . . a substitute for the hypothesis of original sin which gives due prominence to everything that the notion of original sin was rightly enough meant to embrace."[17] All sin is forgivable so long as conditioned by ignorance, or, in other words, so long as it has not hardened into a final rejection of God. We can assert no actual instance of such hardening, identified as the sin against the Holy Spirit, though its real possibility must be maintained. God's love constrains, but Ritschl will not allow that it coerces the will of man.

Evil, in distinction from sin, "signifies the whole compass of possible restrictions of our purposive activity."[18] It cannot in general be regarded as punishment, which presupposes conscious guilt. On the other hand, the Christian may regard evils, retrospectively and presently, as disciplinary or as sent by God for a good end. But Ritschl takes even Schleiermacher to task for knowing too much about the matter. He cautions that we should not expect to find a reason for every misfortune. What we can hold to is trust in providence, confident that in everything God works for good with those who love him. The treatment of this subject supports Ritschl's claim that he never denied mystery, but only desisted from speaking whereof he knew not.

The source of confidence in God's providence is the historical Jesus Christ mediated through Scripture and church. In this

[16] *Ibid.,* p. 340.
[17] *Ibid.,* p. 344.
[18] *Ibid.,* p. 351.

matter Ritschl has been misrepresented through equal and opposite oversimplifications of his position. He has been denounced for trying to strip away faith from the "bare facts" of the original Jesus and, at the same time, for dismissing objective historiography. Actually, he insists on maintaining both history and faith. At the pole of the original datum both the historical figure and the apostolic witness are integral. At the pole of contemporary appropriation, the faith of the church is primary, but historiography has place. Ritschl argues that the facts about Jesus cannot be finally estimated on objective grounds alone. On the other hand, he enjoins and strives for a rigorous employment of scientific criticism and its results. Faith genetically does not hang on these results, but Ritschl could never with Kierkegaard have called them "rubbish." For they do help to clarify faith and relieve it of corruptions. As a biblical scholar he is tendentious, and his work is now dated; but no adequate assessment has yet been given of Ritschl's pioneering effort to combine historical and theological exegesis.

It is not the witness of faith but the pre- and post-historical transmutations of Jesus over against which Ritschl sets the historical figure. The normativeness of the latter stands against Logos speculation and "spiritual-Christ" fanaticism. The idea of pre-existence is not to be wholly cast out, since it expresses the conviction that Jesus and the Kingdom are grounded teleologically in the divine eternity. But what is thus grounded is the historical personal wholeness of Jesus, not an abstracted, somehow previously subsistent element. In an analogous way Ritschl interprets the continuous power of the exalted Lord, although here, there is the severe special problem of conceiving the Easter event. On the resurrection Ritschl is diffident, not to say cryptic, apparently having reached no precise conception. Clear, however, is the principle that the living presence of Christ to faith has for its *content* the biblically portrayed person. The spiritual is bound to the historical. Resurrection and glory do not belong to an abstracted, now independent element, but to the life that was lived and the cross that was borne.

To know Christ is to know his benefits, not to speculate about the union of his natures. But while the person is measured in the work, the work itself is inseparable from the definite features of the historical life: the perfect sonship of trust and love, the dedication of everything independently human to the purpose shared with God, the tested but unbroken fidelity to vocation. These features permeate the life and cannot be isolated in one aspect or moment such as the teaching or the suffering on the cross. Faith, in apprehending this one life as the model and power of its own being, affirms that Jesus is the unique Son and final revealer of God. In the Nicene and Chalcedonian formulae Ritschl senses a detached scientific interest which should not be prescriptive for faith. But he can assert Christ's Godhead as "the worth to be put on those human achievements of his which suffice for our salvation."[19] Ritschl emphasizes Christ's humanity; yet in two ways he maintains the divinity: formally, in the unity of Christ's will and purpose with God's; and efficiently (so to speak), according to the paradox of grace stated by Paul in Phil. ii: 13. Thus, in Christ's human will and purpose God meets us; and we also give thanks to God for the mystery of this uniquely transparent humanity. Scientifically we cannot penetrate to the "special conditions of Christ's dependence upon God, however indefinite the formula in which we might express them."[20] But while Christ is a free and fully human personality, he is *as such* also the Divine Word, which "includes in itself the characteristic working of God, and is simply inconceivable without it. . . ."[21]

In the traditional scheme of the three offices, Jesus is prophet in revealing God's reconciling, Kingdom-forming will. He is priest in that, according to his unique vocation as God's intermediary, he lives and suffers for our sake in founding the community of forgiveness. His kingship, established through the first two offices, is especially manifest in patience and in humble, serving love. The three offices interpenetrate, but Ritschl occupies himself especially with the priestly function. Against orthodoxy the Socinian criticism is cogent, yet it is devoid of the religious and historical consciousness that Jesus is the redeemer and the founder of the community of redemption. The same lack is found in Kant and the ethical philosophy of the

---

[19] *Ibid.*, pp. 437–38.
[20] *Ibid.*, p. 439.
[21] *Ibid.*

Enlightenment. Jesus is reduced to a prophet who announces God's pardon as a timeless truth. But can we have more than this without recourse to the idea of substitutionary appeasement? Throughout his adult life Ritschl struggled earnestly with this problem, keeping it in continuous development through the various volumes and editions of his work. Consequently, at some points it is difficult if not impossible to compose his over-all or even his final view. For instance, the first volume of the major work, reviewing the history of doctrine, leads one to expect that a more strictly "objective" construction of the atonement will be forthcoming than is actually the case in the third volume. But even in the third volume, and in the last edition of it, there is still an unmistakable tension and oscillation. The evolution of Ritschl's thought, as he himself insisted, was strongly conditioned by the biblical investigations of his second volume—especially the inquiry into the concepts of sacrifice and the divine righteousness. Ritschl became convinced that the normative biblical meaning of sacrifice centers in the overcoming of alienation and the re-establishment of communion, not in any kind of payment to God. Divine righteousness he came to understand as the faithfulness with which God carries out his loving purpose to found the Kingdom, not as a separately constituted, fixed justice which requires satisfaction in itself. These insights weighed against any purely objective view of the atonement.

Nevertheless, Ritschl does in two ways assert an objectively grounded atonement. In the first place Jesus gives himself as sacrifice "for us" (in our behalf, not in our place) in living, suffering, and dying for the redeemed community. His deeds of active and passive obedience form the once-for-all established bridge for reconciliation with God. More than mere teaching, they are there for us in history, not as causing God's mind to change, but as providing the concrete means of change in us. In the second place, however, Ritschl wishes to recognize in Jesus' work a more purely objective representation. The Kingdom-forming personal life of Jesus is the end for which God creates and governs the world. In the actuality of this life, therefore, there is a reconciliation of the world to the divine purpose. Jesus sums up, as it were, and offers back to God the justification of the historical and human venture. In accepting this representation God accepts all those who participate in and are identified with it; He sees the world and more particularly the redeemed community through and in Christ.

Ritschl's principal motive in holding out for an objective dimension in the atonement is his commitment to Luther's "in spite of" as a fundamental characterization of the Christian life. The good news of Christ is that sinners are justified and accepted while still in their sins. Thus, as against Roman and Pietist tendencies, the Reformation insists upon the synthetic concept of "pronouncing righteous" (*Gerechtsprechung*) instead of the analytic "making righteous" (*Gerechtmachung*) in describing God's handling of the sinner in Christ. For this reason justification cannot in all respects be identified with reconciliation, although the two are inseparable. Justification is the beginning and the foundation of reconciliation; but it does not imply, in any other sense than the turning to Christ in trust, that reconciliation already is accomplished in the sinner. Justification and reconciliation are a single doctrine, yet a twofold one. Correspondingly, there is the tension between justification by faith and the necessity of good works which Ritschl saw to be determinative of the whole structure of Christian life. For while he gladly embraced the idea of *justus et peccator*, he reproved Luther for unfairness to the Epistle of James. The Christian man is also blessed in his deeds.

"Christianity," accordingly, "resembles not a circle described from a single center, but an ellipse which is determined by two *foci*."[22] Every moment in the circumference of Christian existence is a function both of the graceful indicative and of the moral imperative. Christ restores sinners to fellowship with God, but he also enlists their discipleship for the Kingdom. The imperative defines the sin which alienates us as well as the goal which engages our no longer alienated freedom. The indicative overcomes our alienation and bestows upon us the power freely to embrace the imperative as our own. But the two foci do not coalesce. For justification is in spite of unrighteousness, and the law of righteous love impinges in spite of justification. Yet there

[22] *Ibid.*, p. 11.

is an inner relation between faith and works in the freedom over the world and for God which Ritschl understands as the content of eternal life. For this freedom is concretely given and exercised, not outside the world—in the monastery or the life beyond—but in and for the world, after the model of Jesus himself.

Wherever the liberty of the Christian man is exercised, God's Kingdom is incipiently present. The model of its full realization is Christ, but it comes into being in the measure that Christlikeness prevails among men: in the measure, that is, of reverent trust, humble patience, fidelity to vocation, and serving love. Though he would apply the goal of the Kingdom to the transformation of society, there is in Ritschl no simple progressivism or utopianism. The Kingdom is more within and above history than at the end of it. Nor is it possible to formulate for the Kingdom a rigid code of ethics. For love, the highest righteousness, cannot be translated into prescriptions. It is mediated in incalculable ways through the individual's disposition and is essentially qualified by the individual in his unique contexts.

The church, in Ritschl's view, is not the Kingdom either in fact or in principle. For if it were the Kingdom it would be subject to the perfectionism of the imperative, whereas actually it is grounded in the indicative of grace and is the mediation of the same through prayers and sacraments, proclamation and teaching. The Kingdom is manifested spontaneously from within the church, but it does not define the essential being of the church. Yet Ritschl stresses the church in some respects more than he does the Kingdom. The concrete life of the forgiven, worshiping, aspiring fellowship is actually the first principle of his theology. From within the church Ritschl takes his bearings with respect to Jesus Christ, its ground, as well as to the Kingdom, which is its goal. We do not first grasp the full compass of our sin, then settle accounts with God in Christ, and thereupon wind up in the church. On the contrary, through and within the church we come gradually to understand our sin, and likewise we grow in the knowledge and grace of our Lord Jesus Christ. It is consonant with this orientation that Ritschl appeals theologically to Christian experience and to hymnody, and that he evinces so much concern not only for the history of doctrine

but also for Christian education, for the overcoming of the
church's dividedness, and for a theology of the laity. The
Roman ecclesiology errs not in emphasizing the importance of
the church, but in identifying it with the priestly hierarchy.
The church is the whole body of those who are indwelt by the
Holy Spirit, the Spirit of Christ. This Spirit is nothing less, according to Ritschl, than the very knowledge which God has of
himself in Christ. It is the power of the grace and truth which
the church has beheld and which motivates its mission to mankind: the bread of its own life and the light of the world.

III

Ritschl's theology is certainly not able to save all the phenomena of the historic faith. The sense for mystery and for the
awesome holiness of God registers too faintly. The cross and
the resurrection do not as such retain their traditional centrality. The communion of the Christian with God is inadequately
portrayed—Ritschl could not bring himself to appreciate even
his friend Wilhelm Herrmann's attempt to supply the portrayal.
In general the emotional and quasi-mystical phenomena of the
Christian life are intolerantly handled. In this and other matters a combative will tends to shape exaggerated antitheses. Yet
who would favor wholly suppressing this approach for the sake
of irenic synthesizing? Moreover, it would be smug to assume
that there is today a firm universal position from which can be
read off pat judgments against Ritschl. Even his stricture against
metaphysics remains problematic rather than simply wrong-
headed, and the burden of proof must lie on those who would
tell us that he was no more than a blunderer in philosophy.

Appreciation is confused by the unfinished or fluctuating aspect of some of his key ideas: the relations of eternity and time,
of will and knowledge, of the kingdom and the church. At
these points, of course, one wrestles with perennial difficulties
of Christian understanding; and the same is true with respect
to what surely is a fundamental problem in Ritschl's thought:
Christ's role as the mediator of our salvation. In bringing God
to the sinner, how shall it be that Christ does not stand between
the sinner and God? On the one hand, as Ritschl sees it, Christ

bestows upon us the fellowship with the Father which he himself enjoys; he is the model of our own redeemed God-relatedness. But on the other hand, it is only in or through Christ that God views and receives us, not in terms of our own individuality. In the one image, corresponding to reconciliation, we are in personal communion with our heavenly Father, whose solicitous love misses every lost sheep. In the other image, corresponding to justification, a Christo-monism displaces the concern for our personal response to God. Perhaps the images cannot finally merge. For, as Ritschl knows so well, the Gospel proclaims new being and yet acceptance in spite of our lack of new being, so long as we cling to Christ.

Aside from the great stimulus he gave to the development of critical-historical perspective, a comprehensive estimate of Ritschl's success will depend first and most generally upon how seriously one takes *both* poles of the mediating theological task: the biblical message *and* the human situation. Secondly it will depend, on the one side, upon how biblicistic one insists upon being about the Bible, and, on the other side, upon how practically or existentially (rather than theoretically or ontologically) one thinks the situational base line must be traced. In the third place and quite particularly, it will depend upon how radically one is willing to construe man's subjective autonomy. If one is instinctively hostile to "anthropocentrism," or if one regards Christianity as only a rescue operation, it will be difficult to see much good in Ritschl. But if one believes that creation and redemption themselves have basically to do with human freedom, then Ritschl's theology may well be one of the noblest efforts yet made to reconcile the graceful divine sovereignty with the dignity of truly responsible though sinning manhood.

Bibliography

No books by Albrecht Ritschl have been available for some years.

Hugh Ross Mackintosh, *Types of Modern Theology: Schleiermacher to Barth,* London, Nisbet, 1956, Part V.

FREDERICK DENISON MAURICE

William John Wolf

Frederick Denison Maurice, described by Masterman as "the greatest thinker of the English Church in the nineteenth century," was born at Normanstone in 1805. His father was a Unitarian minister who had once been a younger colleague of Joseph Priestley. Young Frederick with three older and four younger sisters knew an affectionate, tightly knit family until about the age of ten when some of his sisters and finally his mother left Unitarianism for the strict Calvinism of the Baptists. To prepare himself for the study of law Frederick lived for some time in London with a family closely allied to the Wilberforces and to evangelical circles in the Church of England. At Cambridge he took a first class in civil law but could not receive the degree because he would not subscribe to the Thirty-nine Articles. At college he was introduced to Plato and Coleridge. With his lifelong friend John Sterling he moved to London in 1827 to write for and finally to edit a literary journal.

His dissatisfaction with Unitarianism was resolved when he became a member of the Church of England and returned to university study to prepare for its ministry. At Oxford he finished his novel *Eustace Conway* and was ordained in 1834. *Subscription No Bondage,* his defense of the Articles as requirements in the universities, deserves study today apart from its dated controversy as a thoughtful analysis of the theological foundations of education and culture. In 1870 as he drew near the end of his career he indicated its importance in his own understanding of his work. "No book which I have written expresses more strongly what then were, and what still are my deepest convictions."[1]

He exercised a deep pastoral and preaching ministry as chap-

[1] *The Life of Frederick Denison Maurice, Chiefly Told in His Own Letters; Edited by His Son Frederick Maurice,* 2 vols., (N.Y., Scribner's, 1884), I, p. 174.

lain of Guy's Hospital in London. At first he welcomed the Anglo-Catholic revival of the Tractarians, but he was soon drawn into controversy over Pusey's beliefs on baptism.

Maurice married Annie Barton, sister of Sterling's wife. In 1845 she died, leaving him with two small boys. Later he married Georgiana Hare, half-sister of Julius Hare. Maurice was appointed professor of English literature and modern history at King's College, London. Afterwards he accepted the chair of divinity in its newly added theological college. He gave up Guy's Hospital to become chaplain of Lincoln's Inn, a center for students.

His theological masterpiece is *The Kingdom of Christ* (1838), which began as a series of letters to a Quaker "concerning the Principles, Constitution and Ordinances of the Catholic Church." His revision of 1842 was edited in 1958 with helpful notes by Alec Vidler. The first half consists of an analysis of Quakerism, pure Protestantism (Lutheranism, Calvinism, Zwinglianism, Arminianism), Unitarianism, contemporary religious, philosophical, and political movements, and Roman Catholicism. His basic conclusion is that nearly every one of these movements is right and truthful in its positive assertions but wrong in its negations, which are compounded into systems that further divide men and shatter the unity of Christ's church. Rarely has a man been able to live and think himself more imaginatively and appreciatively into the beliefs of others. Maurice is a Christian Socrates meeting other Christians on their own ground. The second half of the book describes the "hidden hunger" of the previous systems and interprets the Bible as the progressive manifestation of covenantal relations between God and man in terms of family, then nation, and finally church as the kingdom of Christ. The "signs of a spiritual society" are then analyzed in the order in which men are drawn into communion with Christ: baptism, the creeds, forms of worship, the eucharist, the ministry, and the Bible. Relations between church and nation are described, and the Church of England, particularly its party structure, is analyzed with respect to the previous problems and concerns. A common misunderstanding of Maurice is to regard this book simply as an apology for the Church of England.

I am not ignorant, also, that the hints which I have offered in opposition to systems may, themselves, be turned by myself or by others into a system. . . . On the other hand, if there be anything here which may help to raise men above their own narrow conceptions and mine, may lead them to believe that there is a way to that truth which is living and universal, and above us all, and that He who is Truth will guide them in that way—this which is from Him and not from me, I pray that He will bless.[2]

The Kingdom of Christ sets forth theological principles which have yet to come into their own in the ecumenical movement. As the Protestant churches see beyond pan-Protestantism to an ecumenism that is genuinely catholic and as the Roman Catholic Church comes out of its isolationism and loses what one of its theologians has called its "anti-Protestant face," Maurice's modestly offered "hints" will become increasingly central to ecumenical discussion and action. Already there are studies of the cosmic nature of the church by French Roman Catholic writers like de Lubac that resemble Maurice's positions. Father Bouyer comments that if anyone has seen the principle that is needed "to resolve the crisis endemic in Protestantism". it is Maurice.

Maurice is often described as the founder of Christian socialism. This description may actually be the source of more confusion than light. Maurice was not interested in a specific set of social goals for which legislation was to be sought. He was interested in a theological analysis of political and economic reform, in providing educational opportunities by founding colleges for working men and women, and in challenging his theological students to concern for the social imperatives of the Gospel. He helped set up a series of workers' cooperatives. "Competition is put forth as the law of the universe. That is a lie. The time is coming for us to declare that it is a lie. I see no way but by association for work instead of for striking. Hence my notion of a Tailors' Association." Maurice with Ludlow and Charles Kingsley was the senior statesman in a group loosely called Christian socialists, who met weekly after the

[2] *The Kingdom of Christ*, 2 vols., rev. ed. (London, Everyman's Library, 1842), II, p. 332.

events of 1848 and later published "Tracts on Christian Socialism." The name had been suggested by Maurice, but his own comment indicated his orientation. The title "would commit them at once to the conflict they must engage in sooner or later with the unsocial Christians and the un-Christian Socialists." He felt that the nation was related to the church much as the law is related to the Gospel. The church must educate "the conscience of the nation." "The time is come . . . when a nation must be felt to be *not* a formal corporation but a spiritual reality, a society of which we *can* predicate spiritual conditions and spiritual emotions, which can repent and be reformed as an individual can."[3] In an Advent sermon for the turbulent year of 1848 he asked: "Do you think that the invasion of Palestine by Sennacherib is a greater event than the overthrow of nearly all the greatest powers civil and ecclesiastical in Christendom?"

Attacked on all sides by the politically conservative papers of both low and high churchmanship, Maurice gave his enemies the opportunity they were seeking to impugn his orthodoxy when he published in 1853 his *Theological Essays,* his second best known work. He had criticized the popular view of the endless (i.e., eternal) nature of future punishment. His own understanding of the word "eternal" was drawn from such Johannine texts as "This is life eternal, that they might know thee the only true God, and Jesus Christ, whom thou hast sent." After much controversy he was dismissed by the Board of King's College for somewhat undefined opinions "of a dangerous tendency . . . calculated to unsettle the minds of the theological students."

In 1860 Maurice was appointed to St. Peter's, Vere Street, London. In 1866 he became Knightbridge Professor of Moral Theology and Moral Philosophy at Cambridge. The remainder of his life was spent in university surroundings where he also had cure of souls at St. Edward's. The substance of his Cambridge lectures is preserved in his immense two-volume work on the history of *Moral and Metaphysical Philosophy* and in his lectures on casuistry entitled *The Conscience.* He died on Easter Monday 1872 as he prepared to receive Holy Communion.

[3] *The Prophets and Kings of the Old Testament,* 2d ed. (Boston, Crosby, Nichols, 1853), pp. 403 ff.

Most of Maurice's writing was called forth by specific controversies. This occasional character of his thought with its demands on the modern reader for a detailed knowledge of Victorian England is doubtless one of the reasons why he has been so neglected until comparatively recent years. Any deep knowledge of him requires a complementary study of his life. Here there is an excellent resource at hand in the two volumes of his *Life* by his son Sir Frederick Maurice. This is largely a collection of his letters.

In 1842 he wrote *Three Letters to the Rev. W. Palmer*, defending the proposal of a Jerusalem bishopric with the German Lutherans. In *The Epistle to the Hebrews* (1846) he replied to Newman's *Theory of Development*. He delivered the Boyle Lectures on *The Religions of the World*, a work that both pioneered in the field and enjoyed immediate popularity. In 1859 he fiercely attacked Mansel's Bampton Lectures in *What Is Revelation?* Mansel was skeptical about our ability to know God, but argued that since the philosophical alternatives to Christian theism became entangled in unsolvable problems we might accept Bible and tradition. Maurice considered this the very worst of apologetical methods and held out for God's gracious self-disclosure as the Word that really enlightens every man.

Maurice's use of the Scriptures was precritical and constitutes a problem to the student today who works through his otherwise excellent commentaries or sermons on the Bible. Some of the more outstanding of these are: *The Prophets and Kings of the Old Testament, The Unity of the New Testament, The Doctrine of Sacrifice, The Patriarchs and Lawgivers of the Old Testament, The Gospel of St. John, The Epistles of St. John, The Gospel of the Kingdom of Heaven,* and *The Commandments Considered as Instruments of National Reformation.* The extent of his writing is amazing. One estimate runs to more than 16,300 octavo pages.

METHOD AND STYLE

The interpreter of Maurice's thought is considerably helped by its inner consistency from the time he sought ordination in the Church of England until his death. Very few changes are to be recorded. He remained loyal to the basic principle of Christ as king, which he had established very early. He found, however, ever more fascinating ways of illuminating man's cultural task in its light. Many times Maurice made clear his opposition to system-building. While he modestly described his vocation as "metaphysical and theological grubbing," this phrase really expressed his deliberated choice of the method of laying bare the theological presuppositions of culture and of dogma. "Now to me these words [system and method] seem not only not synonymous, but the greatest contraries imaginable: the one indicating that which is most opposed to life, freedom, variety: and the other that without which they cannot exist."[4]

Behind this opposition to system is something of Kierkegaard's existentialist protest. The note of struggle in finding "the truth-for-him" is present in a letter: "I can say, I did not receive this of man, neither was I taught it. Every glimpse I have of it has come to me through great confusions and darkness."[5] His chief opposition to systems of doctrine, however, was founded on his respect for the facts of historical existence. In this Maurice expresses both the Englishman's empiricism against the conceptualism of Continental thinkers and the Anglican's respect for historical institutions as points of departure for theological analysis.

> When once a man begins to build a system the very gifts and qualities which might serve in the investigation of truth, become the greatest hindrances to it. He must make the different parts of the scheme fit into each other; his dexterity is shown, not in detecting facts, but in cutting them square.[6]

One of his letters provides insight into his understanding of the theologian's task.

> . . . theology is not (as the schoolmen have represented it) the climax of all studies, the Corinthian capital of a magnificent edifice, composed of physics, politics, economics, and connecting

---

[4] *Kingdom of Christ,* I, p. 238.
[5] *Life,* II, p. 16.
[6] *Ecclesiastical History,* p. 222.

them as parts of a great system with each other—but is the foundation upon which they all stand. And even that language would have left my meaning open to a very great, almost an entire, misunderstanding, unless I could exchange the name theology for the name *God*, and say that He Himself is the root from which all human life, and human society, and ultimately, through man, nature itself, are derived.[7]

An unfortunate hurdle for the reader of Maurice is his style, which can be and often is opaque and confused. Every reader finds himself at times trying to translate his author. This problem is partly the result of Maurice's extensive use of the Socratic method of inquiry, in which it is not always clear whether the evaluation and exposition is to be regarded as Maurice's or that of his imaginary interlocutors. Sometimes it reads like dictation that has suffered from interruptions. In spite of all this, however, there are passages of great emotional intensity and conviction. Every now and then he has the gift for epigrammatic utterance that makes it worth searching for nuggets amid the slag.

THE BASIC CHRISTOLOGICAL PRINCIPLE

No theologian of Christendom has ever expressed with more passionate conviction and sustained throughout a lifetime with more fidelity and richness in his theological analysis of culture the biblical witness to the cosmic setting of Christ's person and work. Christ, the Eternal Son of God, is "the Head and the King of our entire race." That is the heart of the Gospel as Maurice understood it.

In a letter to his son he wrote: "I was sent into the world that I might persuade men to recognize Christ as the center of their fellowship with each other, that so they might be united in their families, their countries, and as men . . ."[8]

The basic principle of all of Maurice's theology is that God has created and redeemed all men in Christ. This he believed to be the basic witness of the creeds and behind them of the en-

---

[7] *Life*, II, p. 136.
[8] *Ibid.*, I, p. 240.

tire biblical revelation. Incarnation-atonement in a trinitarian setting is the key feature for understanding every other Christian doctrine as well as the human situation.

My desire is to ground all theology upon the name of God the Father, the Son, and the Holy Ghost; not to begin from ourselves and our sins; not to measure the straight line by the crooked one. This is the method which I have learned from the Bible. There everything proceeds from God; He is revealing Himself. He is acting, speaking, ruling.[9]

Maurice felt that contemporary theology, whether Roman Catholic or Protestant, whether Anglo-Catholic or Anglican Evangelical, had wrongly oriented itself around the sinfulness of man as the actual (even if not explicit) starting point. He proposed instead the divinity of the early creeds, which do not mention the fall of man. It should be noted here that Maurice held to a literalistic view of Genesis and thus believed in the fall as historical fact. Yet Maurice had understood that we know Adam and man through Christ and not *vice versa*.

Protestants and Romanists, even while they denounce and excommunicate each other, yet appear to recognize the fact of depravity, of Evil, as the fundamental fact of divinity. The fall of Adam—not the union of the Father and the Son, not the creation of the world in Christ—is set before men in both divisions of Christendom as practically the ground of their creed.[10]

The theocratic principle in Maurice's thought that Christ is the head of all mankind is never left in isolation. It is always immediately correlated with the nature of the church and her function in the world. To Miss Williams Wynn he wrote in 1858:

I do therefore anticipate a very deep and searching reformation, one which cannot be attended with less trials, one which I trust is to issue in greater blessings than the Reformation of the sixteenth century. . . . I feel very strongly that the ascension of our Lord into the heavens, and the glorification of our nature in

[9] *The Doctrine of Sacrifice* (London, Macmillan, 1893), p. xii.
[10] *Conflict of Good and Evil*, p. 170.

Him with the corresponding truth that the Church exists to witness of Him, not only as her Head, but as the Head of every
man will be the battle-cry that will rally Protestants and Romanists, hungry seekers after wisdom, lonely tatterdemalions without bread, about the one standard . . .[11]

Maurice held his understanding of *Christus Consummator* in
close association with what might be called *Ecclesia Consum-
matrix*. It remains to underline the significance of this fundamental Christological principle for such other doctrines as
revelation, man and sin, the church and the sacraments.

REVELATION AND SCRIPTURE

In spite of his precritical attitude toward biblical study, Maurice
anticipated many of today's theological commonplaces about
revelation and its modes. He distrusted the scholastic distinction between natural and revealed theology on at least two
grounds. He could not accept the notion that there were two
pathways to the knowledge of God, especially that there could
be one initiated from the side of man by something called "un-
aided reason." In today's terminology we would say that he
believed in general revelation. "I hold that *all* our knowledge
may be traced ultimately to Revelation from God."[12] He repudiated "the contemporary rage for apologetical literature."
In the second place, he refused to class the Gospel as a religion
among the religions of the world. The Bible is not about religion, but about the acts of the living God. ". . . we have been
dosing our people with religion when what they want is not this
but the living God."[13]

Maurice's use of the Bible has sometimes been criticized as
"Platonizing eisegesis." There is no question about the impact
of Plato on his thought. Yet even there the influence is more in
terms of a method of inquiry than of substantive propositions.
The Kingdom of Christ reminds one at once of Socrates seeking
the definition of justice by questioning conflicting schools of

[11] *Life,* II, pp. 316–17.
[12] *Sequel to the Inquiry, What Is Revelation?* (Cambridge, Macmillan,
1860), p. 97.
[13] *Life,* I, p. 369.

opinion. Maurice, of course, is leading his respondents on to the admission that there actually is a Catholic Church in their midst to which each bears a partial witness. Probably the criticism of Platonism is rooted in the recognition that for Maurice the Johannine writings are very much the clue to his understanding of the Bible as a whole. It might even be permissible further to limit the field by saying that within the Fourth Gospel it is the prologue which is the key.

The Bible is the witness to the kingdom of Christ, and that kingdom is the real theme of the Old Testament and the source of half-truths in other religions and philosophies. Actually Maurice in interpreting any passage tried to understand its simplest context as well as its historical context. Then he tried to show how the historical facts therein narrated also were pointers to God's universal kingdom and in particular to the constitution of all men in Christ. He believed that the Holy Spirit would reveal the relevance between these insights and the situation of the preacher or reader of the Bible. He believed deeply in the self-authenticating character of revelation.

I use them [the Scriptures] because I conceive they set forth Christ as the Son of God and the Lord of every man. I do not use them because I think they set forth some standard which is good for a set of men called Christians, who are different from other men, and who have not the same God with other men. I use the Scriptures to show us what I believe is the law and the life for all of us, that law and life of which men in the old world had only a partial glimpse. I should not use them if I thought them less universal and more partial than the books of heathens or of later moralists.[14]

For Maurice the Bible is not a solitary fact. He seeks to lay bare the organic connection that actually exists between church, creeds, and Bible. His Anglican heritage with its respect for Bible, tradition, and reason received a creative reinterpretation in depth.

He who dwells with us and governs us, the Ever-blessed Word, has formed us to be one in Him; He seeks to make us one by

[14] *Epistles of St. John* (London, Macmillan, 1867), p. 14.

bringing us to a knowledge of Himself: for this end He has revealed Himself to us, and has preserved the revelation in a book; this revelation He has entrusted to His Church, that she may impart it to men, and train men to apprehend its contents; the Church, in the exercise of her functions, has from Scripture formed a creed which is the first step in her scheme of education; when men were awakened by this creed, it became her duty to use the Bible, that they might know the certainty of those things wherein they have been catechised; with this Bible, she is able to cultivate the reason, which is the organ wherewith we apprehend spiritual matters; the Church tried what she could do without the Bible, and she became weak; the Bible has been set up against the Church, and has been dishonored; the Reason has been set up against both Church and Bible, and has become partial, inconsistent, self-contradictory. Finally, bitter experience must lead us at last to a conviction, that God's ways are higher than our ways; that a universal Church, constituted in His Son, and endowed with His Spirit, is the proper instrument for using His universal book; and this book the instrument for educating the universal reason.[15]

MAN AND SIN

It is evident from the previous statement of Maurice's Christological principle what his method will be in evaluating the human situation. Christ precedes Adam in the order of being. When it is written in Genesis that man has been created in the image of God, Maurice at once understands that man has been created by the Eternal Son and that this image can therefore not be destroyed by sin. We are "not to think that the world was created in Adam, or stood in his obedience; for the Scriptures of the New Testament, illustrating those of the Old, teach us that it stood and stands in the obedience of God's well-beloved Son; the real image of the Father, the real bond of human society and of the whole universe who was to be manifested in the fulness of time, as that which He had always been."[16]

This means that when Christ comes he comes not as an alien

---

[15] *Kingdom of Christ* (1838), II, pp. 87 ff.

[16] *The Patriarchs and Lawgivers of the Old Testament,* 5th ed. (London, Macmillan, 1878), p. 66.

intruder into the world and to men, but as the redeemer of his own creation. While Christ brings us the utterly new gift of redemption, he does not extricate us from the race but restores us to our true life as men created in his image.

It is clear that such a presentation will entail a different understanding of sin than the traditional one which speaks either of a total loss of the image of God or of certain aspects of the image. For Maurice, sin is to be understood not so much prospectively as in conventional treatments which develop sin as the prelude to redemption, as retrospectively in the sense that we are members of a race that has been redeemed by the incarnation of the Word, by his bearing the sins of the whole world and by his resurrection from the dead on the plane of our history.

There is no minimizing of the Atonement in Maurice's work. Indeed, the opposite is the case, for his firm convictions about the work of Christ in overcoming sin led him to demote the doctrine of sin from its too dominant place in popular theologies. Maurice's view of the Atonement in *Theological Essays* has been characterized as close to the moral theory. This is only a partial description, although perhaps justified because of the obscurity of expression in that work. His own view of the Atonement is best set forth in *The Doctrine of Sacrifice,* one of the clearest of his writings. Tracing the sacrifices of the Old Testament in a way that would need much correction today from newer historical perspectives, Maurice holds that the New Testament asserts sacrifice as the great principle of the divine obedience of the Son before the world existed. What is new here is the careful linking of the Trinity and the idea of creation with the concept of Atonement.

. . . we see beneath all evil, beneath the universe itself, that eternal and original union of the Father and the Son . . . which was never fully manifested till the Only Begotten by the eternal Spirit offered Himself to God. The revelation of that primal unity is the revelation of the ground on which all things stand, both things in heaven and things in earth. It is the revelation of an order which sustains all the intercourse and society of men. It is the revelation of that which sin has ever been seeking to destroy, and which at last has overcome sin. It is the revelation of that perfect harmony to which we look forward when all things are gathered up in Christ . . . when the law of sacrifice shall be the acknowledged law of all creation.[17]

Maurice views sin from the angle of Christ's accomplished work; from this angle he cannot, I feel—contrary to his critics —be accused of underestimating the power of sin. Sin, for him, is to be defined as self-willed isolation from the true constitution of man as created and redeemed by Christ. Sin is man's refusal to acknowledge his true center in Christ, and his desperate effort to establish a false independence. Since Maurice took the fall as a historical event, his interpretation that it must not be the base for theology is all the more remarkable to us who usually describe it as a myth that lays bare deep insights into the human situation. Maurice also believed in the devil, but refused to grant that the world was properly his possession.

Maurice's criticism of Calvinism was that it misinterpreted God's election and predestination in a narrowly individualistic and exclusivistic way that made a travesty of the biblical witness that Christ was himself the elect and predestinated One and that the whole race, not just a favored few, was included in him. This perspective is quite close to Barth's criticism of Calvin. Maurice claimed that the constitution of the race in Christ is the proper background for appreciating the power of Luther's concern for justification by faith and of keeping that cardinal insight uncorrupted. But Protestantism found it almost impossible to submit its doctrine of justification by faith to the *experience* of justification by faith. As a result ". . . when assent to the doctrine of justification was substituted for belief in the Justifier, Protestantism went into the lean, sickly and yet contentious stage of its existence, only to emerge from that into indifference —a mere denial of Romanism."[18]

THE CHURCH AND ITS SIX SIGNS

For Maurice the church was organic to the Gospel. It is the body of Christ, given life by its head, that exists to show the world its true center and by articulating the law of mutual sacri-

[17] *Doctrine of Sacrifice*, p. 194.
[18] *Life*, II, p. 615.

fice to support the unity of both nations and families. Maurice held that the church was really the world when the Christological principle was rightly understood.

> The world contains the elements of which the Church is composed. In the Church, these elements are penetrated by a uniting, reconciling power. The Church is, therefore, human society in its normal state; the world, that same society irregular and abnormal. The world is the Church without God: the Church is the world restored to its relation with God, taken back by Him into the state for which He created it.[19]

It was not customary in Maurice's time to develop the idea of the church as the Israel of God. With a thoroughly scriptural analysis he traced a series of covenants between God and Abraham and the Israelite nation to show that family and nation are preliminary manifestations of church structure. *The Church a Family,* one of his most helpful books, carried on this theme. The ultimate pattern of unity is God Himself who as the Blessed Trinity expresses the ground of the family principle. He described the fundamental position of the *Kingdom of Christ* as follows: ". . . there rose up before me the idea of a *Church Universal,* not built upon human inventions or human faith, but upon the very nature of God himself, and upon the union which He has formed with His creatures."[20]

Just as the church had a history in Israel and in the New Testament period, so it has today. It is to be recognized by concrete facts of historical existence, not just in theological ideas. The theologian does well to accept the historical givenness of the signs of the church. These as facts are more impressive in their witness to the "Universal Society" than in the views men have entertained about these facts.

The fundamental sign of church life is baptism, whereby men are forgiven their sins and are incorporated into Christ and realize their status as sons of God because of the objective and racial atonement effected by Christ. Maurice liked to call baptism "the sacrament of constant union." He stressed the importance of sacraments as demonstrations of the free grace of God

[19] *Theological Essays* (Cambridge, 1853), p. 403.
[20] *Kingdom of Christ,* I, p. 14.

in Christ and as salutary checks to any excessive preoccupation
of man with his own feelings or faith.

> Outward signs and tokens have a great worth. They attest the
> reality and the universality of God's gifts, as in the case of the
> water in baptism and the bread and wine in the Lord's Supper.
> They prevent men from fancying that their thoughts, and im-
> pressions, and beliefs, create the blessings which are bestowed
> upon us by God's free grace.[21]

Baptism interprets to man the human situation. Maurice has
a way of bringing all his previous insights together when he
seeks the depth of his next point. Notice the themes hitherto
separately developed now focused on baptism:

> I have maintained that Christ, by whom, and for whom all
> things were created, and in whom all things consist, has made
> reconciliation for mankind; that on the ground of this atone-
> ment for mankind, God has built His church, declaring men one
> family in Christ. . . . And [we believing] that the mark of that
> universal body or fellowship, appointed by God Himself is Bap-
> tism, do, without fear or scruple, asseverate of ourselves, and of
> all others who will come to this holy Baptism, of all who bear
> the marks and impress of that nature which Christ took, in His
> birth, of the blessed Virgin; that they are admitted into these
> high and glorious privileges; that they are brought into a state of
> salvation; that they are made sons of God and heirs of everlast-
> ing life. . . . And in saying this, we contend that we give faith
> . . . a ground upon which to stand, and which otherwise it can-
> not have.[22]

The second sign of the kingdom of Christ is the fact of the
two creeds which confess the triform name into which we are
baptized. The creeds are not digests of doctrines; they are our
protection against theological systems. To say the creed is to
confess the name, to make an act of allegiance to a person.
Baptism is the sign that we are saved by grace; the creed that
we are saved by faith.

---

[21] *Acts of the Apostles*, p. 188.
[22] *Kingdom of Christ* (1838), I, pp. 88 ff.

The third sign of the church is the existence of set forms of worship such as are collected in the Book of Common Prayer. Maurice is one of the deepest interpreters of liturgics. He rejoiced that the ordinary Englishman expressed his worship in forms derived from the Hebrews, the Greeks, and the Latins. It was evidence to him that the church transcended space and time. Like most engaged today in the liturgical movement he held that "the prayers written in the first ages of Christianity are in general more free, more reverent, more universal, than those which have been poured forth since."[23]

The eucharist is the fourth sign. It testifies that because of Christ's sacrifice once and for all perfected on Calvary a "living and perpetual communion" has been established between God and man. It expresses Christ's "continual presence with His universal family." More significant than the debates over the manner of Christ's presence, Maurice maintained, was the reality of that presence as sheer fact. There was social meaning to the eucharist and an eschatological anticipation of the new age. Here his biblical orientation saved him from any Platonism, although even so he cannot be said to have given to eschatology that weight which it has held recently in biblical studies and theology. He was too Johannine for that. Maurice felt personally that the eucharist expressed a depth and a practicality that man could not find elsewhere, not even in the Bible. "Ask yourself then solemnly and seriously: 'Can I find Christianity—the Christianity I want—a Christianity of acts, not words, a Christianity of power and life, a divine, human, Catholic Christianity for men of all countries and periods, all tastes and endowments, all temperaments and necessities so exhibited as I find it in this Sacrament?' "[24]

The ordained ministry is the fifth sign of the church. It testifies that there is a permanent structure in the life of the church, a representative office of sacrificial service that unless it is kept faithfully may congeal into a hierarchy, making the church only another expression of the world. Maurice wrote that the four Gospels might be described as "The Institution of a Christian Ministry." The historic episcopate, he believed, expressed the

23 *Ibid.*, II, p. 30.
24 *Ibid.* (1838), I, p. 287.

reality of universal communion in the church and was the order
that stood in essential succession to the apostolate.

> I believe that He meant His Church to stand in certain perma-
> nent and universal institutions . . . in a permanent ministry
> through which He should declare His will, and dispense His
> blessings to the whole body, and the main office in which should
> be that apostolic office which belongs characteristically to the
> new dispensation, seeing that it expresses the general oversight of
> Him, who no longer confines Himself to any particular nation,
> but has ascended upon high that He might fill all things.[25]

Although he considered the episcopate necessary, he did not,
like the Tractarians, unchurch those who had lost it. The bond
of communion might be broken and yet many ties with the
universal church might still stand. Unlike the Tractarians he
refused to define the limits of the church. "I cannot answer the
question; I believe only One can answer it; I am content to
leave it with Him."[26] Nothing would more falsify the picture
than to describe Maurice as expounding Anglicanism as a system superior to other systems. He who was *persona non grata*
to all the parties within the Church of England in his day and
who warned against parties and systems, even to the extent of
calling those who said they had no party the expression of the
worst partisanship, was not likely to suggest that Anglicanism
as such was what creation had been awaiting. The power of
Maurice as a reconciler is illustrated in a letter to Erskine of
Linlathen:

> The English *Church* I look upon as merely one branch of the
> true Church; and every *system*, whether called Evangelical, Lib-
> eral, Catholic, or purely Anglican, which has been invented by
> the members of that Church in former times and in our own day
> to express their notion of the Church, I look upon as "of the earth
> earthy," and as much carrying in it the seeds of destruction as
> the systems of the different sects which have revolted from her.
> The Church—it seems to me—is a part, the highest part, of that
> spiritual constitution of which the nation and the family are
> lower and subordinate parts; implied in the acts we do and the

---

[25] *Three Letters to the Rev. W. Palmer*, p. 8.
[26] *Epistle to the Hebrews*, p. cxxiv.

words we speak, established before all worlds, manifested as the true and everlasting kingdom when the Son of God died, rose, and ascended on high . . . testified as the common property and inheritance of men by certain forms and ordinances which convert it from an idea for the mind into an actual reality for all who will enter into it and enjoy it, and which prove God to be true though all men be liars.[27]

Since the sixth sign of the universal church, the Bible, has already been treated in the section on revelation, it remains to make a brief summary and evaluation. In *Christ and Culture* Richard Niebuhr cites Maurice as more clearly expressing the position that Christ is the transformer and converter of culture than "any other modern Christian thinker and leader." In spite of its being largely precritical, his sustained exposition of the Bible anticipates the christological interpretation of history held by many contemporary biblical theologians. Social prophet, yet deficient in eschatological perspective, he may be called "a thoroughgoing Johanninist" in his Christian humanism. His ecumenical theology is just beginning to come into its own with its reconciliation in depth between Catholicism and Protestantism. Maurice many times described his whole ministry and authorship as a search for unity.

The idea of the unity of the Father and the Son in the Holy Spirit, as the basis of all unity amongst men, as the groundwork of all human society and of all thought, as belonging to little children, and as the highest fruition of the saints in glory, has been haunting me for a longer time than I can easily look back to.[28]

[27] *Life*, I, pp. 306 ff.
[28] *Ibid.*, p. 414.

Bibliography

Frederick Denison Maurice, *The Kingdom of Christ,* new ed. based on 2d ed. of 1842, Alec R. Vidler, ed., London, SCM Press, 1958.

Alec R. Vidler, *Witness to the Light: F. D. Maurice's Message for To-day,* N. Y., Scribner's, 1948.

ADOLF VON HARNACK

Wilhelm Pauck

I

Harnack was born on May 7, 1851, in the Baltic city of Dorpat in Livonia, which was then and is now again a Russian province. His forebears had come there from Germany. His paternal grandfather, a tailor, hailed from East Prussia, and his maternal grandfather, a professor in the University of Dorpat and for many years its rector, was a native Westphalian. His father, Theodosius Harnack, a strict Lutheran with pietistic leanings, was a professor of practical and systematic theology, first in Dorpat, then for thirteen years (1853–66) in Erlangen, Germany, and then again, for the rest of his life, in Dorpat (he died in 1889).

Adolf Harnack and his three brothers (they were all unusually gifted) received their education in Erlangen and Dorpat. In October 1872 he left home in order to complete his studies in the University of Leipzig.[1]

In 1873 he wrote and published his doctor's dissertation on an early Gnostic text. Shortly thereafter (1874) he began his academic career as a church historian, first as a *Privatdozent* (1874) and then as a professor-extraordinary (1876), in Leipzig. In 1879 he was appointed to a professorship in Giessen. From there he moved to Marburg (1886). Two years later he was called to the University of Berlin. By then he had already acquired fame as a teacher, researcher, author, and critic and

[1] Hans Lietzmann writes in a commemorative article (*Theologische Literaturzeitung* 76, 1951): "When as a young student I became acquainted with Harnack in Venice, he told me one evening during an unforgettable conversation about his upbringing. As if he were telling a fairytale he said: 'We were four brothers, and when we left home, our father gave each of us one thousand dollars and told us that we should make good. All four of us did make good—and I still have the thousand dollars.' "

86

as an organizer of scientific projects.[2] This call was opposed by the Supreme Council of the Evangelical Church. Being the highest office of the Prussian state church, the council was entitled to exercise a veto right of sorts on appointments to the theological chairs in the universities. However, both the faculty and the Ministry of Education strongly desired Harnack's appointment. On their recommendation and on that of Chancellor Bismarck and his cabinet, Emperor William II, then at the very beginning of his reign, overruled the church office and affixed his signature to the document of Harnack's appointment (September 17, 1888).[3]

The objections of the churchmen were based chiefly on Harnack's *History of Dogma* (3 vols. 1886–89; 4th cd., 1909). They consisted mainly of the following charges: (1) that he doubted the traditional views concerning the authorship of the Fourth Gospel, of the Letter to the Ephesians, and of the First Epistle of Peter; (2) that he was critical of miracles and, specifically, that he did not accept the conventional interpretation of Christ's virgin birth, resurrection, and ascension; and (3) that he denied the institution of the sacrament of baptism by Jesus. No attempt was made to refute these views on the basis of historical scholarship from which they were derived; only the irreconcilability of Harnack's views with the doctrinal authority of the church was stated.

All this cast a dark shadow upon Harnack's academic position. Indeed, it lay upon his entire career. Even at this time, to be sure, Harnack was of the conviction that the gospel of Jesus Christ had nothing in common with the doctrinal authority exercised by an ecclesiastical hierarchy or by a bureau of church officials. But the church to which he belonged felt it necessary to maintain this very authority. He could therefore hardly avoid

[2] In 1876 he founded (with his friend Emil Schürer) the *Theologische Literaturzeitung*, which is still one of the foremost critical reviews of theological scholarship. (Harnack was its sole editor beginning in 1881 and held this post for many years.) In 1881–82 he began (in cooperation with his friend O. von Gebhardt) the publication of the series *Texte und Untersuchungen* which, in the course of time, became a mine of information on the history of the ancient church.

[3] Cf. Walter Wendland, "Die Berufung A. Harnack's nach Berlin," *Jahrbuch für brandenburgische Kirchengeschichte* 29 (1934), pp. 103 ff.

some kind of conflict with it. Nevertheless, it was a source of deep sorrow for him that, throughout his life, he was denied all official recognition by the church. He was not even given the right to examine his own pupils as they entered into the service of the church. Yet for many years he was the most influential theological teacher in the land. Hundreds, nay, thousands of students who later became ministers gave him an enthusiastic hearing, and scores of them were inspired by him to prepare themselves for theological professorships, which then became centers from which his views were spread to ever widening circles. As a member of the theological faculty of Germany's most distinguished university, which was maintained and supported by the state and protected by it as to its academic freedom, he made an incisive contribution to the training of the leaders of the Protestant Church. This church was united with the same state, yet it never invited him to take a seat at its councils, synods, or boards, and it never gave him any assurance that as a theological teacher he was one of its spokesmen. Thus Harnack could not but be deeply disappointed in his strong desire to serve the church.[4]

In a wider sense he served it, of course, through his prolific authorship. Most of his more than sixteen hundred large and small writings were devoted to the study of the history of the church.[5] The New Testament, the Church Fathers, but also the Reformation and Protestantism furnished him the main themes.

Certain of his works have already become classics. His *History of Dogma,* for example, will have a permanent place among the masterpieces of theological literature. Though it will be superseded in specific parts here and there, it will always be recognized as a most suggestive work of historical interpretation, grandly conceived and executed with superior skill as to both

[4] The only opportunity he had to satisfy this wish was given him through his membership in the Evangelical-Social Congress (one of the voluntary associations so distinctive of modern Protestantism), whose purpose it was, outside the official church but through a membership that was recruited from the ranks of church members, to give concrete expression to the Christian responsibility for the social-political order. Harnack was its president (1903–12).

[5] Cf. Friedrich Smend, *A. von Harnack: Verzeichnis seiner Schriften* (Leipzig, 1931), which lists 1611 titles.

style and content.[6] The work on *The Mission and Expansion of Christianity during the First Three Centuries* (2 vols., 1902; 4th ed. 1924) is almost of the same quality. His *History of Ancient Christian Literature* (3 vols., 1893–1904) laid the foundation for all further critical studies in patristics.

Few works of modern theological literature have created as much excitement and stirred up as much furor as Harnack's *Wesen des Christentums* (*What Is Christianity?*, 1900; 15th ed., 1950). It is the transcript of a student's stenograph of a course of lectures delivered to students of all faculties in the winter semester 1899–1900. Troeltsch[7] thought it was representative of all theological work based on historical thinking. It certainly has become generally regarded as the one book which more directly than any other represents so-called liberal Protestant theology.

Harnack continued to publish scholarly and popular writings throughout his life. His authorship extended over fifty-seven years, from 1873, when he published his dissertation on Gnosticism, to 1930, when his publications ended with an article on the name of Novatian. His first important scholarly work had been a prize essay on Marcion (unpublished) for which the University of Dorpat had given him a gold medal; his last significant book was devoted to an interpretation of the same heretical figure,[8] and it stirred up considerable excitement.

In his capacity as a historian, Harnack was elected in 1890 to the Prussian Academy of Sciences in Berlin. Theodore Mommsen, one of its most distinguished members, gave him an enthusiastic welcome. Here he soon became organizer and

---

[6] One of Harnack's admirers, the French Jesuit scholar J. de Ghellinck, wrote about it (*En marge de l'oeuvre de Harnack. Gregorianum* 11 [1930], pp. 513f.): "Everyone knows the three volumes of his *Dogmengeschichte*, though it is perhaps correct to say that more people talk about them than read them." (*Chacun le s connait bien qu'il soit peut-être exact de dire que les trois volumes de sa Dogmengeschichte ont trouvé moins d'hommes pour les lire que pour en parler.*)

[7] Cf. Ernst Troeltsch, *Was heisst "Wesen des Christentums"?* (*Gesammelte Schriften* II [1913], p. 387): *Harnack's Schrift is gewissermassen das symbolische Buch für die historisierende Richtung der Theologie.*

[8] *Marcion: Das Evangelium vom fremden Gott* (Berlin, 1921; 2nd ed., 1924).

chairman of the editorial council of the *Critical Edition of the Greek Christian Authors of the First Three Centuries*. Furthermore, he learned to relate theological scholarship to that of other disciplines. It was a signal honor that he, the theologian, was invited by the Academy to prepare its history which was planned to be published in connection with the celebration of its two-hundredth anniversary, in 1900. Harnack punctually fulfilled the assignment. In three volumes, he offered not only an interpretation of the activities of the Academy but, in connection with it, also a history of modern scholarship.

At the dawn of the new century, he was at the height of his career. When the anniversary of the Berlin Academy was celebrated in a glittering ceremony, he was the official orator. It so happened that, just then, he occupied also the post of rector of the University of Berlin. Moreover, at this time his fame was spreading throughout the world in connection with the publication of the book *What Is Christianity?* He wielded great influence on educational affairs through the office of the Ministry of Education, who frequently sought his counsel.[9] Ever increasingly he became a representative personage. The public saw in him scholarship personified. William II, the German Emperor, gave him special recognition, first by inviting him into his company and then by bestowing special honors upon him.[10]

All this had an effect upon his academic career. To be sure, church-historical teaching and research continued to be his primary love and labor. But in the course of time he came to assume two further professional responsibilities. Indeed, he said of himself that he was active in three different careers. In 1906 he accepted the appointment to the post of Director General of the Royal Library[11] in Berlin, the largest and most important library in Germany. Some of his friends were disturbed; they feared that he might gradually abandon his theological career. But Harnack wrote to his friend Professor Martin Rade in Marburg:

[9] At one time the rumor was abroad that he would be appointed Minister of Education.

[10] He raised him to the dignity of hereditary nobility. Harnack was the last scholar so honored in royal Prussia.

[11] After World War I it was called the Prussian State Library.

You come to know the world only in so far as you influence it. My new position will not make me a librarian so much as an organizer. I hope that my friends will find that theology is not made the loser thereby but that all branches of learning, including theology, will make a gain. I have *done* little in my life, and I should like, in a modest way, to supplement my work of lecturing and writing by a "doing" from which the whole community can profit. The church has not offered me an opportunity of this kind, and if such work were offered to me now, it would come too late for me.[12]

He proved to be an excellent organizer and a brilliant administrator. Hence nobody was much surprised when, in 1911, he accepted also the post of President of the Kaiser Wilhelm Gesellschaft.[13] This was a foundation organized (in connection with the celebration of the centennial of the University of Berlin and sponsored by the German Emperor) for the purpose of launching scientific research institutes in which scholars would pursue pure and applied research of a kind which the universities could not afford to become engaged in, on account of their primary responsibility for teaching and professional training. Under Harnack's leadership and with the support of government and industry, the foundation rapidly established several research institutes. Almost immediately they won worldwide recognition and influence.

Harnack continued to be president of the Kaiser Wilhelm Gesellschaft until the end of his life. He led its affairs when it assumed broader and poignantly practical responsibilities during World War I, and he saw it through the turmoil caused by Germany's military defeat and through the ensuing period of monetary inflation and economic depression. In the spring of 1930 these duties led him to Heidelberg, where a new institute of medical research was to be opened. There he died, after a brief illness, on June 10, 1930.

In 1921 he had become a professor emeritus. He then gave up all administrative duties connected with his professorship and he also retired from the library, but he continued to teach

---

[12] Agnes von Zahn-Harnack, *Adolf von Harnack*, 2nd ed. (Berlin, 1951), p. 325.
[13] Now called Max Planck Gesellschaft.

(on a reduced schedule, of course) for several years.[14] In the spring of 1929 he delivered his last lecture in the University of Berlin and at the same time closed his seminar on ancient church history, over which he had presided continuously for 108 academic semesters. It always had been the center of his work and the headquarters of his professional labors. For in connection with the broad influence he exercised and throughout the deep impact that went forth from him to all fields of cultural endeavor, he always remained first of all a church historian and a theologian. Indeed, he embodied in his person a kind of cultural Protestantism, which was deeply anchored in his personal faith and reached out broadly upon the wide field of human civilization.[15]

II

Whatever may have been the secret of Harnack's power and whatever was the source of his accomplishment as a scholar, administrator, public figure, and representative man, one can say that he was what he was and that he produced his great

[14] In the fall of 1921 the German Government offered him the post of ambassador to Washington, D.C., but he regretfully declined the honor.

[15] Harnack was a person of great charm. This is the impression one obtains from reading the biography which his daughter Agnes wrote with a rare and congenial understanding of her father (cf. footnote 12). It is also the testimony of all who knew him well. At the memorial service held at the University of Berlin, Professor Erich Seeberg spoke of "his dutiful discipline in so ordering his daily life and dividing his time that he was able to accomplish so much—coupled as this discipline was with a chivalrous and objective formality in his dealings with men and in the management of his relations with them." (Erich Seeberg, *Adolf von Harnack*, Tübingen, 1930, p. 25.) At the same occasion the rector of the university, Professor Erhard Schmidt, a mathematician, characterized him as follows (*ibid.*, p. 6): "Harnack was of a noble, aristocratic character; his outward distinction was softened by a generous, considerate, and kind disposition. In conversation, he never let one feel his superiority; on the contrary, he enhanced the self-confidence of the one who was speaking with him by rearranging in a most agreeable way whatever was being said to him and putting it in such a form that the other took great delight in the thought he had expressed." There is a fine characterization of Harnack in Erich Fascher's *Adolf von Harnack—Grösse und Grenze* (Berlin, 1962).

works in the way he did because he was an unusually gifted teacher.

One who was one of his students in Leipzig, at the very beginning of Harnack's career (in 1877–78), wrote, almost fifty years later, in the following enthusiastic way of the impression Harnack (who was then still in his twenties) made upon him and his fellow students:

We had the feeling that a new world was dawning upon us. We had been trained by capable teachers and we were taking courses from eminent professors and well-known scholars. But here we were touched by the aura of genius. Harnack combined in himself in a unique way the qualities required of a scholar with the gifts of a born teacher: concentrated inquisitiveness; tireless industry; the ability of ordering and forming his materials; a comprehensive memory;[16] critical astuteness; a clear and considered judgment, and, together with all this, a wonderful gift of intuition and combination and, at the same time, a marvellously simple, lucid, and appealing manner of presentation. And, to top it all, he also had not infrequently the good fortune of finding and discovering something new. To every subject and field of study he gave light and warmth, life and significance. In both theory and practice he was a master of the teaching method.

He came to his classes only after thorough preparation. He was never without notes, but he spoke extempore . . . without affectation or pathos and never seeking cheap effects. He talked eloquently and from an even inner participation in what he was dealing with, without trying to excite or overwhelm his hearers. Yet he was fascinating and convincing. He was illuminating through the gentle compulsion of complete objectivity. He was conscientious and accurate but not pedantic, nor did he get lost in details. Without minimizing or concealing difficulties, he explained the problems at hand with vividness as to their logical form and material content. He made the past live through the present and let the present explain the past.[17]

[16] Harnack's brother-in-law, H. Rassow, writes (*Christliche Welt* 44, 1930), p. 728: "I asked him once: 'How much time would you need in order to memorize one page of Greek that you had never seen before?' He replied: 'If I read the page slowly, I would know it by heart.'"

[17] *Christliche Welt* 35 (1921), p. 315. The writer was Prof. W. Bornemann.

Many other testimonies prove that these striking words express the experience and judgment of the large circle of Harnack's students and pupils. Among these none is perhaps as telling as that of Dietrich Bonhoeffer, who was a member of Harnack's last seminar and who spoke in the name of his fellow students at the memorial service on June 15, 1930, in Berlin.[18] He said, among other things:

> He got hold of us in the way a real teacher gets hold of his pupils. He shared our questions, even though he confronted us with his superior judgment. We assembled in his home for a serious piece of work on the history of the ancient church, and there we came to know him and his unerring striving for truth and clarity. All mere talk was foreign to the spirit of his seminar. He demanded absolute clarity. This did not exclude the possibility that very personal and inmost questions were raised. He was always willing to listen to questions and to answer them. All that mattered to him was the honesty of the answer. Thus we learned from him that truth is born only from freedom.[19]

We should note that as a teacher Harnack was a historian and that as a historian he was a teacher. The role of the teacher is almost identical with that of the historian. In a certain sense every true teacher is a historian, and nobody can be a true historian unless he is willing to be also a teacher. For, in every present, men find that they must come to terms with the cultural legacy which they have inherited from their fathers. They must take possession of it and incorporate it into their own lives. They must fit it to the requirements of their own situation and thus transform it and then transmit it to their children and children's children.

Civilization is a product of education and a learning process at the same time. Men are engaged in it in order to relate the values produced by past generations to the needs of the present; at the same time, they endeavor to hand them on to future generations. Whoever, therefore, furthers human culture is in a real sense a teacher as well as a historian, for as he hands down

[18] Bonhoeffer was executed because he opposed the Nazi dictatorship. Harnack's eldest son, Ernst, experienced the same fate.

[19] "Adolf von Harnack," *Ausgewählte Reden und Aufsätze*. Berlin, 1951, p. 210.

the cultural traditions of the past to those around him, he acts as a historically responsible educator. In this sense, Harnack was a supreme teacher-historian.[20] His writings as well as his activities clearly prove that he believed it to be the highest task of the historian to prepare his fellow men for right action in the present.[21] "Only that history which is not yet past but which is and remains a living part of our present deserves to be known by all," he wrote.[22] Hence he regarded all history as mute if it is nothing but a display of an antiquarian interest or if it is dealt with only in terms of archaeology, i.e., understood to be the mere record of past human life.[23]

The following statement sums up Harnack's fundamental conception:

We study history in order to intervene in the course of history, and it is our right and duty that we do this, for if we lack historical insight we either permit ourselves to be mere objects put in the historical process or we shall have the tendency to lead people down the wrong way. To intervene in history— this means that we must reject the past when it reaches into the present only in order to block us. It means also that we must do the right thing in the present, i.e., anticipate the future and be prepared for it in a circumspect manner. There is no doubt that, with respect to the past, the historian assumes the royal function of a judge, for in order to decide what of the past shall continue to be in effect and what must be done away with or transformed, the historian must judge like a king. Everything must be designed to furnish a preparation for the future, for only that discipline of learning has a right to exist which lays the foundation for what is to be.[24]

[20] Cf. W. Pauck, "Harnack's Interpretation of Church History" in *The Cultural Heritage of the Reformation*, 2nd ed., Chicago, 1961, pp. 337ff.

[21] Cf. Hans Lietzmann, *Gedächtnisrede auf Harnack. Sitzungsberichte der Akademie der Wissenscheften in Berlin*, 1931, p. LVIII.

[22] In "Sokrates und die Alte Kirche,"*Gesammelte Reden und Aufsätze*, 1951, p. 25.

[23] Cf. *Wesen des Christentums*, p. XVII, and *Reden und Aufsätze*, Vol. IV, p. 5.

[24] *Über die Sicherheit und Grenzen geschichtlicher Erkenntnis. Reden und Aufsätze*, Vol. IV, p. 7.

We would misunderstand the import of these words if we took them to imply that Harnack was not concerned about the objectivity of historical research. He was wont to say that he was doing his work as a historian on three levels, namely, source criticism, representation, and reflection, and that he felt most at home on the third level.[25] And it is a fact that he devoted rigorous and time-consuming effort to the establishment of the accuracy and reliability of his sources, and that he took great care to represent and interpret these sources as diligently and objectively as possible. But he was also painfully aware of the limits that are set to the historian as he attempts to reconstruct, to relate, and to interpret past actions and events. He shared to some extent the skeptical judgment of Goethe[26] who is reported to have said in a conversation with the historian Heinrich Luden: "Not all that is presented to us as history has really happened; and what really happened did not actually happen the way it is presented to us; moreover, what really happened is only a small part of all that happened. Everything in history remains uncertain, the largest event as well as the smallest occurrence."

As a historian, he therefore did not try to tell *wie es eigentlich gewesen* (what really happened), and, indeed, he avoided all biographical history because he suspected that it represented, especially in regard to motivations, a necessarily unsuccessful engagement with insoluble puzzles and inscrutable enigmas. Instead, he chose to study the development of institutions, i.e., states, societies, groups, and corporations and their established practices, customs, laws, codes, and authoritative rules. He interpreted institutional history as a history of ideas, for he felt that one cannot understand the development and the power of institutions unless one knows the direction along which they are moved by the ideas that govern and maintain them. For example, he believed it to be the historian's task to show to what extent an institution has succeeded in incorporating the idea or purpose for the concrete expression of which it was founded, or

[25] The remark is reported by Walter Koehler. Cf. *Theologische Blätter* 7 (1930), p. 168.
[26] Cf. his lecture "Die Religion Goethes in der Epoche seiner Vollendung," *Reden und Aufsätze*, Vol. IV, p. 157.

in what way an institution has striven to maintain itself even after losing the right to exist because the purpose which called it into being became invalid or lost its directive power. He even dared define the norm by reference to which the historian can judge what institutions or institutional functions deserve to be maintained—that within them which preserves life. And he was persuaded that "only that line of action and that power preserve life which liberate men from the 'service to that which passes away,' from enslavement to mere nature, and from servitude to one's own empirical self."[27]

III

Among Harnack's books the *History of Dogma* is the clearest expression of this basic conception of the historian's task. It shows concretely how and to what extent he tried to carry out his historical principles in his own field of study. He himself describes the importance of his interpretation of the history of dogma in the following way:

> By delineating the process of the origin and development of the dogma, the "history of dogma" furnishes the most suitable means for the liberation of the church from dogmatic Christianity and for the speeding up of the irresistible process of the emancipation which began with Augustine. But it also witnesses to the unity of the Christian faith in the course of history by furnishing proof that the actual significance of the person of Jesus Christ and the principles of the gospel were never lost sight of.[28]

In writing the history of dogma, i.e., the history of that authoritative ecclesiastical doctrine concerning the person and work of Christ, God incarnate, which every Christian had to accept on peril of being excluded from the communion of salvation, Harnack desired to show, in the first place, how it happened that the gospel of Jesus Christ, which in its nature has nothing in common with ecclesiasticism and with authoritarian

---

[27] Cf. his lecture "Was hat die Historie an fester Erkenntnis zur Deutung des Weltgeschehens zu bieten?" in *Ausgewählte Reden und Aufsätze*, 1951, p. 192.

[28] Cf. *Grundriss der Dogmengeschichte*. 9th ed., Berlin 1921, p. 5.

statutes and doctrines, became embodied in the cultic-hierarchical practices and, especially, the doctrinal institutions of the church. But, in the second place, he wanted to offer proof, by historical analysis, for the thesis that if the gospel is to retain its living power today, it must be freed from identification with dogma. Indeed, it was his major point that the dogma originated in the effort of the ancient Christians to render the gospel comprehensible in the concepts of the Hellenistic world view and that they therefore expressed it in the thought forms of Greek philosophy and science. Then he drew the conclusion that, after having been maintained for centuries through the doctrinal authoritarianism of the church, the dogma has been coming to an end in the way the various Christian churches and groups have come to deal with it: In Eastern Orthodoxy it has become an uncomprehended relic kept alive only in the cultus and the liturgy; in Roman Catholicism it has become submerged in the hierarchical-sacramental order of the church, culminating in the absolute authority of the Pope; the Reformation invalidated it in principle by the rediscovery of the gospel and by the assertion of its primacy in all Christian thought and life. However, the Reformers failed to recognize the full revolutionary significance of this rediscovery: instead of making room in all Christian thought for the gospel alone, as they said it was their purpose, they coupled the reformation of the church on the basis of the gospel with the conservation of the dogma, in the interest, so they believed, of catholicity. Thus it came about that the churches of the Reformation faiths—Lutheranism, Calvinism, and Anglicanism—exhibit in their orders and practices the religion of the personal faith in Christ's gospel of forgiveness in the context of authoritarian churchmanship. They have always required of the faithful obedient submission to the authority of ministers and ecclesiastical officials who are duty-bound to maintain conformity with the dogma.

It was Harnack's conviction that the Reformation must go on. Inasmuch as "every really important reformation in the history of religion was primarily a critical reduction,"[29] Luther's rediscovery of the gospel must be completed by the emancipa-

[29] *Wesen des Christentums,* p. 160.

tion of Christianity from doctrinal authoritarianism. He believed that the Hellenization of the gospel which began with the formulation of the Logos-Christology and culminated in the promulgation of the Nicene dogma of the Trinity and of the Chalcedonian dogma of Christ, very God and very man, was a historical decision through which the Christian church succeeded in maintaining its identity in its confrontation with Hellenistic civilization and the Roman Empire, but he was also convinced that this Hellenization does not need to be continued forever, especially if this perpetuation can be accomplished only through an authoritarianism and an intellectual servitude which are irreconcilable with the gospel and its spirit. Having in mind Luther and the Reformation, he summed up his basic view in the following words:

> Christianity is something else than the sum of doctrines handed down from generation to generation. Christianity is not identical with biblical theology nor with the doctrine of the church councils, but it is that disposition which the Father of Jesus Christ awakens in men's hearts through the gospel. All authorities on which the dogma is based are torn down—how then can the dogma possibly be maintained as an infallible teaching! Christian doctrine is relevant only to faith; what part can philosophy then have in it? But what are dogma and dogmatic Christianity without philosophy?[30]

He concluded by asking: "How can there possibly be a history of dogma in Protestantism in view of Luther's 'Prefaces to the New Testament' and in view of his writings on the principles of the Reformation?"[31]

And with respect to the various historical forms which Christianity assumed in the course of time, beginning with the so-called Jewish Christianity of the Apostolic Age, he wrote:

> Either Christianity is . . . identical with its first form (in this case, one is forced to conclude that it came and went at a certain time) or it contains something which remains valid in historically changing forms. Starting with the beginnings, church

[30] *Dogmengeschichte*, 4th ed., Vol. III, pp. 896f.
[31] *Ibid.*, p. 898.

history shows that it was necessary for 'early Christianity' to perish in order that 'Christianity' might remain. So too there followed, later on, one metamorphosis upon another.[32]

We must acknowledge that this interpretation is thoroughly historical. By combining historical exposition with historical criticism, Harnack drew the full consequences from the application of the historical method to the Christian religion. In fact, he replaced the dogmatic method, which had been employed for so long a time in Christian thought, by the historical method. In doing so he brought to a culmination the approach which had first been introduced into Christian theology by the historical theologians of the Enlightenment, especially Johann Salomo Semler (d. 1791), and which then resulted in the interpretation of Christianity as a "development" at the hands of Ferdinand Christian Baur (d. 1860) and Albrecht Ritschl (d. 1889), whom Harnack regarded as his immediate predecessors. He relied on the work of these historical theologians and brought it to a climax insofar as, in following out the implications of the historical method, he substituted for the traditional dogmatic norm of Christian theological truth the historical concept of the nature of Christianity (*Wesen des Christentums*). Thus he hoped to replace theological dogmatism by historical understanding.

In the introduction to a new edition of his lectures on the nature of Christianity, he wrote: "Historical understanding is achieved only as one makes the effort to separate the distinctive essence of an important phenomenon from the temporary historical forms in which it is clothed."[33] In these lectures which constitute a summary and a popularization of the results of his scholarly investigations, he tried to achieve this understanding

---

[32] *Wesen des Christentums*, p. xix. Cf. *Dogmengeschichte*, 4th ed., p. 85: "The church historian is duty-bound not to be satisfied with the establishment of the fact that the Christian religion underwent changes but to examine to what extent new forms of it were able to protect, to implant, and to instill the gospel. In all probability the gospel would have perished if the form of 'early Christianity' had been preserved in the church; but, as a matter of fact, early Christianity perished in order that the gospel might prevail."

[33] *Wesen des Christentums*, p. xix.

by identifying the nature of Christianity with the gospel and its influences. He therefore dealt first with the gospel of Jesus Christ, then with the impact which Jesus himself and his gospel made upon the first generation of his disciples, and finally with the main types of the Christian religion as they developed from the changes which it underwent in its encounter with different human conditions. He proposed to discover the common features shared by these movements by testing them at the gospel. Furthermore, he believed that he would be able to define the principles (*Grundzüge*), i.e., the main characteristics of the gospel by verifying them through a study of the various ways by which the gospel was understood in the course of church history.

It is often said that Harnack identified the nature of Christianity with the teachings of Jesus. But this is an undiscriminating simplification of his view. He did not think it possible, it is true, to define the Christian religion apart from the gospel of Jesus Christ, but he did not isolate this gospel from its historical impact, nor did he absolutize it on the basis of the New Testament, where it is recorded in its earliest form. No historical form of Christianity, he believed, should be absolutized or regarded as normative.[34] "One may say," he wrote, "that Paul or Augustine or Luther were right [in their conception of the Christian gospel], yet one must never go so far as to regard their Christianity as Christianity itself."[35] He was persuaded that wherever the gospel of Jesus Christ is actually believed, i.e., where it is really apprehended by way of a commitment to God derived from faith in this gospel (i.e., so that this commitment is a certain trustful disposition of the heart), there Christianity is realized: the impulse which motivates such an actualization and the fountain which feeds it is the gospel—the gospel which Jesus proclaimed and of which he was the concretion in his historical humanity.

Harnack never stated in so many words what he conceived

---

[34] *Ibid.*, p. 113: "The gospel did not enter the world as a statutory religion and it can therefore have no classical and permanent manifestation in any form of intellectual or social expression, not even in the first one."

[35] *Ibid.*, p. xviii.

the nature of Christianity to be (and we should realize that no historian would attempt to offer a final definition!), but he undertook again and again to define the gospel. We must take care not to isolate certain ones of these definitions from the rest lest we illegitimately distort his thought.

He loved to quote Luther's saying, supposedly under the assumption that it summarized the gospel: "In forgiveness of sins there is life and bliss." Or he said: "The religion of the gospel rests upon . . . faith in Jesus Christ, i.e., because of him, this particular historical person, the believer is certain that God rules heaven and earth and that God the Judge is also the Father and Redeemer."[36] In the *History of Dogma* he asserted that the gospel as the New Testament presents it is something twofold: (1) the preaching of Jesus, and (2) the proclamation of Jesus as the Christ who died and rose again for the sake of sin and who gives the assurance of forgiveness and eternal life.[37]

Many, therefore, misunderstand Harnack when they hold that he thought that the gospel consists ultimately only of the teaching of Jesus. There is, of course, no denying that he put great stress on the teaching of Jesus. Indeed he has become famous for the definition he offers in *What Is Christianity?*: in the teaching of Jesus there are three circles of thought, each of which contains the whole proclamation: (1) the Kingdom of God and its coming; (2) God the Father and the infinite value of the human soul; (3) the better righteousness and the commandment of love.[38] He was concerned to emphasize that this teaching must be received with full seriousness. For he was persuaded that it was not something merely provisional which must be differently understood in the light of Jesus' death and resurrection, as if only a certain conception of the person of Christ (for example, that he was the "Son of God," etc.) could ensure the proper comprehension of the gospel.[39]

"Not the Son but alone the Father belongs in the gospel as Jesus proclaimed it."[40] By saying this, Harnack in no way in-

---

[36] *Dogmengeschichte,* 4th ed., p. 70.
[37] *Ibid.,* pp. 65f.
[38] *Wesen des Christentums,* p. 31.
[39] *Ibid.,* p. 86.
[40] *Ibid.,* p. 86.

tended to minimize the significance of Jesus. He wanted only to make sure that the gospel was understood as a religious-moral proclamation addressed to man's conscience which requires from him a decision for or against it and will then bring about a transformation of his inner disposition. He desired thus to avoid the impression that the gospel must be taken to be a revelation of an extraordinary sort which can be maintained only on the basis of certain metaphysical views about God, Christ, man, and the world.[41] He felt it necessary to insist on saying that "Jesus does not belong to the gospel as one of its elements,"[42] for, in fact, he thought of him as highly as possible.

He was the personal concretion and power of the gospel and we still perceive him as such. For none has ever known the Father in the way he knew him, and he gives this knowledge to others, thereby rendering "the many" an incomparable service. He leads them to God, not only by his word but still more by what he is and does and, finally, by his suffering. It is in this sense that he said not only this: "Come unto me all ye that labor and are heavy laden and I will give you rest," but also this: "The Son of Man is not come to be ministered unto but to minister and give his life as a ransom for many."[43]

Throughout his life Harnack was certain that because of this gospel Christianity was *the* true religion. "It is *the* religion," he wrote, "because Jesus Christ is not one among other masters but *the* master and because his gospel corresponds to the innate capacity of man as history discloses it."[44]

In order to do full justice to Harnack's basic conception, we must note also that he frequently pointed out what the gospel

[41] Cf. *ibid.*, p. 122: "For most of us this identification [of the Messiah with the Logos] is unacceptable because our thinking about the world and about ethics does not lead us to conclude upon a Logos as being [*einen wesenhafter Logos*]. To be sure, the affirmation 'The Logos has appeared among us' had an exciting effect, but the enthusiasm and the rapture of soul which it evoked did not lead with certainty to the God whom Jesus proclaimed."

[42] *Ibid.*, p. 87.

[43] *Ibid.*

[44] *Die Aufgabe der theol. Fakultäten und die allgemeine Religionsgeschichte. Reden und Aufsätze*, Vol. II, pp. 172f.

and the Christian religion are not. "The Christian religion is something lofty and simple and is concerned only about one point: eternal life in the midst of time through God's power and in his presence. It is not an ethical or social arcanum for the purpose of preserving all sorts of things or of improving them. Even the mere question of what it has contributed to the cultural progress of mankind does harm to its spirit."[45] It is an error, therefore, to apply the gospel directly to secular affairs and to deduce detailed prescriptions and statutes for their regulation from it.[46] It is something religious; indeed, it is religion itself and as such a disposition of mind marked by worship in spirit and in truth. Hence it cannot and must not be expressed in laws and regulations or in a worship through signs, liturgical rituals, and idols.[47] Its true nature is threatened if it is linked with or confined to authoritative forms of faith and order, dogma and liturgy, law and hierarchy. Ecclesiasticism, so Harnack affirmed, frequently imposed a terrible burden upon the gospel, but it never succeeded in suppressing its power.[48] However, the most momentous conformity which, he thought, ecclesiastical authority has been wont to require and still requires of Christians is the doctrinal one. This is detrimental to the gospel not because of doctrine as such (though the gospel is not a doctrine!), but because of the fact that, from the beginning, Christian dogmatic thought was combined with Greek philosophy of religion and with the intellectualism characteristic of this philosophy. The result was not only that the Christian faith came to be dependent upon metaphysics but also—and this was an observation which Harnack thought was amazing and shocking—that a "fancied Christ was put in the place of the real one." [49]

IV

These several points are an indication of the program which Harnack advocated (explicitly and implicitly) for Christianity

[45] *Wesen des Christentums*, p. 5.
[46] *Ibid.*, pp. 38, 71.
[47] *Ibid.*, p. 141.
[48] *Ibid*, p. 158; *Dogmengeschichte*, 4th ed. p. 82.
[49] *Wesen des Christentums*, p. 140.

in the modern world. In conclusion, we now direct our attention to his major programmatic convictions and recommendations.

We must give priority to a concern which runs through his entire theological work, namely that Christians should be freed from the requirement of holding certain rigidly defined doctrines and of maintaining other traditions only because they are regarded as authoritative in connection with a dogma whose absolute validity is simply taken for granted or affirmed without question. During the negotiations about his call to the University of Berlin he addressed a memorandum to the Ministry of Education in which he made the following declaration:

> Neither exegesis nor dogmatics but the results of church-historical research will break the power of the traditions which are now burdening the consciences of men. Cardinal Manning once made the following frivolous statement: "One must overcome history by dogma"; we say just the opposite: Dogma must be purified by history. As Protestants we are confident that by doing this we do not break down but build up.[50]

Harnack's whole theological work can be regarded as a commentary on this statement. He wanted to see authoritarian dogmatic thinking replaced by historical thinking. He knew how difficult it would be to achieve this goal. For he was aware of the fact that "there is nothing more conservative and unyielding than ordered religion."[51] Indeed, he had the greatest respect for the Roman Catholic Church because it had succeeded in maintaining itself throughout many ages by means of this conservatism. "The Roman Church," he said, "is the most comprehensive and powerful, the most complex and yet most uniform structure which known history has produced."[52]

In order to liberate the gospel from the connection with this powerful institution, Harnack believed that the Reformers had had to renounce in some way the Roman Catholic ideal of building a visible Kingdom of God on earth and of penetrating the realm of nature with the power of grace and holiness; but

[50] November 27, 1888. Agnes von Zahn-Harnack, *op. cit.*, pp. 130f.
[51] *Wesen des Christentums*, p. 104.
[52] *Ibid.*, p. 166.

in order to return the Christian religion to its spiritual core, they had no choice but to effect a tremendous reduction.[53] The result was that the gospel was once more clearly seen in distinction from Roman ecclesiasticism. However, the Reformers did not go far enough. They abolished Roman ecclesiasticism in the name of the Word of God and they assailed its foundations, but they left the dogma intact. Luther had a certain historical sense, and to some extent he was able to apply historical criticism to purely dogmatic authority. For example, he rejected the notion of the infallible authority of the papacy by pointing out that it was the product of changing history. But his thinking was not really determined by historical sense.[54] Hence he was unable to recognize the Scripture as a historical product. For the same reason, he argued that the dogma promulgated by the ancient councils of the church was valid inasmuch as it agreed with the Word of God. The other Reformers, with the exception of a few humanistic representatives of the Reformation's left wing, followed in Luther's train. Hence, so Harnack concluded,

Protestantism was unable, from the beginning, to develop fully, consistently, and strongly. It continued to be heavily burdened with Catholic remnants. When the Enlightenment finally came to its assistance, it brought with it a certain unproductive self-sufficiency which spoiled everything. Because of this, it failed to recognize the historical element through which faith in God the Father is linked with Jesus Christ.[55]

Modern historical theology must, Harnack contended, complete what the Reformation began. The application of historical thinking to all parts and phases of the Christian religion would make it possible, he believed, for the gospel of Jesus Christ to run a free, unhindered course in the world. "It must become possible," he wrote, "that one may openly say that such and such teachings and affirmations of the creeds are incorrect and

---

[53] *Reden und Aufsätze*, Vol. IV, p. 338 (in an address in commemoration of Albrecht Ritschl).
[54] *Dogmengeschichte*, Vol. III, 4th ed., p. 867.
[55] *Ibid.*, p. 906.

that nobody is forced to confess in the Divine Service what outside it he does not need to confess."[56]

He hoped that the time would come when traditional dogmatic Christianity would be replaced by an undogmatic Christianity.[57] At the end of his life he stated that he felt a certain kinship with the Congregationalists and the Quakers.[58] There can be no doubt that his whole theological outlook was similar to that of the "theologians" of the American denominations which represent the so-called free-church tradition.

There are three great themes to which he returned again and again in connection with his advocacy of the undogmatic, historical thinking in religion and theology: (1) the canonical authority of the Old Testament; (2) the doctrine of Christ; (3) the unity of Christendom.

(1) In order to release Protestantism from the shackles of literalistic biblicism and the dogmatics connected therewith, and in order to be consistent with the historical interpretation of the Bible—indeed, in order just to "honor the truth"— Har-

[56] Agnes von Zahn-Harnack, *op. cit.*, p. 315.

[57] In this connection, it is interesting to note that throughout his career, Harnack found himself unable to regard systematic or dogmatic theology with the same seriousness which the "dogmatists" were accustomed to demand for it from themselves and others. For example, Theophil Wurm, later Bishop of Württemberg and widely known as a prominent opponent of Hitler, reports that Harnack said in the course of a seminar which Wurm, then a student, attended in 1894 (cf. *Theol. Blätter* 9 [1930], p. 273) that he would propose the following outline to anyone wishing to write a dogmatic theology: "Part I: The teachings of Jesus and the apostolic interpretation of them. Part II: Mysteries; in this part, he added, one could proceed to speculate as much as one liked." And Karl Barth writes (*Kirchliche Dogmatik* I; II [1938], pp. 403f.) that in the last conversation they had together, Harnack told him that if he had to write a "dogmatics," he would entitle it: "The Life of God's Children." Barth goes on to explain that Harnack intended by this suggestion to propose the substitution of the traditional kind of dogmatic theology by the personal confession of a Christian who had achieved maturity by letting his thinking be centrally determined by the history of Christianity. See also the remarkable book by Walter von Loewenich, *Luther und der Neuprotestantismus*. Witten, 1963, esp. pp. 118–29.

[58] Cf. his correspondence with Prof. Erik Peterson, reprinted in the latter's *Theologische Traktate*, München, 1951, p. 258.

nack felt that the Protestant churches should break with the tradition of treating the Old Testament as a book of canonical authority. In his work on Marcion he wrote (and he was then at the end of his career):

> In the second century, the rejection of the Old Testament would have been a mistake and the Great Church rightly refused to make this mistake; its retention in the sixteenth century was due to the power of a fateful heritage from which the Reformers were not yet able to withdraw; but its conservation as a canonical book in modern Protestantism is the result of a paralysis of religion and the church.[59]

Harnack did not mean, of course, to suggest that Christians, and particularly the historians and theologians among them, should no longer study the Old Testament. On the contrary, he thought that from the historical point of view it would always not only be good and useful but also necessary to read it in relation to the New Testament. But he was convinced that only the New Testament was the basic Christian book and that it alone, therefore, should be held as Holy Scripture.

This view called forth a storm of protest and it still does. Harnack's critics felt that he was assailing the very foundation of Christianity. Karl Barth, for example, responded to Harnack's insistence that Protestantism should "clearly decide" against the canonicity of the Old Testament, by saying: "In respect of this we merely remark that if the Evangelical Church were to do this, it would lose its identity with the Church of the first seventeen centuries."[60] It is difficult to imagine that this point would have greatly impressed Harnack, for his whole proposal was inspired by the realization that, in terms of historical reality, modern Protestantism is not and cannot be "identical" with the church of former ages.[61]

[59] *Marcion: Das Evangelium vom fremden Gott,* 2nd ed., Leipsig, 1924, p. 217.
[60] *Kirchliche Dogmatik* I; II, p. 82.
[61] Agnes von Zahn-Harnack cites (*op. cit.,* pp. 244f.) a letter which her father wrote to Karl Holl with reference to the discussion which his book on Marcion had elicited: "Is it not so that the Ancient Church was not aware of the fact that truth too develops? . . . I did not find it

(2) Of much greater importance to Harnack was his hope that modern Christians would free themselves from the burden of the dogma about the person of Jesus. Even as late as 1925, he said: "By combining all the various affirmations about Christ in the one confession and witness that he is the mirror of God's paternal heart,[62] one can get free from the entire ancient dogma and, at the same time, hold fast to the root of faith."[63] He was sure that it is not possible for any man on the basis of faith or knowledge to make any valid statements about Christ's nature and particularly his "divine nature." Christians must be content with the New Testament and leave room for the same diversity of thought and speech which the early Christians displayed in relation to their understanding of the lordship of Christ.

Harnack looked forward with keen anticipation to the Lausanne Conference on Faith and Order in 1927. He hoped that there the churches would achieve some clarity about Christology. In a memorandum he expressed the opinion that the deliberations of the conference were "a fateful hour of decision for the Christian church" insofar as they would either make a contribution to clarification and unification of a sort the churches had not experienced for centuries or increase the division of Christendom. Then he went on to say:

> There is a significant consensus in Christology. No one denies either the uniqueness or the unity of the person of the Redeemer; nor does anyone deny that the Christian faith is faith in the Father, the Son, and the Holy Spirit and that its universal confession is that in Jesus Christ the Word became flesh. . . . Should we not be satisfied with this consensus as it is expressed in the confessional affirmations that Christ is the "Son of God," the "God-Man," the "Image of God," "Our Lord"? In my judgment,

---

difficult to cause my children to accept the teaching that the Old Testament is now antiquated and only in certain parts still appealing and valuable. It is the law and history of the Jews; *our* book is the New Testament."

[62] This was a phrase of Luther's making (cf. his Larger Catechism). Harnack was very fond of it and used it frequently.

[63] Agnes von Zahn-Harnack, *op. cit.,* p. 161, in an address to the Evangelical-Social Congress.

this should be sufficient, and the churches would leave it to every Christian how he might further conceive the person of Christ. But, as a matter of fact, this consensus is not sufficient in our day; we need a formal decision, for, at the great ancient councils, the churches ordained that one must believe in the *two natures* of Christ and that any statement about him in which this speculation about his two natures is rejected must be considered heretical . . . But, in the course of the last two centuries, numerous Christians have found it impossible to express the faith in Christ through the speculation about the two natures, etc. . . . . The Conference on Faith and Order will have to decide whether it shall demand that the dogmatic affirmation [that] Christ had two natures shall continue to be an affirmation of faith or whether it is prepared to reaffirm the faith in the Father, the Son, and the Holy Spirit and, therefore, also in the God-man Christ, but, as far as the churches are concerned, to make no binding rules about any further speculation.[64]

This expectation of Harnack was not fulfilled and has not been fulfilled to this day. No church body has ever officially renounced or given up or modified any dogmatic decision made by the official bodies of the ancient church.

(3) Harnack ardently believed in Christian unity. He was convinced that the Christian religion was the greatest force for the reconciliation of men with one another. He experienced with gratification the awakening of the ecumenical movement and entertained great hopes for it. But he felt strongly that such unity could be brought about only if all intolerance based on dogmatism and doctrinal authoritarianism would be banished from the life of the churches.

v

After the First World War the fashion of theological thinking changed radically. The leadership of Harnack, the historian, was replaced by that of Karl Barth, the dogmatist. The difference between them as to theological method was so great that Harnack, who was one of Barth's teachers, found himself utterly unable to follow Barth. "He was ready to acknowledge

[64] *Ibid.*, pp. 420ff.

Barth's deep seriousness, but his theology made him shudder."[65]

Barth has explained the difference between his own outlook and that of Harnack by pointing to the fact that, following Schleiermacher, all "modern" Protestant theologians pursued their work by proceeding *von unten nach oben* (from man to God) whereas he advocates a method which goes *von oben nach unten* (from God to man). There is much truth in this distinction. But saying this does not necessarily mean that truth is on Barth's side. He begins his theological interpretation with revelation, and God's revelation remains his theme throughout. But the question is, by what right he can begin and proceed in this way. For he is a man and as such he is bound to history and he should therefore be ready (but he is not!) to admit that like all other knowledge also the knowledge of God can be available to him only historically.

Harnack, by contrast, started with the assumption that, together with everything else that belongs to man's realm, the Christian religion also is something historical, a heritage with which every generation has to deal with respect to the past as well as to the future. Is then truth not on his side insofar as he insisted that the only adequate method of dealing with Christianity is the historical one? The discussion of this question will occupy theology for many years to come, and in this discussion Harnack's views will continue to be important.

[65] *Ibid.*, p. 415.

Bibliography

Adolf von Harnack, *What is Christianity?*, N. Y., Harper, 1957. (Harper Torchbooks).

No full-length studies of Harnack in English are easily available.

ALBERT SCHWEITZER

Fritz Buri

Albert Schweitzer belongs to humanity. His name and his work are known throughout the world. But even so, and despite the fact that, as it turns out, he has spent most of his life in Africa, he is still an Alsatian and Günsbach is still his home. In Günsbach he grew up, and in Günsbach his house stands—the house, built years ago with his Goethe-prize money, to which he always returned during the years when he still visited Europe, and which even today remains a meeting place for his worldwide circle of friends.

Up the Rhine, a two hours' journey by train, lies Basel. This town, already famous in the Middle Ages, has in recent years become known in all the world as the center where the theologian Karl Barth and the philosopher Karl Jaspers carry on their work. Karl Barth returned to this his home town at the beginning of the Nazi regime in Germany, and Karl Jaspers, having withstood the terrors of that regime, settled down there. In recent years students and scholars from all the world have come to this city on the great northward bend of the Rhine to listen to these two men.

Opposite Alsace, on the right bank of the Rhine, stretches the Black Forest. From this region comes Martin Heidegger, the fourth great philosopher of our era. (Ever since his years at Marburg, Heidegger has been a close friend of Rudolf Bultmann, Barth's opposite number, theologically speaking. It was from Heidegger that Bultmann took over the concept of existential interpretation.) Heidegger's name is bound up with that of Freiburg, the intellectual capital of the little land of Baden. As is well known, he was rector of the Freiburg university during the Nazi years, and since then has lectured there. He still lives in the Black Forest—whence the title of his collected essays, *Holzwege* (Woodland Paths).

Geographically, Günsbach, Freiburg, and Basel form a small

triangle. But in this little space a significant part of the most recent history of theology and philosophy has unfolded. For the names of the four thinkers who are associated with these three places must figure prominently in any account of the newest developments in theology and philosophy. The four men are indeed determinative for these developments, and even today are a center of world interest. One could most readily say of Schweitzer that this is not the case; he is the oldest of the four, and his great intellectual accomplishments belong to the first quarter of our century. So far as the theological and philosophical world is concerned, he seems to have vanished in the primeval forest. But from there the image of this *homo universale* and friend of humanity shines forth, casting a radiance stronger than that emanating from any of his three younger contemporaries. At the beginning of the century he spoke the word about the eschatological character of the New Testament —the word that Barth (to be sure, in altogether different form: as theology of crisis) took as the point of departure for his own great achievement. On his part, Bultmann accepts as self-evident Schweitzer's argument concerning the primitive Christian hope of the imminent coming of the end and its disappointment through history; and a great deal of Bultmann's opposition to Karl Barth goes back to this circumstance. Schweitzer's philosophical work, which remains incomplete, cannot stand comparison with that of Heidegger or Jaspers. But on the other hand, Schweitzer succeeded in formulating an ethical principle of elemental force and a view of the "decay and rebuilding of culture" with a clarity and a power of conviction that are matched neither in Jaspers' thought, which brings everything into a state of suspension, nor in Heidegger's existential analysis of existence (*Dasein*) and philosophy of being.

Thus it appears that these four great thinkers of our time form a group whose interrelations are internal as well as external. And this suggests that it would be in order to take a closer look at the significance of Albert Schweitzer in the frame of this "foursome" (to use an expression of Heidegger's). We shall first try to get a clear understanding of Schweitzer's basic concerns, which anticipated those of the three younger men in important respects. Then we shall analyze the relevant positions of the three others in order to show how, precisely against this background, Schweitzer's concerns can be newly appreciated today. In a critical analysis of this kind—an analysis such as Schweitzer himself did not carry out—the significance of his thought for our day can be truly assessed.

I

Schweitzer's theological and philosophical thought moves around two centers: the question of the historical Jesus and the problem of an ethic capable of undergirding culture.

For Schweitzer, the historical Jesus is the eschatological Jesus; that is, the Jesus who proclaims the immediately imminent breaking-in of the Reign of God in the sense of late Jewish apocalyptic. Anticipating the Last Judgment, Jesus preaches repentance, that is, a life lived in expectation of the New Eon. He is convinced that he is destined by God to be the future Messiah, and out of this messianic consciousness of himself he goes to his death, in order to bring in the New Eon and to suffer the tribulations of the End Time vicariously for the elect. Schweitzer arrives at this view of "consequent eschatology," on the one hand, through his research into the history of the attempts to capture the historical Jesus; on the other hand, this seems to him the best-supported hypothesis to clarify the oldest traditions by the methods of modern historical science. The outcome of Schweitzer's research, as stated in his *The Quest of the Historical Jesus,* is the thesis that since the *parousia* failed to eventuate, a de-eschatologizing of the Christian message necessarily set in. This thesis he pursues further in *The Mysticism of the Apostle Paul,* where he shows how Paul can hold on to the eschatological, saving significance of Jesus' death in spite of the contrary course of history: Paul interprets the proclaimed resurrection of Jesus as an emergent breaking-in of the New Eon into the Old, which still persists for a short time. The New Eon thus initiated is continued in the existence (*Dasein*) of the faithful, who think of themselves as those who died with Christ and are awakened to a new life in the Spirit. This is an ethically significant internalization of the Synoptic message of the Reign of God, and one that is in harmony with Jesus' call for repentance. But in John's Gospel it is externalized and made ethically questionable; for in that Gospel the primitive Christian eschatology and the Pauline Christ-mysticism are converted into the sacramental mysticism of the Hellenistic mystery cults—a change that became of decisive importance for the development of the church's Christ dogma.

Using the same methods as in his study of the problem of Jesus, Schweitzer deals with the problem of a worthy culture-ethic. In the two volumes of his *Kulturethik* that are devoted to this theme, and also in his volume on the "world view of Hindu thinkers," he examines the ethical content of various philosophical systems and ascribes positive value to this content in so far as it manifests a will to a culture-informing ethic and seems adequate to that end. Schweitzer shows that this will to culture is weakened, or falls victim to illusions, if it seeks a foundation in events in the world. But neither can it develop a world-forming ethic if, for the sake of its otherness from the world, it retreats from the world. From this problematic, Schweitzer draws the conclusion that ethics, if it is to fulfill its function, cannot take a world view as basis but can issue only out of a thinking will to life. To describe the posture of this will to life, raised to the level of thought and active in all life, he coined the formula "reverence for life." And in our time of decay he sees in that "reverence for life" the foundation for a possible rebuilding of culture.

All sorts of objections could be raised against these theological and philosophical ideas of Schweitzer's; and indeed, though they have been widely accepted and influential, there has been no lack of dissenting criticism of them. But before going on to consider positions held by others—positions from which Schweitzer's points of view might seem outdated and no longer tenable—we must emphasize two aspects of his thought that even today strike us as very modern, because they find parallels in the "foursome" mentioned above.

In his theological research Schweitzer stresses the absolute necessity of a strictly objective historico-critical scientific methodology. And he claims objective validity for his picture of Jesus. But we cannot fail to note that at the end of his *Quest* he speaks of another approach to Jesus. This special approach can be opened up through a single word, a word that, as the expression of Jesus' will, appeals to our will and prompts us not only to translate his message into our own way of looking at things but to obey the call we have thus heard. But, Schweitzer declares, this Jesus—the Jesus whose authority is experienced "from will to will," and in obedience to whom Schweitzer himself undertook his work at Lambaréné—meets us as "an unknown and nameless one"; that is, as one who will not fit into our conceptual schemes. Only as we obey him is the mystery of his personality revealed to us.

In regard to both the understanding of history and the problems of world view and culture, Schweitzer is well aware of the limits of objective, scientific thought and of the necessity and possibility of a direct connection between thought and being. As he sees it, this most intimate connection, which cannot be captured in a system, becomes evident to us as we pursue a way of thought and action determined by "reverence for life": "I am life, that wills to live, in the midst of life, that wills life." The open-endedness of an ethical world view that issues from a thinking experience of the will to life Schweitzer compares on one occasion to a cathedral, incomplete and forever incompletable, in whose choir the spirit ceaselessly worships.

That the formulations of these last two aspects of Schweitzer's thought are questionable cannot be denied. Their character as theology of experience and philosophy of life has been obvious from the beginning. Yet it is plain that they are nevertheless a direct bridge to the theology and philosophy of those three other thinkers—outwardly near to Schweitzer but inwardly very different from him—who have had an important part in helping to stamp the thought of our time through their emphasis on the limitations of science and their insistence on taking the impact of the existential moment into consideration as the basis of every metaphysic and ethic. That indeed is why we see Schweitzer with them as a foursome in the spiritual situation of our time.

II

In its day Schweitzer's "consequent eschatological" view of Jesus and of primitive Christianity had on the whole only a negative reception. It was Karl Barth who more than forty years ago set in motion what might be called a groundswell of eschatologism. This demolished some things that were obviously built on sand, but it has been ebbing for quite a long time now and has become a sort of Black Sea. True, the bibliography of the first edition of Barth's *Letter to the Romans*—which marks the breaking-in of eschatological Barthianism—cites Schweitzer's *Quest of the Historical Jesus*. But the eschatology of dialectical theology has nothing to do with the eschatological Jesus and his message of the emergent Reign of God as Schweitzer worked these out by the methods of scientific history. Even at the time Barth's *Romans* was published, leading New Testament scholars and historians averred that rather than interpret the Roman letter of the apostle Paul, he had put into it the sense of the crisis and impending fall of Western culture that beset him and many of his contemporaries in that first post-World-War period. (Since then, indeed, Barth himself has partly admitted as much.) Barth defended his unhistorical procedure by saying that he recognized historical science and its results as phenomena of this world, which, like everything in this world, stand under the weight of God's word, which breaks in vertically from above. As to the "talk about the nonappearance of the *parousia*," Barth asked: "How could that fail to appear which by its very nature can never come to pass?"—and thereby asked the same question in regard to every theory of salvation history. Every moment stands under the weight of eternity. The essence of the Christian's eschatological situation consists in his becoming aware that all worldly and human things are in a state of crisis. And this is to pronounce judgment on all human cultural activity. According to the theology of crisis, every cultural activity is a new attempt to build Babylonian towers. In this stage of his theology, then, Barth sees only disintegration; he does not admit the possibility of a rebuilding of culture. To be sure, this eschatological nihilism did not remain the final stage of his theology. In one of the later volumes of his *Dogmatik* there is even a section entitled "Reverence for Life." Here the "no" to a world spoiled by sin is canceled by a "yes" to God's good creation, and sin is declared to be nonexistent. But for all its beauty, the old Barth's praise of creation makes us think of a sinking sun that, after the struggle of the day, once more veils everything in a golden glow before it finally goes down and gives way to the night—after which, according to his present concept of eschatology as history of salvation, the true day will break in. Plainly, out of this hopeful but still rather weary evening mood there can develop no ethic that would match the message of him who said: "I came to cast fire upon the earth; and would that it were already kindled!"

III

The case is basically the same with Martin Heidegger. Granted, where Schweitzer took his Jesus-mysticism and his reverence for life as the point of departure for his thought, Heidegger took as his point of departure human existence, which cannot be grasped by the methods of science, and whose statements cannot be confirmed by any world view but stand contrary to all ways of looking at the world. On the one hand, however, in accord with the mood of that time—in which Kierkegaard (against whom Schweitzer had always warned as a sickly thinker) first found real acceptance—Heidegger chose as basis of his existential analysis the desperate situation of man, who sees himself delivered up to nothingness. This stance, of course, makes Heidegger sympathetic to the theology of crisis. On the other hand, Heidegger's existential ontology represents a substitute for the discarded, allegedly scientific world-view systematic; only that Heidegger's system is drafted with other means: so-called existentials of understanding in place of the categories of reason. In the measure that the analysis of this existential self-evidentness is rounded into a basic existential ontology, existence as the starting point is virtually betrayed in favor of a new system, under which the element of risk inherent in existence is surrendered in favor of an absolute standing beyond the subject-object antithesis. That Heidegger has surrendered the concept of existence as something that cannot be objectified but can only be experienced in specific historical materializations, is quite clear now that he has substituted being for nothingness and looks for salvation to a new advent of being—an advent in which being, in defiance of all human attempts to grasp it, will manifest itself in its truth. But this being-event of Heidegger's falls under the same objection that Schweitzer (in *Culture and Ethic*) raised against Hegel's metaphysic of being. Not irrelevant here is the fact that, as Hegel once saw absolute spirit in world history and the Prussian police state, so Heidegger saw the "saving event" in the Hitler regime.

IV

Heidegger's thought became influential in theology chiefly through Rudolf Bultmann. This was, however, his thought in its earliest form, before his "turning"—a way of thinking that, moreover, is probably still misunderstood. Bultmann, to be sure, comes from elsewhere altogether: from that field of theology which deals with historical criticism and history of religion, a field of which Albert Schweitzer was one of the last great consistent representatives. Bultmann never belies his origin. It accounts for his speaking in so matter-of-course a fashion of the nonfulfillment of the primitive Christian expectation of the end and of the obsoleteness of the mythological world-picture connected with it—as if he were totally unaware that, for Heidegger, this kind of scientific understanding of history represents an attempt to usurp being and is therefore a deficient mode of thought.

But as is well known, Bultmann aims not only to demythologize the New Testament proclamation but to understand it existentially—that is, as it bears on (and declares) the self-evidentness of human existence. In this positive part of his basic thesis he purposes to vindicate Heidegger's view of the historicity of existence (*Dasein*): as inner history, in contrast to external history. We are onlookers at external history—as though there were an absolute standpoint outside its relativity; we experience inner history when, waiving such questionable objectivity, we become aware that our life is caught up in it in some indescribable way, that we participate in it. Unlike the categories of external history, the existentials are affirmations of the historicity of our existence (*Dasein*). The eschatological event announced in the New Testament does not take place as an occurrence in the outer and inner world of space and time, an occurrence that can be described in terms of history of psychology; no, that eschatological event takes place where this message is proclaimed and the hearer unconditionally decides for it in his existence. Salvation becomes reality in a faith that newly understands itself.

From the point of view of this existential interpretation of the New Testament kerygma it is clear that Bultmann cannot simply acknowledge the nonfulfillment of the primitive Christian *parousia*-expectation and let the matter rest there; but that, on the basis of form-criticism, he can surrender the last remnants of a life of Jesus in favor of a kerygma of a salvation-event in Christ. (Here he goes beyond Schweitzer, and beyond consequent eschatology, which clung to some shreds of a life of Jesus.) We cannot go back of that salvation-event, because its historical origin—in the Jesus of Nazareth who still belongs to Judaism—is certainly not part of the kerygma's content. The primitive Christian kerygma proclaims not the historical Jesus but the risen Christ—even though in its proclamation of the Easter-event and the results thereof it speaks of none other than this same Jesus of Nazareth.

Today, to be sure, some of Bultmann's pupils are no longer content to accept this *skandalon* as the distinguishing mark of true kerygmatic theology; for in that paradoxical relation between an existentially understood Christ and the historical Jesus they can see no guarantee that this Christ of the kerygma is not after all a myth, no guarantee that the biblical kerygma will not be replaced by an existential anthropology. They fear that the Pauline and Johannine understanding of the kerygma will prove an obstacle to any concern to understand the historical Jesus. So the Bultmannians are setting out again, as Karl Barth mockingly said, to recapture the historical Jesus "with swords and sticks."

Undoubtedly it is possible to set up a picture of the "historical Jesus" on the basis of the Synoptic accounts. But, as is admitted, neither formally (i.e., in regard to the way in which it is arrived at) nor as concerns content (i.e., in regard to what it says) can this picture of the historical Jesus be distinguished from the existentially understood kerygma of the New Testament; rather, it represents only a particular part of this kerygma —that part which comes to expression in the Synoptic witness to Jesus. This method cannot take us back of the kerygma; that is, to the historical personality of the Jesus who speaks in the kerygma; or else we have tacitly discarded the existential interpretation and exchanged it once more for scientific historical criticism. For if we start out from the existential we cannot refer back to the categories of external history for our conclusions. A "historical Jesus" thus arrived at would only be a new edition of the Jesus whom the Ritschlians, in their day, thought they could lay hold of through the experience of faith. Even at that time Schweitzer most decisively rejected the Ritschlian Jesus in favor of a clear distinction between apprehension from history and apprehension "from will to will." Schweitzer's strictures on psychological historicism apply equally to today's existential historicism.

V

That Schweitzer's thought is still relevant today is plain when we compare his positions with those of Barth and Heidegger (and Bultmann and his school). It becomes even plainer when we bring his imitation of Christ through the ethic of reverence for life into juxtaposition with the philosophy of Karl Jaspers. Like Bultmann, Jaspers accepts Schweitzer's insight—which today is largely the common property of Protestant theology—into the significance for dogmatic history of the fact of the non-appearance of the parousia. Though he evinces considerable reserve toward the conclusions which, each in his way, Schweitzer and Bultmann have drawn from this historico-critical point of departure, Jaspers nevertheless counts these two as among today's most important representatives of scientific research into the history of primitive Christianity. True, he emphatically disclaims both Schweitzer's culture-ethic, which he regards as a demythologized form of Christianity, and Bultmann's existential interpretation of the New Testament, which he regards as a consequence of this demythologization. But this disclaimer arises from his basic philosophical position, which is of a different kind and is opposed both to Schweitzer's life-philosophy and to Bultmann's existentialism, as well as to their conception of science.

Schweitzer and Bultmann recognize only two (or three) ways

of understanding: historical science and understanding from will to will (Schweitzer), and faith in response to the kerygma in existential decision (Bultmann). Jaspers recognizes more ways than these. For him, the Schweitzer-Bultmann ways merely represent forms of an Encompassing. This Encompassing, however, takes forms in addition to "presentness" (*Dasein*) with its will to life, consciousness in general, in whose frame all our statements stand; and in addition to existence, which makes an unconditional decision in response to the call of transcendence. But it is not only the more comprehensive nature of Jaspers' periechontology[1] that is important in the context of this essay. What is of the highest importance is that, in consequence of this periechontology, the Encompassing does not in any of its forms reveal itself in an absolute and unequivocal fashion. Whether as presentness (*Dasein*), consciousness in general, or existence (to mention only these three possibilities), in each case it reveals itself as something altogether different from any or all of these, something we cannot grasp from any other point of view either, and dare not absolutize under its special aspect.

This is not the place to consider what this periechontological viewpoint means in regard to the existential ontology of Heidegger and Bultmann. Obviously, Jaspers can judge ontology only as a pseudo science which denics the existential—a pseudo science which in Heidegger's case leads to a romantic-poetic mythology of being, and in Bultmann's (in spite of his intention to demythologize) to a churchly-orthodox kerygma mythology. Where Bultmann does away with mythology, and Schweitzer translates mythology into ethics, Jaspers holds on to the declarative strength of the myth for existence. A science that thinks it can overcome the mythological way of expression not only misunderstands the nature of myth but itself becomes a sort of pseudo myth. And in this Jaspers sees the harmfulness of so-called demythologization.

Viewed in the light of Jaspers' conception of science, even

---

[1] "Periechontology" is an untranslatable coinage, combining the Greek word *periechō*, which means "to encompass, enclose, embrace, contain," and the word "ontology." Dr. Buri relates this term to Jaspers' concept of *das Umgreifende*, which we are here rendering as "the Encompassing."

Schweitzer's concern to translate his consequent-eschatological primitive Christianity into a universally provable ethic of reverence for life represents a sort of pseudoscientific *re*mythologization. The questionable conception of the "thinking will to life" does justice to its real intent only when it is grasped in the sense of Jaspers' conception of existential thinking, i.e., the kind of thinking that is carried on in objective categories—but in that very process revolves around the nonobjectifiableness of the essence of existence, which essence cannot be universally proved but can only be appealed to. Moreover, from the point of view of Jaspers' schema of the Encompassing, reverence for life cannot be developed into a metaphysic of a universal will to life which is in conflict with itself but can be reconciled with itself through human action in love. Only beyond all rationalism and irrationalism can this speculation of Schweitzer's be positively valued as an expression of our understanding of existence. But probably that is what Schweitzer means when he builds a bridge from this crowning conclusion of his ethical thought to the Pauline Christ-mysticism, for in Christ he sees God's love becoming active as a transformation of man into a new creature.

Strangely enough, Jaspers has no sympathy for this eschatological Christ-concept. He sees in it only a God-man mythology which endangers the actualization of existence—a mythology that is evident in the Reformers' doctrine of justification, which was distilled from the original eschatological context of meaning. Because of this ominous misunderstanding of the Pauline Christology—a misunderstanding against which Schweitzer warns emphatically—Jaspers thinks that it is only to the so-called historical Jesus that a positive significance in the history of the human spirit can be attributed. But in this "so-called historical Jesus" Jaspers sees a towering embodiment of the ruin which inevitably befalls the human being (that is, man as an existence) as regards both his understanding of himself and his attempts to realize himself. For Jaspers this inescapable ruin in the border situations of life represents the place whence all patterns of thought are brought into flux and whence man, soaring up to the transcendence that forever eludes him, can experience himself as a present, a gift to himself.

This idea of existence as a present to itself, which man experiences in the flight to the transcendent, is lucidly developed again and again in Jaspers' philosophy. And indeed this philosophical ground-operation is indispensable for all thinking that goes to the ultimate limits if it is to be saved from betraying existence to some massivity or other. Yet in comparison with the vitality and nearness to reality of Schweitzer's thought and work, Jaspers' thinking strikes us as carried on in exceedingly thin air and as comprehensible only in a very abstract fashion. Even so, today Jaspers' philosophy is indispensable for the interpretation and further development of Schweitzer's thought and work. A Schweitzer understood from the viewpoint of that philosophy will not have vanished in Africa's primeval forest so far as we are concerned. Through the medium of Jaspers' thought we are able to understand the forest physician's message as the direct, prophetic message it is, but also to appreciate the continuing importance of his thought and research in the frame of the "foursome" that distinguishes our place in history.

Bibliography

Albert Schweitzer, *The Quest of the Historical Jesus*, N. Y., Macmillan, 1960.

George Seaver, *Albert Schweitzer: The Man and His Mind*, rev. ed., N. Y., Harper, 1956.

SØREN KIERKEGAARD

Martin J. Heinecken

Søren Aabye Kierkegaard was born in Copenhagen, Denmark, on May 5, 1813, the seventh and last child of Michael Kierkegaard, a hosier, and Ane Sørendatter Lund. A distant kinswoman, Ane was Michael's second wife and the mother of all his children. She had been a servant in the house and Michael married her shortly after the death of his first wife. The first child was born four months later. This moral lapse, together with the fact that he had once cursed God because of his cruel lot on the barren Jutland heath, plagued the father all his life. When he came to Copenhagen and by a succession of strokes of fortune became a wealthy man able to retire at the age of forty, live in a great house on the square, and spend his time in security and comfort, he could not rid himself of the thought that he had committed the sin against the Holy Ghost and that God was mocking him. The discovery of the father's lapse played a decisive role in the life of the son, turning him for a while away from Christianity but eventually helping him to see that for a stricken conscience, the cross of Christ is the only answer. In fact, one of the decisive elements in Kierkegaard's development was his relationship with his father. He was the child of his father's old age and himself never knew any youth. He grew up in the strange house in the company of an old man who stimulated him with the power of his imagination and with his dialectical skill in debate with some of the more learned men of the town. But the strain of deep melancholy that plagued him all his life and never allowed the unspeakable joy of Christianity to take full possession thus had its natural roots in his heredity and home environment.

Søren was a precocious boy who made up for his lack of physical prowess by his sharp wit. He had a crooked back and walked with a limp, due probably to a fall in his childhood. He had the usual classical education and matriculated at the uni-

125

versity with the intention of studying theology, but the general liberal arts curriculum (languages, philosophy, physics, mathematics) and aesthetic studies (Faust, Don Juan, the Wandering Jew, fairy tales, Socrates, Mozart) engrossed his attention. He was earnestly in search of a cause to which he could give himself with unstinted devotion. The discovery of his father's guilt, followed by a period of dissipation and estrangement from his father, brought him finally, by what he himself ascribed to divine providence, to a decisive Christian experience. After the death of his father, who outlived all but two of his children and feared that he would outlive them all, Søren finished his master's thesis, "The Concept of Irony with Constant Reference to Socrates," and also passed with honors his examination in theology, which qualified him for a call to a parish.

There were two other events by which he felt that God was guiding him to his life's task. The one was his broken engagement with Regine Olsen and the other was the affair with the *Corsair*. There is no doubt about the genuineness of the love Søren and Regine had for each other, but the day after the engagement Kierkegaard declared he knew he had made a mistake. His diary and long sections of his pseudonymous writings betray the intense struggle he underwent. Finally he broke the engagement in what we can only, by Kierkegaard's own standard, regard as a "teleological suspension of the ethical." There are many surmises as to the reason, but Kierkegaard said he would carry the secret with him to the grave. "But there was a divine protest, that is how I understand it."[1] In *Fear and Trembling* he takes as his point of departure the story of Abraham and Isaac to show how unquestioning obedience to the divine command may involve a man in a "teleological suspension of the ethical" and so isolate him from the universal that it is impossible for him to communicate himself. The knight of faith who, like Abraham, receives back from God that which he gave up to him in trust, is to be distinguished both from the "knight of infinite resignation" who merely resigns himself to his loss and the "tragic hero" who, like Agamemnon with Iphigenia, makes his sacrifice for the sake of a greater gain. Kierkegaard realized

[1] *The Journals of Søren Kierkegaard* (London, Oxford Univ. Press, 1938), p. 93.

that he himself was not the knight of faith, but he did recognize what it meant to be one.

It was his refusal to marry that let loose the floodgates of his literary activity. Henceforth he devoted all his time to writing and in a few short years produced a body of literature which for its rich diversity in the realm of the aesthetic, of philosophy, of ethics, of psychology, of theology, of devotional writing, knows no equal. He praised his mother tongue as the finest and most flexible of instruments with which to give expression to the most profound as well as to the lightest thoughts. His writings abound in wit and humor, they are rich with imagery, they discuss with precision and the utmost dialectical skill the most difficult subjects, they probe to the depths of the human soul. The movement of "existentialism" derives its name from his emphasis upon the unfathomable mystery, the wonder, the terror, the joy and the burden of human existence. Like Socrates, whom he "approached with a palpitating enthusiasm that yielded to none" other than the God-man Himself, he had no interest in the study of the stones and the stars; his interest was in man himself. All his literature was devoted to but one thing. He had found the cause to which he could give himself with unstinted devotion, and that was to make clear in the midst of Christendom what it means to become and to be a Christian.

It was Kierkegaard's conviction that the Christianity of the New Testament was unknown in his day. The theologians and the preachers, led by Martensen, an outspoken Hegelian, were confusing the specifically Christian or biblical categories with those derived simply from the reason of the "natural" or unconverted man. Hegelian philosophy, as was the case with Aristotelian philosophy for Luther, was the object of his ceaseless, scathing attack. It confused God and man, put an end to ethics, destroyed the individual, and for existence as the time of decision it substituted the world historical process in which everything flowed together in a sea of mystification. If the Hegelian interpretation of Christianity were true, then all anyone had to do to become a Christian would be to think straight. Preachers would not be witnesses but professors, and pulpits nothing but lecture platforms. Difficult as some of Kierkegaard's polemic with Hegel is—because it is couched in the same terms—it clearly differentiates individual existence before the living God in the time of decision as man is confronted by the absolute paradox of the God-man, from the sort of monistic pantheism and worship of the state which has culminated in our day in totalitarianism and communism. All these developments Kierkegaard foresaw with amazing clarity. He was the Jeremiah, the weeping prophet of his day, whose clear warnings went unheeded.

The result of the church's proclamation in Kierkegaard's Denmark was that being a Dane and being a Christian were simply equated. Being a Christian meant being a respectable, prosperous, and satisfied citizen, content like a goose being overfed for Michaelmas and with no desire to use its wings and to fly.[2] People lived at the level of either the aesthetic or the ethical and at the level of universally human religiosity, but never became decisively transformed into being Christian.

The second crucial event that finally prevented Kierkegaard from accepting a call to a parish was the attack upon him by a rather dubious scandal sheet, the *Corsair*. Kierkegaard had attacked it in the hope that others would rally to his support. Instead, however, he was left in the lurch when the *Corsair* turned upon him and with a series of articles and cartoons made him the laughingstock of all the north country. It may appear as though Kierkegaard made far too much of this affair, but to one as sensitive as he this was a great blow. It isolated him more than ever and set him with resolution to his single task. Whereas before he had displayed joviality and wit, beneath which was hidden the most frightful melancholy, this was now scarcely possible any longer. He considered this a suffering which providence too had thrust upon him and not a self-chosen martyrdom.

The remainder of Kierkegaard's life was uneventful and was spent almost entirely in writing, until a year before his untimely death he made his uncompromising attack on the church of his day. Fortunately his patrimony was enough to keep him in comfortable circumstances. By the time it had given out, his life, too, was spent—and this, too, he attributed to providence.

[2] *Ibid.*, p. 54.

Except for two brief visits to Berlin and an occasional visit into the north country he never left the city of his birth. But what he lacked in breadth of actual experience in the world he made up for by the prodigious powers of his imagination. One hour on the Jutland heath, he said, was enough to educate a man in the school of possibility, for existence was for him the sphere of possibility where anything could happen and not at all the rationally determined world process necessarily bound to end in the *Kulturstaat*. Necessity, he said, belongs entirely to the sphere of logic, of static relationships, where nothing can happen. But life is not a logical system and history is the sphere of contingency. That is why man, who is free but not absolutely free, can find no security in existence short of coming to rest in the living God.

In order to make clear what it means to become and to be a Christian, Kierkegaard used a method of "indirect communication," sending out most of his books under a series of pseudonyms. This reflects his view that no matter what a man's profession may be, he actually "exists" in a way which may deny his profession. The professor who builds a beautiful castle of thought in which everything follows reason nevertheless lives in the hovel of actual existence by its side. There are thus mutually exclusive levels or stages or spheres of existence. A man will live either at the level of the aesthetic or at the level of the ethical in which the aesthetic is subsumed. Or he will live at the level of the specifically Christian and thus also give the aesthetic and the ethical their place. This is why Kierkegaard was nicknamed by his contemporaries "Either/Or." Either the aesthetic is dominant in a man's life, or he has made the transition by a "leap" to the sphere of the ethical. This "leap" from one existence to another Kierkegaard opposed to the Hegelian principle of mediation. In his view life is not a series of inevitable transitions but of discrete leaps of decision.

The aesthetic life, says Kierkegaard, is the uncommitted life, the life of the moment, the life that recognizes no binding universals but seizes what pleasure and significance it can from day to day. It is typified by the characters in the first volume of *Either/Or* and by some of the characters in *The Stages of Life*, particularly by John, the Seducer. This life, as is evident from the so-called diapsalmata at the beginning of *Either/Or,* is at bottom a life of despair. Instead of presenting such a life in the form of a lecture, Kierkegaard's method of indirect communication lets one see this man in action from the inside and experience with him what it actually means to exist in that sphere. So the reader cannot as a mere spectator know what is meant, but only by inner participation.

The sphere of the ethical is exemplified by Judge Wilhelm in the second half of *Either/Or.* This is the level of the universally human, where a man is guided by the recognition of universally binding ethical norms. It is here that the seriousness of life begins and all of life from the cradle to the grave is a time of trial in which a man must choose either to conform to the universally binding ethical norm or to depart from it. This is the task of life and no one can come to the teacher before life itself is ended and claim that he has finished his lesson and wants something else to do. Present-day interpretations of Kierkegaard which make him responsible for the complete subjectivism and moral relativism of the atheistic existentialists, for whom existence precedes essence and who contend that every individual makes his own values, are seriously mistaken. The ethical existence sphere is for Kierkegaard the sphere in which a man lives actually bound by absolute ethical norms. The ethical man is the one who is related absolutely to the absolute and relatively to the relative, and what makes this life at bottom a life of despair is the recognition that this is for the existing individual an impossibility. But there is a stage beyond the ethical—the specifically Christian—where the categories of sin and faith and love replace those of the universally human ethical norms.

The sphere of the ethical is at the same time the sphere of the universally human religiosity of which all men are capable by virtue of being human without entering into the decisive relation with Jesus Christ. Here lies the crucial difference between a "religion of immanence," in which a man is able to find God (the eternal Truth) within the depths of his own consciousness at any place and at any time because of his basic integrity, and Christianity, the sphere of the paradoxical in which man is forsaken by the hidden immanence of the eternal (the state of sin) and therefore can enter into the right God-relation only by having the Gospel preached to him at a specific time and place. In other words, a man's eternal blessedness depends upon his relation to a contingent historical event: the birth, life, death, and resurrection of the man Jesus. Any man of any generation can become contemporary with this contingent historical event, but only in faith. That is to say, there is no recognition of the revelation of God in Christ and the saving significance of his life and death for the sins of the world unless there is a transformation of existence. Of this transformation of existence any man in any generation is capable in the power of the Holy Spirit. Wherever the Gospel is proclaimed a claim is put upon man's existence; therefore the Gospel is apprehended only in "faith" or in "offense." He who makes the Christian profession cannot do so as a mere spectator, but only by living what he professes and by having passed by means of the leap of "faith" from the universally human religiosity A to the sphere of the specifically Christian religiosity B.

It is these distinctions between the existence spheres which Kierkegaard tried to make clear through his pseudonymous literature. *Either/Or* and *The Stages of Life* depict the first two alternatives. *Fear and Trembling* and *Repetition* point beyond the ethical to the specifically Christian. The *Philosophical Fragments* is his most significant and influential work in terms of establishing, merely as an experiment in thought, the difference between the religion of immanence and the religion of the Christian revelation. This work and its sequel, *The Concluding Unscientific Postscript,* in which the question discussed in the *Fragments*—"Can a man's eternal happiness be decided by his relation to a contingent historical event?"—is given its historical dress in Christianity, have been most important for the break with idealism and the return to the biblical categories which began in Germany with the bombshell of Karl Barth's *Letter to the Romans* (1919). *Fragments* and *Postscript,* written under the pseudonym Johannes Climacus, develop consistently the whole of Kierkegaard's thought. The first book is a model of precision and clarity in writing, coupled with beauty of expression (Swenson's is an excellent translation). There is in the world's literature no apology for the Incarnation that parallels the story of the king who loved the humble maiden and abandoned his throne in order to establish the absolute equality of love. In the second Kierkegaard pulls out all the stops of his genius and uses all the weapons at his disposal— dialectical acumen, sarcasm, irony, ridicule, humor, logic, pathos—in order to demolish Hegelianism and the pseudo-Christianity of his day and make clear the meaning of existence before the living God and the suffering involved in being a Christian who cannot give full outward expression to his absolute surrender to God. Without a grasp of these two books it is impossible to understand Kierkegaard and his influence on both theology and the development of so-called existentialism.

In *The Concept of Dread* and *The Sickness unto Death* Kierkegaard shows his genius as a psychologist of the human spirit, a quite different psychology from that which depends on objective experimentation. Here everything depends on the most astute kind of introspection and nothing is understood about human nature except that which is understood within. In fact all understanding of life itself is seen to be nothing but a form of self-understanding, for man will interpret all of history and its significance always in terms of the way in which he understands himself. True self-understanding, however, is possible only when one is first made known of God. The Socratic maxim "Self-knowledge is God-knowledge" must be reversed.

In *The Concept of Dread* he pseudonymously investigates the psychological state which precedes sin and out of which sin emerges with a leap. This state is that of dread or anxiety, to be distinguished from fear of a definite object and from the various forms of neurotic anxiety as the constant concomitant of man's freedom, which is not absolute. It is this basic undertone of anxiety which is the characteristic quality of man's existence in finitude as a center of responsibility before the living God. Man does not have an essence which is stable and which can maintain itself by itself. The human self is the self in relation to itself and other selves; it cannot maintain itself in equilibrium unless it is properly related to the being that posited it. Thus every man is in his existence confronted with the possibility either of coming to rest in the being upon whom he absolutely depends or of divorcing himself from that being in rebellious self-assertion. It is the latter possibility which every man finds realized in his life of conscious decision. This is the state of original sin in which every man finds himself, having leaped from the state of innocence prior to any decision whatsoever, in which the possibility of being able creates the dread before nothingness, into that of rebellious self-assertion. Adam's story is the common human story. Adam represents himself and the whole human race. At the beginning of human history sin enters by a leap out of the state of dread in which man exists in his finite freedom. Sin is not to be equated with finitude. Sin cannot be explained, but it is to be recognized and repented of. The delineation of the state of sin belongs to the sphere of dogmatics. Psychology can investigate only the psychological state preceding sin, which is the state of dread. The only real escape from the basic anxiety of existence is in the atonement.

In *The Sickness unto Death,* which should be read in close connection with *The Concept of Dread,* under another pseudonym Kierkegaard develops the meaning of selfhood and of the universal sickness of mankind which is despair or, in Christian terms, sin. Every man, whether he knows it or not, is in despair, and this is the only sickness which is unto death, for by it the self is destroyed. The ability to despair is man's superiority over the beast; to be keenly aware of this sickness is the Christian's superiority over the natural man, and to be cured of it is the Christian's joy. With the utmost precision Kierkegaard delineates all the subtle forms which despair takes in the human spirit. Basically all the forms of despair may be reduced to one—the unwillingness to be the dependent self, which in order to realize itself must be grounded transparently in the being that posited it. But this basic form of despair may manifest itself in one's failure to realize that he is a self, so that he merely vegetates instead of existing before the living God; or else in the despair of weakness, which simply succumbs to the fact of its dependency and does not take refuge in the possibility of God; or else the despair of defiance, which asserts itself boldly, making claim to autonomy where this claim is a usurpation. This state of despair is from the Christian point of view sin. It is not ignorance (the Socratic presupposition) but a position willfully maintained. Its only cure is in entering into the right God-relation through the miracle of faith.

While thus developing the meaning of the specifically Christian via his pseudonyms (and it is important for the reader always to keep in mind which pseudonym is speaking), Kierkegaard at the same time from the very beginning published a series of edifying discourses under his own name. These are not sermons, nor are they specifically Christian; though in the sphere of the universally human religiosity, they are for edification and deal with life's crucial situations. Often it is difficult for the reader to see why they are not specifically Christian, but a comparison with the later *Christian Discourses* and *The Works of Love* will show the difference. The difference lies in the mention of the paradoxical faith-relation to the God-Man, Jesus Christ.

When it became clear to Kierkegaard that those to whom he looked for support were not responding to his method of "indirect communication" he moved gradually to more direct address. In *Training in Christianity* and *For Self-Examination* the author calls for a return to New Testament Christianity. He clearly sets forth the nature of the "offense" presented by Jesus who in his lowliness nevertheless called all men unto himself. The Christianity of the New Testament therefore demands surrender to Jesus in his lowliness. There is no entrance to Christianity except through the gate of repentance, the recognition of sin, the surrender of faith, and the willingness to follow in the absolute surrender of obedience. Only then can the Christian life become all joy as it was meant to be. The comfortable life of respectable decency which knows nothing of sin or the offense or of suffering is castigated in no uncertain terms.

When even this more direct speaking failed to produce any response from the responsible authorities Kierkegaard ceased writing and waited. He waited for the death of Bishop Mynster, the respected friend and counselor of his father, whose services he regularly attended and whose sermons he read with the recognition that they were for edification. As long as Mynster was alive he could not bring himself to an open attack on the church. But after Mynster's death, when Martensen at the funeral declared Mynster to have been one of the true witnesses of the faith, the hour for direct action had struck. Even so Kierkegaard waited until Martensen had succeeded to the coveted of-

fice of bishop, but then he spared no one. The articles that
appeared under Kierkegaard's own name and the series of
pamphlets which Kierkegaard himself published under the title
of *The Instant* are published together in English as *The Attack
upon Christendom.* The uncompromising nature of this attack
has been seriously questioned. If everything that Kierkegaard
said is taken at face value then there was no shred of decency
left anywhere in the church of Denmark either among the
clergy, those "shopkeepers souls in velvet," or among the people
to whom their Christian confession meant less than nothing except when it became necessary because of the state regulations
pertaining to weddings, baptism of children, and funeral rites.
According to Kierkegaard, all the priests were cannibals living
off the blood of the martyrs, and he advised the people to stay
away from the services. He himself refused on his deathbed to
receive Holy Communion from a priest, although he would
have received it from a layman—a fact which ought to silence
those who claim that if Kierkegaard had lived longer he would
have returned to Holy Mother Church. Kierkegaard understood
the doctrine of the priesthood of all believers and part of his
insistence was that only through an actual transformation of life
could one come into possession of this priesthood, although
the efficacy of one's witnesses did not depend upon this transformation but solely upon the power of the Word of God, which
effects the transformation.

Many remonstrated with Kierkegaard for the severity of his
attack, but he persisted in the conviction that only if he was uncompromising could he stir the church out of her complacency.
As he said again and again, all he wanted was simple honesty,
the admission that what was being preached and lived in Denmark was not New Testament Christianity. He knew, as no one
else knew, the meaning of grace, and he wanted only that men
should recognize their sinfulness and enter into the kingdom of
God through the narrow gate of repentance and then live their
lives accordingly: "Infinite humiliation and grace and then a
striving grounded in gratitude, this is Christianity." Nor is it
true that he advocated a mournful Christianity, celibacy, and
the monastery. In the *Unscientific Postscript* he contrasts the
Trip to the Monastery and the Trip to the Deer Park. His con-

tention is that Christianity is suffering and that this suffering consists in the fact that it is impossible for a man to give unequivocal outward expression to his inward, singleminded devotion, as he is related "absolutely to the absolute and relatively to the relative." Therefore the medieval trip to the monastery deserves credit only for the seriousness of its intention and not because it succeeds in its purpose. The only alternative is fidelity to whatever calling a man feels himself called to by the exigencies of the moment. For Kierkegaard himself this meant the refusal to marry and his becoming the "corrective," the "pinch of spice" called for by the tasteless concoction being dished up as the "bread of life" in his day.

So Kierkegaard persisted in his merciless attack until one day he fell unconscious in the street. He spent several weeks in the hospital during which time he retracted nothing but, like Socrates, remained true in the hour of death to the manner of life he had lived in the market place. According to eyewitnesses he grew more ethereal as the end approached, and he died in the conviction that the joy which in this life had been denied him would be his in the eternal mansions through the merits of Jesus Christ his Lord. So his life was spent together with his patrimony in the pursuit of one objective: to make clear in Christendom what it means to become and to be a Christian.

KIERKEGAARD'S IMPORTANCE

The immediate effects of Kierkegaard's call to repentance in Denmark were negligible. A few of the clergy took it seriously and effected genuine reform. Some, like Ibsen's Brand, misunderstood and in their fanatic devotion only succeeded in wrecking the lives God alone could heal. Kierkegaard had to wait a hundred years for his day to come. Not only Karl Barth and his followers and in this country the so-called neo-orthodox school but all of Lutheranism, both in Germany and the Scandinavian countries and elsewhere, and particularly the free churches in England, in fact all of Protestantism as well as Roman Catholicism, have felt his influence. The theology of the future must inevitably come to terms with the issues he raised and the answers he gave.

Not only theology but also philosophy and psychology and the whole field of literature and the arts owe their debt to Kierkegaard in the development of that vast proliferation known as existentialism and covering everything from the preoccupation with the sordid side of life to the loftiest humanism in a world where God is dead and man as the only spearhead of freedom must in the full anguish of sole responsibility create his own values. In the vast Kierkegaardian literature there is enough for the greatest extremes to find something on which to capitalize and to outdo the master in following the whims of lonely subjectivity, but Kierkegaard must be allowed to speak for himself and he has made abundantly clear where he stood. In several treatises ("The Point of View," "The Present Age") he clearly elucidates the whole plan of his authorship and prophetically anticipates the course of human events in the development of the mass man and the loss of the individual in the monster of totalitarianism.

In addition to his view of the stages of life and of what constitutes authentic human existence, the following are distinctive elements in Kierkegaard's thought.

Christianity is absolute paradox. A paradox confronts one with a fact that is contrary to appearance, contrary to the general opinion, and also with propositions which are contradictory when used in attempted description of the fact. It is Kierkegaard's contention that while many paradoxes which confront us in life may be resolvable, either by clearer vision or greater knowledge, Christianity presents us with the absolutely paradoxical, i.e., with paradoxes which no existing individual, precisely because he exists in time and space and is not pure spirit, can resolve. For God there is no contradiction, but for the existing individual the contradiction remains. This is true, first of all, of the central fact of Christianity, the appearance of God in the flesh. No docetism, no Jesus of history, no rational Chalcedonian Christology nor any of the other attempts to resolve this paradox have been able to do justice to the full mystery of the incarnation in its once and for all uniqueness. That God was in Christ reconciling the world unto himself is true, contrary to appearance, for God does not appear visible to the senses in the carpenter of Nazareth and the man on the cross. It is true, con-

trary to the general opinion, for it is not the general opinion of
men that the death of one can atone for the sins of all or even
that there is need of such atonement. It is true, but not because
man's reason gives him indubitable certainty that it could not
be otherwise, or because by the accumulation of evidence a
high degree of probability can be established for it. He who
recognizes it to be so must first become transformed in his existence. He needs to recognize his predicament in sin and his
need of a Saviour. Therefore the absolute paradox is that which
blocks the way to a mere intellectual acceptance of certain
propositions about God and confronts man with the living God
Himself, to whom a man must surrender in "faith"—which is
itself a paradox, inasmuch as it is at the same time the work of
God in man that it is a human decision. The only alternative,
therefore, to this God-wrought faith in which a man is absolutely humbled before God is an equally God-wrought "offense"
in which the cross of Christ remains a stumbling block to the
various forms of man's pride. And what is true of the central
fact of the Christian faith, the Incarnation, is true also of all
the specific Christian categories. They are all paradoxical and
as such irresolvable by the existing individual. This is true of
the mystery of the *creatio ex nihilo,* the fact that man remains
lifelong a sinner and at the same time righteous, the fact, above
all, of the resurrection from the dead. In fact, except in terms
of the absolutely paradoxical it is impossible to make clear what
is meant by the absolute miracle of grace in man's creation, redemption, and sanctification without reducing it to the merely
astonishing. Here Kierkegaard was adamant. The only thing that
he understood about the absolute miracle of God's love was that
he did not understand it.

There is an absolute qualitative difference between God and
man. This is the corollary to the recognition of the absolutely
paradoxical, for it is precisely because the difference between
sinful man and the holy God is not one of degree only but of
kind that there is no resolution of the absolutely paradoxical
until the end of the time of decision and the turning of faith
to sight in the resurrection of the dead. It is a misunderstanding
to suppose that this means a denial of the creation of man in
the image of God or that it makes impossible any communica-

tion whatsoever with an absolute transcendent God, cut off by an unbridgeable chasm from his creation. The point is simply that it is not possible to get by degrees from the category "created and sinful man" over into the category "God." God and the world are in no sense necessary corollaries and between them there is no simple continuity. God's creation of the world and of man is a contingent and not a necessary event. It is also possible that if God so chose, God and the world should not be. The fact that God is the creator and man the creature establishes an absolutely irreversible relation and hence an absolute qualitative difference. Unless one begins with this premise there is no avoiding some subtle form of pantheism. The absolute qualitative difference therefore finds paradoxical expression in the fact that God is both absolutely transcendent and absolutely immanent, without any confusion of creator and creature. Moreover when Kierkegaard speaks of the absolute difference between God and man he is thinking not only of man as creature but of man as sinner. If God were perfection and man's predicament lay in his imperfection, then the degree of difference could readily be established and perfection quantitatively attained. But when God is holy and man is guilty before him, the sinner can only be redeemed and so spend eternity singing his redeemer's praise.

Truth is subjectivity. This does not mean for Kierkegaard that there are no truths that are independent of the knower. The truths of mathematics are what they are and are discovered by man with the powers of his reason. All the facts of life and history exist in time and space independently of being known by any particular individual. Above all, God is what he is, and he did what he did for man's redemption whether anyone believes it or not. In the moral realm it does not mean that each individual man is the measure of all things (Protagoras) and that all beauty is only in the eye of the beholder; there are ethical universals binding on all men. What Kierkegaard is insisting, however, is that God, the eternal truth, is not apprehended except in inwardness. There is no such thing as an "objective revelation" if by this is meant a direct visibility of God. It is paganism that believes the gods are directly discernible. God, when he is present in his creation, is discernible only in inwardness, with the eyes of faith. When God does appear he, the absolutely other, appears in the absolute likeness of man. Thus revelation and faith (or offense) are always corollary, and although God is "objectively" present whether discerned or not, there is, by definition, no revelation except where God is actually discerned. This discernment, however, always takes place in inwardness and can never be established in any other way. This inwardness is that of either "faith" or "offense" because revelation always puts its claim upon a person. This is the recognition that the Bible is testimony literature, witnessing to acts of God which do not appear as acts of God except to those who have been apprehended by them or to whom their claim is an offense. Jesus was the promised Messiah only to those who surrendered to his claim. To the others his claim was an offense. So there is no way to "prove," either from the fulfillment of prophecy or the "signs" he performed, that he was the one to come, since both signs and prophecies are susceptible of a different interpretation. Revelation is thus discerned in the inwardness of individual transformation. The Christian is reduced to being a witness to the mighty act of God in Christ. His method is that of "indirect communication." When he witnesses in both word and deed, nothing is communicated directly from speaker to hearer or from actor to observer; but when man witnesses, God communicates himself. This is the work of the Holy Spirit.

Hence Kierkegaard by no means destroys the so-called objectivity of revelation, reducing everything to a form of self-understanding, but he does insist on taking revelation seriously as revelation, and he takes seriously the Holy Spirit.

This also explains Kierkegaard's emphasis upon the individual. Each individual, in the strict isolation of his inwardness before God, must hear God put his claim upon him. Men enter one by one into the kingdom of God through the narrow gate of repentance as the sheep enter one by one into the sheepfold, each one known by his own name. As each one dies his death alone, so each one comes to faith alone in strict inwardness. This, however, is no denial of the fellowship of believers, apart from which no one can be a Christian.

It is in his analysis of existence that Kierkegaard has been most influential in the area of philosophy and psychology. Kierkegaard opposed the Hegelian notion of a world process unfolding with some kind of rational necessity and therefore bound to culminate in a certain way. There was no one quite as repugnant to him as the don who had read off the whole course of history in this fashion. History was for Kierkegaard the sphere of contingency, not of necessity. History, that of the individual as well as that of the world as a whole, is shaped by contingent acts of decision on the part of both God and man. Necessity is a logical category which belongs to the sphere of static relationships in which nothing can happen, as in mathematics and formal logic. Life, however, is not a logical system. This is Kierkegaard's so-called irrationalism—that reason is not the final arbiter, but existence itself in all its arbitrariness. God himself is love and not reason. The Logos that became flesh is not the world reason but the creative Word that brings into being that which it speaks.

For Kierkegaard, therefore, existence means man's peculiar predicament as the creature of God, dependent absolutely for his being upon that God's creative fiat. Yet man is a self, a center of self-awareness and of decision, who shapes himself by his decisions. This is precisely the precariousness of man's existence—that he is free to shape himself. There is no pattern to which he must necessarily conform. This enables an atheistic existentialist like Sartre to declare that in the absence of any God "existence precedes essence" and man therefore is precariously free to make himself into whatsoever he chooses within the limits of the particular givenness of his time and place. Man *is* this freedom, responsible to no one but himself and therefore beset with all the anguish and forlornness each decision entails, inasmuch as there is no God to forgive and no second chance and no way of altering a decision once made and acted upon. Kierkegaard, however, differs from this view, because for him man's existence is always responsible existence before the living God and because man was made in the image of God to reflect what God is, namely, love. All of life is the time and sphere of decision, in which man is on trial for eternity. The basic insecurity of life itself and man's involvement in sin can be escaped only in the "moment" of encounter with God in

Christ. Security is possible only in faith, peace of conscience is possible only in the forgiveness of sins, there is no "beyond" the tragedy of life except in the resurrection of the dead. Man does not escape life's involvements by escape into another realm of the eternal and unchanging, nor can he in this life progressively overcome the limitations of his finitude. He can only move forward into the new possibility that God alone creates in the "moment" of renewal. History remains the stage on which men are on trial for eternity.

Kierkegaard's importance for philosophy lies in the fact that he has turned the attention of the philosophers to an analysis of existence itself, a so-called phenomenological description of the human situation. This is what both Heidegger and Sartre attempt to give, operating, however, on the premise that there is no God and that if there is no God then man has no right either to assume a heaven of ideas to which his life is to conform. Atheistic existentialism takes seriously the alternative to faith in the living God and is thus a sort of vindication of Kierkegaard's *Either/Or*. "Rational metaphysics" is no substitute for faith in the living God. The alternatives are faith in the living God, a resolute nihilism, or a humanism that asks for no help from the skies.

Here lies Kierkegaard's importance in the field of Christian apologetics. There is no cogent rational defense of the Christian faith from outside the circle of revelation itself. Any defense of the faith is shameful and insidious betrayal. Christianity can only be proclaimed, so that it will put men before the clear choice of either "faith" or "offense." Christianity, therefore, must be distinguished not only from all the other religions of the world but also from all reasoned world views. The questions of ultimate concern are not answered by man in the predicament of his sinful existence, but must be answered by God Himself. Jesus is not the founder of a religion, but in him God speaks and acts in the fullness of time. This is where the so-called crisis theology got its impetus. The meeting with Jesus Christ is possible in any generation in the "contemporaneity of faith" (or offense). This meeting (*Begegnung*) is God-encounter and not a reasoning toward God. It creates a real crisis, a turning point, in which "eternity enters time" and creates the new. That is why also all "natural theology" with its reasoning toward God succeeds in producing only idols. God must be met face to face with his unequivocal claim and not arrived at as the end of an argument. There are some philosophers who recognize this and who have therefore given up the building of systems and the attempt to get a view of the whole while still enmeshed in existence. They consider their task to be the much more humble one of analysis, the Socratic task of the clarification of thought and of being the gadfly to all who are trying to understand. To this movement Kierkegaard may be said to have given impetus by his own attempt to make clear distinctions.

Kierkegaard hated what he called the "paragraph vulture," the person who gulps down a man's contribution to thought in neatly packaged form. What he dreaded most of all was to be appreciatively mentioned in the textbooks of the enlightened future and assigned his place in history by some pretentious don. Anyone, therefore, who writes about Kierkegaard must cry for absolution. Kierkegaard should be read himself or he should be left alone. He must be read in the way he intended to be read and in the context for which he wrote. Then the Either/Or with which he confronts the reader will be clear enough, as well as the sense in which he is and remains the "corrective" for every compromising theology and wishy-washy Christianity. Christianity is a radical cure and not a mild, sugar-coated sedative. To read Kierkegaard is to know what he has to say particularly to our age when the individual is lost in the mass and when general religiosity is confused with the specifically Christian and all awe and fear and trembling have disappeared from the God-relation.

Bibliography

Søren Kierkegaard, *A Kierkegaard Anthology*, Robert Bretall, ed., N. Y., Modern Library, 1959.

Walter Lowrie, *Kierkegaard*, N. Y., Harper, 1962, 2 vols. (Harper Torchbooks).

P. T. FORSYTH

Robert McAfee Brown

I ask'd the Lord that I might grow
    In faith and love, and every grace;
Might more of His salvation know,
    And seek more earnestly His face.

Instead of this, He made me feel
    The hidden evils of my heart,
And let the angry powers of hell
    Assault my soul in every part.

Lord, why is this? I trembling cried,
    Wilt Thou pursue Thy worm to death?
" 'Tis in this way," the Lord replied,
    "I answer prayer for grace and faith.

These inward trials I employ
    From self and pride to set thee free;
And break thy schemes of earthly joy
    That thou may'st seek thy all in Me."

              (*Olney Hymns*, 1799, Book III, 36)

These words by John Newton (1725–1807), a twice-born slave-trader turned preacher, may not qualify as great poetry, but they describe an experience that rings a responsive note in the hearts of other "twice-born" Christians. And they furnish perhaps the most important clue to an understanding of the development and mature thought of Peter Taylor Forsyth, who on one occasion referred to them as "one of the greatest and most realistic utterances of Christian experience,"[1] and on another occasion, describing the course of his own spiritual pilgrimage, said that to him the words were "almost holy writ."[2]

---

[1] Forsyth, *Positive Preaching and the Modern Mind* (London, Independent Press, 1949), p. 106.

[2] *Ibid.*, p. 195. This section of his Beecher Lectures is the only place where Forsyth deals in any detail with his own theological pilgrimage.

The title of Newton's hymn is "Prayer Answered by Crosses," and if it is true that in his lifetime Forsyth experienced more than his share of personal crosses, it is even truer that the power to endure them came from his conviction that Christ had endured his cross in such a way that no other cross could finally threaten any of Christ's disciples.

Forsyth can be described in many ways, but perhaps the truest way would be to describe him as a theologian of the cross, provided we immediately add that his concentration on the cross did not mean a minimizing of the rest of the Christian message, but rather that the rest of the Christian message received its most concentrated expression in the cross. The holiness of God, the primacy of grace, the centrality of Christ, the significance of history, the basis of conduct—everything that is the proper concern of Christian theology and living was examined by Forsyth and illumined for him within the shadow of the cross of Christ, a cross that casts a shadow only because behind it is the bright light of the gracious God who has visited and redeemed his people.

BEYOND ORTHODOXY AND LIBERALISM

Forsyth did not come to this faith easily. It was a "hardly won" faith, possible because of a divine gift rather than a human achievement, based, as he once said, on atonement rather than attainment. It was a faith constantly under attack by Forsyth's contemporaries. The orthodox wrote him off because of his espousal of such things as biblical criticism, while the liberals (perhaps smarting under his strong attacks on them) looked on him as hopelessly out of date. The fact that he fits no theological pigeonhole is one sign of his enduring greatness. The gospel, he always urged, cannot be scaled down to any human system of thought. He has been called a forerunner of neo-orthodoxy, a "Barthian before Barth," a liberal evangelical (which is not the same thing as an evangelical liberal). But no tag quite fits, and he remains simply a man immersed in the good news of the Bible, particularly as seen through the eyes of the Reformers and Paul.

Forsyth was born in Aberdeen in 1848 in what were, even by

standards of a century ago, "humble surroundings."[3] He graduated brilliantly from Aberdeen University, spent a semester in Germany studying under Ritschl, and was ordained to the Congregational ministry in 1876. After serving in several important English parishes, he became principal of Hackney College, London, in 1901, a position he held until his death twenty years later. Beneath this apparently uneventful series of happenings an entire theological revolution took place. Reacting against a sterile orthodoxy that was crumbling under the impact of biblical criticism, Forsyth was at first a left-wing "liberal"—unashamedly so, as some of his earliest writings make clear. But in his pastoral contacts and, just as important, in his own life, he found that the liberalism of his time had no power. Its recasting of the Christian faith had a hollow sound. Forsyth gradually worked his way back from liberalism to the Bible, and through the Bible to the "Word behind the words," the gospel of the grace of God in Jesus Christ, a gospel contained in the Bible but not identical with the words of the Bible. "I was turned," he writes in a key sentence, "from a Christian to a believer, *from a lover of love to an object of grace.*"[4] By about 1893 the new position had been secured, and a collection of Forsyth's sermons[5] preached before the turn of the century shows evidence of most of the themes that he was to pursue in his later and larger writings.

Forsyth was genuinely convinced, for reasons we shall presently examine, that the liberalism represented by R. J. Campbell's "new theology" represented the most serious threat to the Christian gospel since second-century gnosticism.[6] But he did not merely indict; he elaborated an alternative to what he rejected. One of his most frequent words in this endeavor was "positive"—he advocated positive preaching, a positive gospel, positive belief. But it must be clear that he did not advocate

[3] A full account of Forsyth's life is given in W. L. Bradley, *P. T. Forsyth, The Man and His Work* (London, Independent Press, 1952), and more briefly in my *P. T. Forsyth: Prophet for Today* (Philadelphia, Westminster, 1952).

[4] *Positive Preaching and the Modern Mind,* p. 193 (italics added).

[5] *God the Holy Father* (London, Independent Press, 1957).

[6] The terms of Forsyth's indictment can be found *inter alia* in *Positive Preaching and the Modern Mind,* Ch. VI.

what now goes by the name of positive thinking—a self-help religion astonishingly similar to the type of liberalism on which Forsyth turned his sharpest polemical weapons. But this word must stand as a reminder that for Forsyth the theologian's task had not been completed when the inadequacy of the alternatives had been exposed. At that point the task had merely started.

Honors came to Forsyth during his lifetime. He was elected chairman of the Congregational Union of England and Wales in 1904, gave the Beecher Lectures at Yale University in 1907, received a D.D. degree from Aberdeen University, and was recognized as one of the outstanding theological thinkers of his generation. But we have already indicated that during his lifetime he swam against the current theological currents. His return to the Reformers, to Athanasius, to Paul, set him against what he called the "sunny liberalism" in early twentieth-century Britain. Fifty years ago he was quoting Kierkegaard approvingly, but when he quoted Harnack it was in an effort to refute him. Men professed to find Forsyth's style too difficult—one critic compared his writing to "fireworks in a fog"—although the complaint may have arisen from his use of such difficult notions as regeneration, atonement, and reconciliation. But Forsyth recognized that a popular following was not the index of the truth of the free grace of God; he often quoted Melanchthon —"Our greatest enemies are the accommodating theologians" —and equally often stated that the proper theological stance in a day like his own must be modeled on Athanasius *contra mundum*.

So he was out of step with his own theological generation. He appears to be rather more in step with the current one, if it is too much to claim that the current generation is finally in step with him. The impact of two world wars has removed the heady optimism that seemed in Forsyth's lifetime to make his "positive gospel" redundant to forward-looking Christians. The external crisis of the 1950's and 1960's only serves to illumine the inner crisis that men always face, the permanent *krisis* of which Forsyth wrote so brilliantly. As a result, there has been in recent years a kind of "Forsyth renaissance" among younger churchmen in the Anglo-Saxon (and, interestingly enough, in the Japanese) Christian world. His major works have all been reprinted, thanks to the imaginative foresight of Independent Press and the indefatigable industry of Forsyth's daughter, Mrs. Jessie Forsyth Andrews, who has edited each volume for republication. Contemporary theologians of all stripes are finding that Forsyth speaks a word to them, and through them he is speaking a word to a wider audience than he ever had in his own lifetime.[7]

THE WORD AND THE WORLD

What is his message?

Forsyth wrote so widely, in the course of twenty-five books and hundreds of articles, that a capsule version of his theology would be impossible. The books alone deal with the following range of subjects: art, the church, the holiness of God, Roman Catholicism, death, grace, homiletics, socialism, missions, prayer, marriage, authority, church and state, theodicy, war, the cross, the person of Christ, the work of Christ, the sacraments, and eternal life. And yet they have a unity. With a consistency almost unbelievable, Forsyth takes every topic with which he deals and examines it in the light of what it means in a world where there has been an empty cross and an empty tomb.

His method of doing this is one of his most important contributions, and this method we can only describe as christological. (Here is where Forsyth clearly foreshadows the emphases of the later Barth.) He insists that Christ is not only the Omega, to whom our thought must finally come and in bondage to whom it must finally be made captive if it is to be truly free, but Christ is also the Alpha, the beginning; and if we do not truly start with him, there is little chance that we will truly end with him. Long before the Continental theologians had made the antithesis popular, Forsyth was writing about "The Word and the World" and urging that the greatest decision the church continually has to make is whether to begin its life and thought with the former or with the latter. Forsyth was convinced that theology starts down a dead-end street when it starts with the

[7] It is a matter of continuing surprise that only one of his volumes— and one of the less significant—has been reprinted in the United States.

world, with man's "natural" experiences and reactions, his philosophies and schemes, and assumes that there is an easy transition from these to the heart of the gospel. In an atmosphere
where this is the prevailing current of opinion, the first word of
the gospel must be a judging and condemning word, pointing
out that such an elevation of man's schemes is no more than
an elevation of man himself, and that it quickly becomes the
primal sin. It is not "natural" to kneel at the cross or see in it
the only adequate revelation of the grace of God. There must
be a radical break from "the speculative reason or the instincts
of the heart" if the gospel of God's grace is to make its way
into man's life.

This is not anti-intellectualism. If we are brought to the place
where we see that our human schemes do not lead us to God
but actually lead us further and further away from him, we may
be brought to a radical change of footing in which we *start* with
God's grace revealed in Jesus Christ and from that vantage
point alone discover that we can proceed in faith and confi
dence. This is Forsyth's way of affirming that the Christian pilgrimage is a matter of "faith seeking understanding," and of
affirming that understanding does indeed increase where faith
is strong. "To begin with the world is to become dubious about
the Word; whereas to begin with the Word is to become sure
about the world. A philosophy can bring us to no security of a
revelation; but a revelation develops a philosophy or a view of
the world."[8]

"The Word," of course, is Jesus Christ, the Word made flesh.
It is not the words of the Bible—here is where Forsyth breaks
with views of plenary inspiration so popular in his day—but
the One to whom the words of the Bible point. Since we could
not know the Word apart from the Bible, any theology worthy
of the name must be a biblical theology. But if we stare too in-
tently at the words themselves we can miss the living Word behind them. Thus biblical criticism is not an end in itself; it
exists, and it exists in honor, as a servant of the Word, as a
means through which the Word can shine forth more brightly
than before. There is a kind of criticism that is destructive of

[8] *Positive Preaching and the Modern Mind,* p. 170.

the gospel; Forsyth felt that Harnack's efforts at reconstruction had been particularly devastating. But rather than letting the radical wing of German critics sweep the field, he met them on their own battleground and used their methods for creative rather than destructive ends.

PROPER THEOLOGICAL METHOD

It was partly in terms of this intramural struggle for a proper understanding of the Bible, as well as in terms of the extramural struggle with contemporary culture, that Forsyth stressed the right of theology to employ methods proper to the nature of its subject matter. He insisted that it was improper and "unscientific" to take methods appropriate to the natural sciences for the investigation of *impersonal* data and insist that they be used to investigate the very *personal* claim about a Saviour of mankind from its sin and guilt. To Forsyth this demand, which is always being pressed upon the church, was a "dogmatism" far outweighing the supposed dogmatism of the dogmatic theologians. To proponents of such a claim Forsyth wrote, "You are doing to religion what you fiercely resent that religion should do to art or science. You are limiting its freedom by a foreign dogma."[9] Christian theology, concerned with One who saves from guilt, has every right to employ categories appropriate to the content of such a claim, and the categories will be categories of will and personality rather than slide rule and test tube.

But we must be aware that this concern was focused not only by the church's extramural battles, but was and is *the* issue within the church as well. It is the perennial temptation of the church to scale down its proclamation to terms that make it compatible with "the modern mind." When this happens, the norm becomes the modern mind, to which Christ must be accommodated, rather than a Christ with whom the modern mind must come to terms. If this is true, then Forsyth's insistence on the priority of the Word, and the legitimacy of the character of the Word dictating the categories of appropriate investigation, is a message the church needs to hear at every stage in its history, even though the precise terms of the basic conflict may differ in different ages.

[9] In *The British Weekly,* February 17, 1910, p. 557.

It must not be assumed that such a conclusion leads to cultural or intellectual obscurantism. There is the patent fact that it did not lead Forsyth to any such obscurantism, but rather intensified his concern in cultural areas, as the mere review of some of his book titles will indicate: *Religion in Recent Art; Socialism, the Church and the Poor; Christ on Parnassus, Lectures on Art, Ethic, and Theology; Marriage, Its Ethic and Religion; The Christian Ethic of War.* But more important is Forsyth's contention that a proper priority of the Word makes possible a proper understanding of the world, so long as the world is seen in the light of the Word. The gospel, Forsyth feels, must take seriously those insights about the human situation that come from the social sciences (e.g., the right of the individual to freedom from external authority) and from the physical sciences (e.g., the indubitable truth contained in the doctrine of evolution). Christians have much to learn about the human situation from non-Christians, and Forsyth wrote long articles about Hardy, Ibsen, and others to prove the point. He recognized that Aeschylus had much to tell the Christian theologian, and that Shakespeare could challenge a weak theology. But culture's gift to man is not so much a providing of answers as it is a showing forth of the depth of the human problem. In doing this it can point man beyond inadequate answers toward the one sure answer to human sin and human guilt (about which Ibsen and Aeschylus know so much)—the answer that is found in Jesus Christ and his cross. There are many schoolmasters besides the Law.

But it is not an easy step from culture to Christ; it is a gap. The gap is finally bridged by the movement from Christ to culture rather than vice versa, and only in the perspective of that movement can the continuities and the discontinuities be properly assessed.

"A GRACIOUS EXPERIENCE WHICH WE MUST DECLARE"

Theology, then, must be the servant of the Word who is Jesus Christ and grant him the priority that is rightfully his. This means neither believing doctrines about him (which was the error of the old orthodoxy) nor reducing his significance to that of an inspired teacher (which was the error of the new liberalism). It means recognizing that in Christ we have to do with "a gracious God" who transforms us through his relationship to us.

> The first feature of a positive gospel is that it is a gospel of pure, free grace to human sin. . . . The initiative rests entirely with God, and with a holy and injured God. On this article of grace the whole of Christianity turns.[10]
> To that gospel of grace, as we are continually sent forth from it, so we must continually return, to adjust our compass and take our course. . . . It is more than our base, it is our source. . . . Our theology is not a fixed system we must accept but a gracious experience which we must declare.[11]

"A gracious experience which we must declare." This raises a point of importance not only for the understanding of Forsyth but for the Protestant venture as a whole. Protestantism is often interpreted experientially; Catholicism is represented as having "fixed dogmas" while Protestantism is represented as a religion of experience. There is a certain truth here, but it is no more than a half-truth. No one inveighed with more fervor against equating Protestantism with "the right of private judgment" than did Forsyth. And yet no polemic against the autonomy of personal experience must be allowed to slip over into a polemic against the fact that faith must be experienced. For if the latter polemic is permitted, acceptance of the gospel becomes no more than acceptance of a number of intellectual propositions about the gospel. Forsyth often tried to indicate the fine line here by pointing out that *what* is experienced is more important than what is *experienced*. If the stress is simply on content, the result is creedalism or orthodoxy of a sterile kind. But if the stress is simply on experience, the result is subjectivism with no strings attached, in which the only norm of truth is vividness.

Faith, then, has a content, and its content is the Word of God incarnate in Jesus Christ who suffered on a cross for the sins of the world and was raised from the dead. But faith must also be an experience of this content, so that the "sins of the world" include "my" sins. In another of Forsyth's distinctions,

---

[10] *Positive Preaching and the Modern Mind*, p. 144.

[11] *Faith, Freedom and the Future* (London, Independent Press, 1955), pp. 119-20.

faith descends *to* experience but does not ascend *from* experience. Faith originates elsewhere than in ourselves; it originates in the decisive act of God in Jesus Christ, and that act has objective reality whether we acknowledge its reality or not. But that act exists in order to be acknowledged by us, and when it is, the life of the believer is changed. The gospel is not dependent on our experience for its validity. But its validity is confirmed in our experience.[12]

It is "a gracious experience," an experience of grace, "which we must declare."

REVELATION AS REDEMPTION

What must we declare? We must declare Jesus Christ. What must we declare about him? To this question the bulk of Forsyth's writings are addressed. There is no one book in which he has said it all systematically, although he comes closer to being a "systematic theologian" in *The Person and Place of Jesus Christ* than elsewhere. But so overpowering was the person and work of Jesus Christ to Forsyth that, as we have already intimated, his understanding of Christology shapes everything he wrote.[13]

Since Forsyth looks upon revelation primarily as deed rather than word, as act rather than declaration, a full understanding of who Christ is will be found not in what he said but in what he did. This does not mean that Jesus' teachings lack importance but that by themselves they are not a sufficient index of his importance. For this reason, among others, we must read the synoptics in the light of the epistles, realizing that it is from within the atmosphere of the epistles that the synoptics were actually written. Furthermore, we must not expect that Jesus will *say* everything that is to be said about who he is and what he does; instead he will *do* it, and the saying of it, the description of it, will be the task bequeathed to his followers.

[12] Forsyth develops these themes with great persuasiveness and in great detail in *The Principle of Authority,* 2d ed. (London, Independent Press, 1952).

[13] In what follows, I am drawing in part on the structure of my chapter on "The Cruciality of Christ" in *P. T. Forsyth: Prophet for Today.*

Christ came not to *say* something, but to *do* something. His revelation was action more than instruction. He revealed by redeeming. The thing he did was not simply to make us aware of God's disposition in an impressive way. It was not to *declare* forgiveness. It was certainly not to *explain* forgiveness. And it was not even to *bestow* forgiveness. It was to *effect* forgiveness and to set up the relation of forgiveness both in God and man.[14]

If Christ did not come to "preach the gospel," he did become a gospel to preach. He did what needed to be done and left to his followers the task of proclaiming what he had done, so that subsequent generations might enter into the orbit of the saving power of his deed.

This has important consequences for an understanding of revelation. It means, as Forsyth put it, that "revelation is redemption." God's revelation is not a report by someone (a prophet, an inspired teacher, or even a Son of God) that God is holy and gracious love; revelation is an act by which, at infinite cost to himself, the God of holy and gracious love restores us to fellowship with himself. It is not merely making plain that there is a chasm between holy God and sinful man; it is itself the bridging of that chasm. It is "creation instead of exhibition," "renovation instead of innovation," "resurrection instead of communication."[15] Revelation effects what it exhibits. A full understanding of revelation, therefore, comes only to those who have in fact been redeemed by it. It is not something that can be examined in an abstract, uninvolved way. The one who knows what revelation is, is the one whose life has been redeemed from sin and guilt and who has become a "new man" in Christ Jesus. "The article of Christ's deity," Forsyth writes, "is the theological expression of the evangelical experience of his salvation."[16]

THE WORK OF CHRIST

What does all of this mean for theology? It means something crucially important. It means that we are first confronted by

[14] *God the Holy Father*, p. 19.

[15] See Forsyth's contribution to *The Atonement and Modern Thought*, p. 80.

[16] *The Person and Place of Jesus Christ* (London, Independent Press, 1948), p. 74.

what Christ *does,* and that only thereafter can we begin to understand who Christ *is.* Put differently, it means that we can understand the *person* of Christ only when we have understood the *work* of Christ. Put still differently, it means that we can understand the meaning of the incarnation only when we have understood the meaning of the atonement. To know Christ is to know his benefits.

Now regardless of how Melanchthon came to feel about the latter statement (which he excised from later editions of the *Loci Communes*), it was a principle of utmost importance to Forsyth. The early Christians, he argued, were first confronted by the fact that in the cross of Christ a new relationship between God and themselves had been established. It was out of their indubitable experience of this new relationship that they went on to ask, "What must we affirm of one who could do this for us?" The work of Christ was and is the key to an understanding of his person. Forsyth felt (and he may have pressed this point too far) that theories about the person of Christ, as embodied in the later creeds and particularly that of Chalcedon, tended to become more and more speculative, and that they stood at a considerable remove from the heart of the gospel. A theory about Christ's person, he reasoned, was a secondary matter when compared to the reality of Christ's work. We must of course, he continued to reason, work out theories about Christ's person once we have been caught up in the reality of his work. Forsyth's most creative single book, *The Person and Place of Jesus Christ,* is an attempt to do just that. But this kind of analysis can proceed only if it is recognized that the redemptive deed has been done and that everything has been changed by it.

Everything. The redemptive act of God in Christ was cosmic in its dimensions. A "subjective" atonement was too weak to bear the burden of the full New Testament, Forsyth felt. An objective deed has been done. The relationship between God and the world has been changed. Men live in this new world, whether they are aware of it or not. This view (which can be compared to the "classic" view of the atonement presented in Aulén's *Christus Victor*) has significance not only for individual men but for the whole race, not only for a personal relationship to God but for an understanding of the meaning and sweep of human history.[17] We live in a redeemed world. Evil is still rampant—obviously. But its power is limited, for the real battle between God and the power of evil has already taken place. It took place on the cross. The last judgment is past. It took place there. Its effects are simply being worked out. This means that the Christian, while he must be concerned about evil in the world and is called upon to do battle against it, need never be overwhelmed by it. He may be perplexed, but not unto despair. Indeed he can be of good cheer, for he knows that Christ has overcome the world.

> The evil world will not win at last, because it failed to win at the only time it ever could. It is a vanquished world where men play their deviltries. Christ has overcome it. It can make tribulation, but desolation it can never make.[18]

Against this vast backdrop, in which Christ is seen as "the center of . . . history,"[19] we must underline certain further things Forsyth says about the cross. Not surprisingly, Forsyth looked upon the cross as something done primarily for the race rather than for the individual. Christ offers a complete and perfect obedience on behalf of all men, and his obedience is more important than his suffering. Part of Forsyth's stress on man's solidarity in guilt, and the need for a solidary deliverance, may have come as a reaction against the overemphasis in his day on religious individualism, but basically Forsyth stressed the point because it was what he found throughout the Bible, where God deals with his *people,* his chosen people, and with individuals as they are a part of that people.

> The first bearing of Christ's work was upon the race as a totality. The first thing reconciliation does is to change man's corporate relation to God. Then when it is taken home individu-

[17] Forsyth develops the implications of this in *The Justification of God* (London, Independent Press, 1948), a book on theodicy published in 1916, in the midst of World War I.

[18] *Ibid.,* p. 223.

[19] Forsyth anticipated Tillich's phrase in a series of Lectures given in 1909 and published in *The Work of Christ* (London, Independent Press, 1948), p. 107.

ally it changes our present attitude. . . . We must, therefore, avoid every idea of atonement which seems to reduce it to God's dealing with a mass of individuals, instead of with the race as a whole—instead of a racial, a social, a collective salvation, in which alone each individual has his place and part.[20]

To say that in his atoning act Christ is effecting (and not merely suggesting) a new relationship between God and man is to say that it is at the cross that we come to know the real meaning of grace. Forsyth was chary of using the word "love" to describe God, since the word had become sentimentalized in his day; when he did talk about God's love, he almost always made plain that he meant *holy* love. Holy love is a love that both judges and redeems. And we shall presently see that for Forsyth the cross is both the judging and redemptive act of God. But it is grace rather than love that most characterizes Forsyth's understanding of the cross. An atonement is not needed to make God's grace a reality; on the contrary, it is because God's grace is a reality that there is an atonement. Grace is not something Christ earns for us; grace is God giving himself to us in Christ. Quoting an author whom he does not identify, Forsyth writes, "Do not say: 'God is love. Why atone?' The New Testament says, 'God has atoned. What love!' "[21] Thus God and man are not "reconciled" by a third party, i.e. Christ, but God in Christ does the reconciling. Later on, to be sure, Forsyth speaks of the atonement as representing a "change" in God, but this has a special meaning for him:

> The distinction I ask you to observe is between a change of feeling and a change of treatment, between affection and discipline, between friendly feeling and friendly relations. God's feeling toward us never needed to be changed. But God's treatment of us, God's practical relation to us—that had to change.[22]

As Forsyth spells this out, using the story of the Prodigal Son as a human analogy, it is clear that what he means is that "The father's heart is the same, but his treatment must be different."[23]

[20] *The Work of Christ,* pp. 87, 96.
[21] *God the Holy Father,* p. 4.
[22] *The Work of Christ,* p. 105.
[23] *Ibid.,* p. 109.

So God needed no placation, but He could not exercise His kindness to the prodigal world, He certainly could not restore communion with its individuals, without doing some act which permanently altered the relation. And this is what set up that world's reconciliation with Him.[24]

The cross, then, does not exhibit God's changing mind; it is a revelation of God's unchanging mind and of the way in which, out of his grace, he deals with men in such a way that their guilt can be met and overcome.

To effect this new situation, the cross must represent both judgment and reconciliation. Sin must be judged, and it is judged there. But it is the judge himself who takes upon himself the burden of the penalty and curse. "There is a penalty and a curse for sin; and Christ consented to enter that region."[25] Forsyth frequently refers to the fact that Christ was "made sin" for us. So there is a judgment upon sin, but the very nature of this judgment means that it is also a reconciliation.

By reconciliation, Paul meant the total result of Christ's life-work in the fundamental, permanent, final changing of the relation between man and God, altering it from a relation of hostility to one of confidence and peace.[26]

The reconciliation does certain important things:

(1) It reveals and puts into historic action the changeless grace of God. (2) It reveals and establishes His holiness, and therein also the sinfulness of sin. And (3) it exhibits a Humanity in perfect tune with the will of God. And it does more than exhibit these things—*it sets them up.*[27]

THE PERSON OF CHRIST

So much, then, in briefest compass, for Forsyth's description of the work of Christ. The question with which we are now con-

---

24 *Ibid.,* p. 109.
25 *Ibid.,* p. 147.
26 *Ibid.,* p. 54.
27 *Ibid.,* pp. 180–81.

fronted is: What must be affirmed of one who could do this? Our treatment of this question can be briefer, for it is a question Forsyth has explored in one piece of sustained writing.[28]

What has just been affirmed about the work of Christ leads Forsyth to three inescapable conclusions about the person of Christ:

1. *His pre-existence.* If a modern man recoils from this conclusion, he must at least try to see the reason why Forsyth was led to make it. The reason is essentially a very simple one: "The soul's saviour could be no less a power than the soul's creator."[29] More fully:

> It was an inevitable rebound of spiritual logic under [Paul's] obsession by the Christ in glory. Such glory, such Godhead, could not be acquired by any moral victory of a created being within the limits of a life so brief as that of Jesus. In a similar application he worked back from the faith that all things were made *for* Christ to the conviction that, as the end was in the beginning, all things were made *by* Christ; and by a Christ as personal as the Christ who was their goal. And so, from the exalted glory of Christ, Paul's thought was cast back, by the very working of that Christ in him and in the whole consciousness of the Church's faith, to the same Christ from all eternity by the Father's side.[30]

2. *His kenosis, or self-limitation.* Once we accept the notion of pre-existence, we are forced to some kind of view of the self-emptying of Christ, if he is to lay aside his glory and become man in the full sense of the word. The problem for Forsyth is not whether there has in fact been such a kenosis but rather how we are to conceive of it. He suggests four human analogies, one of which may be cited here: A student with philosophic gifts has to lay aside his scholarly future because of the death of his father and devote himself to the family business. He gradually forgets most of what he once knew, and the joys of

---

[28] See Lectures 10–12 in *The Person and Place of Jesus Christ,* and also the earlier treatment, "The Divine Self-Emptying" in *God the Holy Father,* pp. 29–44.

[29] *The Person and Place of Jesus Christ,* p. 277.

[30] *Ibid.,* pp. 268–69.

philosophic thought are relegated to the past. Forsyth comments:

> Is this not a case where a moral and sympathetic volition leads to a certain contraction of the consciousness; not indeed by a single violent and direct act of the will, but by a decision whose effect is the same when it is spread over a life? . . . In applying the illustration to the theology of a kenosis in eternity, where a thousand years are but as one day, the element of time between choice and result in the earthly case is negligible.[31]

We can at least imagine, on these terms, how the eternal Son of God could engage in a similar voluntary contraction of consciousness and enter into the status of a real humanity.

A real humanity—even though he could not sin. Here a limit is reached, but it is not a limit that forces a docetic conclusion, for Forsyth suggests, "What if his kenosis went so far that though the impossibility [of sinning] was there he did not know of it?"[32] If this supposition is correct, it means that Christ's moral struggles and temptations were real and that consequently his is a real incarnation and not simply a theophany. In fact, from this perspective, "self-emptying" is not the best way to describe Forsyth's kenotic view. For he does not suggest that the divine attributes in Christ were discarded, but that they were retracted or condensed. Instead of being actual, they became for a time only potential. The "self-reduction" of God better describes the situation than the self-emptying. Omnipotence, for example, is not surrendered in this view; kenosis in fact provides a superior way of understanding what omnipotence really is.

> There was more omnipotence (if we can so speak) concentrated in the person of Christ than was spread in all creation. To appear and act as Redeemer, to be born, suffer, and die, was a mightier act of Godhead than lay in all the creation, preservation, and blessing of the world. It was only in the exercise of a perfect divine fullness (and therefore power) that Christ could empty and humble himself to the servant he became.[33]

[31] *Ibid.*, pp. 298–99.
[32] *Ibid.*, p. 301.
[33] *Ibid.*, p. 315.

3. *His plerosis, or self-fulfillment.* Many christological interpretations stop with kenosis. For Forsyth this is not enough.
The self-humbling of Christ must be matched by an increasing
fullness and glorifying of Christ. Through his entire lifetime,
Forsyth asserts, Christ is growing into what he actually is. If in
his kenosis Christ represents God's movement toward man, in
his plerosis he represents man's movement toward God. In the
latter he comes to fuller and fuller communion with his Father.
His life is not static but dynamic, and the reality of his growth
is assured because of his kenotic ignorance of his inability to
sin. In this single personality, then, we have the movement
manward and Godward that sums up the meaning of who God
is and who man is and how they are related to one another.

What is the point of all this speculation? We may let Forsyth
answer the question:

> What we have to ask about Christ, then, is this, what account
> of him is demanded by that work, that new creation of us, that
> real bringing of us to God, not simply in nearness but in like-
> ness? We are to think about Christ whatever is required to ex-
> plain the most certain thing in the soul's experience—namely,
> that he has given it the new life of God and mercy, and saved it
> from the old life of guilt, self, and the world.[34]

One may disagree with the specifics by which Forsyth carried
out this program, but one cannot deny the validity of the concern to which he here gives such concrete expression. One who
is dissatisfied with what Forsyth has done is under the necessity
of providing a more satisfactory answer to Forsyth's inescapable
question.

THE FACT OF THE CHURCH

But none of this can be left in an individualistic setting. Forsyth
is not only a Christian but a churchman, and a high-churchman
at that. He would, in fact, deny that one can be a Christian
without being a churchman. Rather, he insists (and the italics
are his): *"The same act which sets us in Christ sets us also in
the society of Christ. It does so ipso facto, and not by a mere*

[34] *Ibid.,* pp. 346–47.

consequence or sequel, more or less optional. To be in Christ is in the same act to be in the Church."[35]

The church is not a human club established by like-minded individuals who want to get together occasionally; the church is the instrument established by God through which the fullness of the gospel is manifested. It is not a second chapter in the story of the Christian life, it is part of the initial chapter: "To be in Christ is *in the same act* to be in the church."

And since to be "in Christ" is possible only by the grace of God made known in Christ, so too the note of grace will be the note by which the life and message of the church are known. Speaking to his fellow "free churchmen" in Britain, Forsyth could write as early as 1896:

> The Church's changeless note is grace. The charter of the Free Churches is free grace. And the Free Churches are the inevitable response to that freedom of grace which is the one article of the gospel and the one source of the Church's being and wellbeing alike. If that ceases to be our note, we must cease to be at all.[36]

The place to see most clearly the nature of Forsyth's churchmanship is in his treatment of the sacraments. There is much in the first half of *The Church and the Sacraments* that is now dated, but there are few things in the whole Forsyth corpus more exciting or relevant today than Part Two, which deals with the sacraments.

Since the sacraments are means of grace, they must point unfailingly to the supreme embodiment of grace, the Word made flesh, and make that Word a living Word for us. "The sacrament of the Word is what gives value to all other sacraments. They are not ends, but they are means to that grace."[37] The sacrament of the Word can be communicated to believers by baptism or the Lord's Supper or preaching or Scripture or other means as well. All these can be sacraments of the Word as they

---

[35] *The Church and the Sacraments* (London, Independent Press, 1947), p. 61-62.

[36] *The Charter of the Church*, p. 6.

[37] *The Church and the Sacraments*, p. 141.

"convey" (a favorite word) the gospel to the believer and "bring home" (another favorite) to the believer the reality of the grace of our Lord Jesus Christ.

> The Word and the sacraments are the two great expressions of the gospel in worship. The sacraments are the acted Word— variants of the preached Word. They are signs, but they are more than signs. They are the Word, the gospel itself, visible, as in preaching the Word is audible. But in either case, it is an act. It is Christ in a real presence giving us anew his redemption.[38]

As this quotation clearly shows, Forsyth will not settle for a notion of sacraments as "memorials" or reminders. They may be that, but they are more than that. They are *acts.* They *do* something. In them the Word comes alive with re-creative power. Following Augustine, Forsyth can refer to sacraments as the Word made "visible." Nor is he afraid of terms like "real presence." For the sacraments convey grace and do not merely exhibit it.

His treatment of the baptism of infants is a case in point. At a time when this "ceremony" was being looked upon as a "dedication" of the parents, fittingly observed in a private home, Forsyth insisted that baptism—and particularly the baptism of infants—was an act *of* the church and *for* the church and that it "made visible" the true nature of the gospel of prevenient grace. Where does the church more vividly set forth the true nature of the gospel entrusted to it? The child does not know God, yet God claims him. The child does not choose God, yet in the act of baptism is made visible the fact that God has chosen him. Later on the child will have to do something about what God has already done. But the latter step, taken by the child at confirmation, will be no more than an acknowledgment of the reality of the former step, taken by God at baptism. When faith comes, it will be acknowledged as a gift, a gift made possible because grace has already been bestowed. "Infant baptism is a means of exhibiting to the whole Church and world this right relation of grace and faith, that grace precedes and is

[38] *Ibid.,* p. 176.

the condition of faith, that it is not its reward, and that the element of time between grace and faith does not wither nor change the grace and its power."[39] The act is not so much, at the moment, for the child as for the church. It is still proclamation *by* the church, but it is also *for* the church, since it conveys to those present the true reality of grace, the reality that as it is with this little child, so also is it with all those present whom God has chosen: "You have not chosen me but I have chosen you."

And all of this—church, Word, sacrament, congregation—not for the sake of an institution, but for the sake of a gospel that cannot be separated from earthen vessels like institutions any more than it can be equated with them. So there must always be prayer for the church, as Forsyth well recognized:

> We beseech thee, O Lord, for thy Church throughout the world. May it grow in the faith of the cross and the power of the resurrection. Keep it in thy eternal unity, in great humility, in godly fear, and in thine own pure and peaceable wisdom so easy to be entreated. Make it swift and mighty in the cause of the Kingdom of Heaven. Cover, stablish, and enlighten it, that it may see through all that darkens the time, and move in the shadow of thy wing, with faith, obedience, and sober power.[40]

CONCLUSION

A friend of mine, defending Forsyth's style against an over-rationalistic seminarian, once described it as a typical expression of "celebration theology," meaning by the term that every word Forsyth ever put on paper was an occasion to celebrate the reality of the good news, and call attention to the fact that something had really happened, and that therefore nothing could ever be the same again. This is one reason Forsyth is an exciting theologian; he is so obviously caught up in what he is writing about and so aware that the issues he is discussing are momentous. Many men disagree with Forsyth. Some of them

[39] *Ibid.*, pp. 220–21.
[40] *Intercessory Services for Aid in Public Worship*, p. 8.

accuse him of being hard to follow. A few have even accused him of being dull. But no one could ever accuse him of being trivial. It is the large issues he deals with, and he deals with them in such a way that lesser versions of the Christian faith are made uncomfortable in his presence.

When we are tempted to an individualistic Christianity, he reminds us of the inescapability of the church; when we tire of theology, he reminds us that an undogmatic Christianity is a contradiction in terms; when we want a "simple Jesus," he points out that our reconstructions are at the farthest possible remove from the New Testament; when we reduce the love of God to a magnified version of human emotion, he thunders to us of holiness and judgment and grace; when we scale our gospel down to what is palatable to our hearers, he challenges us with the stark alternatives of the Word or the world, and will brook no middle ground no matter how clever we are in answering him; when our preaching settles into mild exhortation, he confronts us with the necessity of preaching that is vigorous proclamation.

And yet, fortunately, such is the nature of his message that he cannot produce "followers." To be a "Forsythian" would be the greatest betrayal of all. Forsyth was first and last concerned to produce disciples. But not disciples of himself.

Bibliography

P. T. Forsyth, *The Person and Place of Jesus Christ,* Grand Rapids, Eerdmans, 1964.

Robert McAfee Brown, *P. T. Forsyth: Prophet for Today,* Philadelphia, Westminster, 1952.

II
Between the Times

RUDOLF OTTO

Bernard E. Meland

Rudolf Otto was the most memorable figure of my student days at Marburg University in 1928. I shall not easily forget my first glimpse of him. On my first Sunday afternoon in Marburg, having arrived from America only a few days before, I called at his home on Rotenburg Strasse. The maid, having managed to make out my garbled request, said one word, *"Augenblick,"* and hurried away to bring Professor Otto to me. I never actually heard Otto come. He just seemed to arrive, an invasion of hushed austerity. Professor Otto said two words: *"Bitte herein."* His towering, erect figure and kingly head, crowned with white hair that bristled upward, caused one to draw back a bit. Here was a presence! *"Der Heilige,"* as he was called by the students, was all you had expected him to be.

My year at Marburg was the last year Professor Otto lectured in the university. He retired at the close of that school term, having completed thirty years of teaching and research. Despite the fact that a persisting illness plagued him throughout that final year of teaching, I remember his lectures as being crisp and orderly, delivered with a directness that commanded attention. Otto spoke as one having authority. And authority is precisely what he had in the field of his special concern.

Rudolf Otto was born on September 25, 1869, in a town called Peine, twenty miles southeast of Hanover. He was educated at Erlangen and Göttingen, receiving his licentiate in theology in 1898 at Göttingen. In the same year he became a *Privatdozent* at Göttingen and remained on its faculty until 1914. During that time he was a colleague of the philosopher Edmund Husserl (1859–1938) and of the Friesian scholar Leonard Nelson. These two influences were to manifest themselves in Otto's own methodology. He left Göttingen in 1914 to join the theological faculty at Breslau, where he remained

only three years before going to the University of Marburg.
Here he was to rise to eminence as one of the major theological
voices of postwar Europe.[1] And he continued to live in Marburg until his death in 1937.

Otto began as a Ritschlian theologian. Ritschl had been a
member of the Göttingen faculty for a quarter of a century
(1864–89) and his influence was still being felt in that place
and elsewhere when Otto came to Göttingen as a theological
student toward the close of the century. Harnack at Berlin and
Herrmann at Marburg were at the height of their influence as
exponents of the Ritschlian school. Students from America and
Britain, who were to become eminent theologians in their re-
spective countries, were finding their way to these centers for
graduate theological study. Rudolf Otto belonged to the younger
generation of Ritschlian theologians who had begun to turn
back upon some of the emphases which had marked Ritschlianism in its earlier years. In this he was joined by his contemporary Ernst Troeltsch (1865–1923), who, like Otto, was
concerned about the specific nature of religion but resisted the
Ritschlian tendency to identify religion and Christianity. Otto
went further in his deviation from the mainline of Ritschlianism
by renewing a concern with philosophical inquiry preparatory
to his effort to establish the religious a priori, and by acknowledging the mystical tradition as a fruitful source of data bearing
upon numinous experience.

If one were to designate the central vein of Otto's scholarly
concern, to which he directed inquiry along various lines
throughout his theological career, it would be the teleology of
the holy as disclosed in numinous experience. For it was in this
dimension of man's experience, Otto believed, that the mark-
ings of religious specificity lay. The source of this notion is
many-sided. Otto attributes the notion in its modern form to
Schleiermacher who, he claimed, "rediscovered the *sensus numinous.*"[2] Yet his own concern with it, he tells us, was prompted

[1] Cf. C. H. Herford, *The Post-war Mind of Germany and Other
European Studies* (Oxford, Clarendon, 1927), p. 49.

[2] *Aufsätze das Numinose betreffend* (Gotha, 1923). Translated by
Brian Lunn as *Religious Essays* (London, Oxford Univ. Press, 1931),
pp. 68–77.

by his study of Luther early in his theological career.[3] Otto's earliest published work, *Die Anschauung vom heiligen Geiste bei Luther* (Göttingen, 1898), analyzes this problem historically. In later writings he continually refers back to Luther as one who exemplified this quality of apprehension which conveyed the distinctively religious mode of truth, "the truth of feeling." Yet it was Schleiermacher who provided Otto with the initial theological stance by which this mode of truth and this distinctive form of apprehension could be inquired into. Otto cites *The Speeches* as being the primary source in this regard. It is to be preferred, he said, to the later dogmatic work of Schleiermacher, *The Christian Faith*, which he felt to be more speculative. If one will simulate the imagery of Schleiermacher's early work in which the sense of dependence becomes the point or boundary at which the feeling of Infinite Unity is inferred, one will have some notion of the starting point in Otto's own reflections. This is not religious experience in the ordinary sense of the term but an ontological moment or event, as it were, in which human perception and the Wholly Other are in juxtaposition. Otto insisted that Schleiermacher must not be read simply as one appealing to the normativeness of religious experience; nevertheless he was aware that the emphasis which Schleiermacher placed upon God-consciousness in his more mature theological work seemed to open him to this interpretation. Otto's concern was to center upon this ontological moment, this point of juxtaposition, and to find a way of attending to the objectively numinous dimension of that experience. For in this moment, he argued, is to be found the specifically religious occurrence.

Otto was helped in this effort by the philosophy of Jacob Friedrich Fries (1773–1843), whose thought was being urged upon the faculty and students of Göttingen at this time by Otto's colleague Leonard Nelson, an ardent disciple of Fries. Before examining this resource of Otto's constructive effort, however, we need to consider his polemic against Darwinism and the naturalism it implied; for it was in this critique that he forged some

[3] Cf. *The Idea of the Holy* (London, Oxford Univ. Press, 1923), Chap. XII.

essential tools of thought with which to build his case for specificity in religion.

Darwin's *Origin of the Species,* published in 1859, had become a thorn in the flesh of all idealists in the nineteenth century, including the Ritschlians. But the Ritschlians had found a way to circumvent direct argument with Darwinism by designating religion as man's act of defining himself over against nature. In this way the issue between science and religion did not arise in theology. Otto, however, saw this procedure as being too cavalier a way of avoiding the issue. His sympathies were with the Ritschlian solution. In fact one might say that his tendency to define man's spiritual nature over against his physical nature is one aspect of the Ritschlian legacy that persisted in Otto's theology. Nevertheless, his own association with scientists and philosophers led him to feel responsible as a theologian for arguing out the issues, which he did in great detail in his first major work, *Naturalistische und religiöse Weltansicht* (Tübingen, 1904; translated into English in 1907 as *Naturalism and Religion*). Otto's grasp of scientific details bearing upon Darwin's theory of evolution and the various vitalistic alternatives cannot fail to impress any reader. The position he took in discussing this problem is one which had become fairly well accepted among critical thinkers in religion. This was to the effect that evolution is to be acknowledged as an established fact.[4] And the significance of the mechanisms of nature for present forms of personality was in no sense to be denied. What Otto objected to in the Darwinian theory, however, was the claim that the evolution of man as a person is to be accounted for by natural selection, thus ascribing to chance occurrences of adjustment the full credit for man's advance as a human being. In this account of causality, teleology, the phenomenological tract of the Infinite Unity in nature and in human events, went by the board. "Darwin's danger," wrote Otto, "is in its radical opposition to teleology."[5] This is a revealing statement. It not only

---

[4] This notion was a familiar one in theological literature prior to 1859. Lotze's *Microcosmus* antedates the publication of Darwin's *Origin of the Species,* but it is commonly acknowledged that Lotze anticipated the evolutionary theory, as did others.

[5] *Naturalism and Religion* (London, Williams and Norgate, 1907), p. 89.

expresses succinctly the basis of Otto's aversion to naturalism, but it points to the mode of apprehension which he was to emphasize as being appropriate to religion as a numinous event. It implies seeing phenomena not only in relation to the Infinite Unity, but in terms of what that Unity intends, or toward what it tends. Kant's teleological judgment lay back of this way of thinking, and with it, Schleiermacher's view of Christianity as being a teleological religion.

One might assume that, in these remarks and others, Otto was anticipating emergent evolution. It is true that he was aware of the work of Lloyd Morgan, whom he cited as a representative of "the new vitalism." Otto approved of the direction of his thought in so far as it countered the mechanical theory and moved "towards a deeper conception and interpretation of reality in general, and towards a religious conception in particular."[6] The most important contribution which he saw coming from this new vitalism was "the fresh revelation of the depth of things and of appearance, the increased recognition that our knowledge is only leading us towards mystery."[7] A point that Otto was insistent upon, however, was that "the psychical is not derivable from the physical, does not arise out of it, is not secondary to it, but pre-eminent over it, is not passive, but creative."[8] Here he was asserting his transcendental idealism, which was to say that the source of personality and of man's spiritual dimension is the numinous realm. In mysticism and in the phenomenon of moral consciousness and moral freedom, he wrote, "there is implied something that is inaccessible to a purely rational consideration, and is directly related to mystery and divination."[9] In any effort to understand personality, then, Otto argued, "intuition and feeling must always play the largest role."[10]

Otto's concern to pursue the specifically religious dimension of man's experience thus led him to probe intuition and feeling as being the form in which apprehension of the numinous could be anticipated. In this effort he found the philosopher Jacob

6 *Ibid.*, p. 275.
7 *Ibid.*, p. 275.
8 *Ibid.*, p. 306.
9 *Ibid.*, p. 325.
10 *Ibid.*, p. 325.

Fries more helpful than Schleiermacher. In his earlier writings Otto had favored Schleiermacher because of a wider scope in his ideas when discussing intuition and feeling; but in writing his philosophy of religion (*Kantisch-Fries'sche Religionsphilosophie,* 1909, translated as *The Philosophy of Religion Based on Kant and Fries,* 1931) Otto found it necessary to say in a footnote "I am now compelled to withdraw my remarks as to Schleiermacher's superiority to Fries." He had now become of the opinion that "in the philosophy of religion, the points of contact between Fries and Schleiermacher are less important than their points of differences; and where their views agree, Fries is quite original, and closer study proves him to be superior in comprehensiveness, thoroughness, and solidity."[11]

Otto, in discussing Fries's contribution to the understanding of intuition and feeling as modes of apprehending the numinous, points out an interesting linkage between Enlightenment thinking and that of Fries, and thus indirectly with his own in this regard, saying that a characteristic of the theological work of the *Aufklärung* is:

> the conviction that religion must have its own sources and a separate life of its own, not dependent on ingenious scholasticism, on reasoning and logic, on speculation, on learned research, on academic controversy and apologetics, on theological schools, on the grace of philosophers, on toilsome proofs. . . . It has its root in the general emergence of "lay Christianity" at the close of the Middle Ages, which carried the Reformation along with it, was continued in the Independents' Movement in England, and thence progressed towards Deism and "Aufklärung."[12]

In this respect Otto finds the *Aufklärung* to be a continuation "of Luther's way and Luther's mind." "Moreover," he continues,

> Kant's attempts at a philosophy of religion, artificial though they may be, are everywhere a plea for the very simplest lay religion and its assurance. The object of Kant's whole attempt is to make

[11] *The Philosophy of Religion* (London, Williams & Norgate, 1931), p. 15.
[12] *Ibid.,* pp. 34–35.

religious conviction safe from the artfulness of speculative thought and the roundabout methods of scholarship. Here as much as Locke, he appears for the "average man."[13]

It is at this point, Otto observes, and with affinity for this effort, that the work of Fries begins, which "in total contrast to the theosophical systems of his contemporaries" (Otto seems to have Schelling in mind here) "professes to do no more than this: to find a basis for the conviction already given 'by the first simple religious emotion.' "[14]

Fries, building upon Kant's theory of the antinomies, opposed the world of knowledge to the world of faith, demonstrating that "Faith is a form of higher knowledge, with a firm base in the reasoning intellect."[15] This line of reasoning led to his "doctrine of *Ahnung*," expressing "man's deepest need and longing" through feeling—a feeling best expressed as an aesthetic response as in the response to beauty and to sublimity. On the surface this appears to be subsuming religion under aesthetics; but Otto defends Fries against this implication, saying that it is rather a matter of availing oneself of the help which aesthetic judgment affords as a mode of apprehension. In aesthetic judgment we apprehend the unity of things under concepts and ideas in a way that differs from that of logic.

That is to say, in an undefined, obscure manner, by the way of "Ahnung" I gain real knowledge of the universe in a quite particular way, following the supreme laws of its unity and necessity, which are clearly presented in conceptual form in the Categories as a whole, and especially in the completed categories of eternity, spirit, freedom, and deity. In the obscure aesthetic knowledge I recognize, dimly and inexpressibly, ideal existence in the world of phenomena as perceived by the senses, ideal existence in general, without any determination of its particular and individual side. But this is not all. For it is precisely this world, actually known to us under categories and ideas, which is the spiritual world in reality, the world subject to the laws of Good and the Supreme Good, the "best work," the world of the

13 *Ibid.*, pp. 34-35.
14 *Ibid.*, pp. 36-37.
15 *Ibid.*, p. 43.

objective Final Purpose. And thus it becomes clear why the aesthetic comprehension, deep but obscure, is not merely of a "speculative" character; why it presents to the feeling something beyond bloodless forms of unity; why it gives these forms the potent emotional content that goes with them. In aesthetic ideas I gain an obscure comprehension of the unity and connection of true reality in the world of appearance, of this reality in its essential nature; and in so doing I also reach an obscure comprehension of its teleology.[16]

In passing from beauty to the sublime, such comprehension presents itself "with still greater force."[17] This aesthetic comprehension of objective teleology in nature and in individual phenomena, Otto continues, would correspond "to a divination of the world as governed by God in history and in the life of the individual."[18]

Otto is suggesting here that feeling, understood in this ontological context, is a mode of perception which apprehends not simply qualities that are subjective and transitory, but structural meanings, purposes, and tendencies bent on attaining such ends. And in this respect it enables us to see, as through a glass darkly, what is ultimate in the complex of experiences about us. In this sense it provides us with *a feeling of truth,* "the obscure knowledge of the Eternal in general and of the eternal determination of Existence."[19]

Otto's patient delineation of Fries's doctrine of *Ahnung* (a yearning which yields the feeling of truth) can be taken as a preliminary working out of his own understanding of intuition and feeling and of their role in pursuing the specific nature of the religious response. John Moore is correct, I think, when he says: "It is a complete mistake to treat *The Idea of the Holy* as if it were a complete account of Otto's theory of religion, for in it he emphasizes the non-rational aspect of experience in a way which is easily misunderstood unless seen against the background of his other works."[20] It is equally a mistake, I would

---

[16] *Ibid.,* p. 141.
[17] *Ibid.,* p. 142.
[18] *Ibid.,* p. 144.
[19] *Ibid.,* p. 229.
[20] John M. Moore, *Theories of Religious Experience* (N.Y., Round Table Press, 1938), p. 79.

add, to assume that one may move directly from Otto's earlier to his more mature efforts as if his method of "divination" rested back upon philosophical premises developed under the influences of Kant and Fries. To a considerable degree these influences persist and show through; but Otto was continuously restive under the recognition that both Fries and Kant veered off toward Enlightenment tendencies which elevated the rational and formal aspect of religion, tending to make of it one universal phenomenon. Thus he wrote,

> In Fries, as in the Deists, something which is, after all, wholly "Positive," something which is equivalent to Christian belief with its precise historical stamp rubbed away as far as possible, is taken as the religion, which is then placed in opposition to the "Positive religions."[21]

But the thrust of Otto's thinking was more concrete than this Friesian tendency implied. He was already participating in a mood of inquiry that sought to take particular instances of the numinous seriously even as he undertook to identify the nature of the religious a priori implicit in all of them. This was by way of attending to historical religions concretely and thus to see them in terms of their own specific offerings, while being attentive also to the comparative aspects of these several historical forms of faith.

Eight years after his work on the philosophy of religion had appeared, Otto published the book that was to bring him worldwide recognition, the title of which was *Das Heilige* (1917), translated into English in 1923 as *The Idea of the Holy*.[22] What was significantly new and fresh in this work was Otto's recognition of the fact that the "holy" as a category embraces di-

[21] *Philosophy of Religion,* pp. 146–47.

[22] The position developed in *The Idea of the Holy* has sometimes been represented as being in the nature of a theological retort to the interpretation of religion simply as social phenomena, to which the psychologist Wilhelm Wundt had given expression in his *Völkerpsychologie (Folk Psychology)*, which first appeared in 1910. Otto had written a significant review of Wundt's book, which evoked considerable interest. The essence of this critique, under the title "Myth and Religion in Wundt's *Völkerpsychologie,*" appeared in the appendix of the German edition of *Das Heilige,* but unfortunately it was omitted in the English edition.

mensions of reality that go beyond the notion of goodness in the moral and ethical sense. This was one of the early thrusts of theological inquiry breaking through the stereotypes of moralism to which much of liberal theology had become addicted. It had the effect of seeing religious phenomena in a new and strange light, opening up vistas and depths of religious meaning which had long been obscured, and compelling a reassessment of religions, both historically and those near at hand, the dimensions of which had been radically curtailed by an arbitrary imposition of the moralistic measure.

Otto was not dissociating religion from its ethical aspect, any more than he was uprooting it from its rational side. His preliminary effort had been directed toward understanding religion in relation to ethical and rational cateogries. Now he was calling attention to its nonrational and nonmoral aspects. This was tantamount to announcing that religion as a numinous event eludes our human measure even as it participates in human forms. To those for whom all things must be made manageable within human bounds, Otto's thesis implied sheer irrationalism; but Otto was insistent that to speak of the nonrational aspect of the numinous was not the same as declaring religion irrational. It was rather to call attention to the fact that rational and moral descriptions of events are limited ways of speaking about them, viewing them under analogies drawn from human nature and experience and in relation to our human structure of realities. This restrictive way of speaking, he argued, is always distorting to a degree; but the degree of distortion is radically accentuated when we apply our mode of analogical or logical thinking to God and to the holy. In confronting instances which awaken us to these numinous realities, or in simply contemplating them, we encounter "a clear overplus of meaning." It was this "overplus of meaning" in the experiences of the holy which Otto sought to isolate in *The Idea of the Holy*.

We suggested earlier that one will be able to identify oneself with the imagery of Otto's thinking if one assumes the orientation implied in Schleiermacher's *feeling of dependence* in which the noumenal and the human consciousness are in juxtaposition. But this is only a starting point. The direction of Otto's thought is intimated in the correction of Schleiermacher which he. undertakes at this point. For in suggesting the term "dependence," Schleiermacher was employing "what is no more than a very close analogy." Schleiermacher distinguishes the feeling of religious dependence from other forms of dependence in the human situation, but "his mistake is in making the distinction merely that between 'absolute' and 'relative' dependence, and therefore a difference of degree and not of intrinsic quality."[23] The distinction, in Otto's view, is more radical than Schleiermacher implied, for the feeling of dependence in this numinous experience is "qualitatively different from such analogous states of mind."[24]

In this observation one will detect in Otto something of the postliberal emphasis which was to become increasingly more prominent in neo-Protestant thinking. Otto substituted for Schleiermacher's feeling of dependence the term "creature-feeling," which, in his judgment, was more expressive of the objective aspect of the numinous presence and more attentive to the reality outside the self. Furthermore, in applying to the object of this experience of creature-feeling the qualifying adjective *mysterium tremendum,* Otto meant to designate it "a unique 'Wholly Other' reality and quality, something of whose special character we can feel without being able to give it clear conceptual expression."[25]

Having designated the form and quality of the nonrational elements in numinous experience, Otto was at pains to make clear that in all religious discourse the rational and the nonrational traffic together. And all explication of numinous experience in religions takes the form of conveying the simultaneity of these two aspects.

The consciousness of a "wholly other" evades precise formulation in words, and we have to employ symbolic phrases which seem sometimes sheer paradox, that is, *ir*rational not merely nonrational in import. So with religious awe and reverence. In ordinary fear and in moral reverence I can indicate in conceptual terms what it is that I fear or revere; injury, e.g. or ruin in the

[23] *The Idea of the Holy,* p. 9.
[24] *Ibid.*
[25] *Ibid.,* p. 30.

one case, heroism or strength of character in the other. But the object of *religious* awe or reverence—the *tremendum* and *augustum*, cannot be fully determined conceptually: it is non-rational, as is the beauty of a musical composition; which no less eludes complete conceptual analysis.

Confronted by the fact of the non-rational thus interpreted we cannot be satisfied with a mere bare statement, which would open the door to all the vague and arbitrary phraseology of an emotionalist irrationalism. We are bound to try, by means of the most precise and unambiguous symbolic and figurative terms that we can find, to discriminate the different elements of the experience so far as we can in a way that can claim general validity.[26]

Theology, when it is true to its function, is thus "an attempted statement, in conceptual terms and by analogy, of something that at bottom is incapable of explication by concepts."[27]

But along with this sense of the uncanny and the mysterious in religious moments, said Otto, there is the experience of being drawn to this numinous event "as being uniquely attractive and fascinating." This, said Otto, conveys the "qualitative content of the numinous experience," as the *mysterium tremendum* conveys its form. The simultaneity of these two seemingly contradictory effects in the numinous experience, "the daunting and the fascinating," awe and attraction, is what lends depth and power to the religious moment. Man is simultaneously judged and made to stand back before the overwhelming impact of the Wholly Other, yet curiously and irresistibly drawn into its presence as being a visitation of grace. Otto saw in this latter aspect a transition into mysticism. At least mysticism seemed to him to present the most complete instance of "fascination." All religious moments, however, Otto suggested, in which "religious beatitude" or an experience of grace are experienced partake of this dimension of the numinous.

It is instructive to see how Otto dealt with such terms as "sin" and "forgiveness" in this context. These words had all but lost their distinctively religious meaning in the moral and ethical discourse then prevailing. Religion, however much it might em-

[26] *Ibid.*, p. 94.
[27] *Ibid.*, p. 53.

brace moral and rational restraints (and this was an important aspect of it for Otto), was seen to him to be first and foremost a thing of mystery emanating from a numinous realm. And when we speak of religious realities such as God, sin, forgiveness, redemption, we are using terms which connote an order, realm, or level other than that conveyed by rational or moral categories. Whenever we press these terms into rational or moral categories, he suggested, we are guilty of reductionism; we ignore the dimension of otherness which they in fact convey and thus profane their meaning. Rather than rationalizing or moralizing these terms, as he found liberals inclined to do, Otto insisted that we are to seek out helpful analogies that will continue to point our thought to what transcends human thinking, that is, to the realm of the numinous; to do so is to recognize the nonrational as being a qualification upon all rational and ethical categories. Accordingly, the righteousness of God, the work of grace, the fact of sin, the act of forgiveness, form a discourse appropriate to the numinous dimension that supervenes experience. Thus whereas Ritschl had defined forgiveness as an attribute of the Christian community founded by Christ, enabling the Christian to remain identified with the Kingdom of God as an ultimate end even as he participated in the Kingdom of sin, Otto sought to wrest this term from the human community as such. Forgiveness, he said, is a numinous act of the spirit transcending moral and rational good and investing them with a higher goodness through the judgment and grace of the holy.

Similarly, sin, in Otto's analysis, took on import beyond that of moral wrong. Sin, he wrote, is

> not simply, and probably at first not at all, *moral* depreciations, but belongs to a quite special category of valuation and appraisement. The feeling is beyond question not that of the transgression of the moral law, however evident it may be that such a transgression, where it has occurred, will involve it as a consequence; it is the feeling of absolute "profaneness." But what is this? Again something which the "natural" man cannot, as such, know or even imagine. He, only, who is "in the Spirit" knows and feels what this "profaneness" is; but to such an one it comes with piercing acuteness, and is accompanied by the most uncompromising judgment of self-depreciation, a judgment passed,

not upon his character, because of individual "profane" actions of his, but upon his own very existence as creature before that which is supreme above all creatures.[27]

Then Otto adds,

And at the same moment he passes upon the numen a judgment of *appreciation* of a unique kind by the category diametrically contrary to "the profane," the category of "holy," which is proper to the numen alone, but to it in an absolute degree. . . . It is the positive *numinous* value or worth, and to it corresponds on the side of the creature a numinous *disvalue* or "unworth."[28]

Thus Otto opened up the line that he was to follow in pointing to the source of forgiveness, "the means of grace" which "springs directly from the idea of numinous value or worth," the awe of standing in a *mysterium tremendum* of good in contrast to one's unworthiness.

One will see here some survival of Kant's use of "the idea of value," "the idea of good," etc.; yet it is surcharged with the concrete, magnetic, and operational working of "the thing-in-itself." Husserl regarded Otto's *The Idea of the Holy* as an application of his phenomenological method to the study of religious phenomena. And, with qualifications derived from Otto's own history and creative effort, this in fact is what it was.

Otto was led in his study of the numinous to conclude that there is such a faculty as "divination," that is, a capacity "of genuinely cognizing and recognizing the holy in its appearances." He believed that both Schleiermacher and Fries had in their way rediscovered this faculty and described it in their explication of "contemplation" and "Ahnung," respectively. Both Schleiermacher and Fries, Otto pointed out, had represented this capacity of "divination" to be a universal one. Otto, on the other hand, was willing to speak of this capacity as being "a universal potentiality of man," but what appears as such, he argued, "is by no means to be found in *actuality* the universal possession of every, single man; very frequently it is only disclosed as a special endowment and equipment of particular gifted individuals."[29]

[28] *Ibid.*
[29] *Ibid.*, p. 149.

In view of his having come to this conclusion, it is not surprising that Otto was to give so much attention to the study of mystics, both Western and Eastern,[30] and to look upon mysticism itself as a resource of special significance in the study of religions. In these studies his pre-eminent figures were Eckhart and Sankara. Here, as in everything else Otto touched, the juxtaposition of the rational and the nonrational, the ethical and the holy, was in evidence. Thus he sharply distinguished these mystics of his choice from "the illuminists" with their "fantastic visions, occultism, or miracle-hunting" and found in their mysticism an ethical content along with the experience of grace.

Otto's concern with mysticism as a phenomenological study was genuine; and his own temperament, not to speak of his theological orientation, inclined him quite naturally to the pursuit of this study. Yet it would be a mistake so to emphasize Otto's interest in mystics as to obscure the very genuine concern he had in extending and nurturing a more general sensitivity and response to the numinous in all aspects of Christian life, especially in Christian worship. During the year I was in Marburg, Professor Otto was engaged in a remarkable experiment in liturgical reform, seeking to create within the forms of the evangelical Protestant tradition a service of worship in which numinous experience would be made central and commanding. I have described this experiment in worship in my book *Modern Man's Worship*.[31] The distinctive feature of Otto's order of service was the Sacrament of Silence, which came at the close of the service. The idea of a sacrament of silence, he says, was suggested to him while attending a Quaker meeting in Boston during one of his visits to the United States. It was to be the supreme mo-

[30] Cf. his *Mysticism East and West* (N.Y., Macmillan, 1932). (First published as *West-östliche Mystik*, Gotha, Klötz, 1926.)

[31] (N.Y., Harper, 1934.) See also Otto's *Zur Erneuerung und Ausgestaltung des Gottesdienstes* (Giessen, 1925); *Chorgebete für Kirche, Schule und Hausandacht* (Giessen, 1925); *Liturgische Blätter für Prediger und Helfer* (Gotha, 1926–30); *Das Jahr der Kirche in Lesungen und Gebeten* (Munich, 1927); *Eingangspsalmen für die Sonntage des Kirchenjahres* (Munich, 1927). Otto has discussed "The Lord's Supper as a Numinous Fact" and "The Form of Divine Service" in his *Religious Essays*, Chs. VI and VII. See also his essay "Silent Worship" at the close of *The Idea of the Holy*, pp. 216f.

ment in the service when, as it were, the Wholly Other invaded
the presence of the worshipers, confronting them with the magnitude of mystery and beatitude. The service as a whole was
conceived within the pattern of a numinous event in which
Scripture reading, music, and prayers as well as the sermon
were viewed as being preparatory for the period of silence.
Thus the Sacrament of Silence, coming at the close of the service, was the climactic experience toward which everything else
in the hour of worship moved.[32]

Otto's concern with liturgical reform extended to other aspects of worship such as the writing of new hymns and a new
prayer literature. His emphasis was upon creating a sense of
urgency and expectancy in worship, consonant not only with
his emphasis upon the numinous presence but with what he believed to be the insistent message of the Christian witness,
namely, that a new age of salvation had come in Jesus Christ
and is an ever-present reality in the Christian community, giving intimation of the coming Kingdom of God. In this, said
Otto, is the church's charisma. Around this theme, he believed,
a new church calendar should be written, every service addressing itself anew to this expectation.

Otto's concern with numinous experience as a phenomenology of the holy took him also into the field of the history of
religions, where his reading and observations were vast. He had
learned Sanskrit and thus had access to basic materials in the
study of Hinduism and the religions of India, and through his
travels in India he was able to observe and study religions close
at hand. His translations of Hindu writings from the Sanskrit
for the study of Hinduism as well as his studies of Hindu writings form a substantial portion of his published works. In addition to his study of Sankara reported in *Mysticism East and
West,* Otto made a study of the eleventh-century Hindu theist
Ramanuja, the theologian of the bhakti school. He translated
the basic chapters of Ramanuja's system, which he published
in 1923 under the title *Siddhanta des Ramanuja.* His book *In-
dian Religion of Grace and Christianity,* published in 1930,
presents a study of Ramanuja's theology together with a com-

---

[32] I have reproduced one of Otto's Orders of Service in my *Modern
Man's Worship,* showing his use of the Sacrament of Silence.

parison of the bhakti religion with Christianity. Otto also translated a number of Hindu texts into the German for the study of Hinduism, including *Dipika des Nivasa* (1916), dealing with the Hindu doctrine of salvation; *Vischnu-Narayana* (1923), one of the basic works in Hindu mysticism; and a philosophic treatise of Brahmanism, *Die Katha-Upanishad* (1936). In addition, Otto published several studies on the *Bhagavad-Gita*;[33] these appear in English in a translation from the German texts under the title *The Original Gita: The Song of the Supreme Exalted One* (1939).

Otto's last major work was his impressive *Reich Gottes und Menschensohn* (Munich, 1934), translated into English in 1938 under the title *The Kingdom of God and the Son of Man.* While this was a further inquiry into the numinous dimension of experience as a study in the history of religions, it can be said to be a kind of summation of his lifelong study applied to the Christian religion, and specifically to the person of Jesus Christ. As the late Joachim Wach pointed out in his moving essay on Rudolf Otto, this study of early Christian reports of Jesus and his teaching throws new light on this material from a source hitherto unnoted. Whereas scholars previously had discussed the relation of Christianity to Jewish, Hellenistic, Egyptian, Mesopotamian, and Syrian religions, Wach observes, Otto brought fresh understanding of "the influence of Iranian notions upon the concept which played so central a role in the Kerygma of Jesus, the idea of the Kingdom of God."[34] In this work Otto revived the theme of eschatology in the New Testament to which Albert Schweitzer had addressed himself a generation earlier. With his notion of the numinous Otto was able to lift up the meaning of the eschatalogical dimension as the mysterious presence of the end or of ultimate reality operating in the immediate moment of time. Or, as Otto himself put it, "The Kingdom, future and yet already dawning, is in truth a mystery. To grasp this mystery one needs the ability and the desire to

[33] Cf. *Die Urgestalt der Bhagavad-Gita* (Tübingen, 1934); *Die Lehrtraktate der Bhagavad-Gita* (Tübingen, 1935); *Der Sang des Hehr Erhabenen. Die Bhagavad-Gita* (Stuttgart, 1935).

[34] Joachim Wach, *Types of Religious Experience* (Chicago, Univ. of Chicago, 1951), p. 224.

see and hear rightly."[35] Or again, "It was the salvation of the new age which was visible to him who could see the mystery of the Kingdom as already present."[36]

I agree with Wach when he says that "this book actually represents one of the major contributions of the last decade to the understanding of New Testament theology and especially to Christological thought."[37] I would place it alongside Schweitzer's *The Quest of the Historical Jesus* (1910; German edition, 1906) and Bultmann's *The Theology of the New Testament* (German edition, 1948) as being one of three successive landmarks in the study of the problem of eschatology in recent biblical theological thought.

In this work more than in any other, Otto appears to be addressing himself to the specifically constructive theological problem of the New Testament. He does so, however, as a historian of religion, thus allowing his constructive concern to show through only incidentally. What is made clear is that Otto sees "the mystery of the Kingdom" as a persistent and significant dimension of the gospel teaching and thus takes his stand on the side of eschatology—yet in a way that enables him to integrate it with the ethical emphasis. Logically he could see that ethics and eschatology are contradictory notions. Nevertheless, he argued, they go together religiously, and these apparently contradictory dimensions of existence are not to be dissociated. They must be kept together as presenting on the one hand a life of obligation in the present world of existence, and, on the other hand, as holding before us an impending mystery that lends depth and expectancy to our immediate life. This mystery is not just an appeal to the future, but a new reality that in some respects has already come.

Otto followed the route of mysticism in specifying the numinous event, in which the mystery of the kingdom is made known, as the charismatic person of Jesus.

His charismatic gift was not an "accidens" in him, but was of the essence of his person, and helps to reveal its significance.

[35] *The Kingdom of God and the Son of Man*, new and rev. ed. (London, Lutterworth, 1951), p. 138.
[36] *Ibid.*, p. 146.
[37] Joachim Wach, *op cit.*, p. 224.

And only when we understand his person and its meaning is the meaning of his message of the kingdom disclosed. The kingdom for him was the inbreaking power of God into salvation, and he was not a rabbi but an eschatological redeemer, who was an integral part of the eschatalogical order itself. "Charisma" and kingdom of God belong together by their very nature and they illuminate one another.[38]

This much one must say, declared Otto, as a historian of religion; to speak otherwise would be to make a false reconstruction of events. Otto acknowledged that much that the historian of religion concerns himself with in explicating the psychic datum that is presented here will not concern the theologian; however, "the 'charisma', together with the *pneuma*, as an anticipation of the eschatological order is an essential element of a community which is intended to be a church of the Nazarene."[39] For Otto, then, the eschatalogical congregation or community is made the norm of the living church. And he closed with this telling conclusion: "That the church has lost its 'charisma,' that men look back to it as to a thing of past times, that men make it and the inbreaking kingdom belonging to it trivial by allegories, does not show this church is now on a higher level, but is a sign of its decay."[40]

The work of Rudolf Otto has been widely admired wherever an interest in the phenomena of religion has been in evidence and wherever a sensitive concern with the problem of religious faith has been acute. The scope of his influence was worldwide, and the effects of his scholarship, one may venture to say, are to be found among students of religions in all contemporary faiths of the world. Certainly his influence among historians of religion has been deeply felt. And within the period immediately following the publication of his *The Idea of the Holy* the effect of his work upon theology and religious thought, especially in Europe and America, was considerable. It is possible that Otto's chief significance in those years lay in his role as a transitional theologian. The insight which his method disclosed,

[38] *The Kingdom of God and the Son of Man*, p. 375.
[39] *Ibid.*, p. 375–76.
[40] *Ibid.*, p. 376.

making the apprehension of the holy analogous to, yet not coterminous with, numinous moments in experience, represented a revolutionary break through the monolithic world view of liberal theology and philosophy of religion. Otto's achievement here placed him at the forefront of that minority company of sensitive theologians who saw the limitations of the liberal theologians' methodology prior to the 1920's. In fact, among critical scholars Otto's work was the baseline from which other ventures in transcendent thinking were made. It succeeded in restoring to liberal theology a nonrational dimension sufficient to give it overtone and depth. The readiness with which this led to a liturgical renaissance in Protestantism is itself evidence of its re-creative force. For many liberal Protestants of that earlier period Otto pointed the way out of the rational-ethical wasteland into which they had come; yet he did so without denying the claims of either ethical or rational concerns. He restored to Protestant thinking enough apprehension of the holy, as distinct from rational and ethical categories, to enable liberal minds to grasp in contemporary terms the significance of such historic notions as *sacred, tabu, mysterium, demonic.* From this they were moved to recognize the reality of sin as a distinctly religious category to which words like "judgment," "grace," and "redemption" were immediately relevant. The strain, so evident in much of liberal Christianity of the period, to retain these classical words within its rational-ethical vocabulary was thereby relieved if not dispelled. The imagery of Reformation thinking, with much of its feeling tone, was again in force, yet in a way that did not rudely disavow the critical judgment of disciplined, historical thinking.

I think it has not always been recognized how responsive Rudolf Otto was to the stimulus of Luther. His idea of the holy, based upon what he called the numinous experience, was put forth within the context of the ethical problem as a repossession of Luther's sense of sin before the judging grace of a righteous God. His basic intention was to set the ethical category, which in Kantian thought had been made the equivalent of the holy, in a dimension of Otherness, bringing man's own formulations of the good under judgment and rendering it responsive to the higher goodness discerned in the grace of a righteous God.

As a statement of the phenomenology of spirit within that framework of thought it is difficult to see how Otto's formulation of the idea of the holy could be improved upon. For all of Otto's concern with the idea of the holy, however, his thought remains essentially under the dominance of rational-ethical categories. The holy appears as an overtone or supplement to it, but with no radically transforming consequences at the level of rational and ethical activity. Thus the effect upon thought and action appear to be more aesthetic than redemptive. This may not be altogether fair to Otto. Certainly his intentions were otherwise. Yet the ethicism of Kant, however deepened and heightened with a more vivid sense of the Wholly Other, persists. In this respect the dialectical theologians are partially justified in considering Otto to be within the liberal tradition, although some of their statements misinterpret and thereby misjudge Otto's efforts.[41] To identify Otto wholly with liberalism, however, in the static way in which they tend to do, is to overlook the important contribution which his thought made at a critical juncture of theological development. As we have indicated, his thought provided at least an imagery by which the beginnings of a more critical liberalism could be undertaken.

Yet it may not be assumed, I think, that Otto's contribution has been only transitional, his influence limited to the closing decades of the liberal era. What his role in the recent turn of theological affairs has been or now is, may not be readily recognized; nor has it, for that matter, been assessed. There are certain aspects of his thought which appear to participate in the current mood of theological inquiry. This perhaps may best be seen by comparing his thought with that of a theologian whose theology is clearly relevant to the immediate theological scene. The contemporary theologian nearest to Otto in feeling tone and in the formulation of his theology is Paul Tillich. Tillich has acknowledged his affinity with Otto's approach to theology. Speaking of the effects of his own early experience growing up in a Lutheran parish, Tillich writes:

[41] Cf. Emil Brunner, *The Philosophy of Religion* (N.Y., Scribner's, 1937), p. 104; and Karl Barth, *Church Dogmatics* I, (N.Y., Scribner's, 1936), Part I, p. 153.

It is the experience of the "holy" which was given to me at that time as an indestructible good and as the foundation of all my religious and theological work. When I first read Rudolf Otto's *Idea of the Holy,* I understood it immediately in the light of these early experiences, and took it into my thinking as a constitutive element. It determined my method in the philosophy of religion, wherein I started with the experiences of the holy and advanced to the idea of God, and not the reverse way. Equally important existentially, as well as theologically, were the mystical, sacramental, and aesthetic implications of the idea of the holy, whereby the ethical and logical elements of religion were derived from the experience of the presence of the divine, and not conversely. This made Schleiermacher congenial to me, as he was to Otto, and induced both Otto and me to participate in movements for liturgical renewal and a revaluation of Christian and non-Christian mysticism.[42]

One sees many parallels between Tillich and Otto stemming from this common orientation in method. In fact, Tillich's description of himself as being "on the boundary" aptly describes Otto's situation in many respects. This theological stance they both inherited from Schleiermacher, who saw the role of the Christian theologian of the modern period precisely in these terms. And this image of the theological task gives rise to other similarities. For example, Tillich's correlation of *kairos* and *logos* recalls Otto's attempt to hold the nonrational and the rational in juxtaposition. And Tillich's "ecstatic reason" has affinities with Otto's way of speaking about the cognitive element in the act of divination. Despite the fact that Otto resolves the eschatological problem within the mystical pattern, ascribing charismatic powers to Jesus, through whom *an inbreaking of the new order* is made manifest, one may say that at least the semblance of a dimensional theology (to use Tillich's phrase) is indicated here within the compass of historical experience. Tillich expresses this same note of innovation ontologically in his concept of the "New Being." Furthermore, one cannot fail to see that both men, in making the holy their starting point in method, have been driven to a symbolic discourse by way of

[42] Charles W. Kegley and Robert W. Bretall, eds., *The Theology of Paul Tillich* (N.Y., Macmillan, 1952), p. 6.

explicating "something that at bottom is incapable of explication by concepts" (Otto). Both men were indebted to the phenomenology of Husserl, and both men trace their early stimulus back to Schleiermacher, Kant, and Luther. Their distinctions arose chiefly from the fact that Otto followed Jacob Fries in formulating his philosophical method, while Tillich drew upon the ontological system of Schelling.

In so far as a dimensional theology finds it necessary to draw upon the notion of the numinous for its imagery of depth and upon a reconception of the doctrine of eschatology in which the numinous informs the meaning of intimations of depth and newness in existence, Rudolf Otto's contribution to theological thinking will continue to have force and influence.

Bibliography

Rudolf Otto, *The Idea of the Holy*, 2d ed., N.Y., Oxford Univ. Press, 1950.

Robert F. Davidson, *Rudolf Otto's Interpretation of Religion*, Princeton, Princeton Univ., 1947.

WALTER RAUSCHENBUSCH

Robert T. Handy

Walter Rauschenbusch (1861–1918) was a Baptist minister, church historian, and the leading exponent and theologian of the social gospel in America. He came into sudden prominence in 1907, and from then to his death he poured out the stream of lectures and writings on which his reputation rests. Three major and four smaller books from his pen appeared in that period of about ten years during which he was American Protestantism's best-known social prophet. At once deeply religious in personal life and vigorously progressive in social attitudes, Rauschenbusch's central effort was to bring into one the two dominating visions of his life, the religious and the social.

I

Rauschenbusch was born in Rochester, New York, on October 4, 1861, son of Karl August and Caroline (Rhomp) Rauschenbusch, who had migrated to the United States from Germany fifteen years earlier. His pietistic father had come as a Lutheran missionary, but was later converted to Baptist views. Beginning in 1858, he taught for thirty-two years in the German department of the Rochester Theological Seminary, devoting much of his scholarly attention to Anabaptist history.[1] Walter was brought up in the conservative German Baptist tradition. His formal education actually was begun in Germany, where he lived from 1865 to 1869. The following ten years were spent again in Rochester, where he attended a private school and a free academy. Summers were passed working on a farm in Pennsylvania. In 1879 the young man had a conversion experience which led to his baptism on confession of faith. Though later his theo-

[1] Carl E. Schneider, "Americanization of Karl August Rauschenbusch, 1816–1899," *Church History*, XXIV (1955), 3–14; Walter Rauschenbusch, *Leben und Wirken von August Rauschenbusch* (Cleveland, Ritter, 1901).

logical understanding of this event changed markedly, he always acknowledged that this "tender, mysterious experience" had great value for him. The deeply religious tone of his personal life remained undiminished, though his intellectual apprehension of the nature of Christian faith was to undergo a sharp reorientation.

Later in 1879 Rauschenbusch again went to Germany for a period of four years, studying at the Gymnasium at Gütersloh in Westphalia, from which he graduated in 1883 with first honors in classical studies. He mastered Latin, Greek, French, Hebrew, and German in those years, showed great interest in art and literature, enjoyed opportunities for travel on the Continent, and studied briefly at the University of Berlin. Resolving to enter the ministry, he returned to Rochester in 1883. His splendid educational preparation allowed him to complete his senior year at the University of Rochester at the same time that he commenced study at the Rochester Theological Seminary. A summer pastorate at Louisville, Kentucky, in 1884 convinced him that he had truly found his calling. He wrote: "It is now no longer my fond hope to be a learned theologian and write big books; I want to be a pastor, powerful with men, preaching to them Christ as the man in whom their affections and energies can find the satisfaction for which mankind is groaning."[2] He graduated from the German department of the seminary in 1885, and from the regular course the following year. Quite in keeping with the warmly evangelical emphases in which he had been schooled, he volunteered for foreign missions. But he was also acquainted with the critical scholarship of his time to the degree that the soundness of his views on the Old Testament were questioned by conservatives in his denomination, and he was refused.

He went instead to the pastorate of the Second German Baptist Church in New York City. Located on West 45 Street, the church was near the depressed area styled "Hell's Kitchen." The cornerstone of a new building was laid in 1889, but it was only two blocks away. Here he was confronted by the social problem in a most challenging way. Here he saw some of the

[2] Dores R. Sharpe, *Walter Rauschenbusch* (N.Y., Macmillan, 1942), p.54.

terrible human effects of poverty, unemployment, insecurity, malnutrition, disease, and crime. It was consistent both with the individualistic, warm-hearted piety in which he had been reared and also with his own understanding of Christian discipleship to reach out in love to help the victims of social misfortune and injustice. But it was difficult for him to find theological undergirding for the social concerns which he found he could not evade. His awareness of the social situation was sharpened in his very first year in New York by the work of Henry George, author of *Progress and Poverty* (1879) and advocate of the single tax. Rauschenbusch later declared that "I owe my first awakening to the world of social problems to the agitation of Henry George in 1886, and wish here to record my lifelong debt to this single-minded apostle of a great truth."[3] Thus awakened, he read widely in the social and socialistic literature of his day. He edited a short-lived paper for working people, *For the Right.* He played a role in some of the movements for social betterment.

Rauschenbusch was very much aware that his social views did not come from the church but from the outside, from personal contact with poverty and unemployment, from his own association with social reform literature and movements. To the earlier religious passion which had called him to the ministry was now added a social passion that engaged him in reformist writing and action. But how were these two passions of his life to be related? The individualistic, evangelistic interpretation of Christian faith which he had inherited and largely accepted scarcely provided resources for confronting the social problem; indeed, many denied that there could be any connection between the two. The effort to bring them together into a satisfying whole launched Rauschenbusch on the main work of his life, and led him to revise much of his understanding of Christian faith. As he later explained: "All this time my friends were urging me to give up this social work and devote myself to 'Christian work.' Some of them felt grieved for me, but I knew the work was Christ's work and I went ahead, although I had to set myself against all that I had previously been taught. I had

---

[3] *Christianizing the Social Order* (N.Y., Macmillan, 1912), p. 394.

to go back to the Bible to find out whether I or my friends were right. I had to revise my whole study of the Bible. . . . All my scientific study of the Bible was undertaken to find a basis for the Christian teaching of a social gospel."[4] That basis he finally did find in his discovery of the importance of the doctrine of the Kingdom of God, which for him bridged the gap between the religious and the social.

The misfortune of deafness, which befell him in 1888 when he arose too soon from a sick bed to minister to others, in a way contributed to his intellectual achievements, for it partially isolated him and provided more time than he might otherwise have had for concentrated study. But his thirst for a resolution of the tension between the religious and the social concerns of his life led him to take a leave from his parish in 1891. He surveyed conditions of life and labor in England, becoming acquainted with Fabian socialism and other social movements, and then went on to engage in New Testament study in Germany. His theological pilgrimage led him in a distinctly liberal direction. He accepted the critical approach to the Bible and the historical understanding of Christianity. He identified himself with the theological streams associated with the names of Schleiermacher, Bushnell, Ritschl, Wellhausen, and Harnack. During this year there came to him as a unifying concept the ideal of the Kingdom of God on earth. He described this turning point in these words:

So Christ's conception of the Kingdom of God came to me as a new revelation. Here was the idea and purpose that had dominated the mind of the Master himself. All his teachings center about it. His life was given to it. His death was suffered for it. When a man has once seen that in the Gospels, he can never unsee it again.

When the Kingdom of God dominated our landscape, the perspective of life shifted into a new alignment. I felt a new security in my social impulses. The spiritual authority of Jesus Christ would have been sufficient to offset the weight of all the doctors, and I now knew that I had history on my side. But in addition I found that this new conception of the purpose of

[4] *Rochester Theological Seminary Bulletin, The Record* (November 1918), pp. 54 f.

Christianity was strangely satisfying. It responded to all the old and all the new elements of my religious life. The saving of the lost, the teaching of the young, the pastoral care of the poor and frail, the quickening of starved intellects, the study of the Bible, church union, political reform, the reorganization of the industrial system, international peace,—it was all covered by the one aim of the Reign of God on earth.[5]

As a theological liberal he frequently criticized the individualistic and pietistic conservatism with which he had once been associated, though the deeply religious orientation of his life was not shaken but deepened. He remained always an "evangelical liberal," deeply influenced by liberal scholarship but grasped by a personally profound Christianity.

Inspired by his new vision and assured of his direction, Rauschenbusch returned to New York to throw himself into his religious and social tasks with a new enthusiasm. He spoke and wrote on the burning public questions of the day. To the Baptist Congress, of which he was secretary, he presented papers on ethical and economic issues. With like-minded brethren who were passing through crises similar to his, he participated in the organization of the Brotherhood of the Kingdom, a group of "thrice-born men" who met annually to stimulate each other's thinking and to advance the cause of social Christianity. At this same time he took a wife, the former Miss Pauline E. Rother, a Milwaukee schoolteacher. Mrs. Rauschenbusch made it much easier for her deafened husband to be at ease in public gatherings. Five children were born of the union.

In 1897 the pastor was called back to his native Rochester to teach New Testament interpretation in the German department of the seminary; at the collegiate level he also taught courses in natural science and civil government. Five years later he was made Professor of Church History on the regular faculty of the Rochester Theological Seminary. Though he wrote little as a church historian, he was a respected and popular teacher in the field. He utilized the concept of the Kingdom of God in organizing his courses. He gave special attention to the early centuries, to the history of baptism, to the Anabaptists, and to American church history.

The pursuits of scholarship and teaching did not at all blunt

5 *Christianizing the Social Order*, p. 93.

his interest in the social question. He could not forget the sufferings of those among whom he had labored as pastor for
eleven years. To discharge a debt to them he resumed work on
a manuscript which he had started years before, a book "on
social questions for the Lord Christ and the people." He knew
the theme was an unpopular one; he was prepared for a storm
of attack and perhaps even for dismissal. Just as the book was
coming from the presses in the spring of 1907, he left the
country on sabbatical. To his surprise, he returned to find himself famous. *Christianity and the Social Crisis* ran through six
editions in two years; finally there were to be seventeen editions.
The mature effort of a competent man and a brilliant writer,
the book appeared at a time when the Progressive movement
was rising in popularity and was affecting national legislation.
It came at a moment when the muckrakers and reformers had
convinced many Americans that social changes were desperately
needed, and when liberal theology was winning a substantial
following in many churches. Its patent sincerity and thoughtful
merging of Christian and social motifs caught the imagination
of many. Its careful elaboration of the ideal of the Kingdom of
God on earth opened attractive vistas to a generation struggling
with the perplexing social question. So the professor of church
history from the moment of his return found himself in great
demand to speak and write on social questions from the viewpoint of Christian faith. Sensing himself to be in the vanguard
of a social and religious awakening, he responded as best he
could to the many calls coming to him.

His second major work, *Christianizing the Social Order,* was
published in 1912. The bulk of this large work, developed from
his Earl Lectures at Pacific Theological Seminary and from his
Merrick Lectures at Ohio Wesleyan, was devoted specifically to
social issues, but characteristically the author insisted that "this
is a religious book from beginning to end. Its sole concern is
for the Kingdom of God and the salvation of men. But the
Kingdom of God includes the economic life; for it means the
progressive transformation of all human affairs by the thought
and spirit of Christ."[6] In pointing the way to such a progressive
transformation, Rauschenbusch drew heavily on the progressive
social thought of his time.

[6] *Ibid.,* p. 458.

Rauschenbusch's message was also presented through a number of articles, pamphlets, and smaller books. In 1910 appeared *For God and the People: Prayers of the Social Awakening,* a little book which distinctively revealed the depth of his own devotional life. Two years later was published *Unto Me,* a small work addressed to social workers. In 1914 was issued another brief writing, *Dare We Be Christians?* In this commentary on I Corinthians 13 he developed his understanding of the meaning of Christian love. In another two years was produced his most widely circulated writing, a study book entitled *The Social Principles of Jesus.*

The climax of his productive decade came in 1917. In the spring of that year he delivered the Taylor Lectures at Yale; they were then published as *A Theology for the Social Gospel.* In this significant work the prophet of social Christianity took this as his main proposition: "We have a social gospel. We need a systematic theology large enough to match it and vital enough to back it."[7] Though he insisted that he was not a doctrinal theologian either by professional training or by personal habits of mind, he continued in what proved to be his last book to relate Christian faith to social concerns precisely by undertaking with considerable imagination to suggest what an adequate theology for social Christianity would be like. In this effort he drew freely on the liberal tradition in theology, and brought to clear delineation the vision of the Kingdom of God that had inspired him a quarter of a century before.

The outbreak of World War I in 1914 had brought deep anguish of spirit to him. He was almost as much at home in Germany as in America. He hated militarism, was inclined toward pacifism, and hoped that America could remain neutral. In the popular wave of revulsion against things German, some began to question his loyalty, though without foundation. His immense popularity declined somewhat. He was a saddened man; war for him seemed to be the negation both of Christianity and of social progress, the twin passions of his life. While the war was still raging, Walter Rauschenbusch, on July 25, 1918, died of cancer in his beloved Rochester.

---

[7] *A Theology for the Social Gospel* (N.Y., Macmillan, 1917), p. 1.

II

Rauschenbusch's public work was dominated by an effort to bring together things which had been separated to such an extent that many saw them as antithetical. Throughout his writings appear references to realities which many had difficulty in relating to each other: science and faith, culture and church, democracy and Christianity, ethics and theology, dogmatics and the social gospel. All these he sought to bring into a coherent whole; for him the Kingdom of God was the way to such unity. A strong sense of continuity between God and man and between God and the world informed his work. An important part of the reason for the appeal of his writings was that they were informed by a vision of a regenerated world; there was in them an arresting comprehensiveness of conception and understanding. However idealistic and perhaps even utopian they may seem to a later generation, they have a breadth and a boldness that is striking. Rauschenbusch sought to give as full and adequate a philosophy for personal and social life as he could. Thus, though he was not a theologian in the formal sense, and in no sense a theological system builder, his work was done in an effort to supply a whole view of the world and of human life.

In methodology Rauschenbusch was decisively influenced by a modern historical approach. His understanding of the Bible, the Kingdom of God, the Christian faith, the Christian Church, and the social situation was cast in terms of historical development. He was conversant with the critical historical treatments of the Bible and of the institutions of Christianity which stemmed from German scholarship; he was well acquainted with the work of the leading "scientific" church historian of the day, Adolf Harnack. His understanding of history was cast in the light of the theory of evolution; the developmental view was worked into the warp and woof of his thought. It was the historical approach which helped him to understand how the church and the movements for social justice had become separated. As he saw both in historical perspective, he could explain why the church had lost the initial social vision which had been hers, and why, in the absence of proper Christian influences, certain serious social conditions and movements for their amelioration had arisen. His dominating ideal of the Kingdom, which would bring the two together again, was shaped in the light of his historicism and developmentalism. He wrote: "Translate the evolutionary theories into religious faith, and you have the doctrine of the Kingdom of God. This combination with scientific evolutionary thought has freed the Kingdom ideal of its catastrophic setting and its background of demonism, and so adapted it to the climate of the modern world."[8] He further declared that the social gospel is always historically minded, always endeavoring "to see the progress of the Kingdom of God in the flow of history; not only in the doings of the Church, but in the clash of economic forces and social classes, in the rise and fall of despotisms and forms of enslavement, in the rise of new value-judgments and fresh canons of moral taste and sentiment, or the elevation or decline of moral standards."[9] The entire first half of the book which won national prominence for him was a sweeping historical interpretation. He traced the historical roots of Christianity to the Hebrew prophets, analyzed the social aims of Jesus in the light of the liberal historical criticism of his period, surveyed the social impetus of primitive Christianity and accounted for its loss in later centuries. Even in the latter half of the book, in which the modern social crises, the stake of the Church in the social movement, and suitable courses of action were discussed, there were many historical references. The strong stamp of the historical method and the developmental viewpoint can be plainly seen both in his most "social" book, *Christianizing the Social Order,* and in his most "theological" work, *A Theology for the Social Gospel.* Inasmuch as it was the historical approach that was setting the pace and posing the main questions in the American theological world in the early years of the twentieth century, it is understandable why a historian might make the leading theological contribution of the period.

The sources of Walter Rauschenbusch's social-ethical thought have been analyzed in a doctoral dissertation by Donovan E. Smucker, who finds four main influences operating upon him: pietism, sectarianism, liberalism, and transformationism. His

[8] *Christianizing the Social Order,* p. 90.
[9] *A Theology for the Social Gospel,* p. 146.

understanding of Christian faith was initially cast in a pietist framework through the influences of family and church; though he later moved out of this frame of reference, a deep personal piety and interest in evangelism remained. The sectarian influences came through the interests both his father and he himself had in Anabaptist thought; his Baptist understanding of the church and the Christian life have sectarian traces. The liberal thought provided the primary content of his position; the most influential theologian for him was Albrecht Ritschl.[10] Rauschenbusch's mature thought was also tempered by the transformationist outlook as presented by such Christian socialists as Frederick Denison Maurice and Charles Kingsley in England and Hermann Kutter and Leonhard Ragaz in Switzerland. Rauschenbusch drew on these influences in a free and often original way in framing the social gospel. Though he wrote from a liberal frame of reference, he never slavishly followed any one pattern, and he felt free to criticize the weaknesses of all. He could say, for example, "To concentrate our efforts on personal salvation, as orthodoxy has done, or on soul culture, as liberalism has done, comes close to refined selfishness."[11]

Rauschenbusch's theology for the social gospel was not a systematic one; indeed, he showed not a little of the distrust of metaphysical speculation and dogmatic thought that was common in his time. His was a theology of mediation, accommodation, and adjustment. For he could say,

> When the progress of humanity creates new tasks, such as worldwide missions, or new problems, such as the social problem, theology must connect these with the old fundamentals of our faith and make them Christian tasks and problems.
> The adjustment of the Christian message to the regeneration of the social order is plainly one of the most difficult tasks ever laid on the intellect of religious leaders.[12]

[10] Donovan E. Smucker, "The Origins of Walter Rauschenbusch's Social Ethics" (typed Ph.D. thesis, Univ. of Chicago, June 1957), p. 212; cf. his summary article, "Multiple Motifs in the Thought of Rauschenbusch: A Study in the Origins of the Social Gospel," *Encounter*, XIX (1958), 14–20.

[11] *Christianizing the Social Order*, pp. 464 f.

[12] *A Theology for the Social Gospel*, p. 7.

Though the statement came from his last work, it aptly summarizes the main thrust of his religious and theological effort.

The informing center of his work, ever since his vision of it in 1891, was the doctrine of the Kingdom of God. Not only was it the most important doctrine for him, but he insisted that it should bring about the revision of "all other doctrines so that they will articulate organically with it."[13] With great emphasis he could say:

> The Kingdom of God is the first and the most essential dogma of the Christian faith. It is also the lost social ideal of Christendom. No man is a Christian in the full sense of the original discipleship until he has made the Kingdom of God the controlling purpose of his life, and no man is intellectually prepared to understand Jesus Christ until he has understood the meaning of the Kingdom of God.

Rauschenbusch believed that the Kingdom was to come on earth in history; he explained that Jesus "never transferred the Kingdom hope from earth to heaven. The Kingdom is so much of this earth that Jesus expected to return to earth from heaven in order to set it up."[14] He believed that the Kingdom of God is divine in its origin, progress, and consummation, miraculous all the way, the continuous revelation of the power, the righteousness, and the love of God. It is the supreme purpose of God, to be realized not only by the redemption of man through the overcoming of evil but also by the education of mankind and the revelation of God's life within it. The Kingdom of God is always present and future, always coming, always pressing in on the present and inviting immediate action. Every human life can share with God in the creation of the Kingdom. The Kingdom is humanity organized according to the will of God, it is a nobler social order. It implies the progressive reign of love in human affairs, it advances wherever the free will of love supersedes the use of force and legal coercion as a regulative of the social order. The reign of love tends toward the progressive unity of mankind. The Kingdom must be the purpose for which the church exists, and gives the church the power to save.

Rauschenbusch did not neglect the doctrine of the church in

[13] *Ibid.*, p. 131.
[14] *Christianizing the Social Order*, pp. 49, 66.

his theology. He called the church "the social factor in salvation," and indicated the necessity of its being and function. His own church idea was much shaped by his Baptist background and commitments. He favored congregationally ordered, noncreedal, nonhierarchical, fully democratic churches.[15] For him church was always subordinate to Kingdom; the church was a perpetuation of the past while the Kingdom is the power of the coming age.

The Kingdom of God, Rauschenbusch taught, embraces all of life and realizes itself through the family, the economic organizations, and the state as well as through the church. The Kingdom of God is a historical force that can be progressively realized; humanity is on the march to the Kingdom of God. The Kingdom of God is not utopia; there is no perfection but only growth toward perfection. There can only be the approximation of a perfect social order. Yet Rauschenbusch dared to hope that a vastly better, if not entirely perfect, social order was at hand, a social order that would far more fully realize the Kingdom of God than anything the world had known. "The swiftness of evolution in our own country," he said at the end of his first book, "proves the immense latent perfectibility in human nature."[16] Interpreting the eschatological teachings of the gospels in the light of the evolutionary optimism of his time, he explained that Jesus took "his illustrations from organic life to express the idea of the gradual growth of the Kingdom. He was shaking off catastrophic ideas and substituting developmental ideas." Actually, Rauschenbusch was basing his interpretation of the eschatology of Jesus on a view that had already been sharply challenged by certain biblical scholars of the time. Though aware of their work, Rauschenbusch argued that "the professional theologians of Europe, who all belong by kinship and sympathy to the bourgeois class and are constitutionally incapacitated for understanding any revolutionary ideas, past or

---

[15] Cf. his articles, "Why I Am a Baptist," originally published in *The Rochester Baptist Monthly*, XX (1905–1906), 2–3, 85–8, 106–8, 134–6, 156–9; reprinted in *The Colgate-Rochester Divinity School Bulletin*, XI (December 1938).

[16] *Christianity and the Social Crisis* (N.Y., Macmillan, 1907), p. 422. For the full development of his teaching on the Kingdom see *A Theology for the Social Gospel*, pp. 139–45, 165 f., 227.

present, have overemphasized the ascetic and eschatological elements in the teachings of Jesus."[17] Hence he continued to understand Jesus' Kingdom teachings as anticipations of the fraternal ethics of democracy and prophecies of social common sense that were soon to be fulfilled.

The Kingdom is of God, but the theologian of the social gospel did not often touch directly on the doctrine of God. He put the doctrine of the Kingdom of God before the doctrine of God, insisting that the Kingdom is the necessary background for the Christian idea of God. Without denying God's transcendence, Rauschenbusch emphasized his immanence: "God is not only the spiritual representative of humanity; he is identified with it. In him we live and move and have our being. In us he lives and moves, though his being transcends ours." He indicated that the conception of God held by a social group is a social product and that such conceptions can change and grow. The concept of God which is dominant among a given people is influenced by the social relations under which they live; under tyrannous conditions the idea of God was tainted with the cruel hardness of society. But when Jesus took God by the hand and called him "our Father," he "democratized" the concept of God. "He disconnected the idea from the coercive and predatory State, and transferred it to the realm of family life, the chief social embodiment of solidarity and love. He not only saved humanity, he saved God."[18] The social gospel is to continue to free men from wrong conceptions of God, it is to continue what the Reformation began. The religious belief that he is immanent in humanity is the natural basis for democratic ideas about him. Rauschenbusch declared that the idea of solidarity, properly understood, acts as a theodicy; the consciousness of solidarity is the essence of religion. God is the ground of the social unity of all mankind.

Though Rauschenbusch rarely touched on the doctrine of God formally, everything he wrote referred, explicitly or implicitly, to Jesus Christ. The very soul of his own deep religiousness was his loyalty and devotion to Jesus. The following passage from a letter written in 1912 is very revealing:

[17] *A Theology for the Social Gospel,* p. 158.
[18] *Ibid.,* pp. 49, 174 f.

God and Christ may differ for my analytic intellect, but for my religious life they are convertible terms. The God of the stellar universe is a God in whom I drown. Christ with the face of Jesus I can comprehend, and love and assimilate. So I stick to him, and call him by that name. Let others do differently if they are differently made. I prefer to superimpose the two concepts on each other and get more out of each.[19]

His was a quest for the historical Jesus; from the scientific New Testament study of his time he found the Master coming out of the past with greater clarity. He saw the Jesus of history as a teacher of morality and the master of "the greatest and deepest and rarest secret of all—how to live a religious life." Jesus knew the Father; his religion flowed out naturally into all the relations of his life, reconstructing everything it touched. Jesus was the perfect religious personality; he rose above the temptations of mysticism, pessimism, and asceticism. Jesus incarnated a new type of human life; he was the first real man, the inaugurator of a new humanity. The social redemption of the entire life of the human race on earth was always the purpose of all that Jesus said and did and hoped to do. He put the Kingdom of God at the center of all his teaching. Rauschenbusch firmly believed that his own views about the Kingdom were solidly based on what Jesus had taught about it. For Rauschenbusch the social gospel must always be concerned about the progressive social incarnation of God. The Christology of the social gospel therefore focuses on how the divine life of Christ can get control of human society. Its emphasis is not on the speculative questions of the two natures in Christ, but on a real personality who could set the great historical process of redemption in motion. In Jesus the Kingdom of God got its first foothold in humanity; by virtue of his personality he became the initiator of the Kingdom.[20]

Throughout Rauschenbusch's work is to be found a con-

[19] Quoted in Sharpe, *Rauschenbusch*, p. 322.
[20] Cf. Chap. II, "The Social Aims of Jesus," *Christianity and the Social Crisis*, pp. 44–92; Part II, Chap. II, "The Social Christianity of Jesus," *Christianizing the Social Order*, pp. 48–68; *The Social Principles of Jesus* (N.Y., Association Press, 1916); Chap. XIV, "The Initiator of the Kingdom of God," *A Theology of the Social Gospel*, pp. 146–66.

tinuing discussion of the doctrines of sin and salvation, "the starting-point and goal of Christian theology," with special attention to their social dimensions. The climax of this discussion comes in *A Theology for the Social Gospel,* in which he declared that "my main purpose in this book has been to show that the social gospel is a vital part of the Christian conception of sin and salvation, and that any teaching on the sinful condition of the race and on its redemption from evil which fails to do justice to the social factors and processes in sin and redemption, must be incomplete, unreal and misleading."[21] In that book he caught up much that he had said before about the nature of social sin and salvation. For him sin was essentially selfishness, a definition which "furnishes an excellent theological basis for a social conception of sin and salvation." He believed that man rarely sins against God alone. A vision of the Kingdom of God makes clear the social dimensions of sin, for we see the Kingdom of God locked in struggle against the superpersonal forces of evil which together comprise a Kingdom of Evil. As men are turned from self to God and to humanity, they find salvation. A solidaristic religious experience is more Christian, Rauschenbusch believed, than an individualistic one.

Rauschenbusch based his social ethics on the teachings of Jesus concerning love. Hence he "made one of the outstanding attempts in modern Christian history to construct an ethic of love."[22] "The fundamental virtue in the ethics of Jesus was love, because love is the society-making quality," he once wrote, adding:

> Human life originates in love. It is love that holds together the basal human organization, the family. The physical expression of all love and friendship is the desire to get together and be together. Love creates fellowship. In the measure in which love increases in any social organism, it will hold together without coercion.[23]

The fullest development of his philosophy of love is in *Dare We Be Christians?,* which closes with the words: "Those who

---

[21] P. 167.
[22] Smucker, "The Origins of Walter Rauschenbusch's Social Ethics," p. 220.
[23] *Christianity and the Social Crisis,* p. 67.

take up the propaganda of love and substitute freedom and fraternity for coercion and class differences in social life are the pioneers of the Kingdom of God; for the reign of the God of love will be fulfilled in a life of humanity organized on the basis of solidarity and love." The Christianization of the social order will be accomplished by bringing it into harmony with the ethical convictions which we identify with Christ.

When he turned to the task of spelling out the specific details of the social ethic of love, Rauschenbusch drew heavily on the progressive, mildly radical, socialistic thought of his time. Private gain must give way to public good. Competition must give place to cooperation. Special privilege must yield to the principle of equal rights. To his joy, when he surveyed the American social scene in 1912 he could report that "four great sections of our social order—the family, the organized religious life, the institutions of education, and the political organization of our nation—have passed through constitutional changes which have made them to some degree part of the organism through which the spirit of Christ can do its work in humanity."[24] The next thing, he affirmed, was business, "the unregenerate section of our social order." Drawing his arrows from the quivers of the muckrakers, reformers, progressives, and socialists, he analyzed capitalism critically. He wrote of its competitiveness, autocracy, and commercialism. He criticized its tendency to grab for profits to the detriment of human values, its neglect of aesthetic interests, its crippling of the institutions of love. He summed up "the Christian indictment of capitalism" as follows: "Capitalism has generated a spirit of its own which is antagonistic to the spirit of Christianity; a spirit of hardness and cruelty that neutralizes the Christian spirit of love; a spirit that sets material goods above spiritual possessions. To set Things above Men is the really dangerous practical materialism." Against this, Rauschenbusch called for "a collective action of the community to change the present organization of the economic life into a new order that would rest on the Christian principles of equal rights, democratic distribution of economic power, the supremacy of the common good, the law of mutual dependence and service, and the uninterrupted flow of good will

---

[24] *Christianizing the Social Order*, p. 154.

throughout the human family."[25] These goals could be achieved, he thought, through the strengthening of the working class, the development of social insurance, the assurance of the right to employment, and the increasing of economic democracy by trade-unionism, cooperatives, and socialism. Rauschenbusch called himself a Christian socialist, but his was an evolutionary, nondoctrinaire, really nonpolitical form of socialism. He noted the dilemma with which organized socialism confronted Christians: "It is far and away the most powerful force for justice, democracy, and organized fraternity in the modern world. On the other hand, these moral elements are fused with an alloy that is repellent to their Christian instincts."[26] Hence he did not himself become a member of the Socialist Party; he could not identify the Kingdom of God with the socialist state, as some Christian socialists were doing. He recognized the "menace" of socialism, but insisted that the task of Christians was to make its menace small and its blessing great.

Not by revolution or swift overturn but by gradualism did he believe that the Kingdom would come. By shortening hours of work and raising wages, by providing adequate housing, by returning something of the "social dividend" to those who have helped make it, by putting "natural monopolies" under public ownership, could the coming of the Kingdom be speeded. Always he maintained that the social task was religious, and that the religious task was social:

It is not this thing or that thing our nation needs, but a new mind and heart, a new conception of the way we all ought to live together, a new conviction about the worth of a human life and the use God wants us to make of our own lives. We want a revolution both inside and outside. We want a moral renovation of public opinion and a revival of religion. . . . A righteous public opinion may bring the proudest sinner low. But the most pervasive scrutiny, a control which follows our actions to their fountain-head where the desires and motives of the soul are born, is exerted only by personal religion.[27]

[25] *Ibid.*, pp. 315, 323.
[26] *Ibid.*, p. 397.
[27] *Ibid.*, p. 459.

So Rauschenbusch hoped to link the evangelical gospel with the social gospel, to add the latter to the former, and thus to create a public opinion that would bring about renewal of both church and society.

III

Rauschenbusch was the best-known and most perceptive advocate of the liberal social gospel. Not only did he enjoy great prominence in the English-speaking world, but beyond, for writings of his were translated into German, French, Norwegian, Swedish, Finnish, Russian, Chinese, and Japanese. His counsel was sought by many, including such public figures as Theodore Roosevelt, Woodrow Wilson, and David Lloyd George. About two decades after his death Henry P. Van Dusen declared, "It is clear, it seems to me, that the greatest single personal influence on the life and thought of the American church in the last fifty years was exerted by Walter Rauschenbusch. Probably the three most influential men in American church history upon the thought of the church have been Jonathan Edwards, Horace Bushnell, and Walter Rauschenbusch."[28] And more than four decades after his passing, Donald B. Meyer called Rauschenbusch the "greatest spokesman" of the social gospel, the man who preached it "more glowingly and with more reasoned faith than any other of his generation of Protestant leaders." Comparing him with other figures of the time, Meyer concludes: "But it was Rauschenbusch who stood foremost, and although Rauschenbusch was hailed for many things, what stamps him most sharply in retrospect is his estimate of tactics, the first clear, concrete estimate in the annals of the social passion."[29]

After Rauschenbusch's death the social gospel and the liberal theology on which it was based developed in several different and not wholly consistent directions, none of which would probably have had his full approval. The basic synthesis for which he labored did not prove to be lasting. Some representatives of the social gospel tended toward a humanistic orientation and in

[28] Quoted in Sharpe, *Rauschenbusch*, p. 410.
[29] Donald B. Meyer, *The Protestant Search for Political Realism, 1919–1941* (Berkeley and Los Angeles, Univ. of California, 1960), pp. 15, 88.

their attention to the social minimized the religious; others focused their attention on one or two major social problems and neglected the larger scene. In the 1930's positions for which Rauschenbusch had stood tended to disintegrate under the attacks of dialectical and realistic theologians and social ethicists. In delineating what Jesus' concept of the Kingdom of God was, no doubt Rauschenbusch did read in too much of his own progressive and evolutionary views; he minimized the eschatological aspects of the Kingdom. In stressing the centrality of the Kingdom, he was inclined to slight the role and place of the Church in history. In proclaiming the immanence of God, he neglected biblical and theological themes concerning the transcendence, majesty, and sovereignty of God. In defining sin as essentially selfishness, he did not deal adequately with the classic Christian understanding of sin as pride and rebellion against God. In seeking to awake public opinion to the need for greater social righteousness, he relied too heavily on the power of press and platform and did not realistically enough count political costs of change. In estimating the degree to which the nation and its institutions had become Christianized, he was far too optimistic and scarcely read aright deeper undercurrents of criticism and confusion. Yet he avoided many of the pitfalls into which the later social gospel slipped. He understood the tragic character of life and warned that men and nations might take the wrong road. He never neglected personal religion; he never confused social reconstruction, important as he believed that was, with the Christian experience of salvation. Hence, though his formulation of the social gospel had its day and passed, it has made lasting contributions to theological and ethical thought. The man who led the attack on the liberal theology and its social gospel, Reinhold Niebuhr, expressed the hope that his own 1934 Rauschenbusch Lectures would be "an extension and an application to our own day of both the social realism and the loyalty to Christian faith which characterized the thought and life of one who was not only the real founder of social Christianity in this country but also its most brilliant and generally satisfying exponent to the present day."[30] What-

---

[30] Reinhold Niebuhr, *An Interpretation of Christian Ethics* (N.Y., Harper, 1935), Preface.

ever its limitations, the social gospel made a permanent contribution to Christian life and thought in America by effectively calling attention to the social dimension in all religious thought and by emphasizing in a way appropriate to an industrial society the importance of the quest for social justice. This was more the work of Walter Rauschenbusch than of any other one man.

Bibliography

Walter Rauschenbusch, *A Theology for the Social Gospel*, Nashville, Abingdon, 1961. (Apex Books).

Dores R. Sharpe, *Walter Rauschenbusch*, N.Y., Macmillan, 1942.

D. C. MACINTOSH

Herbert R. Reinelt

Douglas Clyde Macintosh was born in 1877 in Breadalbane, Ontario. After doing graduate work in theology and philosophy at the University of Chicago, he went to Yale Divinity School in 1909 to teach theology. On his way to Yale from Canada he was almost denied entrance when a border guard informed him that to enter for purposes of employment was in violation of the Alien Labor law. When he happened to mention that he was to teach theology at Yale, the guard said, "I thought you said you were going to work!" and promptly let him enter. Macintosh was also the center of a celebrated legal case in which he was denied U.S. citizenship by a five-to-four decision of the Supreme Court because of his refusal to agree to bear arms in time of war. He remained at Yale until his retirement in 1942. He died in 1948.

Macintosh's thought focuses on the problem of knowledge, particularly the problem of religious knowledge. His first major work, *The Problem of Knowledge,* is a critical examination of the fundamental alternatives in the theory of knowledge. His most important theological works include *Theology as an Empirical Science, The Reasonableness of Christianity, The Pilgrimage of Faith,* and *The Problem of Religious Knowledge.* He also is the author of numerous other books and articles in the field of philosophy and religion.

Theologically, Macintosh sought to come to grips with the problems that were presented to religion by the significant movements of thought in the nineteenth century. He was clearly disturbed by the extreme rationalism, disconnected from empirical data, which he felt to be a fundamental characteristic of much orthodox theology. He was equally disturbed by the retreat of faith before the advance of scientific knowledge. He felt that the major theological developments of the nineteenth century were inadequate because they failed to provide an adequate ground for knowledge of God and, consequently, for the clear understanding and pursuit of a meaningful religious life. In responding to this situation, he was deeply impressed by the significance of scientific method for the discovery of knowledge. In this he reflects the general character of his time. He was influenced by the attempt of William James to study the varieties of religious experience and to base theological theory on the data studied. However, whereas James's work is disconnected from any specific religious tradition, Macintosh was striving to apply the empirical method to the defense of Christian faith. He was also a participant in the attempt to develop a critical realism in regard to the problem of knowledge, and his resulting theological theory reflects his concern that adequate foundation be given for genuine knowledge of God. In this respect some interpreters see him influenced by the Scottish Common Sense School of philosophy.[1]

PHILOSOPHICAL FOUNDATIONS

For Macintosh there can be no essential separation between theology and philosophy. Philosophical issues are of fundamental importance in the solution of theological problems. No theology is adequately critical which does not face the philosophical implications of theological affirmations. Every theology, for example, makes assumptions concerning the possibility and nature of knowledge, including religious knowledge. The problem of knowledge is crucial for the critical justification of theological thought. This outlook involved Macintosh in consideration of general problems in the theory of knowledge as well as in the development of a specifically religious epistemology.

The whole history of modern philosophy, culminating in the critical philosophy of Kant, had set the stage for consideration of the relationship of things as they appear to us to things as they are in themselves. Do we know reality itself in knowing the objects given in experience, or do we know only the appearances while reality itself remains unknown? For Macintosh

---

[1] Cf. Eugene Garrett Bewkes, "Common Sense Realism," in *The Nature of Religious Experience* (N.Y., Harper, 1937), pp. 1–25.

these are the two fundamental alternatives. The second alternative, that the object which is given in perceptual experience is totally different from the ultimate reality, he calls *dualism*. The logical consequence of this view, according to Macintosh, is agnosticism with respect to the independently real object. Nothing can be known about it. We cannot even know that it is.[2] The fundamental error of the dualist is to overlook the continuity of existence. If the appearance is that of a reality, then it is somehow continuous with it. If it is not in any sense continuous with it, we have no basis from which to call it an appearance of a reality.

The first alternative, says Macintosh, must be the correct one. The view that we know reality itself in knowing the objects given in experience is called *monism*. In monism there is at least partial identity between the object which is known and the independent reality. But within monism there are two alternatives. The *idealist* alternative is that there is complete identity between the object we know and the independent reality. The idealist says that there is complete identity because he holds that reality is idea, and since we directly experience ideas, we therefore directly experience reality. Since nothing in our idea is in principle unknown to us, we can know reality completely. The interpretation of the character of ideas may vary among idealists, but they uniformly hold that there is nothing which exists beyond ideas. Macintosh contends that the idealist's theory is clearly at odds with common sense experience and that for this reason the burden of proof for the theory rests on the idealist. He distinguishes many different types of idealism and examines the arguments for idealism with great care; he concludes that the arguments are inadequate to establish the truth of the theory. The argument is too detailed to be included here.[3]

The other alternative within monism is *realism*. The realist is defined negatively as one who holds that reality is not idea in

<hr/>

[2] Cf. *The Problem of Knowledge* (N.Y., Macmillan, 1915), Chaps. II–III, hereafter cited as PK; *The Reasonableness of Christianity* (N.Y., Scribner's, 1925), pp. 193 ff., hereafter cited as RC; "Experimental Realism in Religion," in *Religious Realism*, D. C. Macintosh, ed. (N.Y., Macmillan, 1931), pp. 349–52, hereafter cited as "ERR."

[3] Cf. PK, Chaps. V–IX; RC, pp. 168–186; "ERR," pp. 341–349.

any common meaning of that term. Since idealism—the attempt to identify appearance and reality by reducing reality to the appearances—has been rejected, some form of realism must be true, that is, there must be a reality which exists independent of experience and which can be at least partially known. *Naive realism* reduces the appearances to the reality—the conclusion opposite to that of the idealist. The naive realist holds that we directly experience realities without any intermediate appearances; thus there is no appearance distinct from reality. The problem with this view is that it is committed to the rationally unacceptable notion that if a person has contradictory experiences of the same object, the object must have contradictory characteristics.

An adequate theory of knowledge, then, must be a *critical realism* which recognizes a partial identity between ultimate reality and the way in which this reality appears to us—a theory that can account not only for the fact that we can know what is external to ourselves and independent of our knowledge of it, but also for the fact that the conditions of knowledge influence the character of the object known. The sensible qualities of objects are not independently real; therefore the perceived object and the independently real object are qualitatively distinguishable. However,

> there may still be such an existential unity or identity between them as to enable one to say with truth that an object which is real independently of our conscious experience has been presented in experience and directly known, even though not all the qualities of the independent reality have been directly presented, and even though not all of the qualities of the object as presented need be thought of as belonging to it in its independent existence.[4]

We know the reality through the appearance; it has at least an existential and numerical identity. We have here what Macintosh calls "perception in a complex"—the perception of a reality in and through the presented content of experience. Instances of such perception in a complex are involved in our

[4] RC, p. 198.

knowledge of physical movement, animal life, consciousness, the self, other selves, and, most importantly for the problem of religious knowledge, God.

Development of Theology as an Empirical Science

The consideration of the logical alternatives in the theory of knowledge lays the groundwork for the development of theology. A dualistic theory with respect to knowledge of God leads to agnosticism or to an uncritical dogmatism—uncritical because it is never possible to test the dogmatic claim with the religious reality. It is precisely at this point that Macintosh is extremely critical of many contemporary theologians—Tillich, Barth, and Brunner, among others—who represent this type of inadequate epistemological position.[5] On the other hand, idealism in religion reduces the religious reality, God, to some form of idea. The consequence of this type of theory is that God does not represent an independently existing reality. It is fatal to religion if true, for once God is understood not to exist the meaning of the religious life would be lost; the religious life has as its very essence the relating of man to God, who is understood to be a reality. Feuerbach epitomizes religious idealism, but Freud, Durkheim, and others are to be included among its adherents.[6] Idealism in religion is subject to the general criticisms of epistemological idealism and to other special objections as well.

If we are to deny neither the possibility of testing the truth of religion nor the possibility that religion is meaningful, we are driven toward some type of realism with respect to religious knowledge. Corresponding to naive realism is mysticism. As the naive realist who holds that we know reality as it is could not square his theory with the diverse experiences we have of reality, so the mystic tends to assert that we have direct knowledge of God and to deny the reality of ordinary experiences of other objects. But in denying ordinary experience mysticism is dogmatic and uncritical. In theology as in other fields of knowl-

---

[5] Cf. *The Problem of Religious Knowledge* (N.Y., Harper, 1940), Chaps. XIII–XIX, hereafter cited as PRK.
[6] Cf. PRK, Chaps. IV–X and RC, pp. 219–224.

edge the only justifiable theory is a critical realism which acknowledges a real apprehension of God through a complex of experience, which builds theology upon the data of religious experience and from which adequately tested truth may be derived. It is in order to meet this need that Macintosh develops his theology as an empirical science.

Scientific theology makes the same basic assumptions that ordinary science makes. It assumes the laws of thought, the methods and principles common to all scientific procedures, the results of other sciences.[7] One presupposition, already substantiated by the criticism of alternative epistemological theories, is the critically realistic view that knowledge of reality in general is possible. Scientific theology also assumes the principle of induction, that is, that the future will be like the past or, to state it otherwise, that nature is uniform. If the scientist is to generalize from his data he must make this assumption.

But there is one presupposition which is unique to theology: that of the reality of its subject matter. Theology of a scientific sort has the right to assume the existence of God. In defending this assertion Macintosh points out that scientific theology is only making the same sort of assumption that every scientific investigation makes. Every scientific discipline at least tentatively assumes the existence of its object from the outset. Without this assumption there could be no such discipline. The initial assumption is based on practical experience of the object in question prior to scientific investigation. Practical experience of religious reality is to be found in the religious life of mankind. In fact, the history of religion might be considered the history of empirical investigation of the divine. Those who would deny the right of theology to make this assumption do so on highly dogmatic grounds. The agnostic generalizes from the basis of his own ignorance of God that there is no such reality, but this sort of dogmatism is not in accord with scientific procedure.[8]

When critics accused Macintosh of dogmatically presupposing the existence of God, he defended the *logical* right of the

[7] *Theology as an Empirical Science* (N.Y., Macmillan, 1919), p. 28, hereafter cited as TES.
[8] TES, pp. 29–31.

theologian to make this presupposition on the basis of pre-scientific experience, just as the physicist presupposes electricity in order to investigate it. Macintosh of course granted that the preliminary presupposition of God is tentative and that any preliminary definition of the nature of God is necessarily minimal and subject to revision in the light of further investigation. However, he also suggested the alternative approach of introducing the consideration of the existence of God as a question to be settled by the empirical data of theology and not as a presupposition of theology. In this case a tentative definition of God would be hypothesized and then tested by reference to the data of the religious life.[9] Even the latter approach must make the assumption that there is meaningful theological or religious material which can be investigated and which will enable one to test theological hypotheses. Again, theology is no different from the other sciences in making this assumption.

The principle of induction or of the dependability of nature is also specified in Macintosh's scientific theology. If God is presupposed, this principle becomes the principle of the dependableness of God. Scientific theology could not proceed without the assumption that God will act in the future in ways consistent with those with which he has acted in the past. No generalization from given data would be possible without such dependableness. As the most fundamental assumption of theological science, this principle is the last to be verified; but no science is possible without it.[10] If God is not presupposed, then it must be assumed that whatever reality is the source of the religious life is consistent in its activity.

These presuppositions of religious inquiry having been acknowledged, the next step is to specify what experiences are religious as distinct from other types of experiences. Some criteria must be used in order to distinguish the data of theology from other data. The establishment of such norms presupposes that we have sufficient discrimination to be able to identify the essence of religion or the divine element in experience. Analysis of religion discloses that there are two fundamental elements in religion: first, our consciousness of ultimate reality as expressed

[9] Cf. PRK, p. 193.
[10] TES, p. 35.

in our feelings of absolute dependence, wonder, and awe, and, second, our sense of absolute values which are universally and finally valid.[11] Religion as a function in human life thus has its own unique concern. "The distinctively religious interest is an interest in the relation of reality to values."[12]

The criterion of the divine, therefore, is the unity of power and of value. Reality is felt as divine when it is felt to act in support of the highest values. Nothing less than a being which is ultimate in power and in concern for value could possibly be the object of religious worship, adoration, praise, confidence, and trust. Underlying Macintosh's theology is the conviction that men can know, at least in a general way, absolute values. Macintosh identifies these values with all those factors which contribute toward spiritual development, including rationality and knowledge of truth, righteousness and good will, true friendship and unselfish love; in short, with those values which contribute to intellectual, aesthetic, social, and moral development.[13] Macintosh, an ethical intuitionist, maintains that these values are "intuitively appreciable as intrinsic, ultimate, and universally valid, whether universally appreciated or not."[14] If a critical philosophy of values discloses absolute values to us and if reality steadfastly supports the achievement of such values, then we have evidence that the religious object exists.

Macintosh has been criticized at this point for subjecting God to human criteria. Does not such a theory define and analyze the nature and function of God in terms of a human value system?[15] Can God be God and be subjected to external criteria more ultimate than himself? Macintosh is quite clear that there can be no separation of the divine from value. Apart from the concern for value, there would be no ground for absolute reverence and devotion. Furthermore, are the criteria really external to the divine? We find not only that ultimate reality supports ultimate values, but also that it forces us in the direc-

[11] "ERR," pp. 307 ff.; cf. PRK, pp. 163–4.
[12] "ERR," p. 312.
[13] "ERR," p. 310.
[14] PRK, p. 374.
[15] H. Richard Niebuhr, "Value Theory and Theology," in *The Nature of Religious Experience*, pp. 93–116.

tion of such values, that is, it lays a claim upon us to realize these values. To seek other ends is to be disappointed and, finally, to be driven toward absolute values.

With these criteria we are able to give a preliminary definition of God. God is "the value-producing factor and behavior in the universe, driving toward right adjustment on man's part . . . ,"[16] "a dependable Factor, favorable to spiritual values, and responding to the right religious adjustment,"[17] "the ultimate Object of religious dependence, or the Source of religious deliverance."[18]

Given this preliminary understanding of God, the next step is to confront those experiences in which such divine ideals are being realized. In entering into such experiences we are in the presence of the divine, "an immanence of the divine within nature or humanity or both."[19] Such experiences are instances of religious perception, that is, experiences in which men feel the presence of the divine agency influencing their lives. This agency cannot be identified with human forces, whether the self or society as a whole, for it is responsible for the emergence of man in the first place and thus is prior to all human activities. The experience of this agency is an "experience of spiritual uplift through religious dependence," an "awareness of the presence and activity, within experience, of a Power that makes for a certain type of result in response to the right religious adjustment."[20] In this way what the divinely functioning reality does is revealed, discovered, and known.

Carefully criticized religious experience is thus the source of our knowledge of God. It is important to note that through religious experience we gain knowledge that God is and, in addition, we are able to gain knowledge concerning what God does. It is only at a later stage that we will construct a theological theory on the basis of experience concerning what God is. The next step, according to Macintosh, is to formulate carefully investigated experience into theological laws, that is, to generalize on the basis of experience.

[16] "ERR," p. 395.
[17] PRK, p. 197.
[18] TES, p. 27.
[19] PRK, p. 164.
[20] TES, pp. 31–32.

What we discover is that the reaction of God to man is conditioned by the adjustment of man to God. This adjustment can be positive or negative, responsive or destructive, depending on whether the motive in the action is directed toward proper ends and utilizes the proper means for seeking religious experience.[21] Positive response by God is contingent upon the right religious adjustment. Macintosh is critical of those theologians who claim that man has no part in the working of revelation. God does not act in such a way that man is a mere pawn in the process. Macintosh finds the analogy of sense perception useful. In sense perception we become aware of reality external to ourselves when we are willing to look, hear, taste, etc. When we allow our senses to work we become aware of the influence of reality upon us. The process of sense perception is the product of the use of human capacities and the action of external realities. The same thing is true in religious revelation or religious perception. Revelation or awareness of divine reality occurs only when men make use of their capacity to apprehend it and divinely functioning reality acts to reveal itself.

Making use of our capacity to apprehend the divine means making the right religious adjustment. The right religious adjustment includes (1) concentration of attention on spiritual and moral ends and upon God as the source of these ends and their realization; (2) absolute self-surrender to God and trust that God is a source of help for the attainment of spiritual development; (3) responsiveness to the guidance of God; (4) steady persistence in this attitude of responsive trust and confidence. If these conditions for religious knowledge are met, one will experience in one's life the effects of the activity of God and will know the reality of the working of God in human experience.[22] The right religious adjustment is essentially the same as the life of true prayer.[23]

What theological laws or laws of the religious life are discovered as a result of this experimental faith? They are in the first instance laws which deal with changes in the personal and volitional life of the individual. Macintosh formulates these in a general way: "On condition of the right religious adjustment

[21] PRK, p. 170.
[22] Cf. TES, p. 144; PRK, pp. 170–71.
[23] TES, p. 147; *Personal Religion* (N.Y., Scribner's, 1942), Chap. III.

with reference to desired truly moral states of the will (such as repentance, moral aspiration, and the moral elements in self-control, courage, victory over temptation, faithful service and patient endurance) God the Holy Spirit produces the specific moral results desired."[24] This is the theological law dealing with the elemental experiences of religious life. Macintosh also formulates a similar law dealing with composite experiences which involve such traditional ideas as regeneration, perseverance, and sanctification; salvation is the general term which encompasses all experience of this type. There are also secondary theological laws which deal with the emotional, intellectual, bodily, and social consequences of right religious adjustment.[25]

Macintosh's formulation of these laws in terms of the actions of God and the Holy Spirit has been criticized as assuming the spiritual or essentially personal nature of the divinely functioning reality. In *The Problem of Religious Knowledge* (Ch. XII) he meets the problem by reformulating the laws. For example, he states the elemental law of empirical theology or the law of the answer to prayer (the basic theological law) as follows: "A divinely functioning reality, on condition of the right religious adjustment for a specific volitional effect (the promotion of the good will) tends to produce a desirable change in that direction in the will and character of the individual concerned, and this may be regarded as the basic, dependable 'answer to prayer.' "[26] Laws are stated for conversion, regeneration, perseverance, spiritual health, sanctification, repentance, religious peace, joy, love; religious assurance, guidance, health; the salvation of social groups and society at large.

These laws are not exact in a quantitative sense; rather they are laws of direction and tendency. But for all that, Macintosh holds them to be truly scientific laws. They state constant relationships discoverable within the religious life. As in all science, there are constants and variables. Macintosh sought to delineate the constant relationships in the midst of experienced variation. The constants include nature with its laws, some aspects of human nature and of the social environment, and the being and

[24] TES, p. 148.
[25] TES, Part II, Chap. V.
[26] PRK, p. 203.

character of God, which is the most important constant for empirical theological laws. Among the variables are such factors as individual training and social environment. Most important, however, is the quality and degree of responsiveness of the individual and his particular religious adjustment.[27]

How does Macintosh avoid the criticism that these laws he has formulated do not refer to any external reality but are simply descriptions of the religious psychology of the individual? His answer is that it is not an either/or question. All of the theological laws are also descriptions of the psychology of the individual and can be formulated as psychological laws simply by dropping the reference to God or to divinely functioning reality. However, he contends that they are also evidences for the existence of God. Through these experiences we discover that reality is the cause of dependable results, and this is a disclosure of the dependable character of religious reality, whatever that reality may be. As already indicated, Macintosh holds that this reality is more than man since it antedates and is the cause of human existence.[28]

Theological laws formulate the character of the processes of our religious experience. But science is concerned with more than this. Scientific theory seeks an adequate understanding of the nature of the reality with which experience acquaints us. We acquire scientific understanding of the objects of the experience through our understanding of how the object acts. The same holds for theology as an empirical science. Once theological theory is formulated, it is then capable of further verification by repeated experimentation. It can be gradually substantiated by further positive results or it can be refuted by the discovery of falsifying facts.

On the basis of empirical investigation and the formulation of laws which generalize the results of that investigation, we can, in Macintosh's view, formulate a theological theory concerning the existence and nature of God. We can say that God is known to exist through the experience which we have of him. In addition we can say that he responds to the right re-

[27] TES, pp. 141–2.
[28] PRK, pp. 198 ff.

ligious adjustment; that he regenerates, maintains and promotes the moral and spiritual life; that he convicts of sin, gives peace, joy, and power to love; that he works not only in the life of the individual but in the life of church and of society. In other words, what is discovered in the theological laws can in theological theory be understood as the character of divinely functioning reality.[29]

We have now seen the general way in which Macintosh develops his scientific theology. But theology for Macintosh is more than an empirical science, as we shall see presently. Something must first be said of the limitations of scientific theology. It is limited to consideration of the uniformities discoverable in the data of religious experience and the understanding of the divine through this data. Though much can be known about the character of the divine processes and therefore something about the activities of the divine, we know little in this way concerning what the divine is. For example, we do not know whether divinely functioning reality is one or many. There may be one divine being which is the cause of these results; there may be more than one such being. Again, we do not know whether this being is personal or impersonal. We do not know whether God is more than the universe and its processes, that is, whether God is a being who in some way transcends the universe even though in his activities he is also immanent within the universe. Scientific theology cannot answer these questions. It formulates what can be scientifically known about divine reality, and it provides the indispensable basis upon which all further theological thought must be based and to which it must conform. But it is not adequate in itself to answer all the important questions with which the theologian is concerned.

Scientific empirical theology is not the whole of theology. Within theology proper we can distinguish scientific theology from normative theology and from metaphysical theology. Scientific theology alone gives us knowledge. In both normative theology and metaphysical theology we are dealing with reasoned belief or faith. Within theology one must distinguish that

[29] PRK, p. 209.

material which is fully verified from that which is practically imperative but only partially verified and that which is apparently valuable and not discredited.[30]

NORMATIVE THEOLOGY

Normative theology goes beyond science. As science has its data given to it through perceptual intuition in which reality is disclosed, so normative theology has its basis in what Macintosh terms religious or imaginal intuition. Such intuition is subjective; it is a strong feeling of the reality of an unperceived presence. It is a conviction concerning the nature of transcendent reality. Critical realism with respect to knowledge has disclosed that the reality we know is known only in part. Through our perceptual experiences we become aware of the existence of reality, and we are able to know something of what that reality does. Aside from this, reality transcends perceptual knowledge. But we do have convictions concerning the nature of transcendent reality. These convictions are largely subjective, based on our imaginal intuitions. An example of such an intuition would be the feeling that many men have that the God who exists is the God who is needed for the satisfactory pursuit of the religious life.[31] Such a belief is not known through experience to be true; nonetheless it is a conviction which is subjectively felt to be true.

Can such subjective beliefs form a part of theology? While they do not form a part of scientific theology, they can form a part of normative theology, provided they are critically evaluated and thus become justified as reasonable beliefs. Such evaluation demands that they be in accord with the criteria which govern scientific theology and that they be conformable to or coherent with what is discovered scientifically. In addition Macintosh introduces a pragmatic criterion to which beliefs must be subjected if they are to be regarded as reasonable. He formulates the principle of religious pragmatism thus: "We have the right to believe that those theological doctrines are true which are necessary for the maintenance of the morality which is necessary for the maintenance of the highest well-being of human-

[30] PRK, p. 201.
[31] PRK, p. 368.

ity."[32] Man must act. In practical life a belief is reasonable if it accords with our active tendencies. An idea is theoretically permissible as an object of reasoned belief if it is a necessary presupposition of actions directed toward realization of our fundamental human purposes. This criterion does not permit any belief which may be supported by false rationalization. Again, it must be remembered that it is one criterion along with those criteria which govern scientific theology and is subject to those criteria as well as to the previously formulated results of scientific theology. The pragmatic principle therefore does not stand by itself;[33] it is, however, a necessary further criterion of rational faith.

Given these criteria for testing our religious intuitions, what intuitions are acceptable in the light of critical evaluation? Meaningful religious life involves the commitment of man in trust and confidence that if his will is right he need have no fear of anything the universe can do to him. This moral optimism is practically necessary in that the commitment of one's whole life makes sense only when one feels that the best aims of man and the purposes of God coincide. Furthermore, such optimism is so inspiring that one may say that it is a condition for the realization of the highest ends.[34] Put another way, there emerges within the life of the religious man the imaginal intuition that God is supremely trustworthy and worshipful, fully adequate for all our religious needs.[35]

We are further justified, says Macintosh, in asserting the oneness, the integrated unity and consistency of God. The divinely functioning reality must be at least one, and the burden of showing that it is more than one is on him who would deny the unity of God. This is also justified by the principle of parsimony (not multiplying entities beyond necessity). The reasonable belief that God is one also includes the unity of the immanent and the transcendent aspects of God. Religious intuition also affirms the personal and conscious nature of God. Personality is the highest type of being that we know, and God,

[32] TES, p. 22.
[33] Cf. RC, pp. 17–25.
[34] RC, pp. 46–49.
[35] PRK, p. 361.

in dependably seeking the realization of the highest ideals, is disclosed to us as purposeful, conscious, and personal reality. He is sufficient in power for man's religious needs; this is the practical meaning of omnipotence. And he can be depended on in whatever place and under whatever circumstances we may find ourselves. We therefore can reasonably believe that he is omnipresent. Since he is able to do for us all that needs to be done in order to meet our practical religious needs, we can say that he is wise and, for every practical purpose, omniscient. God is holy love, that is, so far as his character is concerned the God needed for religious life can be reasonably believed to exist. At this point we are also justified in interpreting the effects formulated in the laws of scientific theology as the work of God, the Holy Spirit, rather than the work of a nonpersonal divinely functioning reality.

In the light of what we can reasonably believe about God we are able to say what we can reasonably believe about many other theological topics. A rational belief in immortality is a consequence of our trust in God. The ultimate conservation of all spiritual values, among which must be included the value of individual moral personality, is involved in the belief that God is great enough and good enough to overcome every ultimate threat or disaster. Man is of potentially infinite value as a means to the creation of spiritual values, and one of our basic intuitions is that he is intrinsically valuable in his own right. The values of character and friendship are inseparably bound up with the existence of the individual. Unless these values are to be lost, there must of necessity be continued existence of intelligence, memory, moral activity, and social relations.

In saying that God can be counted on to do all that needs to be done by him for the attainment of the highest spiritual value, we are dealing with the doctrine of divine providence. General providence has to do with the universal actions of God upon all human beings, bringing dissatisfaction and discomfort to those whose lives are morally evil and gradual growth in human fulfillment to those whose lives are directed toward the morally good. There is also special providence for individuals who make the right religious adjustment to God. The laws of scientific theology state what a providential God does for individuals who make the effort to fulfill the special conditions of the religious life.

Human freedom is implied in the foregoing and may, Macintosh declares, be reasonably believed to be true. If man ought to realize the values of moral and spiritual personality, then he must be able to do so. If this is true, then character and all of the other forces which play upon the life of the individual cannot be such that they determine without remainder the choices that man will make. The question of freedom turns on the question whether, in any given situation, the subject might have given more or less attention to an idea or stimulus than in fact he did. That is, though we act within a situation, our reaction to that stimulation, our evaluation of it, is a matter of self-determination within limits. If this is so, then it is at least theoretically possible that some of man's voluntary acts may transcend his already acquired character; rather than already achieved character simply continuing, a change of character may occur in the process of volition or action. Science cannot deny this possibility, and we are justified rationally in believing it as a requirement of moral faith.[36]

In the light of man's moral freedom, any divine predestination to moral evil or purely arbitrary election or rejection must, says Macintosh, be ruled out. A morally perfect God would not be willing for any man ultimately to perish. We cannot say that such a God would work an arbitrary miracle to help one individual and decline to do the same for another. Nor can we say that the disasters suffered by humanity through the orderly processes of nature are to be interpreted as the will of God. They occur within a context of order in which such events can happen as the result of natural processes, but they are not specifically a consequence of the will of God. The natural processes themselves are good, since they are conditions for consistent and integrated beings. Without stable processes within the universe, we could not plan for the future in any rational way, nor would the moral life itself be possible, for it presumes a world stable enough for us to carry out moral aims.[37]

We now come to the critical question concerning the rela-

---

[36] TES, pp. 68–71; RC, Chap IV.
[37] TES, Part III, Chap. V; RC, Chap. VII.

tionship of Christian faith to Macintosh's theology. Nothing that has been said so far depends uniquely upon the person and work of Christ. What has been said is, however, consistent with the Christian faith and in fact serves to explicate much that is contained within the Christian faith. To that extent, Christian beliefs have been shown to be scientifically verifiable and/or rationally justifiable. The whole of scientific and normative theology to this point can be seen as an apology for the truth of Christian faith insofar as Christian faith affirms these truths of scientific and normative theology.

The person and work of Christ has, however, a place within normative theology. For the Christian community and the Christian man, the life and death of the historical Jesus is apprehended in religious intuition as having normative value as a clue to the character, will, and attitude of the transcendent God. "To employ this idea of the Christ-like as a norm for the criticism of all intuitive faith in God is to make use of what is known as the Christocentric principle."[38] Jesus Christ becomes a principle by which the adequacy or inadequacy of our religious intuitions is judged. This does not mean that the attention of theology centers in concern with doctrines about Christ. The center of theological concern is God. What it means is that God is understood in his inmost nature to be like Christ.

But Jesus Christ is not *the* norm of theology for Macintosh. As we have seen, prior to any norms or criteria which we may use for judging what may be reasonably believed, are the criteria of theology as such. The christocentric principle within normative theology is acceptable because Jesus is found to be the primary example within human history of the right religious adjustment to God. When we study the attempts of man to relate himself in an adequate way to divine reality, we find that the highest fulfillment of this human potential is in Jesus; therefore the fullest revelation of God's will toward man is disclosed in Jesus' life.

Jesus Christ is the true moral example in that his love of man, his recognition of the true worth of men, and his regard for every human life exemplified the highest moral values and

[38] PRK, p. 367.

made morality essentially social. He was also the true religious example in that he exemplified in his life the true way of man to God. Through a moral attitude toward a moral God, Jesus sought a relationship to God as the foundation for his relationship to men as well as for its own sake. His moral and religious life constituted a unity in which his life reflected its basis in the will of God. Moreover, he is the true revelation of God. He reveals God through his commitment to the divine in all that he does. His self-surrender to God and the divine quality in his life which came from this self-surrender means that what he does reveals God's will for man. God works in his life, therefore, so that he exercises the divine function of saving man from his sin. For the Christian community he is historically and psychologically the source of salvation. He is the Divine Man because of this divine immanence in him. In affirming the immanence of the divine in Christ, Macintosh does not mean to deny the immanence of the divine elsewhere. Jesus was united with God in the same way in which every human being ought to be united with God. Conversely, it is possible for others to be united to God in the same way in which Jesus was united to God. But the revelation of God in Christ remains normative for the Christian faith.[39]

Macintosh views the virgin birth story as legend, the messianic notions of the second coming and consequent judgment and election as fundamentally mythological. The doctrine of the Trinity, he holds, can be formulated in the light of this view of Christ. The transcendent God, the Father, is immanent in the universe as the Holy Spirit and in the person and work of Jesus as the Son. The transcendent God disclosed to normative theological faith is not different from the immanent God disclosed to empirical theology, and this one God is revealed in Jesus.

Thus in normative theology the revelation of God in Christ can legitimately become the standard by which other revelations are judged. It is consistent with the best that can be discovered through empirical investigation of religious experience, and it is confirmed practically in the life of the committed Christian. The essence of Christian faith can be subjected to

[39] Cf. RC, pp. 149–53; *Personal Religion*, pp. 112–19.

the most rigorous examination and can be shown to involve a reasonable belief.

METAPHYSICAL THEOLOGY

The final test of theology, according to Macintosh, is the submission of theology to the critical examination of metaphysics. Such final criticism by metaphysics is not unique to theology. Every discipline must finally find its ultimate justification through metaphysical analysis. It is the function of metaphysics to combine the more general results of the various sciences in a comprehensive and self-consistent world view. In the course of developing such a world view each of the various sciences will be subjected to critical examination of its assumptions.[40] Metaphysics will be changed by the inclusion of theological results among the data of metaphysics, and theology will be changed by the confrontation of theology with the other data of metaphysics.

An empirical theology will have both problems to suggest to metaphysics and solutions of problems for metaphysical consideration. Clearly, no final solution to the metaphysical problem of the relation of nature and the supernatural is possible which does not take into account the data of theology. Macintosh tentatively suggests that the answer to this problem may be to understand the physical universe as the body of God. We have already seen something of the consequences of theological thought for the problem of determinism and freedom. In addition to these problems, Macintosh sees the problems of substance and activity, mind and matter, body and mind, creation and evolution, mechanism and teleology, law and chance, the one and the many, the absolute and the relative, the finite and the infinite, and good and evil as fundamental metaphysical questions. In all of these questions theological considerations are relevant and no final answer is possible which does not take into account the results of theology. The problem with metaphysics has been that the natural sciences have developed more rapidly than the social and theological sciences, with the consequence that metaphysical solutions have tended to be

[40] PRK, pp. 374-5.

heavily materialistic. Careful and critical investigation can redress this balance.

Theology must, argues Macintosh, submit itself to metaphysical examination. If it refuses this final theoretical test, it would to that extent undermine if not lose the certitude of faith. Scientific theology has a firm basis in empirical knowledge. Combined with normative theology, it has become subjectively certain and reasonable faith. But this subjective certitude must become tentative for the purpose of metaphysical examination in order that it may pass from subjective certitude to objective certainty. Contrary to what Kierkegaard and Barth suggest, theology need not remain in the permanent tension of certainty and doubt. When every test has been supplied the resulting synthesis will be more and more objectively certain. Macintosh is convinced that the final solution of the problems of metaphysics will leave room for the truth of religious faith.[41]

The theological position which Macintosh developed sought to meet the need of religious man in the twentieth century by being adequately critical while at the same time grounding itself on the foundation of religious experience. He sought to provide justification for theological truths through critical philosophical analysis. He was also aware of the historical and psychological dimension of religion and sought to give a sufficient place to historically conditioned and psychologically important normative religious intuitions. Careful analysis of religious affirmations shows that there are levels of meaning and of truth. The aim of theology is to transform beliefs which rest on subjective certitude, so far as possible, to truths which are objectively certain. His final conclusion is that within the limits of what is logically and psychologically possible, "we have the moral right to believe as we must, if we are to live as we ought."[42]

[41] Cf. TES, pp. 249–62; RC, pp. 251–81.
[42] PRK, p. 382.

Bibliography

D. C. Macintosh, *The Problem of Religious Knowledge*, N.Y., Harper, 1940.

No detailed studies about Macintosh are available.

WILLIAM TEMPLE

Joseph Fletcher

Dorothy Sayers in an essay called "The Greatest Drama Ever Staged" says that official Christianity "of late years, has been having what is known as a bad press. We are constantly assured that the churches are empty because preachers insist too much upon doctrine—'dull dogma,' as people call it. The fact is the precise opposite. It is the neglect of dogma that makes for dullness. The Christian faith is the most exciting drama that ever staggered the imagination of man—and the dogma is the drama."

More than any other Anglican theologian in modern times, William Temple has recalled to modern Christians what strong meat the classical faith of the church can be. The Epistle to the Hebrews tells us that "everyone that uses milk is unskillful in the word of *righteousness,* for he is a babe." Archbishop Temple never failed to remark that in the Greek text the word used here is *dikaiosunee,* or "justice"—troublesome, radical, critical, prophetic judgment, not personal, mystical, private rectitude. "But strong meat belongs to them that are of full age, even those who by reason of use have their senses exercised to discern both good and evil" (5:14).

Possibly the most important lesson we have to learn from Temple's life and thought is that the dogma is the drama. The three areas of Christian leadership in which he was especially active were expository and apologetic theology, radical social analysis, and ecumenical thought and effort. In all these enterprises his contributions were solidly grounded in classical Christianity and in a consistently theological frame of reference. After a brief account of his life we will look at what he did and said in each of these three areas. It will be abundantly plain that he was first and foremost a theologian. Temple treated theology as it should be treated—as a method of faith interpretation applicable to every aspect of human life.

"Theological ideas," it has been said, "are created on the Continent, corrected in England, and corrupted in America." If

233

this tart saying has any basis in fact, William Temple played no conscious part in the theological process it describes. Like F. D. Maurice nearly a century before him, he neither cited nor drew upon any Continental theological sources, and only a very few Continental philosophers had any impact on him. He alone among English-speaking theologians of the twentieth century wrote with virtually no reference to such recent architects of Protestant Christianity as Schleiermacher, Kierkegaard, Ritschl, Troeltsch, Schweitzer, nor to those of our own time—Barth, Brunner, and Bultmann.

It is not that Temple was a provincial or a chauvinist. He was never "a little Englishman" or a Colonel Blimp in outlook and feeling. As a young Oxford don he took a leave to sit at the feet of Harnack and Simmel, and another to study with Eucken and Wendt in Jena. He watched the contributions of Continentals cross the Channel through the journals. He used Greek and Latin freely and had a prodigious memory. No doubt his lack of concern with Continental theology was in some measure due to the Catholic and classical orientation of his theology. At the same time his lifelong role in the ecumenical movement is evidence enough that he was not indifferent or antagonistic to Reformation perspectives. Actually his writing was just as sparing of reference to Roman Catholics and the Orthodox as to Continental Protestants.

Temple once told his wife that his highest wish was to "master the great stream of classical theology," but not the Reformers or the disputes of the Counter Reformation. The plain truth is that Temple was every inch an Anglican, standing between Romanism and Protestantism in the *via media* or bridge-church position, at what the French scholar Father George Tavard has called "the crossroads."[1]

PERSONAL HISTORY

William Temple, Archbishop of Canterbury, was the son of an Archbishop of Canterbury. He was "born to the purple" on October 15, 1881, the second son of Frederick Temple, at that time Bishop of Exeter; he died on October 26, 1944. This was

[1] *Protestantism* (N.Y., Hawthorn, 1959), pp. 91–106.

the only father-to-son line ever to sit in St. Augustine's Chair. After becoming a "scholar" at Rugby he went on to Balliol College, Oxford, where as an "exhibitioner" he won honors in classics in the intermediate "moderation" (1902) and in his final examination or "greats" (1904). At Balliol the idealist Edward Caird—and especially his dialectical synthesis of supposedly conflicting views—was a significant influence on Temple. Of the three major concerns in Temple's life, two were already manifest in his undergraduate days—social redemption and the apologetic exposition of the Christian faith. The third, the ecumenical movement, came almost as early: while a young philosophy don at Queen's he began to take an active part in the Student Christian Movement. In 1910 he went as an S.C.M. steward to the Edinburgh meeting of the International Missionary Conference, and following that made a tour as an S.C.M. lecturer in Australia.

During his Balliol days he was elected president of the Oxford Union, a top university distinction. His involvement in social service through the university settlements in London's Bermondsey and Bethnal Green matured quickly into a conviction that the poor had to produce their own leaders and that education was a vital part of the strategy. For this reason he entered the Workers' Education Association with his school friend R. H. Tawney in 1905 and stayed on faithfully as its president from 1908 to 1924. At the same time he began to fly the flag of the Labour Party, keeping on as its consistent but not uncritical supporter all his life. He formally joined the party in 1918, remaining a "card carrier" until 1925, when he took his seat in the House of Lords. Then he quietly dropped his membership to avoid the side issues inevitably associated with adherence— or seeming adherence—to a doctrinaire position. At a Pan-Anglican Congress in 1908 and in *The Economic Review* he said, in language he later modified, that the alternatives were "socialism or heresy."[2]

Upon receiving his degree Temple was offered some thirty posts. He chose a teaching fellowship at Queen's College, and his remarkable gift for analysis and exposition of both abstract

[2] M. B. Reckitt, *Maurice to Temple* (London, Faber and Faber, 1947), p. 412.

and concrete questions soon marked him as a man to watch. Since early boyhood Temple had meant to be ordained, but in 1906 Francis Paget, the Bishop of Oxford, refused to order him deacon because he was only "very tentatively" inclined to accept the Virgin Birth and the bodily resurrection. Randall Davidson, successor to Temple's father at Canterbury, was less cautious and ordained him in 1908. In 1910 he accepted the headmastership of Repton, an old public school in the Midlands. However, he soon learned that he was out of his proper element, and when in 1914 Lord Chancellor Haldane offered him the benefice of St. James' Church in London's Piccadilly, he accepted it gladly.

In London, Temple's preaching and writing caught on with a socially varied public. In 1915 he was made honorary chaplain to the king, and crossed the war-hazardous Atlantic to deliver the Paddock Lectures (on Church and Nation) at General Theological Seminary in New York. In 1916 he married Frances Anson, secretary of the Christian Social Union, of which he was chairman. (No children were born of their lifelong marriage.)

The First World War and the turbulent years just after pushed William Temple into national prominence. The Church of England as the "established" church was under fire, accused of having sold out to Toryism and imperialism. In response to popular disillusionment with the church, Temple led what was largely a young men's fight for a truer measure of Anglican self-government and self-respect. It began first with the National Mission of Repentance and Hope, of which he was secretary; but after the report of the Archbishops' Commission on Church and State (Temple was its youngest member) appeared, the young men converted the mission into a new and broader program called the Life and Liberty Movement (1917).

Temple was chosen to be the leader of the movement and editor of its magazine *Challenge*. The movement aimed both at widening the Church's role in social and industrial life and at setting up a Church Assembly, or national synod. He resigned the St. James pastorate, dropping his income from 2,000 to 700 pounds a year in order to give full time to stumping the country. He sought life and liberty for the church—if necessary, he said, "even at the cost of disestablishment." Evangelicals and high churchmen alike joined in the campaign. Temple, with his love of causes and his distaste for church party-liners, was in his element. Then, in 1919, the House of Commons passed an Enabling Act for the Assembly—a victory for Temple, though less than what he wanted. Later on he was deeply disappointed by Parliament's refusal to allow the 1928 revision of the Prayer Book (and at his request his own funeral service in Canterbury was conducted according to the Revised Book). But in 1919 the Enabling Act was a great step forward.

That same year Temple was given a canonry at Westminster Abbey. It was an almost certain way-station to a bishopric, and in only two years' time he was nominated by Lloyd George as Bishop of Manchester. By then he had already published ten volumes of apologetics and philosophical theology and had contributed to various symposia, such as *Foundations* (1912), a work by seven Oxford theologians on Christian belief for modern times, and *Competition* (1917), produced by an interdenominational "collegium" dealing with social issues.

During his Manchester episcopacy, Temple began chairing the Archbishops' Commission on Doctrine (1925–38), and in 1924 he headed the Interdenominational Conference on Politics, Economics and Citizenship, held in Birmingham. He tried unsuccessfully to mediate in the national coal strike in 1926. He published eight more books. At the 1927 Lausanne Conference on Faith and Order he continued his ecumenical labors, serving as chairman of its continuation committee at gatherings everywhere in Europe. He also took part in the 1928 Jerusalem meeting of the International Missionary Council. In 1928 Prime Minister Stanley Baldwin persuaded Temple to accept the Northern primacy of York. Temple's exposition of theology to students gave him considerable stature in university circles. Sympathizing with the students' doubts and difficulties, he suggested that the church inaugurate a new "associate membership" for those whose fellowship was a moral and spiritual reality but not yet a settled intellectual certainty.

As Archbishop of York (1922–42) Temple became even more of a world figure. He was sworn in on England's Privy Council; an ardent advocate of the League of Nations, he preached at the Disarmament Conference at Geneva in 1932;

and he took the chair on Christian Unity at his first Lambeth (worldwide) Conference of Anglican bishops (1930). He continued to preach university missions; he delivered the Gifford Lectures at Glasgow (November 1932–March 1934); on behalf of the International Convention of the Student Volunteer Movement he revisited the United States (1935–36), at which time he lectured at Harvard, the University of Chicago, and Washington's College of Preachers. At the same time his energies were equal to meeting the demands of his diocese and his obligations as Metropolitan of his province. And with all this he managed to produce in his York period another dozen volumes, in addition to journal and magazine articles and chapters in such important symposia as *Contemporary British Philosophy, Revelation, Men Without Work,* and *Doctrine in the Church of England.*

Ecumenics was much to the fore in Temple's thinking. He worked for Christian unity on all fronts—in evangelism and missions, life and work, faith and order. In 1937 he was active on two commissions of the Oxford Life and Work Conference on Church, Community and State and drafted its Message. Two weeks later he moved to the chair of the Faith and Order Conference in Edinburgh. His leadership naturally put him in the chair of the provisional committee of the World Council of Churches, which met at Utrecht in 1938. In spite of Anglo-Catholic resistance he succeeded in winning the English church's approval of the World Council. Moreover, he asked the Cardinal Secretary of the Vatican for exchange of information and unofficial consultation with Roman Catholic theologians; the Vatican "saw no obstacles in the way."[3]

Cut off from the Continental churches by the Second World War, Temple marshaled his forces at home for the foundation of the British Council of Churches, saying in his sermon at its inauguration that "the primary need is for more clear and united testimony to Christianity itself. The difference between Catholic and Protestant is very small as compared with the difference between Christian and non-Christian." He attended the Amsterdam World Christian Youth Conference just before war broke

[3] F. A. Iremonger, *William Temple* (London, Oxford Univ. Press, 1948), p. 412.

out in the summer of 1939. His chairmanship of the 1941 Malvern Conference—intended to shape Christian thought for "a new society" as part of the nation's war aims—made it quite plain that as he saw it the Anglican communion was not any longer "the conservative party at prayer."[4]

Temple was enthroned at Canterbury as primate of all England on April 23, 1942, following Lang's retirement. It was, said George Bernard Shaw, "a realized impossibility." In plain fact it was rare indeed for a man of letters and learning to be elevated to that seat—in this case one who was also a social liberal, an irenic Christian, and as much distrusted by the Federation of British Industries as he was trusted by the broad mass of Englishmen. His sobriquet was "the people's Archbishop." In that moment of national struggle Winston Churchill had no alternative but to accede to the appointment.

The demands of a wartime primacy, however, were taxing in the extreme for Temple. With the appearance of his *Christianity and Social Order* in 1942, which in its first edition alone ran to 129,000 copies, all major publication ended for him. He lived only two and a half years longer, moving up and down and back and forth across the land—attending "Religion and Life" and Industrial Christian Fellowship meetings, giving quiet days for clergy and laity, lecturing to philosophical societies and civic gatherings, working in the House of Lords for measures like the Butler Act (an education bill). Many of these addresses were gathered together and published posthumously in a volume titled *The Church Looks Forward* (1944). Ironically, he died of gout in spite of being a teetotaler. His death in October 1944 came peacefully a week before his sixty-third birthday.

Temple was much more caught up in church administration and public affairs than the other theologians dealt with in this volume. The preceding account of his life and enterprise is therefore necessary background to an understanding and assessment of his thought. The full flavor of Temple's contributions to what he called "theological philosophy"—to say nothing of the other phases of his thought—comes only when those con-

---

[4] Cf. *Malvern, 1941: The Life of the Church and the Order of Society* (London, Longmans, Green, 1942).

tributions are viewed within the context of his ceaseless activity as a man of affairs. He believed that our times need what Thomas Aquinas did for his, but he never for a moment supposed this to be his own role. He produced no *Summa;* his extensive treatises *Mens Creatrix, Christus Veritas, Nature, Man and God* were put together in spare moments between speeches in the House of Bishops or the House of Lords, ecumenical meetings, episcopal duties, university missions. Yet the "system" implicit in the scores of volumes and essays he wrote is in nearly every way the most comprehensive, versatile, and lucid achievement by an Anglican theologian of this age. Had he gone into a purely academic career his gifts would have guaranteed him a prominent place in British intellectual life, but very likely at the expense of the scope and concreteness which brought his thinking into such close alignment with both the reformer's vision and the apologist's urgency.

THEOLOGY: EXPOSITORY AND APOLOGETIC

Temple approached virtually everything theologically. For him theology was a method, not primarily a body of doctrines. He was convinced that all human problems and concerns must be theologized, i.e., set in a framework of Christian faith. To do this obviously calls for a vast amount of integrative thought, hence his ceaseless concern with the relations of faith and reason. The Christian starts with faith, he held, then his reason uses faith to illuminate every question. Though sympathetic to Anselm's *credo ut intelligam*, Temple insisted that once the leap of faith is made, reason must come into play as its skillful servant and friendly critic. "Faith is not a conclusion but a starting point; reason will enrich its content." Thus "God is for faith not an interference, but a datum," because "the man of faith does not reach his faith by scientific inference."[5] Faith propositions are decisions, not conclusions; thus the so-called logical proofs of the existence of God are only arguments. God is not to be found through a syllogism or a microscope or a telescope.

---

[5] *Thoughts on Some Problems of the Day* (London, Macmillan, 1931), pp. 6–7.

"The primary assurances of religion are the ultimate questions of philosophy."

Reason is, in Temple's view, the lantern with which faith's light is focused. It is also the link between the Christian's believing and his behaving. In this sense Temple was a rationalist. He would not flout or ignore reasonable tests of faith's internal and external consistency. In his method reason's service to faith is correlation, not verification. He had no sympathy with Luther's reference to "Dame Reason" as a whore. As to Barth's dictum that "God is not only unprovable and unsearchable, but also inconceivable," Temple agreed on the first two points but not on the third. He was confident that "by analogy we make progress" in our pursuit of theological questions, "even though we never reach their ultimate solution."[6] He declared firmly, "I see no alternative to the acceptance of the method of analogy."[7]

Like his Balliol teacher Edward Caird, Temple was a man of coherent convictions; to use a distinction come into use since his day, his aptitude was for coherent rather than analytical reason; he thought inclusively, not exclusively. His amazing ability to find middle terms and to mediate apparently divorced or contradictory views in an irenic and conciliatory reinterpretation—so invaluable to the World Council of Churches in its formative, pre-Amsterdam years—he referred to as his "parlour trick." Dean Matthews said that Temple's "comprehensive" method was "fired" by a "synthetic impulse." Temple himself said it was his "temperamental disposition, fortified by the fact that my master in logic was Edward Caird, to start from the assumption that every conviction strongly held is at least partly true, and that, as a rule, our wisdom is to find out, if we can, where this partial truth fits into the whole fabric."[8] In short, his theological method was a decidedly Anglican one.

Temple's third primary category along with faith and reason was revelation. In his view revelation has two dimensions—divine initiative or self-disclosure, and human response or be-

[6] *Nature, Man and God* (London, Macmillan, 1935), p. 441.

[7] *Religious Experience* (London, J. Clarke, 1958), p. 231.

[8] Intro., O. C. Quick, *Gospel and the New World* (London, 1944), p. xii.

lieving apprehension. God makes His mind and will manifest both in His creation (general revelation or "natural theology") and in decisive direct action, most crucially in the God-man event in Christ (special revelation or "revealed theology"). But the total process of revelation is "the coincidence of divinely controlled event and minds divinely illuminated to read it aright."[9] Even the Bible, the Word of God, is refracted or sifted first through the finite personalities of its writers, then through those of its readers. What it reveals depends partly on how it says what it says, partly on how it is "heard." While this is obviously a theory of revelation by inspiration, it is not a gnostic notion of secret saving knowledge given to some and withheld from others; on the contrary, Temple always held that the "believing interpretation" is not a special gift at all but the work of the Holy Spirit through reason, the fellowship of the church, the sacraments, and character-forming experience in human society and brotherhood.

Temple's starting point in his Gifford Lectures was that the difference between natural theology and revealed theology is one of method only, not of content. By the same token he set aside the division commonly made between "philosophy" and "theology," claiming that it is intellectually unrealistic to call the first an enterprise of reason, the second of faith. He held that since reason and faith cannot be artificially disconnected or pulled loose from each other, the true task of theology is to reason clearly and fully (i.e., philosophize) about faith.

In the last analysis, Temple was convinced, faith is a matter not of holding correct opinions but of having personal fellowship with the living Lord. What is offered to men in revelation is not a truth or truths about God but God Himself. Two cardinal principles in Temple's method of theologizing were: (1) man's finite intelligence can at best only apprehend God, not comprehend Him, and (2) faith is essentially not belief about God but a relationship of trust (*pistis*), that is, a moral rather than an intellectual matter. His last formal counsel to "the younger theologians" was to urge their more serious consideration of experiential rather than propositional theology.

[9] *Revelation,* John Baillie and Hugh Martin, eds. (London, Faber and Faber, 1937), p. 107.

On the doctrinal side Temple's theology was centered in the incarnation. Affirming Jesus' simple statement "He that hath seen Me hath seen the Father," he saw Christian theology as "God in the light of the Incarnation" and Christian anthropology as "man in the light of the Incarnation." God became man and preached and taught and died on a cross and rose again. Temple never hesitated to insist on the absurdity and scandal of it, as seen from the Greek perspective. The God who dared to become not only a man but a criminal in a divine act of shocking sacrificial love—this God was his starting point.

At the same time, like F. D. Maurice, Temple in Platonic fashion declared that "Christ is not only *a* man, He is Man."[10] The incarnation added not merely another individual to the human race; it was the confluence of deity and humanity, which "raised our humanity to an entirely higher level, to a level with His own." Temple espoused a strong christocentric doctrine of man in terms of "solidarism" (cf. Maurice's "He is the Head of the Body"). He was confident that what had been done for man metaphysically or essentially or latently in the saving effects of the incarnation—this at-one-ment in Christ—would become historical or existential or realized. The membership of men one with another would come to be known and acknowledged here or hereafter by all. As to the question of the mode by which the divine and human were to be united, Temple was agnostic. He rejoiced that Chalcedon (A.D. 451) only affirmed the fact without saying how. "It would be disastrous," he said, "if there were an official Church explanation of the Incarnation."[11]

In the doctrine of "the Word made flesh" he found a theological foundation for Christian materialism—a dialectical materialism, not unlike Marxism's, in which the incarnational interpenetration of the spiritual and material, as of the divine and human, is the first principle. It was Temple who made the first major break away from idealism in post-Reformation Anglican theology. God acts in history through and by means of material things. Therefore, he said, "Christianity is the most avowedly materialist of all the great religions."[12] The incarnation

[10] *Christus Veritas* (London, Macmillan, 1924), p. 153.
[11] *Ibid.,* p. 134.
[12] *Nature, Man and God,* p. 478.

is a cosmic dialectic, as every sacrament is a particular dialectic. And why does God so act, giving up His wholly otherness? Said Temple, "Although He had no need of us for the fulness of His being, He has need of us for the satisfaction of His love. . . . The World minus God equals zero: God minus the World equals God."[13] Yet because of His loving nature, God conceives and creates and relates; while He does not need objects, He necessitates them!

Temple adhered too firmly to the biblical ethos to conceive of God as anything so impersonal as Being-itself. Men are men only because they are personal beings, and they are personal only because God is personal; they share this capacity for self-identity precisely because they are made in His image. God is not impassive but loving. Therefore God suffered in true patripassian fashion. "Suffering," Temple said, "is not the ultimate evil. Hate is the ultimate evil." In spite of his almost lyric admiration for Greek literature and philosophy, Temple rejected the classicist orientation at any point where it was in opposition to the biblicist orientation. "Christ," he acknowledged, "does not reveal all that is meant by the word God. There ever remains the unsearchable abyss of Deity. But He reveals what it vitally concerns us to know; He reveals God the Father."[14]

For Temple the concepts of incarnation and atonement were inseparable, that is, he saw the Christ event and its consequences as a unity. Some not too careful students of Temple have held that he strongly emphasized the incarnation but neglected the atonement. On the contrary, toward the end of his life, in a time of wars and revolution, he maintained that the contemporary upheavals in human hearts and societies called more for a theology of redemption than one of explanation. He came to emphasize the saving effect of God's incarnation and only secondarily saw in it the key to meaning and existence, for he wanted to encourage contemporaneity in the younger theologians. At the same time he insisted that these two "theologies" —the incarnation-centered and the atonement-centered—are only emphases, are actually part and parcel of each other.

13 *Ibid.*, p. 435.
14 *Readings in St. John's Gospel*, 2 Vols. London, Macmillan, 1939–40), Vol. I, p. 18.

Thus, as Temple saw it, the atonement has both an objective and a subjective side. The objective side is what God had done for man, His taking up of man's being into His own in a new creation ("redemption") and his incarnational revelation of Himself by word and deed. Yet Temple did not believe that the incarnation (nativity, ministry, crucifixion, resurrection, ascension) restored men to a right relation with God as far as God was concerned. "Christ's death and Resurrection did not cause God to be after their occurrence what He was not before." Nevertheless, the revelation of His love was an objective event and a new fact without which men could not be "saved," i.e., enter into the knowledge, worship, and service of God. The subjective side of the atonement is of course man's response to God's offer of Himself, a response which is free and uncoerced. The completion of atonement "is accomplished through our realization of the love of God."

Temple viewed the so-called "moral influence" theories as part of the truth about the atonement. He insisted that even if he wishes to affirm more concerning the atonement, every Christian can agree with Abelard that "Christ by His manifestation of His love awakens love in us, and that is the Atonement."[15] The unconquerable and creative love of God is manifested in the objective fact of the incarnation. The freedom of man is respected in the subjective side—man's ability to say Yes or No, or to say nothing, to God's redeeming sacrifice. But whether or not men respond, the facts of the "new creation" and the "new life" remain.

In Temple's theology, as in the gospels, the Kingdom of God is the key concept. By "Kingdom" Temple meant not so much God's realm as His rule, though his concept encompassed both. Inaugurated by Christ, the Kingdom is eventually to reorder and rule all the structures of life—economic, political, familial, personal, etc. Temple was no pietist, restricting redemption to purely individual and "religious" affairs. The Kingdom is for this world, though not "of" it. He was a "conversionist" in H. Richard Niebuhr's sense: one who believes that ultimately and progressively God's grace will convert the whole world to

---

[15] *Faith and Modern Thought* (London, Macmillan, 1910), p. 133.

His will for it. Temple never, however, endorsed the nineteenth-century idea of automatic or inevitable progress, or the idea of automatic harmony to be found in laissez-faire social philosophy; this error of the American liberal Protestant "social gospel" made little or no headway in either Anglican or Continental social theology. Temple's theology was neither a "bootstrap" one, claiming that men could build the Kingdom by their own powers, nor a "stalemate" theology, holding that God's will cannot be realized within history even though He is Lord of it, that it is something for "beyond" history only. In short, his eschatology was prophetic rather than apocalyptic or gnostic or "pie in the sky."

The church, as Temple understood it, stands in relation to the Kingdom as a means to an end. "As Christ's purpose was to found a Kingdom, so we should think of the Church as the army of that Kingdom." Temple never swallowed the Catholic "heresy" which treats the Church as an end in itself, the highest good. He held that it is related to the Kingdom as batter is to cake—a chief means and ingredient in God's purpose. Still, Temple acknowledged the importance of the extra-ecclesiastical work of the Holy Spirit and of the power of uncovenanted grace The Swedish bishop Yngve Brilioth remarked after Temple's death that "the criticism against Anglo-Saxon theology as founded on a superficial conception of the Kingdom of God cannot be applied to him."[16]

As a consequence of his personalist theology, Temple's anthropology was personalist. He conceived of both human and divine personality as "purposive will organized for action." Will, he held with Plato and Aristotle, is not a faculty or function like emotion and intellect, but the purposiveness which is released when they are integrated. To ask if the will is free is tautologically to ask, "Has the power to choose the power to choose?" Though almost completely ignorant of modern psychology, Temple had a realistic if unsophisticated understanding of it. He declared that personality is the capacity to choose rather than be "hung up" by conflicting desires and reasoning, and that the power of choice, or freedom, is the key to personal status.

---

[16] Iremonger, op. cit., p. 605.

The end and aim of God's creative purpose, Temple held, is the realization of the full personal potential of every human being. In his view personality is the highest and the only intrinsic value, the only value which is always good in itself. Furthermore, he held that there is no good (value) of any kind at all apart from persons. The goodness of a thing "depends for its actuality upon the appreciating mind."[17] And he was insistent that society or fellowship is the matrix of personality; a person is a socialized individual. As he put it (with no knowledge of Buber's "dialogic" thesis), "I am only I in my relationship with You, and You are only You, or capable of being called an *I*, in your relationship with Me."[18] Community, he was sure, progressively engulfs and repairs all fragmentations—of nations, races, classes, etc.

The logic of Temple's understanding of God as purposive will, of creation as a process, and of the Kingdom as *for* yet not of the world, led him to a developmental view of history and providence. All things exist in dynamic, ascending grades, developing upward from matter to life to mind to spirit. Each grade, he said, develops only as it is indwelt by what is above, though it also depends on what is below it. All of this is a process of value-achievement. His world view was akin to Whitehead's and L. S. Thornton's theistic process-doctrine, and was suggested to him by the creative or emergent evolution of Samuel Alexander and Lloyd Morgan.

Temple's view of history as God's creative process was not only purposive (teleological); it entailed moral as well as technical and cultural progress. This is what it means, he insisted, to speak prophetically of God as the Lord of history. Moreover, he not only rejected "automatic" progress in society and culture but also distinguished sharply between moral progress at the level of nature and at the level of grace. Therefore, while he saw in history evidence of human success in moving from stupid to enlightened self-interest, apart from Christ he saw no possibility of disinterested love.

Contrary to the neo-orthodox emphasis, Temple was certain

[17] *Nature, Man and God,* p. 211.
[18] *Christianity in Thought and Practice* (N.Y., Morehouse, 1936), p. 68.

that modern secularized men are not half so blind to the reality of sin as they are skeptical about the reality of grace. He treated sin (especially "original" sin) as selfishness—"self-centeredness and all the welter of evil flowing from it." Most men, he contended, know this experientially even if they do not conceptualize it theologically. What men do not believe is that there is a power greater than their own to help them. Grace, he pointed out, is God himself—not something God "gives" but something He *is,* just as love is not something God "has" but something He *is.* In our experience of grace God gives Himself, as in the sacrament of the altar. And only God can rescue us from our self-captivity. "Education may make my self-esteem less disastrous by widening my horizon of interest; so far it is like climbing a tower, which widens the horizon for physical vision while leaving me still the center and standard of reference."[19] The Pelagian notion that men can of themselves overcome their selfishness was in Temple's opinion the only intrinsically damnable heresy.

The new self that God's love (grace) has "saved" reaches out for wider fellowship. "The true aim of the soul is not its own salvation: to make that the chief aim is to ensure its perdition; for it is to fix the soul on itself as centre."[20] Fellowship is the consequence of grace, as it is the goal of the creative process. Creation's "one increasing purpose" through the ages is to bring about the practical, conscious solidarity of mankind. It has been so from the start of the world. Temple was always careful to describe the "fall" not as an event but as a myth; he discarded all prescientific notions of aboriginal virtue. Savage men in the "garden" were innocent and therefore without virtue morally; their "fall" was a fall upwards to the knowledge of sin and hence to ethical decision and personal responsibility. At the same time, Temple insisted that "none of these evolutionary theories touches the centre of the problem," for over and beyond our not always seeing the goals and demands of God's will (good will), we often do see them yet turn our backs.[21]

Even though he expressed hesitation about "universalism,"

---

[19] *Christianity and Social Order* (N.Y., Penguin, 1942), p. 50.
[20] *Nature, Man and God,* p. 390.
[21] *Citizen and Churchman* (London, Eyre & Spottiswoode, 1941), p. 64.

on balance Temple was confident that God's love would win all men to full fellowship (sonship) with Him by means of their new creation in Christ—if not in this world then in another. He saw through to the hidden salvation-by-works doctrine lurking in the post-Reformation distortion of salvation by faith, i.e., the notion that men are "saved" by their faith in God, when in fact they are saved by His unshakable faith (*pistis*) in them. "All that we can contribute of our own would be the resistance of our self-will. It is just this which love breaks down, and in so doing does not over-ride our freedom but rather calls it into exercise."[22]

THEOLOGY: SOCIAL AND PROPHETIC

Temple's basic ethical position was relativistic. In his view the good is whatever is right, the right whatever is good, in the circumstances. The ideal or standard in his ethics was love as manifested in Christ. Reason, serving love, must in every situation weigh the factors as wisely as possible. What is right in one set of conditions may be wrong in another: "an act cannot, strictly speaking, be wrong in itself."[23] "Universal obligation attaches not to particular judgments of conscience, but to conscientiousness. What acts are right may depend on circumstances . . . but there is an absolute obligation to will whatever may on each occasion be right."[24] For this reason he opposed absolutist pacifism, even though he defended and protected pacifists. As a matter of Christian ethics he identified justice as the social dimension of the love norm. "It is axiomatic that Love should be the predominant Christian impulse, and that the primary form of Love in social organization is Justice. . . . Love, in fact, finds its primary expression in Justice."[25] In short, Temple regarded justice as love (neighbor concern) facing the fact that we have many neighbors, that rarely if ever is it just one individual whose claims are binding on us.

[22] *Nature, Man and God*, p. 469.
[23] *Essays in Christian Politics* (London, Longmans, Green, 1927), p. 123.
[24] *Nature, Man and God*, p. 405.
[25] *Christianity and Social Order*, p. 75.

A second feature of Temple's ethics was his concept of "natural order," which he sometimes called natural law. Actually, however, his personalistic view of value (it has to be worth something to some person) and his extrinsic, relativistic view of obligation (acts are never right or wrong in themselves) were not consistent with classical natural law theory. He never spoke, as would a Roman Catholic moral theologian, of "natural" moral laws "discernible by human reason" and "given in the nature of things." He believed that this doctrine had lost out when it had sought to fix forever a "special relation to a feudal and peasant society."[26] What he meant by "natural order" was a given God-willed, functional means-end pattern of life. For example, he argued teleologically that in the natural order of economics goods are produced to satisfy human needs, and finance assists the exchange of goods and labor: finance exists for production's sake, production for consumption's sake. When bankers control and even restrain industrialists, and industrialists control and even restrain the supply of goods, ends are subordinated to means, and *inordinatio* (i.e., sin) results.

Temple followed Aquinas and Aristotle in the view that man is a *zoön politikon,* a social being. A person, he said, is an individual in community: a socialized individual. Society is an "order" of creation: it is real or natural in the sense of original or elemental. Hence the social order was of vital concern to his basic relationship theology. The state he insisted, is only an agency of society (although important as such); politically to identify state and society or to subordinate society "is the one great heresy."[27] Hence his theological emphasis on democracy.

To Temple the state was good though corruptible; he did not concur with the libertarian notion that the best government is the least government. In fact, in this regard he stood in the tradition of Plato, St. Paul, Augustine, Aquinas, Luther, Calvin, Hooker, and (interestingly) Marx, rather than with John Milton, Thomas Jefferson, Guizot, Cavour, and the liberal Protestant separationists. This partly explains his genuine preference (even in the Life and Liberty Movement) for a church-state coalition provided it could be maintained on terms suitable to the Gospel's

[26] *Ibid.,* p. 79.
[27] *Christianity and the State* (London, Macmillan, 1928), p. 45.

integrity. "We have a divine commission; we exist as a divine creation. If the earthly State likes to associate with us, let it."[28] Temple was too Anglican and too irenic to embrace a doctrinaire social ideology. He called himself a Christian socialist, in the line of F. D. Maurice, Kingsley, Westcott, Gore, and others. As an Oxford don he was a convinced adherent of evolutionary socialism, and he never abandoned it. Yet in a lecture tour in Australia in 1910 he was already qualifying his socialism by acknowledging some good in private enterprise; he favored "free enterprise conducted in a spirit of public service."[29] By the thirties he was an advocate of economic pluralism or a "mixed" economy. "Our problem," he said, "is to get the best out of both" capitalism and socialism.[30] For obvious theological reasons he was never a Marxist. Yet as a sacramentalist he appreciated the Marxist concept of dialectical materialism and once thought of calling his Gifford Lectures "A Study in Dialectical Realism." "The Christian understanding of history," he said, "has much closer affinites with the Marxist view than with the interpretations of Christianity in terms of idealistic thought."[31] Nevertheless, he found Marx "not a profound or an accurate thinker."[32] And he had a radical distaste for communist dictatorship. As a socialist he recognized that technology and interdependence ("collectivism") constitute an irreversible trend and that planning is necessary; hence, he argued dialectically, we can preserve personal freedom only by planning for it.

Temple thought that the church's task is to teach principles, the individual Christian's to try to find their application; he allowed for disagreement on the latter but not on the former. As to the pietistic objection that the church should not interfere with political and economic policies, he countered that through its members it "is bound to 'interfere' because it is by vocation the agent of God's purpose, outside the scope of which no human interest or activity can fall."[33] Needless to say, he met

---

[28] *The Church Looks Forward* (N.Y., Macmillan, 1944), p. 130.
[29] *Essays in Christian Politics*, p. 44.
[30] *Christianity and Social Order*, p. 102.
[31] *Religious Experience*, p. 254.
[32] *Christianity and the State*, pp. 82–83.
[33] *Christianity and Social Order*, p. 21.

strong and sometimes quite vicious opposition in big business and Tory circles—which only added delight to the English masses' pride in his leadership. Some of his concrete proposals (to be found in the Appendix to his *Christianity and Social Order*)—among them elimination of outside investors in favor of ownership of enterprises by their managers and laborers, public control of production, socialization of credit and banking, a "mutual-export" plan for international trade (a plan foreseeing the European Common Market), public ownership of urban land and control of rural land—are worth attention even today.

THEOLOGY: ECUMENICAL AND MISSIONARY

Christian unity took as much of Temple's time and attention as social witness, but it was a concern that found expression primarily in sermons and addresses rather than in published material. He was fully committed to the Anglican Communion as being both Catholic and evangelical, i.e., encompassing both the genius for order and the genius for freedom and personal decision. In Catholicism he saw the dangers of rigidity, lack of sympathy, legalism and magic; in Protestantism the dangers of sectarian atomization, one-sidedness at the expense of the total Christian heritage, and Pelagianism or self-sufficiency. Anglicanism, he believed, best avoided this complex of faults; it was therefore for him a bridge church to help reunite not only fragmented Protestantism and Orthodoxy but Catholicism too. As between the "high" and "low" wings of Anglicanism, the pluralist Temple usually endorsed their affirmations and discounted their negations.

In accordance with the Lambeth Quadrilateral, Temple held to the necessity of episcopal ordination, but he was always quick to point out that while such ordination confers authority to administer the sacraments, their power or efficiency comes from Christ. He declared that the requirement of administration by a priest has all along meant only that it *should* be, not "can only be."[34] He thought it "a shocking presumption to question

[34] *York Diocesan Leaflet* (July 1931).

the reality of the Sacraments administered, for example, in the Presbyterian Church of Scotland or the Lutheran Church of Germany."[35] Ordination by bishops is, he held, *bene esse* only. And this principle he extended to lay ministrations too—in emergencies, even of the eucharist (as with baptism). And he looked forward to the eventual ordination of women.

Temple worked by discussion and debate for "a fuller and worthier conception of the Church than any of us hold today."[36] In the meantime he held to the Quadrilateral, even to the point of opposing open communion except at ecumenical gatherings. The Church of South India's agreement on limited intercommunion with the Church of England had his full support, as did the C.S.I. itself. Temple was always definite about distinguishing unity from uniformity, and sought, as a good pluralist and dialectician, to avoid the latter. He favored doctrinal and liturgical variety within dogmatic unity. Concerning the C.S.I. he said to his high-church critics that it limited ordination to bishops, which is what the Anglican churches do, and he urged his critics to make sure they do not impose on others more stringent terms of union than obtain among the Anglicans themselves (a simple piece of ecumenical ethics!).

Temple foresaw a united church which would include all three basic principles of polity—episcopal, presbyterial, congregational—as well as the distinctive genius of both Catholic and Protestant Christianity. And his deep involvement in Protestant and Orthodox ecumenics never closed his eyes to Rome and its people. At many church assemblies he spoke of his regret at their absence. (He would have rejoiced at the presence nowadays of Catholic observers at such gatherings. He used to say, "I think reunion with Rome is so far off that it need not trouble us just now; there are other things to do; but I would certainly refrain from anything which made ultimate reunion more difficult. And so I hold fast to my Catholic doctrines."[37] Just as he warned the "party" men in his own communion that their real enemies are "the world, the flesh, and the devil," so he insisted that "the difference between Catholic and Protestant is very

---

[35] *Thoughts on Some Problems of the Day,* p. 112.
[36] Iremonger, *op cit.,* p. 406.
[37] In Harold Begbie, *Painted Windows* (N.Y., Putnam's, 1922), p. 187.

small compared with the difference between Christian and non-Christian."[38] The communion prayer for "the whole state of Christ's Church" is offered alike for Rome, the Eastern bodies, the Reformation churches, and the "sectaries."

The archbishop was twenty-five years ahead of the new emphasis in mission theology—the emphasis that the churches do not *have* missions but are missions. Said Temple: "To be a Christian is to be a missionary," drawing men to or driving them from Christ.[39] As with his view of creation, atonement, the Kingdom and so on, he saw conversion as a process rather than an event, gradual instead of suddenly effected. "The beginning is to admit the Lord to our lives at all. But when that is done there are many doors still to be opened."[40] He listed some of these doors: true citizenship, decent housing, economic democracy, wider education—not the pious abstractions and intimate personal details in the ordinary "devotional" treatise!

There were two cardinal principles in Temple's view of Christian mission. One was that Christian witness must be expressed through socially redemptive action and socially relevant theology, for the setting of today's evangelism is a sick society in need of the Christian remedy. But the remedy has to be offered in relevant terms, else it will be pushed aside; communication of the Gospel calls for social theology. The other principle was "the ministry of the laity"—because the laity constitutes the church in the world, and "the actual leavening of the world's lump with the energies of the Kingdom of Heaven must be done by laymen."[41]

Temple's faith was that God's creation, that is, His spreading Kingdom, was moving toward one world as well as one church. As with the ecumenical effort, so he found ecumenical politics in the League of Nations (and would have found it in the United Nations). In his theistic belief that history's process moves from heterogeneity to homogeneity he went far enough to predict that the Christian-unity effort would some day be superseded by a

---

[38] *The Church Looks Forward*, p. 32.
[39] *Basic Convictions* (N.Y., Harper, 1936), p. 79.
[40] *Personal Religion and the Life of Fellowship* (London, Longmans, Green, 1926), p. 81.
[41] *Citizen and Churchman*, p. 61.

faith-unity development. It gave Arnold Toynbee great satisfaction to quote in his *Study of History* from Temple's *Readings in St. John's Gospel:* "All that is noble in the non-Christian systems of thought or conduct is the work of Christ upon them and in them. There is only one divine light; and each has only a few rays of that light, which needs all the wisdom of all the traditions to manifest the entire compass of the spectrum."[42] Yet Temple was no eclectic. His Lord was, as he put it in the titles of his major expositions, *Christus Veritas,* the source of whatever is valid anywhere, and the *Mens Creatrix,* the creative guiding intelligence of all the world.

[42] *Readings in St. John's Gospel,* Vol. I, p. 10.

Bibliography

William Temple, *Nature, Man and God,* N.Y., St. Martin's, 1960.

Joseph Fletcher, *William Temple, Twentieth-century Christian,* N.Y., Seabury, 1963.

NICOLAI BERDYAEV

Matthew Spinka

Nicolai Berdyaev (1874–1948) has been steadily gaining recognition among the cultured Western circles as the philosopher of the spirit, of freedom, and as a fighter against the contemporary dominant secularist tendencies which deny man his spiritual nature and thus reduce him to a mere psychosomatic being. Accordingly, he stressed man's spiritual nature as against the generally held materialistic conception. He once defined his philosophy as

> the science of the spirit. And the science of the spirit is above all the science of human existence. It is in the human existence that the meaning of being is revealed. . . . And the existential philosophy is precisely the knowledge of the meaning of being through the subject. The subject is existential. . . . In that sense philosophy is subjective and not objective. It is founded on spiritual experience.[1]

But before Berdyaev arrived at this mature Christian and existentialist view of man and reality he had to struggle with views that were quite foreign to it. He was born in Kiev of an ancient Russian noble family. His father, Alexander Mikhailovich, was a retired officer of the Cavalier Guard, who intended his son for the elite military service. His mother was half French and never learned correct Russian. Nicolai had a brother, Sergei, fifteen years his senior, an eccentric, whose son, Alexander, is the sole surviving member of the Berdyaev family, and still lives in the Soviet Union. From childhood Nicolai felt "alone and rootless in this world,"[2] the real world being the one of his imagination. He was naturally of the Platonic bent of mind, and

---

[1] "Ma Conception philosophique du Monde," in *Bulletin de l'Association Nicolas Berdyaeff*, Paris, April 1953.

[2] Donald A. Lowrie, *Rebellious Prophet: A Life of Nicolai Berdyaev* (N.Y., Harper, 1960), p. 21.

this characteristic remained his guiding principle throughout life. He read all sorts of books before he entered the Cadet Corpus school at the age of ten. Left to himself, he developed an exceedingly strong tendency toward self-direction, refusing to accept orders from anyone. He became both physically and intellectually fastidious. In his old age he recorded in his spiritual autobiography: "I often close my eyes, ears, and nose. The world is filled with odors for me."[3] In the school he could not endure the coarseness and ignorance of the other boys as well as the poor quality of the teaching offered him, both of which he regarded as stupid. His philosophical precociousness set him apart from his fellows—a solitary, serious youngster eager to find some sense to life. He confessed in his autobiography that during his school days he was "a regular monster." Nevertheless, he graduated from the school, and at the age of twenty he entered the University of Kiev, enrolling at first in the natural science department—which was then exceedingly popular as being in line with the prevailing materialism; but within a year he transferred to the faculty of law. He continued his private devotion to philosophical studies as before—he had already become well grounded in Kant, Schopenhauer, Hegel, and Nietzsche. His only friend was Leon Shestov, a Jew, who later became a notable philosopher in his own right.

Berdyaev underwent a spiritual crisis which at first turned him against the existing conditions in society, particularly his own aristocratic class, and which led him, in 1894, to accept the then fashionable Marxism. But it was impossible for his independent spirit ever to become a doctrinaire conformist. Because of his unusual philosophical proficiency, he was acknowledged within a few years as the principal ideologist of the Social Democratic party in Kiev and as such was associated with Lunacharsky (later the Soviet commissar of education), and in Zurich he met Plekhanov. He plunged into the revolutionary activity among the workers and his fellow students; but finally, in 1898, the police arrested him along with 150 other students. After two years of imprisonment he was sentenced to

---

[3] *Samopoznanie* (Paris, YMCA, 1949), p. 351. My translation. (An English ed. was published by Macmillan in 1951, under the title *Dream and Reality: An Essay in Autobiography*.)

three years of exile in the Vologda province (an "easy" exile center). Berdyaev lived there in the best room of the best hotel of the town, free to have contacts with other revolutionaries, to order all the books he wanted, and to write and publish almost as he pleased (subject to moderate censorship). He published during this time his first major work, *Subjectivism and Individualism in Social Philosophy.* The book already betrayed a clear "deviationism" from orthodox Marxism of such of his fellow exiles as Lunacharsky and Bogdanov.

During the third year of his exile he was permitted to remove to Zhitomir in Volhynia. After his return to Kiev, Berdyaev made the acquaintance of Sergius Bulgakov, then professor of economics at the Polytechnic Institute, who was already moving from Marxism to Christianity. The latter ultimately entered the Orthodox Church as priest and after his exile from the Soviet Union became the outstanding Russian Orthodox theologian and the dean of the Paris Orthodox Theological Academy. He helped Berdyaev to make the transition to the Christian faith, although Dostoevsky's religious views had been even more influential in aiding him to make the radical change. This is particularly true of the concept of Christianity expressed with overwhelming power in Dostoevsky's "Grand Inquisitor," which Berdyaev made practically his own. Bulgakov was also instrumental in directing two sisters, Eugenie and Lydia Trushev, daughters of a prominent Kiev lawyer, to Berdyaev, who was already regarded as a dominant intellectual leader. He later married Lydia.

In 1904 Berdyaev moved to St. Petersburg and joined there the brilliant literary circle consisting of such luminaries as Vyecheslav Ivanov, Vasily Rozanov, Dmitry Merezhkovsky and his wife, Zinaida Hippius, as well as the symbolist poets Alexander Blok and Andrey Byely. They met weekly in Ivanov's celebrated "Ivory Tower." Berdyaev's definite conversion to Christianity falls within this period (1907), as is witnessed by his chapter contributed to *The Milestones,* a kind of manifesto of the seven contributors who thereby signalized the radical change of their views. Included among the contributors were the two later leaders of the Russian religious movement, Bulgakov and Frank. Nevertheless, the Christianity which Berdyaev now embraced was not the "official" kind identified with the Holy Governing Synod—to which he remained opposed, at times even violently. In his autobiography he writes: "I never pretended that my religious thought had a churchly character. I sought the truth and experienced as truth that which was revealed to me."[4] Along with the other Russian religious thinkers from Alexey Khomyakov onward, Berdyaev distinguishes between the Church composed of all who are truly redeemed and dominated by the spirit of Christ—this being the essential meaning of the Russian concept of *sobornost*, approximating the Western concept of the Church invisible—and the mere external and formal membership in the outward institution of the Church. Only the former compose the real body of Christ. It is this distinction which the official Russian Church repudiates. Nevertheless, Berdyaev did not reject the sacraments of the historic Church and did not neglect communicating in them. "Philosophy is my calling," he writes, "but sacraments of the Church are the very essence of life."[5]

In 1912 Berdyaev went to Italy for a year. It was at Capri that he at last caught a glimpse of his own religious vision of life and embodied it in "one of the most important books of his life, *The Meaning of the Creative Act,*"[6] to the fuller explication of which he devoted his entire subsequent literary career. After his return to Russia in 1913 he plunged into a violent struggle with the Holy Governing Synod by publishing an article titled "Quenchers of the Spirit." He was arrested and charged with blasphemy—an offense then punishable by exile to Siberia for life. But the outbreak of the First World War delayed the trial, and the subsequent catastrophe of the revolution quashed it.

During the war Berdyaev found himself unable to join either the revolutionaries, from whom he had felt estranged ever since his conversion, or the Kerensky regime. After the October Revolution he bitterly denounced the Bolsheviks, writing of them: "The Russian revolution has turned out to be a consistent application to life of Russian nihilism, atheism, and ma-

---

[4] *Ibid.*, p. 199.
[5] Quoted in Lowrie, *op. cit.*, p. 221.
[6] *Ibid.*, p. 134.

terialism. . . . This . . . leads to destruction of all values."[7] He likewise wrote a fierce denunciation of the revolution in his *Philosophy of Inequality*, which, however, could not be published in Russia. Berdyaev likewise refused Lunacharsky's appeal to writers to serve the new regime. Thereupon he and his wife and sister-in-law were compelled to join a labor battalion detailed to clean the railroad tracks in winter, when the temperature often fell to twenty degrees below zero. Nevertheless, he was invited to lecture in a state institution and allowed a free hand in choosing his subjects. He even organized a Free Academy of Spiritual Culture, which was permitted to exist for three years. At one time he was called before the dreaded head of the Cheka, Felix Dzerzhinsky, and in a forty-five-minute speech he frankly expounded to him his religious, philosophical, and moral reasons for the faith that was in him. Dzerzhinsky not only heard him through without interruption but even set him free and sent an escort to accompany him home; Berdyaev could not, however, leave the city without permission. In 1920–21 he was elected by the university faculty to lecture there—a remarkable tribute to him, since he had not finished his university course and hence had no degree. During the four years following the revolution he wrote several books of outstanding merit, characterized by a remarkable freedom of expression: *Worthiness of Christianity and Unworthiness of Christians,* which he had delivered as lectures to large audiences of skeptics and unbelievers; *Meaning of History,* which is also of permanent value for the understanding of his thought; and *Dostoevsky,* still one of the best interpretations of the religious message of the great novelist.

But in 1922 conditions changed for the worse, the men in power no longer "knew Joseph" and consequently decided not to tolerate those former intellectual leaders who still refused to conform to the new order. Berdyaev was imprisoned and banished along with others from the Soviet Union, and forbidden ever again to return on pain of death. He was at first taken to Berlin, which was then the intellectual center for the one and a half million Russian émigrés. Berdyaev always insisted that he

[7] Quoted in *ibid.,* p. 146.

was not an émigré but an exile, and as such was not well received by those who had left Russia voluntarily. But with the collapse of the German currency he could not make his very slender means suffice and moved, along with others of the intellectual elite in similar dire circumstances, to Paris, where he lived for the rest of his life. An English lady, Mrs. Florence West, an admirer of his religious philosophy, left him a legacy with which he was able to buy a small house in Clamart, a suburb of Paris, which thus became his permanent home.

The Paris period was Berdyaev's most fruitful in literary production. He published here in Russian the large number of books which in French, English, German, and many other translations made him famous and established him in the West as one of the most notable of contemporary Christian thinkers. He also engaged in other activities: he became the editor of the Russian publications issued in an astonishingly large number by the Y.M.C.A. Press, and which made it possible for the exiled Russian intellectuals to engage in literary work. Nowhere else had a similar opportunity been offered them. He also edited a periodical, *Put'* (The Way), which contains many valuable articles both by him and others. Furthermore he lectured extensively, particularly among the Russian youth, and entertained discussion groups in his own house. He did not participate to any great degree in the political activity of his fellow countrymen, and in turn was severely criticized by them. He even refused to follow Metropolitan Eulogius of Paris, the ecclesiastical head of the Orthodox Russians in the West, when the latter cut himself off from the Moscow patriarchal jurisdiction and placed himself under the authority of the Patriarchate of Constantinople. Nevertheless, Berdyaev continued to hold the metropolitan in high personal esteem. Toward the end of his life he conceived a great admiration for Father Stefan (Svetozarov), despite the latter's return to the Soviet Union. Father Stefan wrote of Berdyaev after the latter's death: "I consider him a faithful member of the Orthodox faith."[8] This testimony contrasts favorably with the adverse judgment of some outstanding Russian churchmen who denounce him as heretical,

[8] Quoted in *ibid.,* p. 221.

or at least insufficiently Orthodox. It must be remembered that in the religious sphere Berdyaev was isolated even from his wife, Lydia, who had been converted to Roman Catholicism before leaving the Soviet Union. He died in 1948 at his writing desk as he was ready to engage in his customary daily task.

We may now turn to a succinct summary of his religious thought, chiefly on the basis of his works published after his removal to Paris. They represent his mature thought, for they were written after he reached his fiftieth year. He always insisted that he was a religious philosopher, not a theologian. As such it was paramount that he establish, first of all, firm philosophical foundations for his religious faith. Starting with Kant, whose critical distinction between the phenomenal (scientific) and noumenal (ethical) realms he accepted as the basis of his own existential philosophy, he blazed a path to an apprehension of the spiritual realm—a position not reached by Kant, although the latter prepared the way for it. Accordingly, Berdyaev regarded Kant as the philosopher of freedom. Berdyaev makes a fundamental distinction between the world of objects and the world of the spirit. The former is subject to natural laws and therefore determined by them: there is no freedom in it. It is only in the latter, the spiritual realm, that freedom exists. He writes: "The chief characteristic of my philosophical type consists above all in that, that I have placed as the basis of my philosophy not being, but freedom. Not a single other philosopher has done that in such a radical form."[9] Man is a unique being in so far as he is the meeting point of both the material and the spiritual realms: he is thus a microcosm. Nevertheless, in him as in all reality the spiritual is primary; the objective, the ontological, is secondary. Being is identified by him with matter, while existence is synonymous with the spiritual realm, which is freedom. "Existence is not essence, is not substance; it is a free act."[10] "Spirit is not being, but the existent, that which exists and possesses true existence, and is not subject to determination by any being at all. Spirit is not a principle, but personality, in other words the highest form of existence."

[9] *Samopoznanie*, pp. 58–59.
[10] *Truth and Revelation* (N.Y., Scribner's, 1953), p. 12.

"Freedom cannot have its source in being, nor be determined by being: it cannot enter into a system of ontological determinism."[11]

Accordingly, in Berdyaev's view to identify the objective with the real, as is often done in scientific systems and is always done in materialism, is a fundamental and pernicious error. Science properly delimited deals exclusively with objects, matter, things, and as such is justified in its methods; however, this is far from including all reality, the existence proper where alone meanings are found. There are no meanings as such in objects, in mechanical contrivances, no matter how ingenious they might be. Meanings are imparted to objects solely by persons who alone are capable of conceiving them, since they partake of the spiritual realm: hence meanings are subjective, not objective.

The common misunderstanding of the proper character and function of these two realms results in "objectifying" the spiritual into the material, converting a subject into an object, a thing. To Berdyaev this represents the origin of most if not all the evil in the world. This is in essence what materialism invariably and necessarily does. The commonest example of this universal practice is the treatment of human beings as if they were merely psychophysical organisms, a chemical laboratory walking on two legs and driven by a variety of impulses all of which are physical. This denies man's spiritual nature and results in his being looked upon as a commodity: "in short, whenever man is used as a means rather than an end, objectification takes place."[12] This is for Berdyaev the "fallen world." And the worst about it is that it is we who create it; God does not. He afflicts no man, for there is no evil in Him.

Objectification of the world takes place through our agency and for our sakes, and this is the fall of the world, this is its loss of freedom, and the alienation of its parts. . . . Objectification is the ejection of man into the external, it is an exteriorization of him to the conditions of space, time, causality and rationaliza-

---

[11] *The Beginning and the End* (N.Y., Harper, 1952), pp. 103–4.
[12] Matthew Spinka, *Nicolas Berdyaev, Captive of Freedom* (Philadelphia, Westminster, 1950), p. 107.

tion. But in his existential depth man is in communion with the spiritual world and with the whole cosmos.[13]

Consequently man, by being denied his spiritual nature and treated only as a physical being, is degraded, dehumanized, and his personality destroyed. No genuine community is possible where spiritual communion, the I-Thou relationship, is absent. All intercourse is reduced to a lower, impersonal level and thus "objectified."

It is on the basis of these considerations that Berdyaev constructs his concept of God and man. As for God, or rather the Godhead, He is in Himself beyond all possibility of apprehension by the human mind: for as well could a child scoop up the ocean in his sand pail as man by his mind grasp God in His essence. Nevertheless, it has pleased God to reveal Himself in such a way that man can grasp something of the divine. But Berdyaev never tires of warning men—particularly theologians—against assuming that they can construct a neat logical system in which to enclose and delimit even the revealed God. This is the distinction he makes between the "apophatic" and the "kataphatic" ways of knowing God—God apprehended in a mystical experience of the human spirit meeting with the divine Spirit, and a logical construct of a purely intellectual or philosophical system. Thus God has revealed Himself to some degree in nature and history, but this revelation is so variously conceived by men as to be self-contradictory, a matter of opinion and therefore relative. It is only in His revelation by incarnation in Jesus Christ that we possess an authentic, supreme, and final self-revelation of God, even though this is likewise but inadequately apprehended by men. We are thus reduced to a personal encounter with the divine in the depths of our consciousness—to an intuitive apprehension of God. "Christian dogma is merely a symbolism of spiritual experience."[14] God cannot be known by reason alone, or by some scientific method of analysis, for He is not an object, a thing, but Spirit, a subject. "Our knowledge of God is, therefore, basically intuitive, subjective, experiential, or, if you will not blanch at the word, mys-

[13] *The Beginning and the End*, pp. 56, 60.
[14] *Spirit and Reality* (N.Y., Scribner's, 1939), p. 140.

tical. It is neither exclusively intellectual, emotional, volitional, nor intuitive, but rather integral, combining all these four together with the additional element that results from this integral approach."[15]

But Berdyaev's rejection of the ontological interpretation of reality, his insistence on the primacy of existence as against being, leads him to reject the current doctrine of God as creator. God is *not* Being or the Ground of being, for He is Spirit.

> God does not act everywhere in this objectified world. He was not the Creator of this fallen world. He does not act and he is not present in plague and cholera, in the hatred which torments the world, or in murder, war and violence, in the trampling down of freedom or in the darkness of the ignorant boor. Doctrines of that sort have even led men to atheism. . . . God is present and God acts only in freedom. . . . God is to be found in Truth, in Goodness, Beauty and Love, but not in the world order. . . . God is Spirit and he can operate only in Spirit and through Spirit.[16]

But in that case, how was matter created and by whom? This stark, unexplained dualism, even though it asserts an undoubted truth when applied to the perverted thought of man and the many evils consequent upon it, fails to account for the cosmic objective reality, which certainly cannot be ascribed to man's "objectification"! For it surely cannot be asserted that it was the perverted thought of man that created the material world. Whence then evil? The only glimpse of relief of this dilemma is in defining as evil only that which is the direct result of man's evil will, while designating the natural evils as calamities inseparable from the very nature of matter.

Accordingly, Berdyaev rightfully rejects any causal connection between evil and God. He traces it to the nature of freedom: "Evil and suffering exist because freedom exists; but freedom has no foundation in existence, it is a frontier. But because freedom exists, God himself suffers and is crucified. The Divine love and sacrifice are an answer to the mystery of free-

---

[15] My article on Berdyaev's existentialism in Carl Michalson, ed. *Christianity and the Existentialists* (N.Y., Scribner's, 1956), p. 63.

[16] *The Beginning and the End*, pp. 151-52.

dom wherein evil and suffering have their origin."[17] We are here touching upon some of the most difficult and controversial aspects of Berdyaev's thought: since evil originates in freedom, is God not responsible for making evil possible by creating spirits with the fatal endowment of freedom? In order to parry this thrust commonly made against his thought, Berdyaev resorts to Jacob Boehme's cosmogonic speculations and asserts that freedom is *uncreated, not* created by God. But it seems that this is more of an evasion than a solution of the mystery; it would have been better had Berdyaev followed his own advice and treated the mystery in the apophatic, rather than the kataphatic, fashion. He himself admits that the idea of "uncreated freedom" has been generally unintelligible to his readers, although for him it "has become ever more clearly etched." Nevertheless, he confesses that "I remained altogether alone in my view."[18] Perhaps he best expressed the necessity of such a view when he wrote: "Freedom cannot be derived from being, for it would then be determined."[19] Moreover, without freedom, men would not be intelligent, morally responsible beings, but mere automata.

Turning now to his conception of man, he asserts, following Kant, that human personality is the greatest value in the world: "I became a Christian not because I ceased to believe in man, in his dignity and supreme destiny, in his creative freedom, but because I sought a much deeper and more actual basis for that faith."[20] But it is the human personality that he identifies with the supreme value, not the psychosomatic organism that he calls individuality. Only as man secures spiritual victory over his physical nature—what Apostle Paul calls the flesh—does he become a person. Accordingly, personality is an attainment, not an endowment, and presupposes a struggle. Many, perhaps most, individuals never become persons. Nevertheless, the three elements composing man—body, soul, and spirit—form a unity.

The individual is born within the generic process and belongs to the natural world. Personality, on the other hand, is a spiritual

[17] *Spirit and Reality,* p. 115.
[18] *Samopoznanie,* p. 239.
[19] *Toward a New Epoch,* p. 98.
[20] *Samopoznanie,* p. 191.

and ethical category. It is not born of a father and mother, it is created spiritually and gives actual effect to the divine idea of man. Personality is not nature, it is freedom, and it is spirit.[21]

Man is a whole creature, an organism compounded of spirit, soul and body. . . . *Spirituality* is not opposed to *body* or *matter* but implies its transformation . . . personality. Its realization is achieved through the victory of spirit over the chaotic elements of soul and body. . . . The spirit is derived from the Logos, while the soul is cosmic.[22]

Berdyaev thus accepts the Christian dogma of the "fallen" state of man, although he places the "fall" in the spirit's pre-existence.[23] The spirit fell by a free choice, not by any divine fiat of predestination. In its earthly existence it likewise remains in the "fallen" state by its own act of self-assertion. Therein consists its individuality. But man may be saved by the grace of God, which is ever available, ever offered to him, were he willing to accept it. Thus man's salvation from the state of alienation consequent upon his self-assertion is likewise an act of his own will, or rather an act of cooperation with the proffered grace of God. For God ever yearns that man should not perish but have eternal life; and He has revealed His gracious purpose supremely in Jesus Christ. For Christ is not only the revelation of God as *agape*—the love that seeks those who are not worthy of that love and could never deserve it by their own efforts, no matter how heroic; he is also the divine revelation of what man may and ought to be. The incarnation of the divine Logos reveals the God-Man and makes possible the transformation of the merely human into the divine-human. This is the doctrine of Godmanhood, taught by Eastern theologians from Irenaeus onward, but particularly in the recent Russian religious renaissance by Feodor Dostoevsky, Vladimir Soloviev, Sergius Bulgakov, and Nicolai Berdyaev. To use the latter's philosophical term, this is the process whereby an individual attains the status of personality. In it the spirit dominates the flesh and thus attains to freedom—for the spiritual realm is one of freedom. In it all action is freely chosen, not

[21] *The Beginning and the End*, pp. 135–36.
[22] *Spirit and Reality*, p. 40.
[23] *The Destiny of Man* (N.Y., Scribner's, 1935), p. 328.

governed by necessity or determinism: man is free from all fetters—his own passions which enslave him as well as from the "objectification" which prevails in the unredeemed society.

> The mystery of Christianity is the mystery of Godmanhood, the mystery of the meeting of two natures, united but not co-mingled. Man does not cease [to exist], does not become divine, but retains his humanity in the eternal life. I think that this idea is wholly orthodox, even though it is inadequately revealed in Orthodoxy and is often obscured by a monophysite tendency.[24]
>
> Man ought to be free, he dares not be a slave, for he ought to be man. Such is the will of God.[25]

> This deification or theosis . . . is neither a monistic identity with God nor a humiliation of man and the created world. Theosis makes man Divine, while at the same time preserving his human nature. Thus, instead of the human personality being annihilated, it is made in the image of God and the Divine Trinity.[26]

It follows, therefore, that since the attainment of personality is equivalent to salvation, those who do not attain it are necessarily excluded from this state, even though it is not by some inscrutable decree of God, or His predestination, but by their own failure to act redemptively. "Man is immortal and eternal as a spiritual being belonging to the incorruptible world, but his spirituality is not a naturally given fact; man is a spiritual being in so far as he manifests himself as such, in so far as the spirit in him gains possession of the natural elements. . . . Immortality has to be won by the person and involves struggle for personality."[27] Nevertheless, Berdyaev does not accept the tenet that the failure to win salvation in this terrestrial life is final: he clings to the possibility of other opportunities in the life beyond the grave (although he does not accept Origen's notion of universal salvation; that to his mind constitutes a denial of human freedom). Moreover, he shares the Eastern Orthodox hope in

---

[24] *Samopoznanie,* p. 195.
[25] *Slavery and Freedom* (N.Y., Scribner's, 1939), p. 48.
[26] *Spirit and Reality,* p. 149.
[27] *The Destiny of Man,* p. 325.

the cosmic redemption that includes in its scope all creation. "My salvation," he writes, "is bound up with that not only of other men but also of animals, plants, minerals, and every blade of grass—all must be transfigured and brought into the Kingdom of God."[28]

The redeemed society, then, consists solely of transformed men and women and is impossible on any other basis. As long as men are dominated by selfish motives they cannot create a good world. Accordingly, mere external change—cultural, political, economic—is inadequate because it does not transform basic human motives. All social achievements in the present era are only relative: they may improve the prevailing conditions and lessen some evils, but they do not cure them. It is for this reason that Berdyaev rejects Marxism, which he regards as "a lie." "Marxism is a lie, because God exists; that is, there exists a supreme power and the source of all power; there exists a spiritual, and not only an economic power."[29] But the bourgeois ideal of capitalism is equally materialistic, extolling economic well-being as the highest good, and therefore equally unacceptable. "Bourgeois life is dominated by money and social position. Another of its characteristics is a complete disregard of the human personality."[30] Thus the Christian ethic of redemption, of the transformation of the mainsprings of human conduct, is incompatible with the prevailing sociological and political notions of the world order. A radical improvement of society cannot be attained without a spiritual transformation. And this is a process that cannot be forced or imposed on society from without: it must be voluntarily undertaken by each individual. As long as men insist on doing their own will, so long will social evils, injustice, war, and misery afflict humankind. The Marxist dream of a perfect society that does not involve such a radical change is utterly naive, lacking in the elementary perception of the necessary conditions of its realization.

But this does not imply a rejection of the cultural, political, and economic means as subsidiary to the transforming process,

[28] *Ibid.*, p. 367.
[29] *Khristianstvo i klassovaya borba* (Paris, YMCA, 1931), p. 17.
[30] *Spirit and Reality*, p. 120.

provided they are guided and dominated by the redemptive motivation. In fact, Berdyaev places an extraordinary emphasis on such creative action on the part of redeemed men: he calls them to creativity. If Christian men should fail in the task of redemptive creativity, then the forces of evil would surely take over. In fact, that is exactly what is happening in the contemporaneous world where arts, literature, and cultural life generally are largely subserving the demonic rather than the divine aims. Because Christians have failed to exercise creative activity in arts, sciences, politics, and economy to a sufficient degree, these fields have been pre-empted by the forces of evil. Berdyaev castigated this creative lag in his early work in which he developed the thesis of "the worthiness of Christianity and the unworthiness of Christians." He has never tired of insisting that Christianity is not a passive and static but a dynamic and creative religion.

> It would be wrong and impossible to abandon society to the free play of evil forces and passively to await a miraculous transformation of the world, a new heaven and a new earth. . . . Society must struggle against evil, but in doing so it must preserve the value of personality and spiritual freedom.[31]

The task of the Christian Church consists primarily of bringing men to God who alone can act on their wills in the gracious process of spiritual transformation. And since God compels no one but awaits his free acceptance of the proffered grace, salvation is a synergistic process.

Berdyaev is also deeply concerned with history as far as its spiritual meaning is concerned. History is a record of humankind's wrong choices. It is the tragic story of the misuse of human freedom, of the self-assertion of the proud, strong, ruthless, grasping, ambitious, and the power-mad over the weaker or less well endowed of their fellows. This applies both to individuals and nations, or rather to the rulers of nations. All the suffering, misery, cruelty, injustice, and inhumanity originate from this root cause. But despite this tragic character of the story of humankind, it is not devoid of meaning. God reveals

[31] *The Destiny of Man*, p. 284.

His purpose in it, especially in Jesus Christ, in whom the divine has broken through into the human sequence of historical events. The goal and aim of history—properly speaking, of the *Heilsgeschichte,* the history of redemption—is the transformation of the human into the divine-human, the theanthropy. History is meaningless unless one sees the world order in the light of God's purpose. There can be no "progress" unless there exists a goal toward which humankind is tending. And the goal cannot be set by mere mechanical evolutionary process, because natural forces are determined by the natural law of cause and effect and therefore cannot foresee the goal and thus direct themselves toward it. They lack purposiveness, teleology, and therefore are devoid of meaning. Only God can set a goal for His world and humankind and thus impart meaning to the historical process. Accordingly, only those who believe in God and in His providence can discern a purpose in an otherwise meaningless and purposeless universe. They alone can hold the notion of "progress" without being guilty of an absurdity.

Berdyaev concludes that the present humanist-secularist era has exhausted its original creative energies and has for the past century turned upon itself in repudiating man as the measure of all values. Secularism, by denying God, has also destroyed man as a spiritual being. He writes:

> Man faces the threat that nothing shall be left of himself, of his personal and intimate life, no freedom for his spiritual life or his creative thought. He is submerged in huge collectives, subject to non-human commandments. It is demanded of man that he give himself up without reserve, to society, the state, the race, the class, the nation.[32]

I find myself in complete rupture with my epoch. I sing freedom, which my epoch hates; I do not love government and am of religio-anarchistic tendency, while the epoch deifies the government; I am an extreme personalist, while the epoch is collectivist and rejects the dignity and worth of personality; I do not love war and the military, while the epoch lives in the pathos of war; I love the philosophical mind, while the epoch is indifferent

[32] *The Fate of Man in the Modern World* (London, SCM Press, 1935), pp. 12–13.

to it; I value aristocratic culture, while the epoch degrades it; and finally I profess eschatological Christianity, while the epoch recognizes only traditional-contemporary Christianity.[33]

In other words, Berdyaev holds that only Christianity properly apprehended may entertain a valid hope of creating a good and just society, a society of spiritually transformed men and women, voluntarily accepting the rule of God in their hearts— a veritable Kingdom of God. That Kingdom is realized at present in the hearts of those who have submitted their lives to God, and it will so continue to come to the end of time. But since it cannot be reasonably expected that *all* humankind will accept God's rule at any time in the future any more than it had accepted it in the past, the Kingdom of God shall never be completely realized on earth within the scope of human history. "The Kingdom of God cannot be thought as existing in time, it is the end of time, the end of the world, a new heaven and a new earth."[34] Thus Berdyaev's grandiose concept spans time and eternity. Nevertheless, the man who is committed to this glorious vision of the ultimate goal of the divine purpose need not sit in passive, idle expectation of it as if he could do nothing to bring it about or to hasten its coming. In fact, the spiritual transformation which he undergoes is an essential part of the transformation of the world. Since this "fallen" world has ever been created by man's "objectification" of it, the end of history will be brought about by the cessation of this perversion of reality. As this process is of human contrivance, its end must likewise be effected by human cooperation. This is Berdyaev's vision of the transformed humanity, and along with it of redeemed cosmos, at last realizing the original intention and purpose of God.

[33] *Samopoznanie,* pp. 280–81.
[34] *The Destiny of Man,* p. 367.

Bibliography

Nicolai Berdyaev, *The Destiny of Man,* N.Y., Harper, 1959. Harper Torchbooks).

Donald A. Lowrie, *Rebellious Prophet: A Life of Nicolai Berdyaev,* N.Y., Harper, 1960.

KARL HEIM

Carl Michalson

The thought of Karl Heim, late professor of systematic theology at the University of Tübingen in southern Germany, exhibits an astonishing range and versatility. Over a period of more than fifty years he wrote on the history of religions, philosophy, and natural science with the same vigor and skill that characterized his theology and ethics. He also produced biblical expositions and historical studies, including a treatise on Alexander of Hales and another on the problem of certainty in Christian doctrine to the time of Schleiermacher. Scores of his sermons were published, several volumes of which are in English. They reveal a fascinating combination of tender piety and disciplined penetration into personal and cultural needs. No crisis in the life of the German people seemed to escape his theological scrutiny. A fat volume, *Faith and Life (Glaube und Leben,* 1926), which someone has called "a thesaurus," embraces these essays over a period of twenty-five years.

Heim saw the care of the soul portrayed in the ministry of Jesus. Contrary to the stereotype of the German theologian, he made such pastoral concern central to his own vocation. Ecumenical involvement begun in his youth as secretary of the German Student Christian Movement persisted throughout his most mature work. To the very end of his life he deliberately resisted what he felt to be the theologian's cardinal ambition— the writing of a *Dogmatik.* During an Oxford Group meeting in England that ambition was revealed to him as a sin of pride and he surrendered it. In 1931 he began his closest approximation to a *Dogmatik,* a six-volume work entitled *The Evangelical Faith and the Thought of the Present (Der evangelische Glaube und das Denken der Gegenwart).* The first volume, *Faith and Thought (Glaube und Denken),* is his most significant work. In his preface he announced that he was definitely not writing "in the form of a *Dogmatik.* . . . We have enough text-

273

books on dogmatics." At least one theologian in Europe found it impossible to take that announcement lightly, for Karl Barth just four years earlier had launched his own leviathan.

Probably best known to the English-speaking world of the pre-World War II period was Heim's Protestant manifesto, *Spirit and Truth* (*Das Wesen des Evangelischen Christentums*, 1925). This was written in open dialogue with his famous Catholic colleague at Tübingen, Karl Adam. Since World War II Heim has been known across the world for his writings on natural science. This is a calamity, for it by-passes his most distinctive contribution, which is the methodological structure underlying his entire literature and which, more than the concerns of piety, dictated the direction of his theological writing. Heim aimed his communication of the Christian faith at levels of the human spirit which are often left untouched by the theological traditions stemming from seventeenth-century Protestant orthodoxy and from nineteenth-century liberalism. It is not mysterious, therefore, that a majority of the pastors in Germany today regard him as their principal teacher.

Here the mystery begins, however. The Continental theologians who remember him have appended him to their courses in the history of doctrine. His phenomenal life-span has made that a possibility. He was over eighty years of age when he died. But what of the contemporary pertinence of his work? I believe there are mainly two reasons for the relative neglect of Heim's thought among his colleagues today. The more immediate reason seems to be that the Barth and Bultmann circles have almost completely absorbed current theological attention. The less evident but equally instructive reason is that the theologians have been too disconcerted by Heim's method to sustain their interest. My account of Heim's contribution will attempt to provide the key to both circumstances. It can be found in what Heim conceives to be the responsibility of Christian apologetics.[1]

---

[1] In December 1953 the *Scottish Journal of Theology* printed my article on Heim entitled "The Task of Apologetics in the Future." I am indebated to the editors for permitting me to draw heavily upon the substance and language of that article.

I

The theologians who have noticed Heim have exhausted themselves attempting to locate his position within some standard camp. One group has labeled him "a rationalist." Did he not develop a philosophical basis for the Christian view of life? Was he not concerned with the intellectual possibility of the certainty of faith? Did he not restlessly seek for a "category" by which to express the Christian faith in terms comprehensible to contemporary culture? Is not that device reminiscent of the Schleiermacher-Troeltsch-Otto succession, with its tactic of religious a priori?

The testimony of this group is very confident. "Anyone who accepts Heim's world view is not yet a religious man," says one interpreter. "Heim's whole effort is a blunder which can be traced to his preoccupation with artful abstraction," says another. "Insoluble logic is more important to him than personal relations. His God is an 'it' and not a 'Thou.'" "He employs the experience of despair as a device for securing the certainty of faith." "In his desire for a science of the ultimate he wishes to stand where only God can stand." "He does not speak from a place within the Church." He "fails to follow the proper task of theology, reflection on the testimony and message of the Bible."[2]

These charges would be serious were it not for the almost comical fact that another block of interpreters arrives at a completely opposite conclusion about him. His tendencies, they say, are those of "an irrationalist." Does he not elevate God beyond the reach of human reason? Does he not exemplify a simple trust in the biblical revelation with its miracles and unique revelation? One rejects him because he denies that man is able to

[2] Paul Kalweit, *Die Christliche Welt*, J. 21, p. 562; Th. Steinmann, *Zeitschrift für Theologie und Kirche*, n.f., XIII, p. 49; W. Thimme, *Theologische Studien und Kritiken*, J. 105, pp. 25, 35–36; Karl Barth, *Die Kirchliche Dogmatik*, II,1, p. 225; Dietrich Bonhoeffer, *Christentum und Wissenschaft*, H. 12, p. 435; Hermann Diem, *Die Christliche Welt*, J. 46, p. 546; H. Obendiek, *Scottish Journal of Theology*, Vol. 5, No. 3, p. 259.

have communion with God outside of Jesus Christ. Another says, "He imports a *deus ex machina* into a sceptical philosophy." Another, "He is a reactionary irrationalist." Still another, "He neglects the rational in order to found religion on an irrational source."[3]

By these contradictory testimonies the critics fall against each other and the Heim mystery deepens. The more patient and discerning critics see both rationalist and irrationalist tendencies in Heim's work, but they fail to see how he has resolved these tendencies. He presents the puzzling appearance of one who attempts contradictory aims. Therefore, these analysts ask, "How can one combine in a single viewpoint an emphasis both on what is beyond the reason and what is a necessity within the reason," as Heim seems to do? "How can an intellectual impossibility become the basis for the intellectual possibility of Christianity?" "How can one express Tertullian's fideism in the patterns of pure mathematics?" Has not Heim "vacillated indefinitely between an austere metaphysical theology and a theology of individual experience"?[4]

Those more cautious and well-balanced critiques are as misguided as all the others, however. All seem to miss a central key which unlocks the mystery of Heim's theological significance. One may state it briefly. Heim's theological method is instructed by a sensitivity to the polarity, the tension, in human existence which is ineradicable from within existence. How does he know about this tension? In not one but two ways. He both lives as a man and is the beneficiary of the revelation which names the truth "Jesus Christ." These two standpoints are nowhere held in separation in Heim's position. The human situation is seen to be riddled with the agonies one associates with doubt, social hostility, suffering, guilt, and death. These agonies are the more acute for the fact that there appears to be

[3] Fernand Ménégoz, *Le Problème de la Prière*, p. 203; Friedrich Traub, *Theologische Studien und Kritiken*, n. j., 1917, p. 191; D. C. Macintosh, *The Problem of Religious Knowledge*, p. 350; Rudolf Paulus, *Zeitschrift für Theologie und Kirche*, n. f., 1922, p. 201.

[4] Karl Beth, *Theologische Rundschau*, V. 20, p. 94; Otto Hoffmann, *Theologische Studien und Kritiken*, 1922, p. 267; Julius Kaftan, *Studien zur systematische Theologie T. von Haering*, pp. 37, 39; Erich Przywara, *Stimmen der Zeit*, 1926, p. 353.

no satisfactory relief from them within the human situation. How does Heim know that? Has he personally played all the registers of life? That is not required of a man who has heard from within his life as a man the message of justification by faith alone. It is precisely the priority of faith in his method which makes it possible for him to participate profoundly in the life of the world.

For instance, he wrote as a *phenomenologist;* indeed, his first book in 1902 was an analysis of Husserl's phenomenological method. That means he dealt with the problem of life *as it appears,* and not simply as a deduction from the Christian revelation. Yet it was his position from within the faith that gave him his warrant for proceeding as a phenomenologist does, in honest pursuit of the problem of life as it appears, for that process of fundamental questioning would surely culminate in thirst for a meaning which does not necessarily appear. He also wrote as an *existentialist.* Heim was one of the first theologians in Europe to introduce Kierkegaardian insights, as well as one of the first to take up the work of Heidegger into theological reasoning. Yet it was as a steward of the faith that he had the confidence that the pursuit of meaning involves *all* one's faculties and commits one to decisive action upon the results of his search. And he wrote as an *ontologist.* That means he was not simply a metaphysician seeking for the origin or causes of things, for first principles. In that regard he was instructed by Ritschlianism. To say he was an ontologist means he examined and illuminated the fundamental structure of being in such a way as to relate the whole of one's life to the ultimate meaning in the whole of life. Along with Tillich and others in the days between the wars he defended the role of ontology in theology. However, it was clearer to him than to some others that theology precedes ontology and makes it possible, as even Plato and Aristotle seem to have believed. Finally, he wrote with a *hermeneutical* accent. By that is meant that the fundamental realities with which a theologian has to deal are meanings. This accent ought not be confused with a variety of Gnosticism for which sheer theological information was held to be redemptive. The intellectual propositions of a hermeneutical theology are different from those which specify that life means this or that.

The meanings which resolve the manifest and hidden agonies of life will be breathed with intimacy through such confessional language as "You mean everything to me!" and by that communication change the structure of life.

II

The primacy of faith in Heim's system ought to safeguard his otherwise secular methods from being dismissed, as Barthian-influenced theologians tend to dismiss them. Karl Barth has said *"Nein!"* to almost every major theologian of this century, and he has done it, as he himself says, like a roaring lion. His main prey have been theologians with an *Anknüpfungspunkt* mentality, which is a species of natural theology, deriving theological insight from sources other than God's special revelation in Christ. Therefore, to join forces with Heim would seem like an invitation to annihilation at Barth's hands, considering Heim's apparent deafness to the Barthian warning. The following typical citations from Heim's works are impressive evidence of his apparent methodological flirtation with natural theology:

"All reality speaks a common language." "Morality and religion are one and the same movement of life under two different viewpoints." "Every fleeting wish is indeed already a religion in miniature." "The demand of human relations is for another who himself needs no other." "There are only two possible reactions for the man in battle—stupefaction or prayer." "There is no experience of despair that does not give light to the horizon." "The despair which the conscience experiences is the foothold in the visible for the leap into the invisible." "Every forcible suppression of doubt is a direct blow at conscience. It destroys our reverence for truth, the highest faculty within us, which must be kept alive if we wish to know God." "An atheistic ontology is only possible on the grounds of an abstraction which neglects the why and wherefore of the existence of the real man." "We must find an answer to the question about how we may find a way from creation to the creator." "The leading of God can come to one in an entirely reasonable and commonplace form in which, after a laborious rational process through which I examine a given situation according to my best knowledge and conscience and enumerate all the reasons *pro* and *con,* I become stamped with the seal of certainty: 'This way must in the name of God be taken.' "[5]

Barth's own critique of Heim was relatively benign until he read Heim's statement disavowing works on dogmatics as acts of pride. It can truthfully be said of Barth that he never fought an offensive war. In the case of Heim, the casual sentence in his Preface provoked Barth's counterattack. In an open letter to Heim appearing in the periodical *Between the Times,*[6] Barth asked Heim to explain what he meant by that statement. But he said more. The students who moved back and forth between the two universities where Heim and Barth were teaching had told Barth some of the things Heim was saying about him in his lectures. Apparently Heim said that Barth's *Dogmatik* is "the summit of the unpleasant pride of modern secularism." To that Barth replied that Heim's theology was "the most recent form of the equally unpleasant humility of modern pietism." While Heim's personal history is laden with pietism, as his recent autobiography quite explicitly reveals, Barth's charge was theological in intention. Heim's approach to the Christian faith, Barth said, is a form of "psychologism," the very kind of anthropological exaggeration which makes bedfellows of nineteenth-century liberalism, pietism, and scholasticism. Each is a trend toward "point of contact" thinking, or natural theology.[7]

Barth's criticism of Heim is wrong. Heim's theology has never

[5] *Das Weltbild der Zukunft,* p. iv; *Leitfaden der Dogmatik,* 2nd ed., Vol. 1, p. 64; *Das Weltbild,* p. 193; *Glaube und Leben,* pp. 518–19; *ibid.,* p. 623; *Glaubensgewissheit,* 1st ed., p. 39; *Glaube und Leben,* p. 650; *Spirit and Truth,* p. 113; *Zeitschrift für Theologie und Kirche,* n. f., Vol. 11, p. 330; *Die Wandlung im naturwissenschaftlichen Weltbild,* p. 18; *Glaube und Denken,* 2nd ed., pp. 335–36.

[6] *Zwischen den Zeiten,* J. 9, h. 5, pp. 451–53.

[7] *The Doctrine of the Word of God,* p. 21. In one of his last written statements Heim conceded that pietism dominated his thinking, but defined pietism as "the conviction that there is such a thing as Christianity only on the basis of a 'conversion,' which means a turning about through which I cease to lead myself and by complete surrender put my whole existence under the leadership of Jesus Christ. If a conversion is the only way a man can be certain of his eternal salvation, then a theology can only have meaning if it serves the end of leading man to this decision." *Ich gedenke der vorigen Zeiten,* 1957, pp. 315–16.

been anthropological, except in the sense that his Lutheran Christology is anthropological. To begin with God's word in Christ, however, does not prohibit taking one's humanity with theological seriousness. Since the Enlightenment, of course, any alliance between revelation and human discernment has been looked upon with suspicion by both theologians and philosophers, for at that time philosophy declared its independence from theology and theology felt obliged to return the compliment. Therefore, in modern life philosophies have tended to absorb the functions of faiths. Barthianism alone of all the theologies today has attempted, like medieval scholasticism, to absorb the functions of philosophy.[8]

Heim's understanding of the relation of theology to non-theological disciplines antedates this curtaining off of the human and the divine disciplines. It is probably best exemplified in the philosophical theology of Augustine. Karl Heim can really be understood only in this setting. For that reason, judgments aimed at him from within the philosophy-blind post-Enlightenment theology are apt to miss the mark. If theology is separable from other spheres, it is insulated against their judgment. At the same time, however, in such a relation the judgment of theology upon other spheres is blocked by its own defenses. If theology is in any way dependent upon other spheres, its autonomy is threatened, being subject to the judgment of these other spheres. One of the rewards of that risk, however, is that the methodological lines by which theological perspective is communicated to other spheres are at least kept open.

It would be better to find a new name for what theologians used to do than to allow the theological task to be pinched by restrictions forced upon it by either secular or sacred sciences. Heim believed this so firmly that he entertained the notion of a completely different name for theology, namely, the "Science of the Ultimate." Such a science is interested in but one question: "What are the ultimate presuppositions which support our life

[8] Kazuo Mutō, a Japanese Christian teaching philosophy at Kyoto University, has helped me understand this about Barth. See my *Japanese Contributions to Christian Theology* (Philadelphia: Westminster, 1960), p. 133.

and how is the certainty of this foundation established?"[9] Heim would not concede that there is a distinction between theological responsibility and the type of search for a basis in life which goes on outside theology, such as in the novel and the drama, or even in newspapers and in politics. All are concerned explicitly or implicitly with the ultimate in existence, be they inside or outside the church.[10]

Heim believed he was able to achieve as a result of his method at least the outlines of a Christian ontology. There does seem to be a convincing overlap between the human situation as lived through by the concerned man and the divine revelation as witnessed within the Christian church. One would expect, therefore, that the effect of Heim's method would be to break down the wall, if not to construct a bridge, between the church and the world, between theology and philosophy, between faith and culture. It should be carefully noted that Heim proposed no theological bridge "between God and man." That task is out of the theologian's hands and, where attempted, is nothing but a *Schneebrücke*, a bridge of snow.

Two major data dominate Heim's ontology. One is the thoroughgoing relativism of human existence. The other is what he calls God's "dimensional" transcendence. These data are complementary. If there is a God of the sort confessed by the Hebrew-Christian faith, then man has a permanent basis for his life. The basis, however, would be not in man's life but in God's. Therefore Heim could press man relentlessly with the question of ultimate meaning because he knew from the outset that a life unrelated to God is relatively meaningless. "A man must have something permanent," Heim believed.[11] Human experience needs it, not because it feels the need, but because the need is revealed to be inherent in the very structure of life.

By relativism Heim meant that in existence, as one can know it by himself, there is no absolute point of reference. The ontology underlying this assertion is constructed out of a view of time. Man is completely embedded in time, or better, time

[9] *Glaube und Denken*, p. 22.
[10] *Die Wandlung*, p. 13.
[11] *Leben aus dem Glauben*, pp. 3, 4.

is completely embedded in man. The very structure of existence is time, and, like time, existence is running out. Within existence there is no security for existence. Man's life is a continuous trek across a never-ending watershed. Behind him is the irrevocable and certain past, powerless to help him in the present. Ahead of him is the uncertain future. Without the help of any final knowledge, man must act decisively toward the future. In the nature of time, moving forward as it does irreversibly, suspension of decision would be itself a decision to let time decide. The mistake of man is either to accept something in time as if it were final, or to fail to despair of its lack of finality. Either state would be a condition of "radical godlessness," which Heim describes as the lack of an Archimedean point for the orientation of one's life.

How does the human reason function within this time reference? Reason leads man restlessly from island to island but never finds a continent on which to build firmly. Within the ever-receding infinity called existence, the reason comes upon nothing which is not staggered by the question, Why? But the conscientious reason, the moral reason, the reason which is concerned with the total destiny of the person on behalf of whom it functions, is not content with this situation and tantalizes itself in an endless and exhausting search for a clue to transcendence beyond the situation. Life under these conditions can result only in either the crushing spiritual poverty one has learned to call despair, or a leap into some sort of saving faith. No faith could be regarded as a saving faith which does not transcend the limitations of the "time-form" from which it professes to bring deliverance. In his autobiography *Ich gedenke der vorigen Zeiten* (*I Remember the Days of Old*), Heim recapitulates the sheer geographical and political relativity he experienced in a trip around the world just after the First World War. Add to this experience his knowledge of Einstein's theory and you have what he called "the fundamental negative idea at the base of my whole theological work."[12]

The Christian belief in the transcendence of God both explains the relativity of the time-form and brings deliverance

[12] *Ich gedenke der vorigen Zeiten*, p. 224.

from it. Where there is only one God, all else is related to him, that is, all else is relative. Where there is only one Absolute, all else presupposes this Absolute. The very effort to know the Absolute depends upon the prior existence of the Absolute. Is God so transcendent, then, that He is out of touch with human experience? On the contrary. God is transcendent because he is so near, not because He is so remote. He sustains man's whole life, and one cannot see the place on which one stands. Is man therefore destined to live in ignorance of the one reality the knowledge of which can bring authenticity to his life? Not at all. The experience of thoroughgoing relativism is the presupposition for the raising of the question about the ultimate. The question simply waits upon the answer which only the ultimate can give, and give in its own way. The Christ-revelation is taken to be the answer of God to the question implicit in the structure of man's life. As such, it is an answer which arises not from the relative situation but is transcendent of the situation.

Yet throughout Heim's work he makes the claim for the rational certainty of the Christian faith. What could that mean within this ontological scheme of human relativism and divine transcendence? The allusion to certainty is a residuum in Heim from another day. The meaning, however, does not hinge upon the language. Heim is convinced that it is rational to affirm what is needed to make experience possible. The Christian revelation, then, notwithstanding man's inability to come upon it by himself, is a "rational event"—as Barth himself once called it.[13] For Heim it is not revelation but only the need of revelation which is given in human experience. When Barth complains that one cannot end with faith-certainty unless one has begun with it, he requires exactly what Heim has proposed. His theology begins from within the human situation at the point where the Christ revelation brings the ultimacy of the transcendent God to the contingency of existence.

III

The general lines of Heim's ontology were present in his theology from his earliest work. Pertinent elements in the new physics

[13] *The Doctrine of the Word of God*, pp. 152–53.

and biology, in existential philosophy, and in the political fortunes of the world have been blended with Luther's doctrine of justification by faith. The result has been no flatulent philosophy in waiting for some doctoral candidate to place it in the history of thought. Heim's work has been a spur at the flank of Continental life for over half a century.

The mobility of Heim's intellectual forces during this time is most impressive. In each succeeding decade he has shifted his key concept, always improving without essentially changing his fundamental structure. To shift the figure, he has felt it important to erect a readily traversible bridge between the Christian message and the world. It must be remembered that the bridge connects the Church and the world, not God and man. To use an Augustinian figure, the bridge is traversible when illuminated, and one who believes in the Christian doctrine of justification by faith or—what is the same—the doctrine of the Holy Spirit, knows that this is a *lumen aeternae* for the coming of which one can only wait. This primacy of God's action, however, in no way obviates for Heim the importance of building bridges.

In *Psychologismus oder Antipsychologismus* (1902) Heim set the pattern for his entire theological literature. In this very difficult little study of Edmund Husserl's pioneering work in logic, he attempted to show how it is possible to do theology without either metaphysics on the one side or the logic of the natural sciences on the other. An epistemology is required which will allow that at the base of thought processes there are presuppositions which are themselves unknowable. In his recent memoirs he notes how Martin Heidegger's *Sein und Zeit,* which virtually attempted the same kind of analysis, has now made that early work of his superfluous. I cite this comment simply to observe that he makes no such statement with reference to his other works.

Das Weltbild der Zukunft (1904) established Heim as an author at a time when he would rather have become a professor. The book was a study of reality documented from the modern sciences and from philosophy. His thesis was that in reality as it appears one has to do only with relationships, never with ultimate data. This very relativity of phenomena forces men to make decisions, even though a secure basis for such decisions is not given in the phenomena. It does not seem unreasonable, therefore, that there would appear to man what man himself needs but cannot voluntarily conjure up—the revelation of an absolute basis for decision in God's own decision.

Heim does not hide his disappointment at not being called to a chair of systematic theology as a result of this work. Actually, it was not the kind of work expected of dogmaticians in Germany at that time. Just to show that he could do it, he subsequently turned to more traditional historical studies, one on Alexander of Hales and another on the problem of certainty. Karl Barth is said to have confessed a similar motive behind his own *Anselm* study. Not until 1914 was Heim finally called to a professorship at Münster. Because of the war he could not take up this call until 1918. Two years later he won the post at Tübingen, which he held until retirement. I say "won" because a contest actually ensued with Rudolf Otto for that position. In his early student movement days Heim felt shunned by circles in Germany which associated him with an American brand of practical Christianity and a Methodist brand of evangelical piety. On one occasion when he sought the advice of Reinhold Seeberg concerning his vocational possibilities as a professor of theology, he was shocked when this famous teacher told him he should seek a chair of practical theology.

In 1916 his original insights concerning the decisional character of reality were sharpened in the direction of more fundamental theological concerns in the volume called *Glaubensgewissheit* (*The Certainty of Faith*). In the second edition of this work, appearing in 1920, the first significant shift in his position occurred. The "decision" category was replaced by a "destiny" category. Man's windowless decisions do not simply presuppose some transcendent light. They suffer a light burning in upon them. This category, suggested by Oswald Spengler, offered Heim the occasion to introduce into his method the more aggressive connotations of revelation, theologically expressed in the doctrines of predestination, grace, and the witness of the Spirit.

Within three years a third edition of *Glaubensgewissheit* appeared, which further clarified the structure in the relation which

God's destinating decision sustains to man's relative decisions. God is "the nonobjective perspective," drawing all visible experience up into the unity of His being, but Himself remaining invisible. This perspectival unity is at the ground of all experience as the very possibility of experience. One cannot know the nonobjective perspective point of all objective perspectives, but one cannot know anything else without it. The dependence here upon motifs from Kant is avowed.[14]

This development of categories prepared the way for the emergence of the category on which Heim based his magnum opus, *The Evangelical Faith and the Thought of the Present.* I refer to his most famous category of "the dimension." Heim believed that one who understands the meaning of the "dimensions" has come upon the primary and most important basis for understanding the mystery of existence. The illustrations are patent. The two-dimensionally minded primitive man was unable to make sense of his universe until someone announced the existence of the third dimension. The third dimension was nothing he could see, for one's perception presupposes it. Width and height stretch out before us, but depth is a straight line. If we observe it we see only the end of it, a pinpoint on the two-dimensional width-height surface. If we observe on the basis of it, however, the surface becomes deep with perspective. To say it more technically, on the basis of two-dimensional experience it is contradictory to assume that more than two straight lines may meet at right angles. Analogically, the God-relation is the depth dimension which, when one hears of it, comprehends all other dimensions and clarifies existence, without itself being perceptible.

The God-dimension is hidden, and it is the presupposition of a meaningful existence. But it is not a silent relation. It is characterized by "the word," an encounter similar to the relation between persons. Hence the analogy from dimensions serves an additional function. Heim has used it to express in somewhat logical language the poetical insights of Martin Buber's *I and*

[14] In 1932 G. C. Berkouwer wrote discerningly of Heim's theology as "the theology of the nonobjectifiable." See his *Geloof en Openbaring in de Nieuwere Duitsche Theologie (Faith and Revelation in the New German Theology)*, pp. 84–103 and 182–92.

Thou. There are two kinds of spaces: I-spaces and it-spaces. It-spaces are filled with contents which are exclusive of all other spaces, like the spaces on a checkerboard. The conflict in personal relations is a result of attempting to make it-spaces out of I-spaces. Either we draw circles around ourselves in such a way as to exclude others, or we introject the others into the circle of our own existence in such a way as to rob these others of their independence. I-spaces, however, are not content-spaces. They are dimensional-spaces. Therefore there may be an infinite number of these spaces without their excluding one another. An infinite number of lines may converge perpendicularly at the same point if there is a third dimension beyond height and width. At the same time, these dimensional spaces can meet without losing their distinctive identity. Two infinite planes may intersect without jeopardizing either their infinity or their distinctness. It-spaces meet by contact. I-spaces meet by encounter. The God-relation is of the nature of I-spaces.

The analogy from space has not overlooked the time analogy in which Heim's ontological structure was conceived. It-spaces are past time and I-spaces are present time. God Himself is an I-space with the unique character of eternal presentness. God is the "dimension of dimensions" which comprehends all other dimensions. That dimension actively confers meaning on all reality when the word of God, which is the point at which the world of experience is related to God, is present.

With the rise of National Socialism in Germany, Heim's categorial bridge-building suffered a moment of uncertainty. Since 1902 his method had assumed the ontological impossibility of relativizing the absolute and absolutizing the relative. Obviously it was always considered *morally* possible to invert the structure of life, to exchange the truth about God for a lie and worship the creature rather than the Creator. National Socialism, however, seemed to illustrate the possibility of embracing relativities as absolute without undergoing existential despair. Hence in the third edition of *Glaube und Denken,* which was the first volume of his six-volume work, Heim stressed what had nonetheless always been implicit. This volume is translated into English as *God Transcendent.* In it Heim indicated that analogies from the world are too weak to turn man from preoccupation with the world to faith in God. Man cannot by any observation of his own attain to the Christian knowledge of God. "We are thrown back on God's own revelation."[15] As Heim had said in his *Glaubensgewissheit,* "The hammer with which the smith strikes the anvil cannot forge itself. . . . Nor can thought prove its own presuppositions."[16]

IV

The best clue for understanding Heim's theology is what he believes to be the responsibility of a Christian apologetic. At this point he is most clearly different from the two dominating figures in Continental theology, Barth and Bultmann. The questions that emerge from a comparison of these three theologians are now helping to form the theology of the future.

In Heim's method an apologetic has three obligations. The first is to unmask the idols which the world destructively reveres. This is the offensive phase of apologetic. As such, it is simply a propaedeutic to Christian preaching. The second obligation is to preach the positive Christian message. The third is to provide a Christian view of life, a Christian ontology, a science of the ultimate that would relate the Christianized world meaningfully to its total environment. This is the phase of consolidation, organic to apologetics in general.[17]

The old variety of defensive apologetic in which the theologian felt called upon to justify the Christian message before the so-called bar of reason is utterly foreign to Heim's method. As he said, "We need an attitude which we do not need to defend . . . indeed, which can change the strategy from defense to attack."[18] Equally foreign is the still older method of rational attack upon non-Christian systems, characterized by Franz Overbeck as the intellectual equivalent of the medieval crusades. Heim is rather in the tradition of Pascal and Kierkegaard,

---

[15] *God Transcendent* (N.Y., Scribner's, 1936), pp. 230-31.

[16] Second ed., pp. 129-30.

[17] The strategy was outlined by Heim in an article called "Der gegenwärtige Stand der Debatte zwischen Theologie und Naturwissenschaft," *Theologische Studien und Kritiken,* 1908, pp. 402-29.

[18] *Der christliche Gottesglaube und die Naturwissenschaft,* Erster Teilband, p. 33.

applying a relentless critique to the roots of man's existence, and always upon the presupposition that the God revealed in Christ can alone re-establish the uprooted man on the soil of His truth. Apologetic attack is analogous to the way a physician attacks an illness. He is not so intent on defending his professional reputation as he is in effecting a cure.

Apologetic can lead only to the threshold of a Christian solution. Even then the threshold is no closer to heaven than to hell. The method is informed by Socratic midwifery, the maieutic method which Kierkegaard introduced into theology through his concept of irony. But where Socrates used the process of fundamental questioning to deliver the mind of its own innate wisdom, the great Christian apologists have simply disabused the mind of its barriers against the coming of the revelation.[19] The revelation itself is *sui generis*.

Heim's apologetic can be clearly seen in his latest work, his three volumes on natural science and the Christian faith, which are volumes four to six of his *Evangelical Faith and the Thought of the Present*. Following a lead from German physicist Pascual Jordan—that the language of today is the language of the natural sciences—Heim has gone to the trouble to think through the faith as it relates to the latest sciences and to communicate the faith in juxtaposition to scientific questions. Motifs in contemporary thought, inspired by classical materialism and Newtonian mechanism, attributing absoluteness and causal necessity to the objective world, do not need to be attacked by theology. The newer science has already discredited them. Physics, it seems, has been forced to become more philosophical by its successive reduction of matter to an indeterminate element, of space and time to relativity, and of mechanical necessity to acausality. The theologian in this context does not ask science to listen to the dogmatic conclusions of faith but simply to the wistfulness of science itself. After science has been allowed to interrogate itself, the faith introduces the meanings

---

[19] Emil Brunner's works also illustrate this method. He has given it the name "eristic" or "Christian Socratism," and he refers to it as "theology's other task," which was his way of saying that the writing of a *Dogmatik* does not exhaust the theologian's responsibility. *Zwischen den Zeiten*, 1929, pp. 255–276.

which are essential but inaccessible to science. The universe is sustained by a living God who relates Himself to the ongoing process as He will. That, roughly, is the thesis of volume five, *The Transformation of the Scientific World-View.*

Volume six, *Weltschöpfung und Weltende (Creation and Eschatology),* takes up the problem of the origin and end of the world. Here again the new science has destroyed the Laplacian and Newtonian concepts of a universe that is closed and self-existent. The universe is open at both ends. It has its beginning in an indefinable fog and its ending in what the scientists themselves call a "natural science eschatology," such as the notion of the heat death of the universe. The interpretative value of natural science in these instances, however, is candidly negative. It clears the air for what we need desperately to know about our universe but cannot know even from science. God is at the beginning and at the ending of time. While this affirmation cannot be made on the basis of a scientific method, it shockingly corresponds to the deepest though unanswered questions of science.

There is a vast difference between apologetic in this sense and natural theology. Natural theology, as Karl Barth has rightly called it, is a species of intellectual works-righteousness where the mind arrives at the truth of God, not independently of God perhaps, but independently of God's revelation in Christ. It is, therefore, a kind of theological peeping-tom act which spies on God independently of the manner in which God wishes to reveal Himself. It may succeed in finding out God's hands and feet, but as Calvin has said, it will not find His heart. The heart is the sole master of its secrets.

Why, then, an apologetic? Why not simply a quiet, patient waiting for God to break into our perception when and where He will? Apologetic proceeds neither out of skepticism of God's ability to make Himself known independently of apologetic nor on the basis of a theory of natural revelation. Apologetics answers to the call of Christ to preach the Gospel to the world. It is not difficult to be a man of the world to the men of the world if one is a Christian, for a Christian is always at the same time a worldling. Apologetics simply calls upon a man to do earnestly what comes quite naturally—to talk to one's neighbor in the terms of one's neighbor about the matter of our life and death. A man in Christ knows much more about his neighbor than the neighbor knows about himself, not by virtue of his neighbor-relation but by virtue of the transcendent perspective of the Christ-relation.

A man is never asked, however, to step from his false though orderly world view into an esoteric faith-relation whose contacts with the rest of reality are allowed to remain amorphous and chaotic. The Christian man has the privilege of living within a church which is constantly developing "an honest theology of cultural high standing," to use Paul Tillich's phrase. This is no longer apologetics in the sense of establishing a bridgehead on enemy territory. It is the consolidation of gains. Nor is it simply dogmatics or systematic theology in the sense of the exposition of the faith of the church. It is avowedly secondary to dogmatics, but not thereby without importance. It is a frankly bifocal enterprise which, while informed by the substance of Christianity, is patterned by the dominant issues in the culture of the time.

Despite my valiant effort to keep Heim's most respectable side forward, I must confess that I find his more popular later writings theologically inferior to his earlier work. Some might explain this apparent decline by the fantastic manner in which Heim wrote these books. Confined to bed with a heart ailment, he was permitted to dress and sit at his desk for but one hour daily. Whatever the reason, this later work deviates from his self-announced apologetic method. Until this time he had created categories which had theological and existential durability. Except for the first of his six volumes, these works abandoned categorial and analogical reasoning for sheer homily and illustration. The second volume, *Jesus der Herr* (*Jesus the Lord*, 1935), adds little to the understanding of christology and soteriology except sermonic lessons drawn from the feeling of need for a strong leader which National Socialism inspired. *Jesus der Weltvollender* (*Jesus the Fulfiller of the World*, 1937) adds even less to eschatology and supports a rather traditional view.

Most vulnerable of all are the three volumes on natural science. Due to his serious illness during the time these volumes were composed, Heim's publisher kept negatively critical reviews from him. Thus the benefit which comes from vigorous challenge was lacking in this process of composition. The most manifest difficulty is that the latest insights of natural science are used by Heim to justify traditional views of creation, miracle, and eschatology, views which many exegetes and theologians are no longer able to purvey as either mandatory or meaningful. An apologetic method which began with the capacity to sting the life of man with the sense of his inadequacy and to illuminate his life with the realization of God's adequacy ended in defense of doctrinal forms which had already begun to lose their meaning.[20]

How, then, does Heim stand up alongside the giants of the contemporary theological scene? A detailed comparison of the apologetic emphases of Barth, Bultmann, and Heim would be highly instructive. Suffice it here to make several generalizations.

Barth dismisses Heim's apologetic as a scholastic residuum in Protestant theology. Heim, however, believed that Barth defaulted in his leadership in the church's conflict with the unbelieving world. There is no disputing the fact that Barth has warmed the heart of the believing community. For that Heim recurrently professed his personal debt to Barth. Whether Barth has chilled the life of modern man with a "sublime monotony," as Heim has claimed, is a serious charge whose validity the future must appraise. At the same time there is already impressive evidence that a strategy such as Heim's could lead the church "out of the stuffy air of a closed space in which it spoils miserably, into the full expanse of world events."[21]

In the last years of his life Heim felt he had to choose between two projects, his memoirs or a critique of Bultmann. He wrote his memoirs. Bultmann was an enigma to Heim. That fact may indicate that Heim never really learned his lessons well from Heidegger. For Bultmann, hermeneutics is the sum and substance of the theological task. In that single discipline are embraced all the tasks which other theologies splinter into exegesis, dogmatics, apologetics, and preaching. Bultmann would

[20] Cf. also my analysis of Heim in *The Hinge of History*, esp. pp. 70, 71.

[21] Kurt Leese, *Zeitschrift für Theologie und Kirche*, J. 24, p. 120.

not have criticized Heim, as Barth did, for flirting with natural theology; he would have recognized the thoroughgoing Christo-centrism of Heim's position. Bultmann would have criticized Heim for developing Christian world views which had no neces-sary relation to man's self-understanding and which therefore amounted to nothing but cosmological speculation. Barth is just as disconcerted as Heim by Bultmann's disavowal of apolo-getics. In his little writing on Bultmann, Barth admits that every time you mention apologetics in Bultmann's presence Bultmann "hits the ceiling." Barth cannot understand this, and says that "in some one sense all theologians in all times have been and even must be apologists as well."[22] What Bultmann means, however, is that the method of theology is no different from the tactic of exegesis or of apologetic. It is simply in the light of the Scriptures to understand the meaning of human existence.

Barth, by his exclusive preoccupation with the Christian gospel in its own terms, has run the risk of moving parallel to modern culture, although he himself understands that the con-nection between God and the world is a circuit which God, not the theologian, completes. Bultmann, with his concern for the meaning of human existence, has run the risk of changing the traditional form of the gospel, although not the gospel itself. Heim has run no risk. He has attempted to reach the world without jeopardy to the traditional form of the Christian gospel. Not even the pietistic community of Württemberg questioned his orthodoxy. He moved with no noticeable sense of intellectual agony back and forth from the existential needs of the modern world to what he took to be the historical facts of the first-century gospel. Behind the appearance of dialogue with the world, he has come close to maintaining a parallelism as sharp as Barth's while at the same time pursuing the interpretive task less courageously than Bultmann.

The great merit of Barth is that he has developed in theology today a conscience about the unique source of the Christian faith in the reality of God and His revelation. The merit of Bultmann is that he has been willing to lose his faith in its

---

[22] "Rudolf Bultmann: Ein Versuch ihn zu verstehen," *Theologische Studien,* Heft 34, p. 43.

traditional form in order to find it as a meaningful reality. It may well be enough to say of Karl Heim that he stood at a point of transition between these polar passions.

Bibliography

Karl Heim, *Jesus the Lord*, Philadelphia, Fortress Press, 1961.

No detailed study of Heim is available in English.

III
Recent Theological
Work

ANDERS NYGREN

Warren A. Quanbeck

Anders Nygren (1890–   ) is the most influential representative of the Lundensian school of theology, so named because of its origin in the University of Lund in Sweden. Gustaf Aulén and Ragnar Bring are other well known theologians of this school.

Nygren was ordained to the ministry in the Church of Sweden (Lutheran) in 1912 and served as a parish pastor until 1921, when he was appointed docent (instructor) in the faculty of theology at Lund. In 1924 he was appointed to the chair of Systematic Theology and Ethics. In 1948 he was elected bishop of the diocese of Lund, continuing in this position until his retirement in 1959. He has been active in the ecumenical movement since the Conference on Faith and Order at Lausanne in 1927. He played a leading part in the Edinburgh Conference in 1937 and served as chairman of the Faith and Order Commission on Christ and the Church for more than a decade. He was among the leaders in the formation of the Lutheran World Federation, and served as its first president.

Nygren's range of theological interests has been broad, including the philosophy of religion, historical theology, ethics, and biblical exegesis. Until quite recently English readers had access only to his writings in historical theology and exegesis, a situation which has prevented a proper understanding of the purpose and development of his thought. His earliest writings were in the field of philosophy of religion, and in these works Nygren lays down the program which is carried out in the later works.

The first years of Nygren's work at the university were devoted to study and writing in philosophy of religion. His first major work was *Religious Apriori; Its Philosophical Presuppositions and Theological Implications* (1921). Condensed and popularized versions of this work appeared in Swedish and Ger-

297

man in 1922 and in English in 1960. During this period he also wrote *The Scientific Foundation of Dogmatics* (1922), *The Question of Objectivity in Theology* (1922), *Philosophical and Christian Ethics* (1923), *Basic Questions in Ethics* (1926) and *Religiosity and Christianity* (1926).

His work in the history of thought includes his *History of the Christian Idea of Love,* appearing in two parts (1930, 1936) and in English translation as *Agape and Eros* (1932, 1939). He also wrote essays on *Primitive Christianity and the Reformation* (1932) and *The Atonement as a Work of God* (1932).

Later Nygren turned to biblical theology, publishing his *Commentary on the Epistle to the Romans* in 1944 (English edition 1949) and a pastoral letter to the clergy of the diocese of Lund (1949), translated into English in 1951 with the title *The Gospel of God.* In 1956 followed the volume *Christ and His Church,* closely related to the work of the World Council of Churches' Commission on Faith and Order. He also made important contributions to two volumes of essays: *A Book about the Bible* and *A Book about the Church.*

During Nygren's days as a student of theology there was serious question about the method, scope, and even the possibility of theology. The historical study of the Bible had brought into question the traditional doctrine of biblical inspiration and authority. The theology based on the traditional use of Scripture was further undermined by the philosophical work of Kant and his successors. The scholastic method of using the theological propositions of the Bible to construct a well-integrated picture of the transcendent realm was discredited. Some theologians were persuaded that with the disappearance of the transcendent realm as an object of study, they could only duplicate the efforts of students of philosophy or psychology of religion, comparative religion or ethics. Nygren set himself the task of discovering whether there is a legitimate scientific task for the theologian and what methods should be used to establish valid knowledge in this realm.

Nygren accepts the judgment of historical studies and critical philosophy on the traditional theological method, agreeing with Kant that there can be no science of the transcendent. What lies beyond the limits of human experience cannot become the object of scientific thought. Science must be based on the realities of human experience. If theology is to claim to afford valid knowledge it must meet two requirements: (1) it must first have its own subject matter for investigation and not be parasitic on some other discipline; and (2) it must have a scientific method of study which is appropriate to its subject matter. These requirements provide the starting point for Nygren's early essays in philosophy of religion. He seeks first to answer the objections of those who claim that religion is illusion and that a scientific study of religion can only end by demonstrating this fact. He also grapples with the objections of those who claim that theology is only a masked version of some other discipline, such as ethics, philosophy, or psychology.

Beginning with an examination of philosophy itself, Nygren insists that the requirements of scientific method be applied here first of all. Inasmuch as philosophy lacks the data for a study of the transcendent realm, it must forego metaphysical speculation and assume the humbler but more useful task of a critical examination of language and presuppositions. Philosophy is not a quest for some ultimate reality beyond experience, but an examination of the validity which is to be found within experience itself. The examination of language is designed to assist clarity in communication by eliminating ambiguity and confusion as far as possible.

When the critical examination of language has been accomplished, Nygren holds, the philosopher can undertake a second task: the examination of presuppositions. These are the concepts that underlie all our thinking and speech, but of which we are most frequently unaware. They are the unspoken assumptions of a period or a culture, judgments of fact or value whose truth or validity is not questioned, simply because everyone in a society accepts them. Nygren argues that it is the task of philosophy to uncover these hidden presuppositions, examine them, and make plain what are the basic principles or fundamental categories with which a period or society carries on its task of reflection.

Through his use of critical philosophy Nygren observes that there are four main areas of meaning, each corresponding to one of the inescapable questions which are fundamental to the life of the spirit. The first is the theoretical question, the question of truth. It is easy to show that this question is fundamental and essential, for if there were no difference between truth and falsehood, research would be meaningless, the search for causes and relationships pointless, speech and reflection in vain. The question of truth points to the area of the scientific. The second question is that of right and wrong, and the closely related question of good and evil. This too is obviously fundamental, for apart from it social life would be impossible and even individual character would be without foundation. The third question is that of the beautiful. It is more difficult to establish its fundamental character and less easy to refute aesthetic skepticism, but it is nevertheless an all-embracing form of the spiritual life. The fourth question is that of the eternal, the religious question. Positivism challenges the validity of this question, interpreting religion as a relic of an earlier and outworn stage of human existence. Nygren replies that this is to confuse religion with a primitive world view, and insists that the question of the eternal can be shown to be fundamental to the life of spirit. Each of the questions claims to be valid, and not simply for a single time or place but for all time. But none of these spheres —theoretical, ethical or aesthetic—realizes this presupposition in itself. Only in religion is this presupposition of the life of the spirit realized. Each of the other realms therefore ultimately depends upon the realm of religion, the question of the eternal.

By this analysis Nygren has attempted to establish the existence of four distinct areas of meaning: science, ethics, art, and religion. Each has its own distinctive approach to the data of experience. Each has its own use of language, must be dealt with in its own terms, and resists reduction to one of the others. The areas may indeed overlap, in the sense that a person may be concerned with several of them at the same time. The physician may be concerned as scientist with the nature of the ailment afflicting his patient, as ethical thinker may be troubled about the problem of informing his patient of his condition, and as religious man be seeking divine guidance in his dilemma. But his scientific thinking will not solve his ethical problem, nor can his ethical or religious reflection solve the scientific question.

The purpose of this analysis is to show that religion is an independent form of experience with its own context of meaning. Those who regard religion as strange ritual practices or merely mythological notions fail to understand it in its fullness and reality. For religion is not something accidental imposed upon human life from outside; it is the spiritual life itself in the deepest meaning of the term. Nygren points out that the independent status of religion has frequently been overlooked—by Kant, for example, who treats it as identical with ethics, or by Hegel, who identifies it with philosophy. But to understand religion the scholar must study it as it grows on its own ground and in accordance with its own laws. It can be rightly understood and expounded only from an essentially religious point of view, and any attempt to construe the meaning of religion by the application of laws which govern other spheres of the spiritual life is bound to fail.

Nygren points out an important difference between the scientific area and the other contexts of meaning. The scientific realm is "theoretical"; the others are "atheoretical." A statement in a scientific context can be verified empirically, and its truth or falsity conclusively demonstrated. But this does not hold in ethics, aesthetics or religion. Statements in ethics and religion are true or false only in relation to ultimate standards, and these standards cannot be verified empirically. There are different ethical and religious ideals, and which of them is right and true is a matter not of empirical verification but of personal decision and commitment. This does not mean that statements in these realms are unimportant or meaningless, but that they must be judged by standards different from those which prevail in the scientific context of meaning.

For the study of religion this means that a religious assertion is not to be dealt with in abstraction or removed from its context. There are different religions and each of them forms a complete constellation of meaning. Each has its own conception of the eternal and from this develops its understanding of the religious relationship, man's communion with the eternal and its social and ethical implications. For example, both Christianity and neoplatonism speak of the love of God, but this does not point to agreement or identity. What the love of God means in each of them must be understood in the context of the total constellation of meaning. One then discovers important differences between the religiosity of late Hellenism and that of early Christianity.

But in order to understand what is essential in religion, it is not enough to undertake a logical analysis of the concept of the eternal. Because the realm of religion is autonomous, by being subjected to logical analysis it can only be falsified and confused. It is important rather to turn to an examination of historical religions, and from a study of their features learn what content is to be put into the question of the eternal. Nygren contends that examination of the religions which have existed during the course of history does not support an evolutionary scheme in which there is unbroken development from primitive religion to complete "ethical monotheism." But he perceives that the question of the eternal occurs everywhere in certain fairly constant forms, and he singles out four of them: (1) All religions claim to unveil the eternal. Some religions have no idea of God, but there is no religion which lacks the idea of revelation, the disclosure of the eternal in the world of time. The revelation takes varied forms, ranging from fetishism and animism to mysticism, but in all there is a concern to open up the experience of the eternal. (2) All religions express the disquiet or judgment of the eternal. The eternal is regarded as mysterious and powerful, and he who approaches it must do so with gravity and earnestness. (3) Religion seeks to overcome the tension between the awareness of the eternal and man's knowledge of his unworthiness. It seeks ways to bridge the chasm between man and the eternal, to remove the barriers that separate them, to seek atonement or ways of purification. (4) Religion claims to be genuine fellowship and union between the eternal and man. The two cannot stand opposed to one another, but must be brought into union. The ways of doing so are very diverse, from totemistic eating of the deity at one extreme to the most sublime mystical awareness of union with God. With this analysis Nygren believes that he has detected the essential structure of religious experience. The four aspects appear in varying degrees and emphases in concrete historical religions, but all are present. But like the concept of the eternal, they are abstract—

tools to be used in the analysis of actual religions to see what content they are given.

With the task of philosophical analysis accomplished, Nygren turns to the second main part of his theological work, the task of developing systematic theology as a scientific discipline. It is the task of science to examine and comprehend a given subject matter. The science of systematic theology, according to Nygren, is given the task of understanding and expounding the Christian faith as it has developed over the centuries. It must show the essential content and meaning of the faith, pointing out its specifically Christian features and showing what makes it different from other religions. It is *systematic* theology in that it expounds the fundamental character and unity of Christianity and shows the relationship, structure and coherence of all the parts to each other.

Nygren's proposals for a scientific systematic theology are simple and for this reason attractive. But formidable difficulties stand in the way of carrying out this program. The great number and variety of theological expressions of Christianity seem to doom any project for finding the essence of the Christian religion. Viewed in the perspective of the contemporary church one sees Roman, Orthodox, Anglican, Lutheran, Calvinist, free church, and sectarian versions of Christianity. Historical perspective shows us the versions of Irenaeus, Origen, Augustine, the scholastics, Luther, Calvin, Schleiermacher, Barth, and others. Even if one limits the quest to the New Testament there is a bewildering variety: Christianity according to Paul, James, Peter, Matthew, Luke, John. What is to insure that Nygren's version shall not be merely another addition to an already long list of interpreters of Christianity? Nygren's answer is to propose motif research as the tool of the systematic theologian.

Motif research is a technique for discovering the fundamental idea or category of a religion. It seeks to set aside what is unique to individual interpreters of a religion and fasten on the elements which are essential and formative. Its procedure is to examine the historical evidence at hand for the understanding of a religion, form a hypothesis as to the fundamental element amid all the diverse expositions, and then test the hypothesis by checking it against the evidence. If the facts are not accounted for adequately, the hypothesis must be refined or reformulated. If the hypothesis does stand up to the facts, the indications are that it expresses the fundamental character of the religion being studied, and not merely peripheral matters. Nygren maintains that this is the proper scientific approach to the study of religion, and that it is capable of yielding valid results.

In the volume *Agape and Eros* we can view the method at work. The work has two parts, one dealing with the New Testament and the apostolic age, the second examining the history of theology to the Reformation in the sixteenth century.

Nygren begins with the recognition that Christianity is a religion and is therefore concerned with the question of man's relationship to the eternal. He then asks how communion with the eternal is achieved in Christianity, in order to see what content is given to the fundamental category of all religion. His hypothesis is that the fundamental category of Christianity is *agape,* the unmotivated love of God. The communion of man with God is brought about by God's manifesting his *agape,* by the fact that he takes the initiative, offers man his love in Jesus Christ, and invites man to receive the life which is thus proffered to him. Nygren proposes to show that this is the fundamental category of Christianity by demonstrating that it is (1) the unifying principle of the diverse theologies of the New Testament, (2) the common center of all the theologies which have developed in the life of the church, and (3) the essential meaning of the great dogmas of the Christian tradition, such as creation, incarnation, and resurrection.

He begins with the materials witnessing to the ministry of Jesus and shows how agape appears as the distinctive thrust of Jesus' teaching and of his understanding of his own ministry. On the basis of this material he formulates four characteristics of agape: (1) It is spontaneous and unmotivated. Christ shows his love by establishing fellowship with social and religious outcasts. (2) It is indifferent to value. God's love is not an irrational craving for spoiled goods. His love is addressed to the proud and complacent as eagerly as to the tax collector. (3) It is creative. What has no value in itself becomes valuable because God's love is directed to it. Man is not in himself of infinite value, but is invested with value because God cares for him. (4) It initiates fellowship with God. The greatest marvel of the divine love is not that it annuls death penalties or accomplishes deliverance, but that God gives himself to his creatures.

Where the older liberal theology liked to point to the contrasts between Jesus and Paul, Nygren shows that Paul's development of the agape theme is in full harmony with that of Jesus. The vocabulary is different, but the same central theme comes to expression, as in Paul's vivid awareness that the love of God met him just as he was acting most rebelliously, on his way to persecute the Christians of Damascus. Paul's proclamation of the cross is nothing other than an exposition of God's agape. This is plain also in his use of the term agape to describe the Christian's relation to his neighbor, and in his contrast between the way of knowledge which puffs up and the way of love which builds up.

The third movement in the analysis of biblical materials is the examination of the Johannine literature. Nygren regards this as the climactic formulation of the agape motif in the New Testament, although he points out the duality of the presentation. The strong concentration on the Christian love of the brethren achieves a high level of intensity but runs the risk of narrowing its scope to members of the community.

The analysis of biblical materials is followed by a systematic exposition of the *eros* motif in Hellenistic civilization. Nygren examines the writings of Plato as an unfolding of the religious outlook of Hellenism, and then studies the development of the theme in Aristotle and in neoplatonism. The closing section of the work is a contrast between biblical and Hellenistic modes of thought, sharpening the differences in the different dimensions of God's love, love toward God, love of neighbor, and love of self.

The second volume traces the development of the idea of love in the history of the church. A new element, inexplicably absent from the first volume, appears here: the *nomos* motif, the fundamental concept of rabbinic Judaism. The nomos type is exemplified in the writings of the Apostolic Fathers and Tertullian, the eros type in Gnosticism and Alexandrian theology, and the agape type in Marcion and Irenaeus. The discussion here is a tacit correction of the first volume, where the discussion of the agape motif in Paul had little to say about conflict with the nomos concept, even though Paul's theology was formulated in a struggle with rabbinic viewpoints concerning the proper interpretation of the Old Testament.

The remainder of the volume unfolds the development of a new synthesis in the theology of Augustine, and the twofold challenge to this synthesis in the sixteenth century. Augustine is viewed as a pivotal theological figure who combines elements of biblical and neoplatonic religion in a new formulation, the Caritas synthesis, which then dominated the history of theology for the next millennium. The Renaissance offered an effective challenge to it, seeking to return to the religious ideals of Hellenism. A second challenge appears in the Reformation, which attempts to renew the biblical agape motif.

The *Commentary on the Epistle to the Romans* is an eloquent testimony to Nygren's many-sidedness and versatility as theologian. He is not only a philosopher and historical scholar of distinction, but shows remarkable gifts as an expositor. The *Commentary* does not enter upon questions of textual criticism or an examination of literary forms and traditions, but comes to grips effectively with the religious content of the epistle and expounds it with clarity and simplicity. His treatment of the development of the argument of the letter is persuasive, even in such difficult and debatable sections as chapter seven or chapters nine to eleven.

The volume *Christ and His Church* also shows Nygren as an able organizer and expositor of complex and difficult biblical materials, and it illustrates the wide influence he has exercised on the character of theological discussion within the ecumenical movement. When after forty years of discussion of comparative ecclesiology the Commission on Faith and Order turned to study of the centrality of Christ and his relation to the church, Bishop Nygren's voice was one of the most effective in urging the change.

The Gospel of God, first written as a pastoral letter to the clergy of the diocese of Lund, shows yet another aspect of Nygren's theological work—his pastoral orientation and concern.

However intense his preoccupation with the problems of scientific theology, he has never permitted himself to overlook the central concern of the church, the communication of the gospel. An earlier work, *The Church Conflict in Germany,* shows another aspect of this concern. Written after a visit to Germany in 1933, the year of Hitler's accession to power, it shows Nygren's early perception of the true character of the Nazi movement and his anxiety that the church not be trapped into compromise.

But while we are impressed by the versatility of Nygren as theologian, it is highly probable that his most enduring contribution is to the history of Christian thought. *Agape and Eros* promises to be a lasting source of illumination on the meaning of the Christian theological tradition. His contribution to philosophy of religion may well increase in popularity among the devotees of linguistic analysis, especially if a projected volume on theological method is published. Others will agree with the criticism that the task of philosophical criticism is not done stringently enough, and that the formal questions addressed to the Christian tradition are not sufficiently formal, but ascribe an alien content to the Scriptures and thus distort the biblical message. Support for this contention is to be found in Nygren's neglect of the Old Testament as the background of the Christian community and his overlooking of the tension between *nomos* and *agape* in the development of the biblical message. He has also been criticized for being insufficiently radical in his proclamation of the kerygma to his own age, being so occupied with research into Luther's theology as to permit the historical presentation of that theology to serve as proclamation to the twentieth century.

Bibliography

Anders Nygren, *Agape and Eros,* Philadelphia, Westminster, 1953.

Gustaf Wingren, *Theology in Conflict,* Philadelphia, Fortress, 1958.

GUSTAF AULÉN

Gustaf Wingren

Gustaf Aulén was born on May 15, 1879. After receiving his early education in Kalmar, on the east coast of Sweden, he matriculated at the University of Uppsala, where he became an assistant professor in 1907. For the subject of his doctoral thesis Aulén chose the life and history of Henrik Reuterdahl, professor of church history at the University of Lund in the nineteenth century. After serving as an assistant professor in Uppsala from 1907 to 1913, Aulén transferred to the University of Lund, where he was a professor of dogmatics from 1913 to 1933. While in Uppsala, Aulén had continued his interest in the theological tradition of Lund, and so in 1914, as a young professor, he was quite prepared to deliver an inaugural lecture on the theme "Den Dogmatiska Traditionen vid Lunds Universitet" (The Dogmatic Tradition at the University of Lund). During his twenty years as a professor in Lund Aulén himself left his mark on that university's tradition. His personality and his books helped immeasurably to define what is meant by the term "Lundensian theology."

In 1933 Aulén's university work was broken off by his appointment as bishop of the Strängnäs diocese, a position he held for almost twenty years (1933–52). But even during these two decades he continued to engage in theological research. In 1937, at Edinburgh, he officiated as a vice-president of the World Conference on Faith and Order. Liturgy and church music have always been of great interest to Aulén; while he was a bishop the Swedish Church acquired a new hymnbook, a service book, a gospel book, and a missal, and he played an active part in shaping all four.

After retiring from the bishopric, Aulén returned to Lund and immediately busied himself in writing. Several books have come from him during his emeritus years, and in spite of his advanced age all of them suggest a youthful spirit. Aulén is still a member of the editorial staff of *Svénsk Teologisk Kvartal-*

skrift (Swedish Theological Quarterly), a periodical he began in 1925. Although it continued to be printed in Lund, Aulén remained its chief editor during his first year as Bishop of Strängnäs. Now he is the only surviving founder of the journal. Some important articles by him are to be found among its early volumes.

Aulén's most important work before he became a professor was *Den Lutherska Kyrkoidén* (The Lutheran Concept of the Church), published in 1912. At that time, unlike today, it was not customary for a European theologian to deal with the doctrine of the church. But Aulén was interested in that doctrine from the very beginning, and for two reasons. In the first place, it had been a dominant concern of the old Lundensian tradition dating from the middle of the nineteenth century. Aulén was well acquainted with this tradition and its outstanding figure, Henrik Reuterdahl, the subject of his doctoral thesis. In the second place, in Uppsala Aulén had been a pupil of Nathan Söderblom and Einar Billing, theologians for whom the concept of the church was central. The influence of these two sources is still evident in Aulén's emeritus work *Hundra ars Svensk Kyrkodebatt* (One Hundred Years of Swedish Discussions on the Church), published in 1953.

In 1917 Aulén published his first major work as a Lund professor—a textbook titled *Dogmhistoria* (History of Dogma). Designed primarily to aid students of theology, only at a few points does the book present results of independent theological research. Relying on synopses by such German scholars as Harnack, Seeberg, and Loofs, it traces the development of Christian doctrine from the first till the twentieth century.

Aulén's next book, *Den allmänneliga kristna tron,* appeared in 1923. Although this was also intended as a textbook, in it Aulén builds on a basis distinctively his own. The book, which has had five Swedish editions (the latest in 1957), appeared in 1948 in a U.S. edition under the title *The Faith of the Christian Church.*[1] Its influence has been important within as well as outside Sweden. The major sections of the work are "The Liv-

---

[1] The first American edition (Philadelphia, Muhlenberg, 1948) was a translation from the fourth Swedish edition (1943); the second American edition (Philadelphia, Fortress, 1961) is a translation from the fifth Swedish edition (1957).

ing God," "The Act of God in Christ," and "The Church of God." It is evident from this work that Aulén has his roots in Einar Billing's theology; it has the same basic structure as Billing's *De etiska tankarna i urkristendomen* (Ethical Ideas in Original Christianity, 1907) and his *Försoningen* (Atonement, 1908)—neither of which, unfortunately, has been translated into English. History, declares Aulén, is the workshop of God. In history, God presents himself as the "living God," accomplishing his utmost in his act in Christ, and out of this act arises the church. The book's three parts, it may be noted, make for a marked trinitarian theology.

Aulén's next work in the area of the history of Christian thought, *Den kristna gudsbilden* (The Christian Conception of God), first appeared in 1927 and was published in German translation in 1930 as *Das christliche Gottesbild*. In it Aulén manifests for the first time his concern to divide the history of dogma into distinct periods and to place the first Christian centuries and the Reformation on the same level. Both these periods he views as valid expounders of the biblical message. For both, God is the subject—the "living God" and the God of action in Christ. At the same time Aulén is critical of medieval scholasticism and Lutheran orthodoxy, which he sees as relatively similar. Thus he does not draw a line from Luther to Lutheranism but instead is inclined to note points at which Lutheranism withdrew from Luther—for instance, its tendency toward a juridical, legalistic interpretation of the atonement. For Aulén, then, Luther is to be allied more with the Fathers of the early church than with Lutheranism. Indeed, in Aulén's view, Luther belongs to the universal church. It is no accident that Aulén's theology has had wide acceptance outside Lutheranism in spite of its being grounded in Luther. Aulén believes that in this work he further developed the view of Luther held by Einar Billing and Nathan Söderblom. Nonetheless in certain respects his interpretation is independent of theirs.

Aulén's next important work also was of a monographic character: a historical study titled *Den kristna försoningstanken* (The Christian Idea of the Atonement), based on a series of lectures delivered by Aulén at the University of Uppsala in 1930 and published the same year. It was published in English in 1931 under the title *Christus Victor,* and since then it has appeared in several editions in English and likewise in French, Dutch, and Chinese. Presumably it is Aulén's most famous book. It presents much the same view of the periods of Christian dogma as his "The Christian Conception of God." Irenaeus, bishop of Lyon during the second century, is here regarded as the great Father of the Fathers. Aulén contends that Irenaeus and Luther essentially share the same understanding of the atonement. Both conceive of it not primarily as a sacrifice offered to God, delivered by man to a receiving God. Rather, they conceive of it as an act performed by God himself, an act accomplished by God in Christ in struggle against the evil powers of sin and death which have enslaved man. Divine struggle and divine victory characterize the work of atonement. Luther modifies the idea of struggle by introducing divine "wrath" and "law," but he nonetheless adheres to the view Aulén calls the "classic" idea of the atonement, which emphasizes a "line leading downwards from God."

Contrasting to the classic idea of the atonement is what Aulén terms the "Latin" idea, which views the work of atonement as a line "from man upward," accomplished primarily by Christ in his human nature and offered to a receiving God. Again we are confronted by the relationship between medieval scholasticism (Anselm) and Lutheran orthodoxy. Both espouse variations of the Latin idea and hence are alien to the theology of the Fathers and the Reformation.

The chief criticism to be made of Aulén's interpretation of the classic idea of the atonement is that it tends to ignore the human nature of Christ. His exposition never clearly answers the question why Christ had to fight against and triumph over the evil powers of the world as a tempted *man.* The reason for this weakness in Aulén's analysis may be that he begins with the second article of the Creed rather than the first, that of Creation. Irenaeus rightly delineates the act of God in Christ as *recapitulatio,* as an act which involves a restoration of man, a return to the purity of the creation.

Of the books Aulén has published in Lund since his retirement we have already mentioned *Hundra års svensk kyrkodebatt* (1953), which is not likely to be translated since it deals with a Swedish subject. Two other books from his retirement years, however, have already been translated into English: a work on the Lord's Supper, *För eder utgiven,* published in 1956, and a work on the ecumenical problem, *Reformation och katolicitet,* published in 1959. The former appeared in English translation in 1958 as *Eucharist and Sacrifice,* the latter in 1961 as *Reformation and Catholicity.* These works from the past decade must be seen against the background of the situation in the Church of Sweden. A vocal high-church group within it, influenced by foreign liturgical movements, at times takes positions contrary to some of the central emphases of Luther and the Swedish Reformers. This high-church wing is especially influential in the middle-Swedish dioceses, which at one time were primarily low-church in orientation.

Not least among them, the diocese of Strängnäs, where Aulén served as bishop, has acquired a high-church clergy in parishes which have been virtually without traditions and which often have very few churchgoers. Aulén himself holds a rather ambivalent position in relation to this Swedish high-church movement. His theology is decidedly on the side of the Reformation and Luther. But owing to his work in connection with liturgy and church music he is at the same time in rapport with the high-church group. Thus it is not surprising that Aulén's writing during the 1950's has sought to achieve peace and to give guidance to church groups of differing opinions.

Eucharist and Sacrifice is concerned with the controversial idea of sacrifice in the Lord's Supper. *Reformation and Catholicity* analyzes the place of the tradition and deals at length with the creeds of the Patristic period and the Reformation. Though Luther figures centrally in the latter work, the Lutheran reformation is regarded—as always in Aulén's works—from an ecumenical and catholic viewpoint.

What is characteristic and distinctive about Aulén's thought? His mentors Söderblom and Billing concerned themselves with the Bible and with Luther. In their biblical research they benefited from findings in the field of history of religion, and they had a positive attitude toward historical-critical exegesis. At the same time they used the then new knowledge of the Near East religions in such a way as to focus on what was uniquely biblical.

In this respect Aulén is very much their pupil. Throughout his works he is concerned to delineate the characteristics of the genuinely Christian faith. But quite new is Aulén's interest in the history of dogma, an interest that he manifested from the very beginning of his professional career. His first work during this period was a survey of the history of dogma, of the development of church doctrine from the earliest days to our own time, and he has retained his historical perspective, his interest in "periods." He is concerned to delineate the characteristic features of the early church, the medieval period, the Reformation, and so on. The uniqueness of Christianity he sees as involved in constant struggle throughout the different periods—for example against juridical, legalistic attitudes or against idealistic, subjectivistic conceptions of life. Sometimes what is genuinely Christian appears purely and clearly, sometimes it is obscured. This desire to maintain a historical outlook was not to be found in Billing or Söderblom.

Consequently Luther also is seen in a new light by Aulén; he emerges as a renewer of the biblical inheritance, whereas the periods before and after him—the periods of medieval scholasticism and Lutheran orthodoxy—were, in Aulén's view, unable to keep this inheritance fresh and vital. Both Billing and Söderblom did work on Luther, but they never placed him in such a perspective. Particularly new is Aulén's interest in the Church Fathers, primarily in Irenaeus, who had been of little interest to Aulén's teachers in Uppsala.

Aulén's predilection for the historical outlook and the dividing of church history into periods is best understood in the light of the Swedish theological examination system. As a rule in European universities, the study of the history of dogma and of Christian thought constitutes a part of the discipline of church history; the church historian deals with both the happenings and the thought of past eras. Systematic theology—for instance in Germany and Switzerland—is a quite independent discipline. In Sweden, on the other hand, the history of dogma and the history of Christian thought are subsumed under the discipline of systematic theology. While studying past periods seminarians also study systematic theology. Thus historical study is given a systematic orientation. The problem with this approach is that it tends to regard the uniqueness of the faith as resting in history; it never finds its way to the present age. In Sweden there is no effort comparable to Bultmann's program which regards the interpretation of the kerygma as the main task of theology. A Swedish scholar in the field of systematics is likely to devote his best years to historical research—a feature of Swedish theology which has been emphasized by Aulén's successors. Aulén's work *The Faith of the Christian Church,* however, is systematic in character yet presents the Christian faith to the man of today.

The "Lundensian theology" which thus came into view utilized much more than the old theology of Uppsala, historical theories shaped through contact with church historians and historians of dogma on the Continent. Of special influence was Adolf von Harnack. Harnack regarded the early dogma of the church as a corruption of the simple doctrine of Jesus. Aulén, however, has given much attention to the christological conflicts of the first four centuries, and he is convinced that the resulting dogmatic system served to guard the Gospel of the Apostolic Age against Gnostic and Arian inroads. This kind of positive valuation of the earliest dogma of the church has long been typical of Anglican theology; it is therefore understandable why Aulén's works have been widely read and appreciated in England.

In regard to the historical view of the theology of Luther, Aulén made use of German research, especially that of Karl Holl and his pupils. But exegetics and the theology of the Bible have always formed the basic ground of Aulén's work. Increasingly Aulén has cooperated with the exponents of the so-called realistic exegesis, established in Uppsala in the 1930's by Anton Fridrichsen. The symposium *En bok om kyrken* (A Book on the Church) is a result of the cooperation between systematic theologians in Lund and exegetes in Uppsala. When this book appeared in 1942 Aulén was no longer a professor at the University of Lund. But most of its articles were originally delivered as discourses at a conference in Nyköping in February 1942— and Nyköping is situated in the diocese of Strängnäs where Aulén was a bishop. That this place was selected for the meeting was no accident.

A number of scholars have raised questions concerning this cooperative effort between systematics and exegesis. Over the years there has arisen a strange alliance between, on the one hand, exegetical scholarship executed by young New Testament scholars in Uppsala and, on the other, certain doctrines of the Anglican and Roman churches. These scholars tend to put aside Luther's exegesis with arguments derived from high-church views. Against this background it is easier to understand Aulén's writings of the 1950's, which have helped foster a split between Swedish exegesis and Swedish systematics and have underplayed the Reformation inheritance. How to remove this crisis in Swedish theology is a problem which cannot be treated here.

When Aulén appeared on the scene soon after the First World War the situation was altogether different. At that time a liberal and subjectivistic theology was posed against a conservative and confessional theology, and Aulén found his own way between them. At about the same time dialectical theology made its way on the Continent. Aulén's emergence is not so distant but what many of us can remember the atmosphere in which his theology appeared. Those who were rooted in the liberal tradition at first regarded Aulén's theology as but a new form of conservative confessionalism. Aulén made no attempt to discover the "historical Jesus" or to anchor faith in a "religious disposition" or in subjective experience. He did not see a demarcation between the Gospels and Paul; on the contrary, he held that the act of God in Christ, as related in the Gospels, was properly interpreted by Paul and by the early Church Fathers.

Those rooted in the conservative tradition, on the other hand, viewed Aulén's theology as a new form of liberalism. Aulén did not reject historical-critical research on the Bible; indeed, he sought to learn from the exegetes—even from some of the most radical ones. He was respectful of scholars in the field of comparative religion and sometimes used their work in support of his own theses. Conservative readers were again distressed when they learned what Aulén had to say about Luther and Lutheranism. Just as Holl had emphasized the difference between Luther and Melanchthon and thus driven a wedge between Luther and Lutheranism, so also did Aulén criticize Lutheran orthodoxy, especially in regard to the view of the atonement which by stressing juridical "satisfaction" theories obscured "the unabridged act of God in Christ."

One might expect that a theology which thus disappointed both liberals and confessionals would have difficulty gaining acceptance. But such was not the case with Aulén's. After the First World War disillusionment with both confessionalism and liberalism set in, and Aulén's unfamiliar theology came as something of a relief—a theology that upheld both the classical dogmatic system and the right of free research into biblical texts. Especially appealing was Aulén's unusual coordination of incarnation and atonement. The Fathers' christological formulas concerning divine and human nature were reintroduced as bearers of the Gospel, witnessing to the act of God in Christ, to an atonement performed by God himself and offered as a free gift to all men through the church.

But the difference between Aulén's theology and the dialectical or "crisis" theology of Germany and Switzerland is also apparent. In his 1927 work, *The Christian Conception of God,* Aulén himself indicates awareness of this difference—a difference which can be traced to divergent historical sources. In the theology of Karl Barth the influence of Calvin and of medieval scholasticism, particularly Anselm, is considerable, while Aulén has been influenced instead by the antignostic Fathers of the early church. This means that the creation holds a more central position for Aulén—and in connection with creation the law also emerges as an essential concept. In the 1930's both Aulén and Barth analyzed and criticized the political situation in Germany and were staunchly anti-Nazi during the Second World War. Of personal importance to Aulén in this connection were his relatives and friends in occupied Norway. But the theological basis for opposition to Nazism was different for the two men. Barth's criticism of Nazism proceeded from the Gospel and from the second article of the Creed. Aulén's criticism had a much wider basis and was grounded in the fundamental theological concept of *Skaparene lag* (The Law of the Creator).[2] The Law of the Creator, ac-

[2] The lectures delivered by Aulén in the United States in the spring of 1947 are characteristic of this phase of his work. The lectures are gathered in a book titled *Church, Law and Society,* published in the U.S. in 1948 (N.Y., Scribner's).

cording to Aulén, is a guardian of the interests of the neighbor but is also a law for society as a whole. Aulén sees this law as a basis for cooperation between Christians and non-Christians. Clearly this idea relies on Luther's "two-realm" theory—an approach explicitly rejected by Barth.

It is evident that Aulén has influenced the whole of Scandinavian theology; his work has modified theological work in both Scandinavia and Finland, and as a result a new way of posing questions has emerged. To this should be added Aulén's influence on Anglican theology, primarily through *Christus Victor*. It is yet too early to give an opinion of Aulén's influence on American theology; study of his work began later in the U.S., but it continues to grow there. Especially interesting is Aulén's role in the inner circle of his former colleagues at Lund. Anders Nygren, beginning as a philosopher in the 1920's, wrote little in the area of systematics. In the 1930's, however, beginning with *Den kristna kärlekstanken* (*Agape and Eros*), he turned to a form of systematic theology termed "motif research." Nygren sees three motifs—agape, eros, nomos—as fighting for domination through the centuries. Sometimes the early Christian agape motif emerges, sometimes it is obscured by hostile motifs. In Nygren's view, to write systematic theology is to write the history of the conflict of these basic motifs. The division of church history into periods becomes also for Nygren a chief concern. But most importantly, once again the early church and the Luther period emerge as similar. According to Nygren's 1936 study, Irenaeus and Luther are history's two best proponents of the agape motif. This conclusion of Nygren's strikingly accords with Aulén's conclusion in his 1930 work on the atonement. Nygren's dependence on the Lundensian tradition is to be noted in two books by myself written in the 1940's: one on Irenaeus (translated into English in 1959 as *Man and the Incarnation*) and one on Luther (translated in 1957 as *Luther on Vocation*).

It is rather difficult to state in what respects Aulén and Nygren have influenced each other. They belonged to the same faculty during the years 1924–33. Aulén was the first to use the "period" approach and no doubt influenced Nygren in this regard. Nygren's work in philosophy of religion, however, is of primary and pioneering importance. His motif method has been most exhaustively developed by Ragnar Bring, his successor as professor of dogmatics at Lund. But it is also true that Aulén has remained somewhat aloof from the later Lundensian theology and uses the term "motif" quite differently than does Nygren. Aulén sometimes views the motifs as composing a unity; a universal conception of Christianity would, for example, bring together "motifs" which might otherwise move in different directions. Aulén seeks to hold together that which is inclined to separate. A typical expression of his is "tension-filled unity." A sound theology, he maintains, holds together the wrath of God and the love of God—unites God's almightiness and his love. But Aulén's effort to hold together opposing elements preserves rather than smooths over tensions; he would sacrifice no element to attain a deceptive harmony.

Aulén is the connecting link between the theological renaissance in Uppsala after 1900 and the theological renaissance in Lund after 1920. He not only stands between those two revival periods but also belongs to both; while he remains faithful to his inheritance from his student years in Uppsala, he also adds to it his wide historical outlook, his work with periods of church history, his study of the Fathers and of classical dogma. All this is characteristic of Lundensian theology and is to be found again in the writings of Anders Nygren, who in turn has added his own contributions to the inheritance, notably his wide philosophical framework and his "basic motif" approach. Aulén has not a little to learn from the younger man Nygren; nonetheless Aulén, though drawing on the tradition of Billing and Söderblom, has furthered that tradition in a quite original and creative manner.

It might seem as if Aulén—viewed in this way as coming between Billing and Nygren—were a figure bound in time, tied to the first half of this century. Strangely enough, in Sweden Aulén is viewed in almost opposite fashion; his contributions to the present theological discussion seem fresh and alive: his words fit the present situation, they break down false contrasts, they point forward. Why is Aulén so well received? For one thing, it is evident that what was a new theological stance at the beginning of this century—that represented by Einar Billing and

Nathan Söderblom—does not today seem antiquated; indeed this older theology has come to life again. The fact that it has returned to life seems to be a part of a general European phenomenon; one can observe in several European countries a considered examination of that theology which tried to take seriously the historical-critical method in exegesis, in the conviction that just in this way the evangelical faith can be more fully comprehended. Furthermore, Aulén in his books of the 1950's has directed his attention to actual problems in today's theological situation—problems of Christian ministry, of Scripture and tradition, of the sacrifice in the Lord's Supper, which in Sweden are at the center of theological controversy. Owing partly to high-church opinions, partly to trends in New Testament exegesis (particularly in Uppsala), the question of the relation between the Reformation and the early Church Fathers has become paramount. On the basis of his previous research Aulén is exceptionally well suited to deal with this problem, and his frank and straightforward way of doing so is evidence that he is well aware of his responsibility.

When Aulén thus directs his attention to the state of affairs in Sweden he is at the same time expressing interest in the theological situation internationally. In *Eucharist and Sacrifice* he deals with several Anglican theologians, and in *Reformation and Catholicity* he discusses Roman Catholic contributions to the ecumenical discussion. The current theological situation in Sweden is such that discussion of foreign contributions seems to be the only hope of untangling the skein of persistent problems. It is significant that Aulén's books are so promptly translated into English. This fact also is evidence of the strength and relevance of his theology.

Bibliography

Gustaf Aulén, *The Faith of the Christian Church*, rev. ed., Philadelphia, Fortress, 1961.

No full-scale study of Aulén is available in English.

C. H. DODD

George B. Caird

Charles Harold Dodd was born on April 7, 1884, at Wrexham in Denbighshire, North Wales. At the age of eighteen he won a classical scholarship to University College, Oxford, and four years later was awarded his B.A. with a first class both in Honours Classical Moderations and in the Final School of Literae Humaniores. From 1907 to 1911 he was engaged in research, first in Roman Imperial Numismatics at the University of Berlin, subsequently in Early Christian Epigraphy at Magdalen College, Oxford. Concurrently with these studies he took a course of theological training at Mansfield College, Oxford, which led to ordination in 1912. After three years as minister of the Congregational Church at Warwick he returned to Mansfield College as Yates Lecturer (afterwards Yates Professor) in New Testament Greek and Exegesis. In 1930 he was appointed Rylands Professor of Biblical Criticism and Exegesis in the University of Manchester, and in 1935, with his election as Norris-Hulse Professor of Divinity at Cambridge, he became the first non-Anglican to hold a chair of divinity at either of the ancient English universities. Besides these regular appointments he has held a number of special lectureships: he was Grinfield Lecturer in the Septuagint at Oxford (1927–31); Speaker's Lecturer in Biblical Studies at Oxford (1933–37); Shaffer Lecturer at Yale (1935); Ingersoll Lecturer at Harvard (1935); Hewett Lecturer at Episcopal Theological Seminary, Cambridge, Mass., Union Theological Seminary, New York, and Andover-Newton Seminary (1938); and Olaus Petri Lecturer at Uppsala (1949). He was elected Fellow of the British Academy in 1946. After his retirement in 1949 he was for a time Visiting Professor in Biblical Theology at Union Theological Seminary, New York, and during this stay in the United States he was also Bampton Lecturer in America, Stone Lecturer at Princeton Theological Seminary, and, for the second time, Ingersoll Lecturer at Harvard. He returned to England in 1950 to become general director of the New Translation of the Bible—"The New English Bible," as it was later to be called. Since then he has been Syr D. Owen Evans Lecturer at the University College of Wales, Aberystwyth (1954), and Sarum Lecturer at Oxford (1954–55), and has been the first non-Anglican to preach the University Sermon at Oxford since the days of the Protectorate. His distinguished contribution to biblical scholarship has been recognized by honorary degrees from Oxford, Cambridge, London, Manchester, Aberdeen, Glasgow, Wales, Harvard, Strasbourg, and Oslo, and by honorary fellowships at Jesus College, Cambridge, and University College, Oxford.

Dodd's publications include over twenty books and about seventy articles, essays, lectures, and reviews, which between them cover a very wide range of New Testament study. But within the whole series may be discerned a leitmotif or principle of unity: the conviction that God is Lord of history, and that the word of God spoken in Scripture is so inextricably interwoven into the fabric of historical events that it can be let loose into the modern world in the fullness of its relevance and power only through historical criticism exercised with the utmost integrity and thoroughness. The importance of this principle can be seen if we set Dodd's work over against each of the five great schools of New Testament thought which have held the hegemony during his lifetime: the radical criticism represented by Wellhausen and Wrede and more recently by Loisy and Goguel; the *Religionsgeschichtliche Schule* of Reitzenstein and Bousset and their modern disciple Bultmann; the thoroughgoing eschatology of Weiss and Schweitzer; the form criticism of Dibelius, Schmidt, and Bultmann; and the revival of biblical theology, heralded by Barth's commentary on Romans. Dodd belongs to all of these schools and to none of them. He has responded to the stimulus of each of them, yet always with originality. He has frequently spoken and written with warm appreciation of their leading exponents, maintaining at the same time his critical independence.

In its inception radical criticism was a movement of emancipation from the dogmatic tradition of centuries, which had almost totally overlaid the real humanity of Jesus, except as an article in the Creed. The critics believed that by employing the methods of the secular historian they could probe behind the Christ of faith to find the Jesus of history. What they in fact did was to produce so many conflicting portraits of the Jesus of history that the whole quest ended in historical skepticism. In the reaction that followed there were many who turned for security to the verbal inerrancy of the Scripture, to the fortress of creed and ecclesiastical council, or to a theology of transcendence unassailable by the doubts of the historian. Dodd has been one of those who unswervingly maintained that, for those who believe in an incarnation, there is no avoiding the historic quest, and that it was not the methods of the critics that were at fault but their presuppositions.

> If we are bound to criticize the great critics of the last century, we are also bound to confess that where we have gone beyond them it is by standing on their shoulders. It is a testimony to the scientific integrity of the critical school that by applying their own methods more strictly it was led to discard many of the presuppositions upon which it formerly relied, and to arrive at what I believe to be a juster estimate of the material with which it deals. Be suspicious of any suggestion that we can afford to by-pass criticism. The way of advance lies through and not round the critical problem.[1]

The history-of-religion school thought that they had found the way through the critical problem. Christianity, they pointed out, did not come into existence in an intellectual vacuum. It had its roots in Judaism and spread rapidly into the gentile world of cults and philosophies, a world where there were "gods many and lords many." They hoped that by stripping off all that Christianity had in common with contemporary religions they would arrive at its essential core. Under their hands the picture of the first century background of Christianity was filled in with an immense wealth of detail. Dodd has hailed their labors as "the most distinctive contribution of the first quarter of the twentieth century"[2] and has himself provided a most important

[1] *The Bible Today* (Cambridge, The Univ. Press, 1946), p. 27.
[2] *The Present Task in New Testament Studies* (Cambridge, The Univ. Press, 1936), p. 14.

addition to them with his own researches into the Septuagint and the Hermetic literature. Nevertheless he has also criticized these scholars because they too readily believed that parallels were evidence of dependence, and because they envisaged early Christianity as an amalgam of beliefs and practices drawn from contemporary Jewish and pagan religion, whereas if they had regarded it in its wholeness they would have been struck by its coherence and distinctiveness. "To establish the derivation of an idea is not to explain it as an element in a new complex."[3]

Schweitzer's rediscovery of biblical eschatology had a transforming influence on the whole of New Testament scholarship, for it opened up the possibility, ignored by previous generations of scholars, that the apostolic faith of the New Testament, in which eschatology figured so largely, might actually be an accurate reproduction of the mind of Jesus, formed as it was by the expectations of apocalyptic Judaism. But Schweitzer carried out his reconstruction of the Gospel with an uncritical reliance on the least trustworthy strands of Synoptic tradition, never stopped to consider whether the Jews, Jesus, or the early Christians took their eschatological language with pedantic literalness or with an understanding of its symbolic character, and completely overlooked the fact that whatever concepts Jesus inherited were transmuted in the crucible of his experience. It was Dodd's concept of realized eschatology, the product of accurate and imaginative scholarship, that rescued Schweitzer's work from futility, as we shall see more fully below.

Form criticism began as a protest against the skepticism of the radical critics and ended by surrendering to it. The form critics believed that the Gospels were compiled out of small units of tradition which, during the period of oral transmission, circulated independently in a limited number of stereotyped forms; and they hoped that by classifying these *pericopae* according to their formal characteristics they would obtain a reliable index of their historical validity. They started from the well-established principle that the contents of the Gospels were preserved out of a larger mass of available material by a process of natural selection, since the early Christians remembered and

[3] *Ibid.,* p. 15.

recorded those sayings and stories which were relevant to their current needs and interests. Every *pericope* therefore had an identifiable *Sitz im Leben* or setting in the life of the primitive church. The next step was to attribute larger and larger powers to the community, which was supposed not merely to have preserved and molded the units of tradition, but in many cases to have created them to meet its own needs. The end of the process was Bultmann's conclusion that very little can be confidently asserted about the historical Jesus. The form critics used criteria which were far too subjective, ignored the established results of literary criticism, overlooked the presence of eyewitnesses in the early church, attributed incredible powers of invention to the community, and unjustifiably depreciated the historical value of Mark's outline of the ministry of Jesus. The positive results of their work would be meager indeed had not Dodd shown how their methods could be turned to more constructive use. He has used the form-critical classification of *pericopae* to demonstrate that, at one point after another in the Gospel narrative, sayings and stories with a wide variety of forms present us with a convergent testimony, which encourages us to think that we are in touch with authentic history and not merely with church tradition.[4] He has shown that the parables, though they may have had a setting in the life of the church in which they were given a general, moral interpretation, had their original setting in the tumultuous ministry of Jesus, as interpretations of the crisis and opportunity which his coming had brought upon Israel. Above all he has acknowledged the great service done by the form critics in drawing our attention to the period of oral tradition between the life of Jesus and the writing of the earliest documents, and has devised a reliable technique for recovering the content of Christian preaching and teaching during that formative generation.

Barth's *Romans,* published in 1918, was a great blast of the prophetic trumpet, recalling New Testament scholars from their preoccupation with details of literary and historical criticism (what the Germans call *Historismus*) to their proper task of expounding the Scriptures as the Word of God. In the excite-

----

[4] *History and the Gospel* (London, Nisbet, 1938), pp. 91–103.

ment of new discovery it had been all too easy to forget that the Bible is above all else a book about God. "Paul knows of God what most of us do not know; and his epistles enable us to know what he knew."[5] There can be little doubt that we owe to Barth the healthy revival of theology which has characterized biblical scholarship during the past forty years. Yet there were dangers in his exegetical methods which have become more apparent in his later work. While Bultmann has been telling us that it is impossible to attain a reliable historical picture of Jesus, Barth has been assuring us that after all this does not matter, since the Jesus of history is irrelevant to faith in Christ the Lord. As a historical figure Jesus is even "a little commonplace" in comparison with the founders of other religions and some of his own followers.[6] The revolt against *Historismus* has become an indifference to history.

Dodd was one of the first to respond to Barth's challenge. Within two years of the appearance of Barth's *Romans* he had published his first major work, *The Meaning of Paul for Today.* Here already we can find the distinctive note which Dodd was to sound so clearly in his later writings. The Word of God in Scripture is not a series of eternally valid propositions which can be disengaged from their temporary setting. It comes to us in the writings of individual men about particular events and situations; and both the individuality of the writers and the particularity of the events are an essential part of the divine revelation. We cannot claim that the Bible is God's word, unless we are prepared to allow its authors to speak for themselves in their own native accents; and we shall find what they say relevant to ourselves only when we have taken the trouble to discover how it was relevant to the circumstances of their own day.

The emphasis on the unity of revelation is salutary. But the question of the historicity of the Gospel narrative is not so easily disposed of. For better or worse, Christianity grounds itself upon a

[5] Karl Barth, *Epistle to the Romans* (London, Oxford Univ. Press, 1933), p. 11.
[6] See Barth's *The Doctrine of the Word of God* (Edinburgh, T. & T. Clark, 1936), p. 188.

revelation *in history*, and history consists of events (including the meaning borne by events, but necessarily including what actually happened). It remains, therefore, a question of acute relevance, what actually happened.[7]

Dodd's own doctrine of history was adumbrated in 1927 in a paper communicated to a conference of English and German theologians and subsequently developed in a series of three books, published between 1935 and 1938. The major premise of the argument is that history consists not of bare facts but of facts plus meaning, facts selected by the historian as worthy of record, because they seem to him to be significant. Some events are more significant than others; and it is not incongruous with the nature of history that there should be a unique event, an event of such absolute and universal significance that it could give meaning and purpose to all history. The minor premise (minor logically, but theologically far-reaching) is that according to the teaching of Jesus the Kingdom of God had become through his ministry a present reality, confronting men with an offer of redemptive power and a demand for instant response and unconditional obedience. The Law and prophets had held sway till John the Baptist, but now the Kingdom was being proclaimed, men were seeing and hearing that which prophets and kings had desired to see, something greater than Jonah the prophet and Solomon the king; already the guests were being summoned to the messianic banquet, already the strong man was bound and his house plundered, already the harvest was ripe for the sickle; and the night of crisis was at hand when the servants must be awake and prepared for the coming of their Lord.

The Jews had always believed that God was Lord of history, but, recognizing that God's intentions were never fully disclosed, let alone attained, in the actual events of their national life, they looked for a Day when God's reign of justice and peace should be established; and in that Day they found the meaning and purpose of all history. But for them it remained an ideal, an unfulfilled aspiration, sometimes even a phantasy. Jesus, in a

[7] *The Study of Theology*, K. E. Kirk, ed. (N.Y., Harper, 1939), p. 241.

great variety of most vivid imagery, declared that this eschatological Day had arrived. Thus, taught by Jesus, the early Christians believed that they had been witnesses to an event which was nothing other than the visitation of God, an event which was capable of giving meaning to all other events. The story of Jesus was sacred history, which carried with it the possibility that all history might be taken up into the same transcendent order.

> Whenever the Gospel is proclaimed, it brings about a crisis, as in the experience of the individual, so also in the experience of whole communities and civilizations. Out of the crisis comes a new creation, by the power of God. Every such occasion is the "fullness of time" in which the Kingdom of God comes. Thus history reveals its meaning as an order of redemption and revelation.[8]

The concept of realized eschatology rests on such overwhelming evidence that it must be regarded as one of the permanent gains of modern scholarship; but it has corollaries which have provoked a storm of controversy. If in the coming of Jesus the meaning of history is fully revealed and its purpose fully achieved, what are we to say about subsequent history, and in particular about the expectation of the New Testament that the historical process would end in a Day of the Son of Man? The *eschaton* of the Jewish hope was final chronologically as well as teleologically, as Dodd himself has pointed out. "It is such that nothing more could happen in history, because the eternal meaning which gives reality to history is now exhausted. To conceive any further event on the plane of history would be like drawing a cheque on a closed account."[9] Except in a highly figurative sense we can hardly be asked to believe that the world ended in A.D. 30! Dodd's answer is that the language of eschatology is figurative, that the end of the world, like its beginning, is a myth used to convey that which is essentially beyond history. "Jesus declares that this ultimate, the Kingdom of God, has come into history, and He takes upon Himself the 'eschatologi-

---

[8] *History and the Gospel*, pp. 181 ff.

[9] *The Apostolic Preaching and Its Developments* (London, Hodder and Stoughton, 1936), p. 206.

cal' role of 'Son of Man.' The absolute, the 'wholly other,' has entered into time and space." In so far as the Gospel writers speak of a future crisis, their tenses are a mere accommodation of language. "There is no coming of the Son of Man 'after' His coming in Galilee and Jerusalem, whether soon or late, for there is no before and after in the eternal order. . . . So far as history can contain it, it is embodied in the historic crisis which the coming of Jesus brought about."[10] This elimination of futurist eschatology creates exegetical and theological difficulties. The early church did not merely believe in the life everlasting, they expected as a coming event the *Parousia* of the Lord; and other scholars have not found it easy to follow Dodd in attributing this expectation to a wholesale revision of the teaching of Christ. Again, if the purpose of God is fully achieved in Christ, what meaning can we attach to the continuance of the historical order? Dodd does indeed grant that the *eschaton* is a beginning as well as an end, but it is the beginning of an otherworldly order not to be confused with history; yet his own emphasis on tradition in the life of the church implies that historic continuity has a place in the divine scheme of things. He allows, as we have seen, that those who in any age accept the Gospel, and with it "the whole rich content of the historical process," are to be taken up into the eternal order; but does not this mean that God is still working his purpose out, until the day when he declares it complete?

For such reasons as these some scholars have suggested that for "realized" we should substitute "proleptic" or "inaugurated" eschatology. By these terms we should be depicting the ministry of Jesus either as an anticipation of that which in essence remains future or as the beginning of a process yet to be consummated. Dodd has given a qualified assent to these suggestions, and in one of his latest works has declared that the Johannine formula, "the hour comes and now is," "probably represents the authentic teaching of Jesus as veraciously as any formula could," though he insists that both in the Fourth Gospel and elsewhere in the New Testament the emphasis remains on the "now is."[11]

[10] *The Parables of the Kingdom* (London, Nisbet, 1935), pp. 107–8.
[11] *The Interpretation of the Fourth Gospel* (London, Cambridge Univ. Press, 1953), p. 447.

It is important, however, that minor adjustments of this kind should not cause us to lose sight of the excellent reasons Dodd had for his original statement of his thesis. He was clearly anxious to avoid the quite unbiblical notion that with the coming of Jesus something was injected into history which would thenceforth work itself out by an evolutionary process to the ultimate denouement. He wanted also to underline the mythical nature of all eschatological language; and much work is still to be done on the relation of the literal to the symbolic in the language of the Bible. He was undoubtedly correct in saying that the first Christians thought of the life, death, resurrection, exaltation, and second advent of Christ as a single divine event, God's day of salvation in the midst of which they were living; and that it was only with the passage of time that they learned to distinguish the part of this event which was past from that which was future, the fulfilled from the unfulfilled. Even then it continued to be a permanent element in New Testament teaching that Jesus had died and risen as the inclusive representative and head of mankind, so that in him all men had vicariously attained their divinely allotted destiny. The eschatological problem turns out, in fact, to be a christological one—the relation of humanity to him who so identified himself with them as to undergo their judgment and achieve their salvation. This central theme of our faith will continue to exercise the minds of exegetes and theologians; and those that are wise will start at the point to which Dodd has led us.

In his inaugural lecture at Cambridge Dodd laid down a program of the three most pressing tasks awaiting the attention of New Testament scholars: the closing of the "gap between the facts of the life of Jesus and their earliest literary record"; the solving of the Johannine problem, earlier criticism's "most signal failure"; and the balancing of the centrifugal movement of analytical study by a centripetal movement which would recover the original unity of New Testament thought. It is characteristic of the man that what he preached to others had already been adopted as the agenda of his own future research, and that from the start these three tasks were seen to be intimately related to one another and to the problem of history as the arena of revelation.

The Fourth Gospel may well prove to be the keystone of an arch which at present fails to hold together. If we can understand how it came to be and what it means, we shall know what early Christianity really was, and not until in some measure we comprehend the New Testament as a whole shall we be in a position to solve the Johannine problem.[12]

The bridge designed to close the gap between the life of Jesus and the earliest written records had three main supports, strongly interlocked: the *kerygma* or apostolic preaching of the early church; its *didache* or ethical instruction; and the principle of selection and interpretation which enabled the first Christians to use the Old Testament as Christian Scripture.

Dodd's reconstruction of the apostolic kerygma begins with the earliest available evidence, the Epistles of Paul. In dealing with the pastoral concerns of the churches Paul occasionally refers to his own preaching or to the traditions which he received from those who were Christians before him, and occasionally also uses formulae of an almost creedal nature, from which he argues as though they were necessarily familiar to his readers. He carefully distinguishes between the foundation and the theological superstructure which he and others have built upon it, and, in spite of his claim to independence of the other apostles, he is insistent that his Gospel does not substantially differ from theirs. A similar pattern of preaching is to be found in the early speeches in Acts, where the author, whatever editorial freedom he may have used elsewhere, was apparently relying on traditions drawn ultimately from the Aramaic-speaking church of Palestine. The evidence of these two primary witnesses is confirmed by parallels in other New Testament writings, since what is common to several of the New Testament writers is likely to have formed part of their common background. The conclusion to be drawn from this is that behind the books of the New Testament there lay a common preaching tradition, which proclaimed that in the life, death, and resurrection of Jesus God had fulfilled his ancient promises given through the prophets, that Jesus was now exalted at God's right hand as Messiah and Lord, in token of which he had sent upon

[12] *The Present Task in New Testament Studies,* p. 29.

his followers the gift of the Spirit, that he was destined to be Judge of all men, but that in his name salvation was now offered to those who would repent and accept the Gospel. The nucleus of this kerygma was a series of events which had happened *sub Pontio Pilato* before many witnesses. But, as Dodd has repeatedly reminded us, bare facts become history only through the significance which the historian discovers in them. The early Christian preachers found a key to the meaning of the events they had witnessed in the eschatological expectations of their native Judaism. The Day of the Lord had arrived; and they pointed to the resurrection of Jesus and the gift of the Spirit—both eschatological events—as evidence that they were living in the midst of the *eschaton,* the final crisis of history, which could be expected to draw swiftly to its close.

The eschatological character of the primitive kerygma has one implication of immense importance. The early church did not invent realized eschatology. They were hardly capable of the drastic remolding of accepted ideas which this concept involved. Moreover, the concept is present throughout the recorded teaching of Jesus, and especially in the parables of the Kingdom, from which not even the most radical criticism can now reasonably excise it. Realized eschatology is thus our strongest guarantee that the apostolic faith of the New Testament had its origin not merely in the common kerygma of the primitive church, but in the preaching of Jesus himself.

The oral traditions of the early church included not only kerygma but *didache,* the ethical instruction by which the life of the community was governed. On this subject Dodd has been chiefly concerned to emphasize two facts. Jesus was known to his disciples and to others as Rabbi, and regularly displayed those qualities which were normally associated with the prophets; and it was expected both of a rabbi and of a prophet that his teaching would be committed to memory by his followers. Not only in the Gospels but in the Epistles as well we find ample evidence for the existence of an authoritative historical tradition, to which appeal could be made to settle matters of dispute. But the ethical teaching of the Epistles is also thoroughly eschatological. It is regularly introduced by a "therefore," which makes it a consequence of God's definitive act of grace. Browning might mock at the grammarian who "properly based *Oun*" and then had no more that he could do; but Dodd has raised *Oun* to theological status. "In the word 'therefore' lies much virtue: it implies that the direction of Christian action, in the variety of situations to be reviewed, is always to be determined by reference to what God has done for us in Christ."[13] But this eschatological character was stamped upon Christian ethics by Jesus himself. His teaching expresses the absolute obligation laid upon men by the presence of the Kingdom of God.

One of the most fascinating and convincing pieces of recent scholarly detection is Dodd's work on the use of the Old Testament in the New. For forty years this area of study had been dominated by Rendel Harris's theory that one of the earliest literary products of the church was a book of testimonies or proof-texts collected at random from the Old Testament for the benefit of Christian preachers, catechists, and apologists; and that it was from this book rather than from the Scriptures themselves that the New Testament writers drew their citations. To test this hypothesis Dodd worked through the New Testament and wherever he came to an Old Testament citation or reference, he turned to the Old Testament passage and underlined it. If Harris's theory had been sound, the underlinings should have been evenly scattered throughout the Old Testament. What Dodd in fact found was a heavy concentration of underlinings in a comparatively small number of passages of varying length. This suggested that the early church considered these whole contexts to be peculiarly relevant to the interpretation of their Gospel. The passages proved to be of three types: (a) Apocalyptic-eschatological Scriptures—Joel 2-3, Zechariah 9-14, and parts of Daniel; (b) Scriptures of the New Israel—certain prophecies of Hosea, Isaiah, and Jeremiah; (c) Scriptures of the Servant of the Lord and the Righteous Sufferer—the latter part of the Book of Isaiah and a group of psalms. The first group describes the supreme crisis of history in which Israel is to be delivered from her humiliation at the hand of evil powers through the vindicating action of God. In the second group Israel is humiliated by God's judgment on her sins, but

---

[13] *The Bible Today,* p. 82.

is to be redeemed by his forgiving grace and restored to ultimate sanctity and glory. The third group portrays Israel as an innocent sufferer who, at least in the Isaianic prophecies, is called upon to endure vicariously the judgment of God on the sins of others. Thus all three groups have a common plot, which enabled the early church to find the fulfillment of all the Scriptures in the drama of the suffering and subsequent exaltation of Jesus. But such a use of Scripture was a complete departure from all Jewish methods of exegesis; and it involved the assumption that Jesus had somehow identified himself with Israel in such a way as to fulfill her divinely appointed destiny.

> Very diverse scriptures are brought together so that they interpret one another in hitherto unsuspected ways. To have brought together, for example, the Son of Man who is the people of the saints of the Most High, the Man of God's right hand, who is also the vine of Israel, the Son of Man who after humiliation is crowned with glory and honour, and the victorious priest-king at the right hand of God, is an achievement of interpretative imagination which results in the creation of an entirely new figure. . . . This is a piece of genuinely creative thinking. Who was responsible for it?[14]

It was not the creation of Paul; he does not argue for this type of exegesis, but argues from it, as something already familiar to his readers. Either there was in the pre-Pauline church an anonymous genius who laid down the substructure of Christian theology without leaving any clue to his identity, or else, as the Gospels repeatedly affirm, the great theologian was Jesus himself. "To account for the beginning of this most original and fruitful process of rethinking the Old Testament we found need to postulate a creative mind. The Gospels offer us one. Are we compelled to reject the offer?"[15]

Dodd's *The Interpretation of the Fourth Gospel* is divided into three parts. In Part I, assuming that this Gospel was directed primarily not to Christian readers but to the serious pagan who could read it intelligently without any previous knowledge

[14] *According to the Scriptures* (London, Nisbet, 1952), p. 109.
[15] *Ibid.*, p. 110.

of Christianity (though he would find vastly more in it if he read it a second time after associating himself with the fellowship, traditions, and sacraments of the church), Dodd takes a series of soundings in the religious literature of the period to see whether he can identify these hypothetical readers. He concludes that the Gospel has affinities with the higher religion of paganism, exemplified in the writings of the Corpus Hermeticum, and with the Hellenistic Judaism represented by Philo. He does not suggest that the evangelist has derived the content of his message from such sources, but that he has deliberately adopted a theological vocabulary and imagery likely to appeal to "a wide public consisting primarily of devout and thoughtful persons . . . in the varied and cosmopolitan society of a great Hellenistic city."[16] Only by allowing for these affinities is it possible to distinguish the specifically Christian elements in his thought.

In Part II Dodd takes up one by one the leading ideas of the Gospel, adduces Hermetic and Philonic parallels, and traces them to their source in the Old Testament. In one instance after another he is led to conclude that the Hellenistic reader would find beneath the superficially familiar language something provocatively new. "The current conceptions of the higher religion of Hellenism have been taken up but entirely transformed."[17] This is not simply because John's thought is fundamentally more Jewish than Greek (though this is true), for Jewish ideas undergo at his hands a similar transformation. The transforming power is the apostolic tradition of the historical Jesus. Other commentators on the Fourth Gospel have in the past claimed that John transformed the apostolic Gospel by expressing it in terms of Greek philosophy. Dodd is suggesting that this is the exact reverse of the truth. It was not the apostolic tradition but the Logos doctrine of Philo and Poimandres which was transformed by the proclamation that the Logos became flesh.

In Part III, in defiance of all theories of dislocation, interpolation, and redaction, Dodd seeks to show that the Gospel, in the form attested to by all manuscripts, has a coherent struc-

[16] P. 9.
[17] P. 212.

tuie dictated partly by the apostolic tradition, partly by the intricate pattern of ideas woven by the author, and partly by the theological program laid down in the Prologue.

Finally, the book has an important Appendix on the historical aspect of the Gospel, which is a shadow of good things yet to come. Dodd rejects both apostolic authorship, whether direct or indirect, and the dependence of John on the Synoptists, and declares himself in favor of the hypothesis that John had inherited an independent Judaean tradition which contained some material that reached the Synoptists by different channels.

A generation ago it was almost axiomatic that similarities between books of the New Testament were due to literary dependence of one author on another. The author of I Peter copied from Paul, John from the Synoptists; there were many who doubted whether Luke could have written Acts because of his manifest independence of the Pauline Epistles; and it was even suggested that John the Divine compiled his letters to the seven churches in imitation of the newly published Pauline corpus. Today, thanks largely to Dodd and those who have followed his lead, we have a more adequate picture of early Christianity. Whatever elements the New Testament writers have in common, whether kerygma or *didache,* Old Testament exegesis or catechetical and liturgical forms, are to be attributed to their common background in the traditions, the life, and the worship of the Christian community. This does not mean that we are to find the unity of the New Testament in a highest common factor, ignoring the intensely individual character of the various authors. No one who has taken seriously what Dodd has to say about the particularity of historical revelation could be content with such a view. It means rather that at the heart of the Gospel is a life, and the writers of the New Testament bear their particular but consentient witness to the meaning of that life and its impact on those who were most directly affected by its creative impulse. Only by understanding what it meant to live in that creative moment of history, from which all other history draws its meaning, can we ourselves come into touch with him who was its origin.

The ultimate test of New Testament scholarship is the picture of Jesus which emerges at the end of the process. From Dodd's writings we gain a picture adequate to justify Christian faith and worship. Jesus is first of all a historical figure deeply immersed in the affairs of his own time. His parables reveal "an untrammelled interest in real life," so that "the literature of the Roman Empire contains no other such vivid picture of the life of common men under its rule."[18] "He lived intensely in a particular historical situation, and the relevance of His teaching to that situation is part of its eternal significance. He dealt not with general abstractions, but with issues which the time raised acutely for the people to whom He spoke."[19] At the same time he was conscious of a unique calling—to be the eschatological Son of Man through whom God was to confront Israel with the ultimate crisis of her destiny. He was a profound and original thinker, capable of reminting the currency of theological speech, of transforming the eschatological hope of his nation into a present experience, and of grasping the Old Testament Scriptures entire, so as to find in them a new conception of God's purpose for his people and his Messiah. He was a man of faith, prepared to translate his vision into practice even at the cost of tragedy, in the conviction that God would honor his promises and vindicate his Servant. He was a man of love, who so totally identified himself with his wayward people that his heart was broken by their disobedience at the very moment when in their name he was offering to God the obedience they had failed to pay. To be with him was to be in the presence of God, to hear his words of pardon was to experience the divine forgiveness, and to understand his love was to have a new conception of God.

The spirit which has inspired Dodd's erudite and humane scholarship is best expressed in his own words. "The ideal interpreter would be one who has entered into that strange first-century world, has felt its whole strangeness, has sojourned in it until he has lived himself into it, thinking and feeling as one of those to whom the Gospel first came; and who will then return into our world, and give to the truth he has discerned a body out of the stuff of our own thought."[20] It is appropriate

[18] *The Authority of the Bible* (London, Nisbet, 1928), p. 148.
[19] *Ibid.*, p. 234.
[20] *The Present Task in New Testament Studies,* pp. 40 ff.

that one who has set himself this lifelong ideal should have devoted the first ten years of his retirement to the *New English Bible*, helping to translate into the language of today not only the words of Holy Scripture but the accumulated wealth of dedicated learning.

Bibliography

C. H. Dodd, *The Authority of the Bible*, N.Y., Harper, 1958. (Harper Torchbooks).

No full-length study of Dodd is available.

OSCAR CULLMANN

S. C. Guthrie, Jr.

Oscar Cullmann was born in Strasbourg, February 25, 1902. He was baptized in the Lutheran Church of Alsace, and is still a member of the Lutheran Church (he was never ordained). He was educated in his home city, receiving from the University of Strasbourg in 1920 a bachelor's degree in literature for his work in classical philology, in 1924 a bachelor's degree in theology, and in 1930 a doctorate in theology for his dissertation on the Pseudo-Clementine writings. After teaching Greek and German in a Parisian secondary school in 1925–26, he returned to Strasbourg to become instructor in Greek at the university. From 1930–38 he was professor of New Testament and ancient church history there. Since 1938 he has been professor of New Testament and ancient church history at the University of Basel. Besides his work in Basel, he also teaches regularly at the École des Hautes-Études, in the philosophical faculty of the Sorbonne, and at the Protestant theological seminary in Paris. In Paris, as well as in Rome, where for a number of years he has lectured periodically at the Waldensian seminary, Cullmann has had fruitful contact with Roman Catholic theologians which has contributed in his writings to a renewed Protestant-Catholic conversation. Cullmann, who is not married, directs with his sister a theological student house in Basel.

Cullmann is a so-called biblical theologian. That is, he is first of all a New Testament scholar whose works are all primarily exegetical studies of the New Testament writings. But he does not consider his task to be exhausted by an analytic investigation of the language and historical setting of the early Christian writings and the comparison of the "religion" they embody with other contemporary religions. He seeks beyond this to identify and describe the unique theological character and central message of these writings. In order to understand his work, there-

338

fore, one must understand both his exegetical method and the theology which results from it.

THE THEOLOGY OF HEILSGESCHICHTE

How does one discover the essence of the early Christian faith? Cullmann never tires of repeating that the task of the biblical interpreter is simply to listen to what the authors of the New Testament have to say to us. He must guard against reading into the New Testament writings, or judging them by, his own philosophical or theological opinions. However difficult this may be, he must try to set aside all his preconceptions and presuppositions (including those he believes to be "Christian") and even his concern about whether what he hears is possible or believable. He has to be willing first of all to take the trouble to understand and present what is in the texts, however strange or contradictory it may be to what he thinks he already knows or can accept as a modern man. For Cullmann, this means especially that one must avoid the false methodology and therefore also the false conclusions of nineteenth-century historicism and of Bultmann and his school.[1]

While he agrees with the great biblical scholars of the past century that the only legitimate method of exegesis is the philological-historical one, and while he seeks the same "objectivity" they were concerned to achieve, Cullmann accuses them of finding in the New Testament only the preconceptions they brought to it. They stripped off as dispensable "form" whatever did not agree with, and discovered as "kernel" whatever did agree with, their own ideas about which of the events and words of the New Testament were scientifically and historically demonstrable, rationally and morally acceptable. As a result the "historical Jesus" they were so concerned to discover turned out to be only a reflection of nineteenth-century idealism.

[1] For Cullmann's description of his own methodology, see especially the prefaces to his various works and the article "The Necessity and Function of Higher Criticism," in his *The Early Church* (Philadelphia, Westminster, 1956). See especially *Christ and Time* (Philadelphia, Westminster, 1950) and *The Christology of the New Testament* (Philadelphia, Westminster, 1959) for his running criticism of Bultmann.

Against this kind of exegesis Cullmann has welcomed form criticism. With other form critics, he recognizes that the New Testament does not offer us only "historical sources," a collection of "facts" to be proved or disproved. It is the confession of faith or preaching (kerygma) of the early church. By its very nature it is *theology*, a biased *interpretation* of Jesus and his message, which we can see only through the eyes of the faith of the early church. In order to get to the real center of the New Testament, Cullmann contends, we cannot distinguish between what is historically genuine and false, essential and nonessential, primitive shell and eternal truth. We must seek to understand the faith of the early Christian community, the forms in which it expressed its faith, and the development of these forms in its life and worship.

But Bultmann's existentialist method of interpretation Cullmann sees as an equally false approach to the New Testament writings, and equally inadequate to get to the real center of the New Testament theology. Despite the fact that Bultmann also rejects the historicism of the past century, Cullmann accuses him of being finally guilty of the same basic error. He also refuses to let the New Testament speak for itself. He also reads into it his own philosophical presuppositions. The only difference is that the presuppositions are now those of existentialist philosophy. Specifically, what Cullmann finds wrong with Bultmann is his reduction of the "objective" events of God's revelatory action in Christ to subjective descriptions of the "self-understanding" of the biblical writers. We must speak again of this criticism of Bultmann, because it plays an increasingly important part in Cullmann's writings; first, however, we must speak of Cullmann's own concept of the center or essence of the New Testament which appears with this general rejection of Bultmann's methodology.

When one is willing to set aside all preconceptions and let the Scripture speak for itself, he discovers that the distinctive content of its proclamation is the *historical* witness it bears. The message of the New Testament is not just a metaphysical speculation, or philosophy of one kind or another, or general theological "truth" which comes to us in the *form* of history. It *is* history. It is not just some abstract propositions about God and man and their relationship, or about "authentic existence," but it is the proclamation of concrete historical events which took place at a particular time in a particular place. Every misunderstanding of the New Testament (whether that of the nineteenth century or Bultmann or any other) is the result of an interpretation which either does not understand or is not willing to accept this historical character of the message of the early church. This is the reason that Cullmann sees docetism as *the* biblical-Christian heresy.

"History" here means of course a special history: "biblical" or "revelatory" or (most often in Cullmann's writings) "redemptive" history (*Heilsgeschichte*). It is the history of God's self-revealing, saving action in the events which lead up to and follow from *the* self-revealing, saving event of the life and death and resurrection of Jesus Christ. This particular history, though unique in general world history, is nevertheless of the same character. It is different from history in general in that the events which compose it are the direct intervention of God in the world, and can therefore be perceived only by faith. They cannot be disproved or confirmed by scientific investigation as can the "facts" of "secular" history (here Cullmann follows the form critics). Yet these events are real historical events in time. They have to do above all with a real "historical" Jesus, not just with a mythological process of salvation described in terms of a historical figure. While we cannot use the New Testament writings to construct a "biography" of Jesus, we can show that the early church did not simply "make up" the content of its faith; rather, its faith resulted from words which Jesus actually spoke and events which actually happened concerning him (here Cullmann qualifies his acceptance of form criticism). Moreover, so decisive is this revelatory history that *all* history both before and after must be understood and judged in the light of it, so that history in general is only the working out of the plan of salvation made known and realized in the particular history recorded in the New Testament.

The theology of the New Testament, therefore, is the theology of *Heilsgeschichte*. All Cullmann's writings are devoted to explaining what *Heilsgeschichte* means and to fitting all theological concepts into the temporal scheme defined by his view of it.

THE BIBLICAL VIEW OF TIME

If the content of the early church's faith and proclamation by its very nature is *Heilsgeschichte,* then one can understand the theology of the New Testament only when he understands the concept of time it presupposes. Cullmann devoted his first major work, *Christ and Time,* to this problem, and all his subsequent works only develop in detail the position formulated here. According to the biblical view, time is understood in analogy to a straight line. The line is formed on the one hand by linking the individual moments of time (*kairoi*) in which God chooses to reveal himself and realize his plan of salvation; and, on the other hand, by linking whole periods of time (*aion*) which these particular actions mark off. Even eternity, "God's time," is not to be distinguished qualitatively from the time which falls between the particular acts in which God creates and ends the world. It is only quantitatively different, to be distinguished from "historical" time only by the fact that it is unlimited, stretching in unending duration "before" and "after" the beginning and end of time as we know it. The time line of the Bible, then, may be divided into three sections: the period stretching endlessly (eternally) backward from creation, the "limited time" between creation and end of the world, and the period stretching endlessly (eternally) forward from the end. This concept of time means that for biblical thought, time has meaning. It is "going somewhere" (in contrast to the "circular" time of the Greeks, which is meaningless because it is only the constant repetition of events and periods without direction or goal). This also means that salvation is expected to occur in time, and that although it will be finally realized only after the "present age," even then it will have a temporal character (in contrast to the Greek idea that salvation comes only by escaping from the prison of time into a "timeless" eternity which is understood in spatial terms of "this world" and "beyond" rather than in temporal terms of "now" and "then").

Judaism and Christianity share the idea that time is the framework for the execution of God's plan of salvation in such a decisive way that all history is at its deepest level the history of salvation. They also share the threefold division of time. Further, both superimpose on this threefold division a twofold one between the "present" and the "coming" age. That is, on the three-part time line of redemption they both locate a "mid-point," which is *the* event of salvation, the one event which gives meaning to and marks the fulfillment of the whole process of salvation which God has been progressively working out not only in and since creation, but even before then in his eternal predestination. The difference between the Jewish and Christian concepts lies in the *placing* of this mid-point. For the Jews it lies in the *future* with the still expected coming of the Messiah, and it coincides with the end of history. For the early church, however, the mid-point is no longer future, nor does it coincide with the chronological end of history. It is identified with the appearance and especially with the death and resurrection of Jesus Christ. The decisive event of salvation which the Jews still look forward to only at the end of time is seen by the early church to have happened before the end. And this means that the coming of the "future age" in which God's plan of salvation is to be fulfilled can no longer simply coincide with the end of time, but has broken into the middle of the "present age." Present and future can no longer be simply distinguished in the Jewish way. Although with Judaism the church also looks forward to the end of time which has "not yet" come, it claims in opposition to Judaism that the decisive center of time, the "fulfillment" of time, has already happened. The end can only be its final completion or confirmation. Salvation or the Kingdom of God to come at the end will only be the final realization of the Kingdom or salvation which has already come.

Cullmann often uses the following analogy to illustrate this complex situation: the decisive battle of a war may be won before the enemy is willing to acknowledge or even knows about it. Fighting may therefore continue for a time, although the outcome of the war has already been determined. The final "cease fire" and declaration of victory are only the inevitable result of the decisive battle already fought. For the Jews the battle which means God's victory and man's salvation has not yet been waged. It will be fought only at the end of time. For the Christians, however, Christ's triumph over death and sin in his resurrection and ascension means that the deciding battle has already been won. Although resistance may continue for a while, the final vindication of God and his gracious will can only make clear to all the victory already achieved.

According to Cullmann, all the theology of the early church is determined by this tension between present and future, "already fulfilled" and "not yet consummated." All periods of the time line must now be understood in the light of the new interim period which began with the resurrection of Christ and which will be concluded with his second coming at the end. Whoever cannot or will not recognize and respect first the linear concept of time which the Jews and the early church have in common, and then the radical change the event of Christ makes in this time scheme, will not be able to understand or share in the uniqueness of the faith and thinking of the New Testament.

Cullmann emphasizes in this context that this "already but not yet" theology of *Heilsgeschichte* is not only the early church's evaluation of the importance of Jesus. A careful exegesis of the Gospels shows that this temporal tension between present and future existed also for Jesus himself. He himself saw the future as already fulfilled in his person: with his coming, the Kingdom of God had come and the victory of God over Satan's kingdom had been realized. And yet he also anticipated a lapse of time (though not a long one) between the fulfillment he accomplished with his earthly work and the end of time when this fulfillment would be finally consummated with his coming again. Therefore Schweitzer, though right in seeing that the whole message of the New Testament is a thoroughly eschatological one, is wrong in seeing Jesus' own eschatology as only futuristic, and in attributing the "already fulfilled" side of the dialectic in the New Testament to the church's invention resulting from the "embarrassment" caused by Jesus' failure to fulfill the Jewish messianic hope for the end of time. C. H. Dodd is equally wrong in resolving the dialectic in the other direction with his "realized eschatology" which leaves no room for a final consummation still to come in the future. Bultmann, while maintaining a tension between the "present" and the "coming" age, reduces (demythologizes) it from a genuinely temporal tension between the now past historical event of Jesus Christ and the future historical event of the end to the "existential" tension in the subjective experience of the man who must decide "now" for or against the Kingdom.

CHRISTOLOGY AND HEILSGESCHICHTE

The mid-point which Christ marks in the time line of redemptive history is so important that the whole line may be called the "Christ line." Every point and every period in it must be understood as Christ-history. All *Heilsgeschichte is* Christology. To move, therefore, from Cullmann's *Christ and Time* (1945) to his later and most important work to date, *The Christology of the New Testament* (1956), is not to change the subject of discussion but to get to the heart of the matter.

It would be quite incorrect for us to be influenced by the Christological controversies in the church after the New Testament period to think that the earliest Christians were interested in the problem of the "nature" of Christ. For the early Christians the question "Who is Christ?" meant not "What is his nature?" but "What does he *do?*" They were not interested in his person as such, but in his work—or rather only in his person to the extent that it is revealed in his work. The Christology of the New Testament is "functional" Christology. It has to do not with philosophical speculations but with historical events. In other words, if *Heilsgeschichte* means Christology, then it is also true that Christology means *Heilsgeschichte*.

The early church had at its disposal certain concepts already familiar in Judaism with which to interpret the meaning of the work of Jesus and the events of his death and resurrection. They were the various messianic titles—titles which dealt not so much with the "person" or "nature" as with the function of the one who should come bringing salvation. The early church worked out its Christology primarily in terms of these Jewish titles. It also used some concepts and titles which came not exclusively from Judaism but also from Hellenistic religion. Nonetheless it is very important to see, Cullmann insists (especially against

Bultmann), that nothing of the Christology of the early church *originated* with these concepts, which were primarily mythological and gnostic; and that when it did take up these concepts, the church poured a new meaning into them, above all by relating them to real historical events having to do with the flesh-and-blood Jesus of Nazareth. Moreover, even the Jewish concepts were not in themselves adequate to express the uniqueness of Jesus but had to be adapted to what actually happened in him. The Christology of the early church is not an attempt to fit Christ into *any* conceptual scheme, but to adjust all concepts, of whatever origin, to the events connected with him. Only when we recognize this can we see the radical newness of the theology of the New Testament and its radical difference from a timeless mythology or nonhistorical kerygma.

We cannot discuss here Cullmann's careful investigation of the various titles with which the New Testament writers worked out their Christology. We may, however, see the results of his work by summarizing his reconstruction of the development of the Christology of the early church. Again in this context Cullmann emphasizes that all New Testament Christology is founded upon and begins with the life of Jesus himself, not with a ready-made mythology or eschatology, and not even with the experience and theology of the early Christian community after Easter. Jesus himself was conscious that he had to carry out God's plan of salvation. He knew that he had to do this by accomplishing the forgiveness of sins "for many" through his obedient death in fulfillment of the role of the "Suffering Servant of Yahweh." He knew that he had to introduce the Kingdom of God in fulfillment of the eschatological role of the "Son of Man," who had existed with God from all eternity and who would appear "on the clouds of heaven" at the end of time to judge and renew the world. In fulfilling this double function of humiliation and exaltation, he was so aware of his complete and unique oneness with the will of God that he was conscious beyond all human possibilities of being the "Son of God."

Already among Jesus' disciples during his life there were flashes of insight into his real identity and mission. But despite Jesus' allusions to his self-consciousness, his disciples generally could think of him only in terms of the political-nationalistic concept of the "Messiah." It was really only in the light of the events of Good Friday and Easter that the disciples began to understand who Jesus was. They now began to understand the meaning of the earthly life of Jesus and his role as Servant, and they were all the more interested in the future now that the Jewish messianic concepts had to be qualified by the fact that the Coming One was the Jesus who *had* come. But it was finally not so much the past or future events of redemptive history as the *present* upon which the thinking of the church concentrated, the time *between* the "comings." The community worked out its interpretation of the role of Christ in the present, above all in terms of the concept "Lord." What is the risen and coming Christ doing *now?* He rules as living and present Lord over his church, the world, and the life of each individual. This understanding of Jesus as Lord is not to be traced to the use of this title in other contemporary religions; rather, it grew directly out of the worship of the earliest community in which the presence of the risen Lord was directly experienced.[2]

So profound was this cultic experience of the present Lord, Cullmann believes, that it really was from this center that the whole line of redemptive history was given its Christological interpretation. All other titles must be seen in the light of the fact that the Jesus who *was* crucified and who *will* come again *is* the living Lord over both Church and the whole world. Indeed, not only must the past and future periods of *Heilsgeschichte* be related to this realization, but also the periods before and after history. If Jesus is really Lord, this must point to his oneness with God himself in eternity—to his "deity." He can therefore be called the pre-existent "Logos" or "Son of God" or even "God." Wherever in all periods of *Heilsgeschichte* God is at work revealing himself, there Christ must be. He *is* God in his self-communication.

The development of the New Testament Christology, then, is the direct traceable path from the self-consciousness of Jesus and the occasional premonitions of his disciples, to the Easter experience of the disciples, to the community's experience of

[2] See *Early Christian Worship* (Naperville, Illinois, Allenson, 1953). Also *The Earliest Christian Confessions* (London, Lutterworth Press, 1949).

the Lord in worship, to a deep theological reflection (especially in the Gospel of John and Hebrews) upon the connection between Christ and *all Heilsgeschichte.*

CHURCH AND WORLD IN THE PRESENT PERIOD OF HEILSGESCHICHTE

We have seen that for Cullmann the biblical *Heilsgeschichte* includes and gives meaning to all periods of the time line. And we have seen how he relates the Christology of the New Testament to all these periods. Yet it would not be correct to think that all these periods and Christ's work in them receive equal emphasis in the New Testament. We have also seen that Cullmann believes that the early church was above all interested in the *present* period and in the function of Christ as Lord in this period. Indeed, all other periods of redemptive history and all other functions of Christ were first understood and interpreted on the basis of the early Christians' belief that they stood already in the future age although the end had not yet come, and of their experience of the risen Christ in their common worship. Cullmann's works on the theology of the New Testament bear a corresponding emphasis. If his two major works, *Christ and Time* and *The Christology of the New Testament,* discuss the whole stretch of *Heilsgeschichte* and the Christological significance of it, most of his other works are devoted to an interpretation of the New Testament understanding of this present period. Even in the two big works this problem occupies a disproportionate amount of Cullmann's time and effort. A glance at his view of the church and the world in this period will at least indicate the direction in which he points in this context.

The period of *Heilsgeschichte* between the resurrection of Christ and his return is the period of the church.[3] The church began with the appearance of the risen Lord to his first disciples and it will end with his return. The meaning of its existence, its faith and life, its task in the world, can be properly understood only in terms of this position in the history of salvation; that is,

[3] For detailed discussions of the church, see *Christ and Time,* pp. 144 ff; *The Christology of the New Testament,* pp. 203 ff. Also *Baptism in the New Testament* (Naperville, Illinois, Allenson, 1950).

only in terms of the church's consciousness of living "between the times," in the eschatological tension between the "already fulfilled" but "not yet consummated" reality of the new age. The presence of the Holy Spirit in the church is a sign of this tension. Because of the Spirit's presence, the new life of the Kingdom of God which will come finally at the end is already realized in the members of the community, and yet it is a new life only provisionally realized, which can only be believed in, because the church is made up of men who are still sinners. The Lord's Supper is another sign of this tension, for at this celebration the church prays for the coming of the Lord at the end and yet experiences his presence already now in the gathered community. Preaching, the one great task of the church, is still another sign of the "already—not yet" dialectic. It is the call for all men to accept the Good News of the decisive battle won on Good Friday and Easter and of Christ's already effective rule over sin and death; and it is a call of promise and warning about his final victory which is coming. So important is the preaching of the church that one can say that the "between times" exists for its sake. It *is* the time of God's gracious patience which grants men still time to hear, repent, believe. The church thus actually participates in and carries forward the divine redemptive activity in history. It is the earthly center from which the lordship of Christ becomes visible, the center from which Christ the Lord rules and does his work in the world. However insignificant it may seem in world affairs, the existence of the church is the clue to what is going on in the world and what God is doing not only in "church" history, but also in the secular history of our time.[4]

What *is* going on in the world? Cullmann is not so much interested in the relation of *Heilsgeschichte* and Christ's lordship to secular history or culture in general as in their relation to

---

[4] This high evaluation of the church does not mean that the church itself may be absolutized. The church has authority only as it submits itself and its traditions to the proclamation of the unrepeatable event of salvation and the apostolic tradition concerning it which lie not *in*, but in the past *before* the time of the church. See Cullmann's criticism of the Roman Church at this point in his *Peter* (Philadelphia, Westminster, 1953, rev. and expanded ed., 1962) and in "The Tradition," in *The Early Church*.

political history. The problem of *Heilsgeschichte* and world history thus becomes the problem of church and state.[5]

The New Testament understands also the existence and history of the state in the light of the dialectic between the decisive battle already won and the final victory yet to come at the end. The lordship of Christ between these events is not only his rule over the church, but also his rule over the world of political powers—and at a deeper level over the invisible demonic "powers" which the New Testament sees as standing behind the state. Christ's victory on Easter was also his victory over the "princes of the world" who were ultimately responsible for his death. Therefore they and their empirical organ, the state, are now subject to Christ and are his "ministers." The difference between church and state is not that the members of the former serve Christ while the members of the latter do not, but that the former know of his lordship and willingly serve him, while the latter do not know of it and serve him unconsciously or even against their will. Not only the church, then, but also the state is God's instrument in the working out of his plan of salvation. Although it may not even know it, the state exists for the sake of maintaining the order and peace in which the preaching of the church before the end may be carried on. Christians for this reason have greater respect than any other citizens for the state, and are more concerned than any others that it be obeyed. They know that the state is subject to Christ and exists to fulfill his will.

This does not mean, however, that the state is absolutized. While the decisive battle over the powers of the world has already been won, in the present period of *Heilsgeschichte* the final victory has not been achieved. The "powers" are only "subjected," not yet "destroyed." They can still do damage. They constantly threaten to attempt to free themselves from the authority of Christ, and sometimes for a time seem to do so. Then the state, instead of creating order and peace for the church's work, becomes totalitarian, becomes the "beast" of Revelation 13, persecuting the church, which refuses to give to

[5] See *The State in the New Testament* (London, SCM Press, 1957) and "The Kingship of Christ and the Church in the New Testament," in *The Early Church.*

Caesar the absolute obedience which belongs to Christ alone. When the state thus oversteps its legitimate limits the church can only disobey it to that extent. Thus while Christians have greater respect for the state than anyone else, they are also more watchful for signs of self-deification in the state, and are more opposed to it, for they know about the dangerous demonic forces threatening to break loose there, and they see this political totalitarianism for what it really is, rebellion against the lordship of Christ.

On the ground that the New Testament does not do so, Cullmann does not attempt to answer the question how we know just when the state does or does not remain within its proper limits. The only clear case we are given in the New Testament is the situation in which the state claims emperor worship. Moreover, while he suggests that resistance is allowed in the case of totalitarianism, he offers no help about what the church's attitude should be when a state is simply unjust. This way of dealing with the problem of church and state is a good example of the way in which Cullmann relates all theological problems to *Heilsgeschichte,* particularly the present phase of it; and his willingness to let difficult problems which are not solved in the New Testament itself simply stand.[6]

CONCLUSION

One of the greatest virtues of Cullmann's work is his ability to deal with difficult problems of exegesis and theological interpretation in such a simple, clear way that not only technically trained scholars but any beginning student in theology can understand him. But this virtue is also the ground of most of the criticisms of his work: is not his theology of *Heilsgeschichte* too simple and generalized, too neatly schematized, to do justice to the complexity of the New Testament writings and their theological content? The most general criticisms in this respect

[6] While Cullmann is not so much interested in the life of the individual Christian as in that of the Christian and civil communities, when he does deal with the individual, it is also in terms of the "already–not-yet" dialectic. See especially his treatment of death and the "afterlife" in *Immortality of the Soul or Resurrection of the Dead?* (N.Y., Macmillan, 1958).

probably relate to his concept of time and to his Christology—precisely to the central themes of all his work.

Can the biblical concept of time really be so nicely diagrammed as Cullmann's time line suggests? Above all, can eternity legitimately be said to be only quantitatively different from time? Is not eternity in the Bible something different from both Greek timelessness and Cullmann's endless time? If God's and man's *time* are only quantitatively distinguished, what does this do to the relationship between God and man? Granted that Cullmann successfully shows that it is improper to read the Greek cyclical (or any other philosophical) concept of time into the New Testament, is he himself free from preconceptions about time? Is his own concept of time in terms of chronological succession not a modern concept read into rather than a concept derived from the Bible? To put the question in an even more radical way: even properly understood, is the biblical concept of time really the central concept which determines the meaning and content of all other concepts? Is everything in the Bible not related rather to *God* and to his acts than to time as such?

The same basic charge of oversimplification lies behind most criticisms of Cullmann's understanding of New Testament Christology. Granted that the Church has often separated the person and work of Christ in such a way that Christology has wrongly become a matter of metaphysical speculation about "substance" and "nature," is it a valid alternative to think only of a "functional" Christology? If Christ *is* what he does, is it not necessary on the basis of the New Testament itself to attempt some "ontological" statements about him? Or again, is not Cullmann's construction of the development of the Christology of the New Testament too neat and easy? Can everything be so certainly traced back to Jesus himself? Does so much depend on our being able to demonstrate a direct continuity between the theology of the church and the "historical Jesus"? Is the "self-consciousness" of Jesus a sound beginning point for ascertaining the "real facts" about who he was and what he did? Is Cullmann convincing when he grounds his opposition to the theory of a Hellenistic influence regarding the Christological thinking of the church on the "cultic experience" of the earliest community?

Behind some of these objections to Cullmann's work lies the difficult problem of the relationship between "biblical" and "systematic" theology. When his understanding, for instance, of time and eternity, or functional Christology, or the church-state relationship is criticized as inadequate, Cullmann answers that a New Testament scholar must permit questions that are not solved in the New Testament itself to stand as questions. He fulfills his function just by refusing to answer them, and by handing them in their proper form over to the systematic theologian. Is he right in so limiting the task of the biblical theologian, or is this also an oversimplification of his task?

Despite all criticisms, Cullmann's work will undoubtedly stand as an important contribution to the biblical-theological thought of our time. His careful, disciplined work of philological-historical research in the texts of the New Testament places him in line with the great critical scholars of the past and present centuries. His theology of *Heilsgeschichte,* with its constant emphasis on the fact that for the New Testament revelation has to do with concrete time- and space-bound historical events, is a formidable obstacle to the gnostic-docetic heresy which also in our time is a threat to a genuinely Christian theology. His consistent demonstration that Christology lies at the heart of all New Testament thought and his refusal to think of the person of Christ apart from his work has contributed significantly to the new understanding in this century of what is unique and central in the New Testament. His treatment of New Testament eschatology in terms of the "already–not yet" paradox offers a constructive alternative to the one-sidedness of Schweitzer and Dodd, and at the very least a serious challenge to the existentialism of Bultmann. Perhaps his most helpful insight has been his understanding of the greatly neglected importance of the meaning of the resurrection of Christ and his function as "Lord" for the "present" period of *Heilsgeschichte.* At this point Cullmann's theology of *Heilsgeschichte* becomes immediately relevant to the situation in which *we* live. *Our* church as well as the New Testament community, *our* world as well as that dominated by the Roman Empire, *myself* as well as the first century Christian—*we* are touched by this lordship. Here Culmann's theology ceases to be merely academic research and becomes itself the proclamation of Good News. Finally, his active and sympathetic participation in the renewed discussion between Protestant and Roman Catholic theologians during the past few years will certainly earn for Cullmann an important place in a new chapter in the history of Protestant-Catholic relations.

Much of what Cullmann has said has also been said by others, perhaps occasionally in a better, more nearly complete way. But he has never been concerned to lead the pack in discovering and defending the newest and most radically different theories of New Testament interpretation. He has never attempted to be "original" or to draw a school around himself. He has been content simply to work at the New Testament itself and patiently to report his findings. New Testament scholarship in the years to come will not be able to ignore or bypass him.

Bibliography

Oscar Cullmann, *Christ and Time*, rev. ed., Philadelphia, Westminster, 1964.

No detailed study of Cullmann is available in English.

REINHOLD NIEBUHR

Hans Hofmann

There are two interrelated aspects of the church's theological task: that of intellectual self-reflection, whereby the church seeks to give coherent, systematic expression to its faith, and that of articulating that faith, which it affirms has definite implications for man and his life in society. Dogmatics is the term used to refer to the former aspect of the church's theological task; ethics, moral theology, apologetics to the latter. And it is in this latter aspect of theology that Reinhold Niebuhr has made an impressive contribution to twentieth century Christianity. However, as significant and perceptive as his thought has been, it is his approach, his stance, which is unique. Though other Christian thinkers, notably Karl Barth and Paul Tillich, appear to have eclipsed Niebuhr in popularity, to ignore his thought is to miss something that is crucial if the church is to retain and deepen its vitality. This essay, while attempting to delineate the major themes of Niebuhr's theology, also seeks to bring into prominence that in his thought which, owing to the almost idolatrous hold which dogmatics has come to have on thinking Christians on both sides of the Atlantic, has not received its full measure of recognition.

Reinhold Niebuhr was born in Wright City, Missouri, on June 21, 1892. His ancestry reaches back into the solid German stock of creative thinkers who anticipated and welcomed rational liberalism. Their faith and insights merged into a vision of a democratic realization of the Kingdom of God, in which the creative grace of God would cooperate with the well-meaning efforts of man to bring about a free and constructive unfolding of human potentials. However, neither Germany nor the Europe of the time was ready for such a development as was evidenced by the reaction to the Revolution of 1848. Reacting against the forces of nationalistic imperialism and political conservatism, Niebuhr's forebears immigrated to the United

States. On arriving they settled in the Midwest among other recent arrivals to the New World. The piety and vigor of these people gave every promise that they would be successful in the kind of venture that had been rebuffed by the Old World.

Such was Niebuhr's background. After attending the college and seminary of his denomination, the Evangelical and Reformed Church, Niebuhr enrolled as a graduate student at the Divinity School of Yale University. However, the needs of his family and his boredom with academic studies led him to set aside his plans for a teaching career. Instead, he accepted an assignment as pastor of the Bethel Evangelical Church, a newly established mission in Detroit. At the time, Detroit was in the throes of industrialization and was rapidly becoming the "motor capital of the world." It was his thirteen years' experience as a minister to people caught up in the juggernaut of American industrialization that shaped Niebuhr's development as a critic of both the church and American society.

In 1928 Niebuhr accepted a call to be Professor of Applied Christianity at Union Theological Seminary in New York City. During the years since, his thought has developed and matured, but its focus has not shifted. Through his lecturing and preaching as well as through countless books and articles, Niebuhr has devoted himself to analysis of and prescription for the problem which so forcefully confronted him during his pastorate in Detroit.

People who today exclaim that the church does not come to grips with the actual problems of its people should be reminded that over a generation ago a young pastor turned "tamed cynic" lamented that what he had learned at seminary was of little use to him in his ministry and that what he now needed to know had not been taught him. Tamed was his youthful idealistic conviction that his task was simply to apply his recently acquired theories; cynical was the doubt that he and the church had any future in Detroit's rising industrialism. Yet Niebuhr set himself the task of exploring the meaning and significance of the Christian Gospel in the context of modern industrial society. His experience in Detroit forced him to grapple with the problem of religion and society. He had seen at first hand both the plight of men caught up in industrialization and the failure of the church to minister effectively to them. For him the most pressing task facing the church became that of investigating the various forces which come into play when the Gospel confronts the world. Hopefully, such an analysis might be of genuine assistance to those who were seeking to be faithful to the New Testament injunction "to be in, but not of, the world." For Niebuhr, a stance for such an analysis that would both recognize the complexity of the problem and be faithful to the Christian perspective would have to be taken precisely at the point at which the Gospel and the world confront each other. To a great degree, Niebuhr's importance as a thinker rests on his skill in identifying that point of contact and his consistency in viewing all things in terms of it.

For Niebuhr the precise point at which the Gospel and the world confront one another is in man. Thus the focal point of Niebuhr's interest is man. Though he does not ignore other facets of theological concern, from the start it was the doctrine of man, theological anthropology, that consumed his attention. The title of his chief work, *The Nature and Destiny of Man,* delivered as the Gifford Lectures when he was at the zenith of his influence, summarizes what was Niebuhr's central concern. But before turning to Niebuhr's mature treatment of human nature, it would be helpful to our understanding of his thought if we became acquainted with the approach and major themes set forth in his first two important publications: *Does Civilization Need Religion?* and *Moral Man and Immoral Society.*

In *Does Civilization Need Religion?*, written just before his resignation from the pastorate, Niebuhr focuses on the problem of the relation of the Gospel and the world by investigating the nature and purpose of religion in human life. At this point he is not concerned to distinguish religion and Christianity—a distinction which has recently become quite fashionable in theological circles—since he still regards the latter as but a specific expression of the former. It was only after he began wrestling with the problem of revelation that Niebuhr became more circumspect in his view of Christianity as a specific expression of the religious consciousness. Nevertheless, it could be argued that Niebuhr was aware of the distinction between religion and Christianity very early in his career. For from the start the word "religion" had a twofold, almost ambiguous, meaning for Niebuhr. On the one hand, he uses the term when referring to the source of man's religious consciousness, i.e., God and his will for man. On the other hand, he often uses "religion" to refer to that which man constructs in order to blunt, domesticate, and replace true religion. These two meanings of religion, which he later distinguishes as prophetic religion (Jesus is interpreted as standing within this tradition) and priestly religion, really are the nub of the current distinction between Christianity and religion. However, especially in the earlier works, Niebuhr does not make this distinction clear and the student of his thought must discern from the context the specific meaning he has in mind.

The first point that Niebuhr examines is the place of religion in modern life. Niebuhr's answer to the question, Does religion have much of a place? is in the negative. Pointing to the tremendous changes which have marked the growth of modern society, he declares that religion has shown itself to be almost helpless in the face of the impact the technological revolution has been having on man, both individually and corporately:

> There are indeed many forms of religion which are clearly vestigial remnants of another day with other interests. They have no vital influence upon the life of modern man, and their continued existence only proves that history, like nature, is slow to destroy what it has found useless, and even slower to inter what it has destroyed.[1]

Nevertheless, despite the dismal performance of contemporary religion, Niebuhr does not conclude that religion has outlived its function and is thus only of antiquarian interest. To the contrary, he asserts that, because of what has been happening to man and society as a consequence of the Industrial Revolution, man needs more than ever before the resources provided by religion.

Niebuhr's experience as pastor to Ford workers made him keenly aware that a by-product of industrialization is the cheapening of the value of personality. It is in the face of this

[1] *Does Civilization Need Religion?* (N.Y., Macmillan, 1928), p. 3.

trend toward the devaluation of personality that he sees religion as making a basic contribution. Far from being outmoded, religion plays a crucial role in life in modern industrial society. To put the matter succinctly, it is Niebuhr's view that if religion is taken away from man, the integrity of his personality is undercut. When that happens, society loses its cohesiveness and integrity. Thus, since society requires religion for its own survival, one would expect to find religion wherever one finds men living in community. Concludes Niebuhr:

> Whatever may be said of specific religions and religious forms, it is difficult to imagine man without religion; for religion is the champion of personality in a seemingly impersonal world.[2]

Having suggested that religion and society come into focus in terms of man, Niebuhr devotes considerable attention to spelling out how the two interact in and on man. On the one hand, religion provides human personality with the foundation that enables it to function in society. It does this by stressing that there is a God who is personal and that God, society, and man are related in organic, personal fashion. By emphasizing the personal nature of the cosmos, religion underwrites the value of human personality. However, in modern society it is just this emphasis which comes most into question. Not only does the philosophical presupposition of modern society—naturalism—run contrary to that of traditional religion by depersonalizing the universe and nature, but, as Niebuhr saw so clearly in Detroit, the forces of modern civilization themselves depersonalize society and the individual. Hence in order to defend the sanctity of personality, religion must carry out the battle on two fronts. As well as demonstrating on a metaphysical level that the notion of a personal God is intellectually defensible, religion must also bring its forces to bear on society itself, seeking to make the latter more humane. Religion must bring its ethical insights to bear on the problems of modern society. In this regard Niebuhr insists that the forces of religion must do more than simply concern themselves with the nurturing of the individual in isolation from his involvement in the social matrix. Important as the

[2] *Ibid.*, p. 4.

personal development of the individual may be—and Niebuhr never overlooks this concern—it is his view that the individual can never be understood or helped except from within the social context, since its forces exercise a decisive influence on the individual's development.

It is this view that lies behind Niebuhr's involvement in the burning social issues of the day. Because he believes that the church has erroneously thought it possible to minister to the individual in isolation from social forces, Niebuhr has sought to redress the balance by involving himself, theoretically and personally, in social questions. In this regard he has come to exercise a great influence on the social and political thinking of the day. It is important to note, however, that he has been no mere social activist. He is well aware that individual as well as social factors are involved in the development of human personality.

Niebuhr has described himself as not a theologian but one concerned with ethics and apologetics.[3] However, his concern for ethics and apologetics must be understood in terms of his conviction that in the battle against the forces depersonalizing man the church has been engaged almost wholly on the metaphysical level. It is because the ethical front, which he regards as just as important as the metaphysical, is being ignored that he plunges into the battle at that point:

> The fact is that more men in our modern era are irreligious because religion has failed to make civilization ethical than because it has failed to maintain its intellectual respectability. For every person who disavows religion because some ancient and unrevised dogma outrages his intelligence, several become irreligious because the social impotence of religion outrages their conscience.[4]

On the other hand, Niebuhr is too subtle a thinker to view the problem of man in modern society simply as a matter of religion's providing man with the resources that will enable

---

[3] Charles W. Kegley and Robert W. Bretall, eds., *Reinhold Niebuhr: His Religious, Social, and Political Thought* (N.Y., Macmillan, 1956), p. 3.

[4] *Does Civilization Need Religion?* p. 12.

him to achieve personal integrity and build a more humane society. If Niebuhr insists that the notion of God as person is
necessary in order that there may be a community of persons,
he also recognizes that one's ability to regard God as personal
depends on one's living in a society in which "person" has
some meaning. Religion is not the panacea which has only to
be applied in order to effect a cure for the human condition.
Such a view is far too naive. To work against those forces in
modern society which prevent the individual from becoming a
person is not to play the part simply of the prophet decrying
the fact that society has turned away from its Lord and suc-
cumbed to evil ways. Rather, to involve oneself actively in
working for a more just and humane society is to give credence
to the view that God is personal. It is to maintain the concept
as viable for modern man. If society ceases to be personal, then
it becomes nonsensical to talk of God as personal.

Niebuhr's view that religion and society are interdependent
categories which come into focus in man provides the starting
point and impetus for the task that has come to occupy his attention during his mature years—the analysis and elucidation
of man's nature and destiny. It is in man that the gospel and
the world come into direct confrontation. Hence, if one would
understand the gospel and its relevance for life in the world,
one must understand man.

Before we turn to an exposition of Niebuhr's doctrine of man,
the reader should be reminded of the way Niebuhr uses the
term "society." His understanding of the term is to be contrasted with that which it bears in modern social theory. As opposed to the social scientist, Niebuhr does not view society as a
self-governing entity which exercises autonomy and supremacy
over the individual. Nor does he accept the view that man, the
individual, and society are mutually exclusive entities. Rather,
society for Niebuhr is no more and no less than a collectivity of
individuals. It possesses no reality apart from its reference to
people. Its characteristics are those of man-as-such. It possesses
no special mystique. The significant difference between man and
society is that in the latter are revealed more nakedly the qualities possessed by individual man. For example, whereas the individual possesses one set of ethical norms, as a member of a

group and as a consequence of interacting within the group, he subscribes to a morality of a much lower level. This situation exists for a very simple reason:

> In every human group there is less reason to guide and check impulse, less capacity for self-transcendence, less ability to comprehend the needs of others and therefore more unrestrained egoism than the individuals, who compose the group, reveal in their personal relationships.[5]

Thus Niebuhr's interest in society is partly motivated by his conviction that one can arrive at a clearer, more realistic understanding of human nature by analyzing group behavior than by analyzing the individual in abstraction. At the same time, it is important to remember that for Niebuhr the individual does not exist apart from the group. Fulfillment of life requires association with others. Yet such association creates as many problems as it solves. This leads Niebuhr to say that "the society in which each man lives is at once the basis for, and the nemesis of, that fulness of life which each man seeks."[6]

Having made these points at the outset of *Moral Man and Immoral Society,* Niebuhr then describes man's nature and function as they are revealed in the various forms of group life that make up what we call "society." The gist of his argument is that man, as a reasoning creature, has a capacity not only for self-consciousness and thus for selfishness, but also comes to the awareness that he counts for nothing in the universe. The latter discovery motivates man to seek to increase his power over others in order to win an illusory victory over his own insignificance. His will-to-live becomes transmuted into a will-to-power. Within the human soul, in self-consciousness, lies that which is at the root of the inhumanity and corruption that is everywhere so evident in human society. And in his analysis of the demonic nature of the groups which compose society, Niebuhr does not exclude a consideration of the corporate forms of religion. They, too, can be used as vehicles of man's will-to-

---

[5] *Moral Man and Immoral Society* (N.Y., Scribner's, 1932), pp. xi-xii.

[6] *Ibid.,* p. 1.

power and its resultant vitiating of human life. As history has shown, man has been all too ready to make religion "his" religion and to use it for his own selfish purposes. The main burden of Niebuhr's study is to demonstrate that at the root of the malfunctioning and breakdowns so obvious in social life is a split within man himself. Only when man is himself healed, Niebuhr insists, can the structures of his societal life function in a healthy and constructive fashion.

Just as the close interrelation of religion, society, and man is to be seen from a realistic appraisal of what is going on in the world, so, for Niebuhr, is that interrelation to be demonstrated by the manner in which society's splits and fractures are overcome. Since man is the center of the disturbance in society, when he is healed he mediates that which in turn renews society. Man is the connecting point where all the conflicts of society arise and the disturbances in the social order converge, but he is also that which mediates the forces which redeem society. It goes without saying that the resources which man makes available for the renewal of society are those of society.

Yet Niebuhr does not simply assert that it is religion which, through man, provides the wherewithal for the renewal of society. He comes to this conclusion only after investigating the question whether man is able to redress the grievances of the social order on his own. Though it is Niebuhr's central position that man mediates that which renews society, he nevertheless contends that man must look beyond himself for the resources of renewal. Society must be integrated if it is to be renewed. But man himself is in need of integration. He lacks the objectivity of judgment that would form a basis for social integration. Though man is the center of renewal, he is also the center of the disturbance. He must receive something from beyond himself which he can in turn mediate to society. It is at this point that religion becomes significant. Its function is to provide the resources which integrate man and through him integrate society. Its function is thus twofold.

Niebuhr understands the primary resource which religion makes available to man as that of a self-transcending goal: that which lifts him out of his narrow, self-centered preoccupations. This self-transcending goal not only helps man to see how narrow and self-seeking he is—and so enables him to be more equitable in his dealings with others—but also enables him to evaluate more fairly what is good for society. Freed from his own prejudices, man will be enabled to mediate between the rival claims which lead to the conflicts on the corporate level. Indeed, given a new perspective which transcends both the self and society, man will see that it is precisely the tendency in society to split into warring camps that makes it impossible for society to rectify human problems. One of the main insights given by religion is the realization that in social conflict there is never simply a right and a wrong side. To make such a division is not only to oversimplify but to preclude at the outset the possibility of solving any problems. It is only when man realizes that society is one that there is any possibility for true social progress.

In being given a new vantage point from which to view both himself and society, man should, says Niebuhr, manifest a humility born out of repentance. Freed from an exclusive concern for self, realizing with pain what his egocentrism has done to himself and others, man is filled with an understanding of and a self-giving concern for the needs of others. More important, he is freed from captivity to the notion that the true and the good function exclusively through him. He is open and ready for change that comes from elsewhere. Further, his awareness concerning the pervasiveness of self-love and the subtlety of its expression makes him humble as to the achievements he believes are possible in society. While working actively for the betterment of the individual and society, he realizes that the Kingdom of God lies in the future and that it is built by God. His realism concerning that which motivates the individual, not to mention social groups, makes him wary of any attempt by men, even churchmen, to build the Kingdom themselves. But at the same time he understands the idea of the Kingdom in corporate terms. He knows that true religion is no private affair. He works to change society, knowing full well that he can build nothing durable and lasting. Acknowledging the fact that he lives in a world vitiated by pride and self-aggrandizement, he recognizes that true religion is one of the forces encouraging change.

From the above general outline of Niebuhr's understanding of the interaction of religion, society, and man, and his view that man is simultaneously at the center of the conflicts disrupting society and the channel through which they are healed, we can see the focus and direction which his thought is to take. The focus is to be on man—his nature, his destiny, how the resources of religion are made available to him, etc. But the interest of Niebuhr in man is in man-in-society. For Niebuhr, there is no other man. Thus throughout his discussion of man's nature and destiny, he does not lose sight of the social dimension. Indeed, one of Niebuhr's greatest accomplishments is the single-minded thoroughness with which he devotes himself to the task of spelling out his doctrine of man as mediator between God and society. We now turn to a more systematic discussion of his understanding of that doctrine.

The sources of Niebuhr's understanding of man are the biblical revelation and his realistic appraisal of the human situation. He accepts the notion of "general" as well as "special" revelation. The former is synonymous with individual, private revelation, while the latter refers to God's self-revelation to man in history. He regards both types of revelation as essential and as implying each other:

> Without the public and historical revelation the private experience of God would remain poorly defined and subject to caprice. Without the private revelation of God, the public and historical would not gain credence.[7]

Thus while Niebuhr is quick to acknowledge that the biblical revelation is determinative as regards man's understanding of God and his ways with men, he is in essential disagreement with the more orthodox tradition, which affirms that it is only within "the circle of faith" that man, or God, is understood. Niebuhr believes it is possible to arrive at valid insights concerning man's nature and destiny apart from the biblical revelation (though these can easily be misunderstood). Here we can see in the background Niebuhr's concern to keep God and society in re-

[7] *The Nature and Destiny of Man* (N.Y., Scribner's, 1953), Vol. I, p. 127.

lationship. Because he affirms this tension he is ready to learn about man from other sources besides Holy Scripture. Yet he does view the latter as determinative.

For Niebuhr the unique and crucial contribution of the biblical tradition to the understanding of man is its myth of creation. According to the Genesis account, man is created "in the image of God." Niebuhr understands this to mean that man is placed between the Creator God and the rest of the created order. Man shares with the former the creative spirit and with the latter inescapable participation in matter. Man's uniqueness lies in his partial self-transcendence. By means of his understanding, man can rise above his immediate involvement in his life-context, but he cannot completely disentangle himself from it. Contrary to the Greek understanding of man, correct understanding, from the biblical point of view, does not necessarily result in correct action. For between man's knowing what is objectively constructive and destructive and his acting accordingly comes the lustful desire of man to prove himself God-like; i.e., independent and all-powerful:

> Man is insecure and involved in natural contingency; he seeks to overcome his insecurity by a will-to-power which overreaches the limits of human creatureliness. Man is ignorant and involved in the limitations of a finite mind; but he pretends that he is not limited. He assumes that he can gradually transcend finite limitations until his mind becomes identical with universal mind. All of his intellectual and cultural pursuits, therefore, become infected with the sin of pride.[8]

This assertion of independence alienates man from God and makes him a slave to the potentials of creation, rather than their master, which was God's original intention in creation. Niebuhr sees the myth of the tower of Babel as illustrating the perennial temptation of man to be completely autonomous and the confusion that results therefrom. But what is there about man which forces him to yield to temptation?

In answering this question Niebuhr attempts to understand and interpret the fall of Adam in such a way that it will be

[8] *Ibid.,* pp. 178–79.

readily accepted by modern man, and to this end he makes use of concepts drawn from the behavioral sciences. Of course, he does not regard Adam's fall as an historical event, in the sense that a specific person disobeyed God's command and implicated the rest of mankind in the consequences of his action. Adam means simply "man" and connotes the normal human propensity for inordinate self-concern. In attempting to explain why man is so unduly concerned about himself Niebuhr is led into an analysis of the nature of sin. Like Kierkegaard, he does not believe that it is possible to set forth the etiology of sin. Sin posits itself. This being the case, one can only trace the phenomenology of sin in human behavior and point to its consequences. This Niebuhr docs so extensively that some critics regard his doctrine of man as sinner as his central contribution to contemporary Christian thought.

Departing from the traditional understanding of Pauline theology—that "the wages of sin is death," i.e., that death is the consequence of sin—Niebuhr does not view sin and death as having any direct cause-effect relationship. Rather, he speculates that, had man not sinned, death would not be an insuperable problem for him. But, since man is already sinful, death comes to exercise a tyranny over him. Death represents the unpredictable termination of man's opportunity to fulfill his life's ambitions. It is this insoluble tension between "finis" and "telos" that fosters man's anxiety. The injustice and competitiveness that mark human interaction on all levels are the paramount fruits of this anxious self-seeking.

In holding that sin posits itself Niebuhr means that man carries within himself a dual awareness. While man knows of his insurmountable finitude, he is also conscious of the totality of which he is a part. The resulting tension creates an anxiety in man which is unbearable but inescapable. This anxiety in turn gives rise to an insatiable temptation to escape the predicament of being human. Niebuhr locates his understanding of man as sinner in this ambivalence:

> The fact is that man is never unconscious of his weakness, of the limited and dependent character of his existence and knowledge. The occasion for his temptation lies in the two facts, his

greatness and his weakness, his unlimited and his limited knowledge, taken together. . . . His sin is never the mere ignorance of his ignorance. It is always partly an effort to obscure his blindness by overestimating the degree of his sight and to obscure his insecurity by stretching his power beyond its limits.[9]

Many have stumbled over Niebuhr's ambiguous statement that "man sins inevitably, but not necessarily." Since he has insisted that sin posits itself, Niebuhr now has to avoid the logical conclusion that God is the author of evil and man a predetermined sinner. This he does by means of his concept of temptation. Niebuhr views God as providing the setting, while man inevitably responds. Temptation implies not a causal necessity but an empirical inevitability. In short, Niebuhr does not explain the nature of sin, but describes its setting and ingredients. The basic manifestation of sin is pride, which tempts man to abuse his freedom. Standing at the juncture of nature and spirit, man recoils into a dehumanizing identification with nature when the strain of proud self-assertion becomes too great. This, which represents an escape from freedom and responsibility, Niebuhr calls sensuality. The two basic forms of sin are pride and sensuality, the latter a derivative of the former. They constitute the two ways by which man attempts to deal with his position between God and the world. Man is created to obey God, but he attempts to "play God." Rather than using this world as he was intended to, man loses himself to it.

According to Niebuhr, the final proof that God is not the author of sin is man's feeling of guilt. On this point Niebuhr makes a sharp distinction between the exterior and interior points of view concerning sin. What to the external observer may appear to be the necessary outcome of prior decisions is in reality the result of conscious choice by the agent reflecting upon himself:

The fact of responsibility is attested by the feeling of remorse or repentance which follows the sinful action. From an exterior view not only sin in general but any particular sin may seem to be the necessary consequence of previous temptations. . . . But

[9] *Ibid.*, p. 181.

the interior view does not allow this interpretation. . . . It discovers that some degree of conscious dishonesty accompanied the act, which means that the self was not deterministically and blindly involved in it.[10]

Niebuhr sees no difficulty in both maintaining human responsibility for actions and asserting their inevitability. Thus he avoids the unending debate between the idealistic contenders for absolute human freedom and the pessimistic advocates of mechanistic determinism. Niebuhr holds that man is not free as such, though he is free in his awareness of his limitations. At the same time, man is not determined in his awareness of motivation and decision, although the external observer, by hindsight, is able to establish a causal nexus between the two. For Niebuhr, freedom is always personal, while determinism is a scientific abstraction. He concludes his discussion of human freedom by asserting: "We cannot, therefore, escape the ultimate paradox that the final exercise of freedom in the transcendent human spirit is its recognition of the false use of that freedom in action. Man is most free in the discovery that he is not free."[11] Implied here is the assumption that in his actions man is always bound by his past and influenced by his expectations. Man's freedom centers in his acknowledgment that he must live in full recognition of his condition.

Niebuhr's discussion of man's status as sinner will be misunderstood if we lose sight of his insistence that man is the point of contact of the natural, social, and religious orders. Niebuhr's interest in analyzing man's nature is motivated by his concern to bring the resources of religion into play in society. As noted earlier, Niebuhr views man as the unique agent who mediates between religion and society. However, though man in his original state is depicted as being able to do so, man-as-sinner is not only unwilling but also unable to carry out his God-given assignment. In addition to describing man's plight following the fall, the Genesis myths depict the natural and social decay which follow upon man's disobedience. Interpersonal innocence gives way to deceit. Peaceful cooperation turns into

[10] *Ibid.*, p. 255.
[11] *Ibid.*, p. 260

competitive annihilation. Social tolerance degenerates into national and international rivalry and turmoil. The story of the flood portrays the depths of man's corruptive influence on both himself and nature. Yet at the same time this myth prefigures the saving grace of God. Just as the natural and social orders are vitiated by sinful man, so the grace of God will be brought to bear on these orders by man. Niebuhr continually attacks any religious understanding, be it pietism or moralism, which is preoccupied with the individual to the detriment of the corporate dimension.

It goes without saying that Niebuhr is well aware that only he who already stands convicted by the loving judgment of God is able to appreciate the full dimensions of man's sinfulness and its reverberations throughout the created order. Even —and perhaps primarily—man's religious notions constantly lead him to justify himself on the basis of his corrupted values. Niebuhr is vehement in stressing that Jesus of Nazareth was persecuted and delivered to his execution by the religious people of his time. But only by hindsight, after one has experienced the redemptive love of God, does one recognize that he has not only fallen short of any standard of perfection, but that his best deeds themselves have added to the corruption. Repentance thus has for Niebuhr the New Testament meaning of a radical about-face in attitude. The grace of God and the faith of man can bring this about.

At this point it must be reiterated that Niebuhr is not particularly interested in a full doctrinal exposition of either Christology or grace. Although he is pre-eminently interested in the work of the Spirit through man, Niebuhr does not intend to minimize the significance of Christology. He acknowledges that the penal theory of salvation on the cross must be kept in careful balance with the view of grace as the inner work of the Spirit. However, more christocentrically oriented theologians have pointed out that Niebuhr has been less than successful in maintaining the proper balance.

With respect to Christology, Niebuhr's interest centers in its ethical significance for man. The revelation of God's love in Christ denies once and for all the human ambition to self-justification—even that of the most pious. Niebuhr views the

Sermon on the Mount as underlining the fact that man, even regenerate man, is unable to fulfill God's law of love. The difference between the sinner and the redeemed is that the latter no longer aims at self-justification. Justified by grace, the redeemed man concerns himself with the real ethical question —how the law of love can be realized in human living. He knows this to be an ongoing task. Regenerate man realizes, on the one hand, that one can never prejudge how the law of love will function in human living, nor, on the other hand, can he claim to have fulfilled its demand in any given instance. He knows that Jesus' ethic is an "impossible possibility"; i.e., one is unable to prejudge the form love will take and to fulfill it in the concrete instance. Yet it is always relevant:

> The ethical demands made by Jesus are incapable of fulfillment in the present existence of man. They proceed from a transcendent and divine unity of essential reality, and their final fulfillment is possible only when God transmutes the present chaos of this world into its final unity. . . . The Kingdom of God is always at hand in the sense that impossibilities are really possible, and lead to new actualities in given moments of history. Nevertheless every actuality of history reveals itself, after the event, as only an approximation of the ideal; and the Kingdom of God is therefore not here. It is in fact always coming but never here.[12]

Niebuhr's ethic is a creative relativism, demanding that the Christian always consider the significance of the love of God in terms of his specific circumstances. Because he no longer aims at self-justification, the Christian can be realistic in his analysis of the problems before him and can accept the necessity for compromise. In this regard, Niebuhr quite properly can be called the "father of contextual ethics." His understanding of ethics has become dominant in American Protestantism.

Niebuhr's emphasis on the context of ethical decision leads him to investigate the two main components of human existence: history and the life of institutions. For him, the former connotes the temporal setting in which man functions. The

---

[12] *An Interpretation of Christian Ethics* (N.Y., Meridian, 1956), pp. 59–60.

latter, in their rise and fall, are the forces with which man must contend. As man's temporal setting, history is constituted of God's providence and man's ambitions. God uses man's ambitions to achieve his penultimate ends. Man, however, identifies his ambitions with God's will. The result is confusion. Dimly aware that his aspirations outrun his individual potentialities, man creates institutions in a vain attempt to transcend his limitations. Very quickly, however, these institutions, intended to be man's means of realizing his Promethean dreams, develop a life of their own and enslave him to their whims. The result is that man no longer controls either his individual or his corporate life. Institutional life apes the life of the individual by pursuing its own goals of dominance and permanence. And it does so with terrifying intensity.

As the institution seeks dominance and the assurance of its own survival it becomes increasingly susceptible to corruption and tyranny. Inordinate force calls forth counter-force. Unfortunately, the latter, though having begun as a redeeming corrective of the existing institutional injustice, itself becomes caught up in the inevitable process of seeking to be permanent. There is thus a vicious circle of degeneration at the heart of institutional structure. Every institution, the religious included, contains within itself the seeds of its own destruction.

Although the process described above assures that no institution can forever outlive its usefulness, such a control mechanism is purchased at an immense price in human suffering and despair. Aware that nature does not destroy as quickly as it creates, man attempts to alleviate his condition by taking matters into his own hands and subverting the established order. War and revolution, which really offer man little recompense, are the logical outcome.

Having described human life in society in these terms, Niebuhr asks himself what are the implications for the Christian who would live in such a world realistically but not cynically. It is at this point that eschatology assumes a special significance for Niebuhr. Christian man lives with a dual awareness which is succinctly expressed in the Johannine notion of "being in, but not of, the world." Though God's judgment will be revealed in its fullness only beyond history, Niebuhr nevertheless maintains that it has real implications within history. For the Christian, the eschatological parables bear witness to the only valid criterion for responsible human conduct. He is aware that God uses the changes and catastrophes of history to exercise his Lordship. Change and misfortune are not simply the result of man's blindness or of chance. They reveal God's judgment on man's individual and corporate pride.

Because he is aware that his true citizenship is in a Kingdom that will be realized only at the end of history, the Christian is able to withstand the buffeting that is his lot in this life. His realization that the Kingdom is not built by men's hands frees him to be a realist. He is saved from cynicism, however, by the knowledge that he has a God-given vocation. Niebuhr never tires in his insistence that, while the Christian cannot build God's Kingdom in history, he cannot escape involvement in God's ongoing action in history. Niebuhr's emphatic declaration that the Christian cannot abdicate responsibility for critical social involvement arises in this context. To be a Christian means to be radically in the world.

The limited scope of this essay precludes any discussion of Niebuhr's extratheological political theories. It must be pointed out, however, that Niebuhr has devoted considerable attention to the problematics of politics, especially in recent years. His theologically grounded suspicion of all ideologies has allowed him to raise a prophetic voice whenever there is a widespread tendency to interpret complex social movements in simple black-and-white terms. His wise insistence that crusading fanaticism, be it Communist, capitalist, or nationalist, always represents a terrible oversimplification, has had considerable influence on political thinking, both here and abroad.

Since there already exists a considerable body of critical literature concerning Niebuhr's work, we can limit ourselves to a brief estimate of his significance. There is no question but that among contemporary Christian theologians, Reinhold Niebuhr is the only native American to have achieved world-renown. His ability to combine unswerving realism and keen analysis has enabled him to cut through speculative theological systems in order to focus on the essential problem—how man is to understand himself as a citizen of two worlds. While some of his insights concerning man's nature may be inadequate in view of more recent findings, he has made a major contribution to theology by his concentration upon man as the point of contact of the Gospel and the world. Today, when systematic theology is regarded by many as the whole of the theological enterprise, Niebuhr's approach stands as a necessary and important corrective. In addition to reminding the church that it must ceaselessly struggle to relate itself to what is going on in the world, Niebuhr challenges us to develop a more comprehensive and creative understanding of man. To view man simply as a "child of God" and a product of society is no longer sufficient. As Niebuhr himself would readily acknowledge, the task which he embarked upon is still for us unfinished business.

Bibliography

Reinhold Niebuhr, *The Nature and Destiny of Man: A Christian Interpretation*, N.Y., Scribner's, 1946.

Reinhold Niebuhr: His Religious, Social, and Political Thought, Charles W. Kegley and Robert W. Bretall, eds., N.Y., Macmillan, 1956.

H. RICHARD NIEBUHR

Clyde A. Holbrook

Helmut Richard Niebuhr[1] has been called "a theologian's theologian"—a cryptic title signifying that by high professional competence he commanded the respect of his peers. Yet the title may be misleading. It suggests a pretentiousness of manner which found no counterpart in the man himself; it implies that his thought could be grasped only by theological experts; and in the popular imagination it may even tend to anchor him too securely in the role of a technician in theology, whereas his intellectual concerns ranged into the territories of ethics, sociological analysis, history, theological education, and on occasion, metaphysics. However the title be understood, it is intended to affirm that Niebuhr stood in the forefront of contemporary American theologians, and some would say he was the most influential, if not the most widely recognized, among them.

MAJOR PUBLICATIONS

Niebuhr came to the attention of the theological world with the publication of his sociological study *The Social Sources of Denominationalism* (1929). This work ruthlessly exposed the secular factors which have fragmented and distorted the Christian movement in America. It showed incisively how national-

---

[1] Born, Wright City, Missouri, 1894; graduate of Elmhurst College (1912), Eden Theological Seminary (1915), Washington University (1917), Yale Divinity School (1923), Yale Graduate School (1924); D.D. degrees from Eden Theological Seminary, University of Chicago, Wesleyan University; Litt.D., Franklin and Marshall College; S.T.D., Oberlin College. Ordained minister Evangelical and Reformed Church (United Church of Christ), 1916; pastor, 1916–18; professor, Eden Theological Seminary (1919–22, 1927–31); president, Elmhurst College (1924–27); 1931 member of faculty, Yale Divinity School; died 1962 while Sterling Professor of Theology and Christian Ethics at Yale University.

istic, economic, racial, and regional influences had molded Christianity into their own images. The book was not a "bestseller." Its impact remained largely restricted to the seminaries. Even there the prevailing liberal mind-set of the period greeted it with mixed feelings. Its strong critical tone appealed to many, but its implications for theological and ethical reassessment had yet to win their way. Whatever else his first major publication accomplished, it undoubtedly helped to bring Niebuhr to Yale Divinity School, where he wielded a potent influence upon the development of theology and Christian ethics.

If his first book rehearsed excessively the theme of the church's bondage to social forces, the balance was rectified in his contribution to *The Church against the World* (with Wilhelm Pauck and F. P. Miller, 1935) and in his study *The Kingdom of God in America* (1937). In the latter work he analyzed the several motifs of religious revolution which have guided and energized the Christian movement in its unending dialogue with American culture. Whereas his first book, he observed, had helped to explain why the religious stream had taken certain denominational configurations, this book showed the initiating forces in the religious stream itself, the nature of its unity and its capacity to mold rather than be molded by culture. By the use of the themes of the "sovereignty of God," "the reign of Christ," and "the kingdom on earth," he interpreted the Christian movement as a dynamic process rather than "as an institution or series of institutions." And in this light he showed the shaping and meaning of American history itself. Here Niebuhr displayed his talent for moving penetratingly in the fields of cultural analysis and theological construction. He had marked out the area where culture and faith interplay as a domain peculiarly his own. Here also had begun the tutelage of American theological students in the lively art of dialectical thinking, which moves back and forth between the relativisms of man's cultural productivity and the convictional options of Christian faith.

The broad theme of culture and faith never lost its appeal for Niebuhr. In a book which might be called the most technically theological of his major publications, *The Meaning of Revelation* (1941), he set his conception of revelation against the background of cultural relativism. He found that the absoluteness of Christian revelation does not call for a repudiation of this relativism but for its intensification, because the absolute God who reveals himself in Jesus Christ and through the Christian community relativizes all finite entities, including even the theologian's statements about the absolute! Therefore no place remains for the exaltation of man's historic actions to the level of the absolute and universal. But neither was Niebuhr content to leave revelation itself as a purely private and subjective act. Since revelation takes place within the Christian community, the individual's views on the universal deity are subject to the cross checking and correction of the Christian community in its historic and contemporary forms. Thus the historical and societal factors continue to be influential preventives against sheer eccentricity and antinomianism on the part of individual Christians.

Niebuhr's emphasis on the communal setting of revelation did not lend itself to the idea that all Christians will interpret the interplay of revelation and cultural forces in the same manner. The question of how the Christian and the Christian community are related to culture at large is not settled by recourse to revelation. Rather the Christian finds himself moving between the demands of God derived from revelation, the structural necessities of the Christian church, and the calls of the culture in which he lives his life. To this triple problem Niebuhr turned his attention in what is probably his most widely read book, *Christ and Culture* (1951).

In this work he traced the types of relations which the church has historically adopted in relating its understanding of the mandate of its Lord to culture. He built upon the foundation laid by Ernst Troeltsch's typology of the relation of Christianity to culture, but amended and supplemented it. In place of Troeltsch's threefold pattern—the church, sect, and mystical types—Niebuhr's treatment yielded a fivefold pattern. The two extreme positions he identified as Christ against culture and Christ in agreement with culture. These two types enter into the remaining three, but are reduced in their radicalness by their mutual interaction. The possibility of Christ in agreement with culture is exploited in the synthetic pattern, but here Christ is also regarded as above culture, acting as the supernatural transformer and goal of human aspirations and values. The dualistic type leans more heavily upon the Christ-against-culture pattern, as the Christian is subject both to the authority of the institutions of society to which he properly owes allegiance and to the Christ who is the judge of that society. The fifth type, the conversionist position, also maintains the opposition between Christ and culture, but in spite of man's fallen nature, which appears in various cultural embodiments and is transmitted by them, it maintains that Christ can effectively enter into the transformation of culture. It refuses to lead either to the extremes of a Christian separation from the world or to the inexorable agony called for by the dualistic pattern. The conversionist position was obviously most congenial to Niebuhr himself, although his identification with the position is something less than explicit.

In *Radical Monotheism and Western Culture, with Supplementary Essays* Niebuhr once more attacked the problem of culture and faith. Here he set forth, more fully than he had in *The Meaning of Revelation,* his conception of radical theocentrism as a form of human faith.

> For radical monotheism the value-center is neither a closed society nor the principle of such a society, but the principle of being itself; its reference is to no one reality among the many, but one beyond all the many, whence all the many derive their being, and by participation in which they exist. As faith, it is reliance on the source of all being for the significance of the self and of all that exists. . . . It is the confidence that whatever is, is good, because it exists as one thing among the many, which all have their origin and their being, in the One—the principle of being which is also the principle of value.[2]

In these abstract terms one can detect the overtones of the Augustinian and Edwardian modes of thought which have suffused much of Niebuhr's theological work.

In his exploration of the relation of this radical faith to competing objects of loyalty found in the religious, political, and

[2] (N.Y., Harper, 1960), p. 32.

scientific worlds, he showed the crucial battle of faith which is to be waged between the polytheisms of culture and the high and austere faith called for by the One God. Man's natural religion, as he was fond of pointing out, is polytheism or henotheism, each of which builds about itself exclusive societies between which struggles for power and influence continue. The faith of radical monotheism challenges the exclusiveness of these societies by virtue of its lodgement in the One who is the undergirding source of all being and value.

The supplementary essays which conclude the book have for the most part been previously published. They include his contribution to the definition and role of theology, the nature of value, the approach to the problem of God's existence, and the moral element in contemporary science. Although these essays appear as an addendum to the volume, each serves as an expansion or commentary upon themes broached in the main segment of the book.

Niebuhr did not confine his attention to theology and Christian ethics. In 1953 he was appointed the director of a major study of theological education in this country and Canada. With Daniel D. Williams and James M. Gustafson he helped prepare and edit three volumes and several bulletins dealing with the nature of the Protestant ministry, its aims and methods, as well as the criticisms launched against seminary education and recommendations for improvement. These books, published in the years 1956–57, comprised a thorough and searching analysis of the needs of the churches and theological schools, and they pointed the direction for theological studies.[3]

BACKGROUNDS OF NIEBUHR'S THOUGHT

Only with great hesitation can an attempt be made to designate several of the factors which provide a context for Niebuhr's

[3] A full bibliography by Raymond Morris of Niebuhr's writings and reactions to them may be found in *Faith and Ethics,* edited by Paul Ramsey (N.Y., Harper, 1957). *Radical Monotheism and Western Culture* and *The Responsible Self* (the latter published posthumously, N.Y., Harper, 1963) appeared after the bibliography was prepared and therefore were not included.

thinking. His was an evangelical heritage whose roots run back through the classical affirmations of the Protestant Reformation to Augustine and Paul. As a matter of personal conviction and thought, the sovereignty of God stands to the foreground. The God who is unapproachable in his awesome power, authority, and justice approaches man in Jesus Christ with a mercy which is powerful and a love which is just. Nothing escapes this One's searching eye; nothing in all creation falls outside the bounds of his care. The church dedicated to his service and worship is itself ever under the divine judgment and hope. It is called to be an obedient community under its Lord, yet its ranks number sinners whose obedience and trust, weak and fragile as these may be, are accepted by the grace of its Lord. Although there has always been in this heritage a danger of an ingrown pietism, a preoccupation with the soul and its travail, there stands beside this tendency a robust intent to infuse and transform the structures of civilization with that sense of prophetic judgment and loving mercy which the Christian community experiences in its own life. From its Calvinist sources this tradition draws its social passion to make the kingdoms of this world the Kingdom of its Lord. Yet it knows that within the limits of historic time and the conditions of human sin, this consummation remains a hope which judges the inadequacy of human effort yet energizes men to fresh assaults upon moral evils. The ethical notes which resound throughout this movement are those of gratitude and responsibility: gratitude for divine acceptance, which frees from self-interest, and responsibility to the source of men's hope and for the neighbor.

At the end of the First World War a vigorous theological movement, associated with the names of Karl Barth and Emil Brunner, broke upon the Continental theological scene. With its return to the Reformation insights of the transcendent divine sovereignty, the Lordship of Christ, the sinfulness of man, the importance of revelation, the sense of the significance of the church, and the reawakened exploration of what Barth called the "strange new world of the Bible" where "the Word of God" is anchored, the prevailing theological liberalism received a serious setback. In this country, which had known the "empirical" theology of D. C. Macintosh and the religious naturalism of H. N. Wieman as well as less radical forms of liberalism, there were few who were ready to understand or appreciate what seemed to many a perverse attachment to doctrines supposedly long since sent to the limbo of dead theological contentions. "Postwar pessimism," "failure of nerve," "retreat from reason"—these were some of the expressions which quickly sprang to mind to explain this strange treason to the conceptions of a benevolent deity, a prophetic Jesus, and a rationally humane human nature.

Among those on this side of the Atlantic whose sensitive minds were ready to catch the deeper meaning of the "crisis theology" were the Niebuhr brothers. The reading of man's situation found in the new movement was not for them a nostalgic return to the Reformation, nor a "bloodless dance of categories" extracted from Scripture by pedantic, closeted exegetes. Nor was it merely a transitory phase induced by postwar discouragement, soon to be replaced by a renascent confidence in man's upward social and moral progress. Rather it was a realistic description of contemporary man's condition when the inherited values of the Renaissance and Enlightenment had proved incapable of preventing war's horror, economic depressions, and incipient political anarchy. The value center of Western civilization had given way; it was time once more to reassess man's image of himself, to seek out once more the points where modern man's ailments arose and to rediscover the grounds of hope resident in the commanding convictions of once-powerful religious traditions.

The evangelical tradition in which the Niebuhrs were reared was of course congenial to the offerings of the neo-Reformation theology. And from this common ground, they each in his own way broke down the American wall of theological isolationism. They provided an opening for a two-way intellectual commerce between Continental theology and American liberalism, without themselves becoming mediating theologians. They did not give up their liberal concern with society's problems or the need for study of social structures; they did not yield to the biblicism inherent in much of the Continental movement; their terminology, though redolent with traditional concepts, was also a translation of a foreign theological jargon into a language which could be understood by the educated American. Together with Paul Tillich, whom they were instrumental in introducing to this country, they brought about a virtual theological renaissance, whose impact has been felt not only in the churches of America but among the "cultured half-believers and active disbelievers."

The richly varied academic tradition of nineteenth-century Protestant theology has also provided substantial fare for Niebuhr's theological stance. One may detect in his writings the impact of Kant and the post-Kantians, who had raised in an especially provocative way questions about the nature of theological knowledge and evidence as well as that more general distinction between theoretical and practical knowledge with which Niebuhr dealt in *The Meaning of Revelation*. Schleiermacher also continued to hold interest for Niebuhr as the pivotal figure whose treatment of theological method and revelation provided the setting for the development of both liberal theology and the reaction against it as seen in the early Barth. With these problems Niebuhr continued to wrestle in the development of his own theological style and his views on revelation. In the development of the latter, Kierkegaard, the creative, nonacademic mind of the nineteenth century, wielded a major influence. In Kierkegaard's existential stance and sharply dialectical thought, Niebuhr found re-enforcement and stimulation for his own conceptions of decision, reduplication in life of thought and in thought of life, participative knowledge, and of the importance of understanding faith in ontological rather than simply noetic categories. But perhaps no figure of the recent past laid so lasting an impress upon Niebuhr as did Ernst Troeltsch. On the one hand, Troeltsch struggled with the problem of historical method and its assertions, and on the other, the claims for the truth and uniqueness of Christian insights as based on historical events. The issue of universal validity as it stands confronted by the intransigent relativism of all historical phenomena, including the observer and interpreter as posed by Troeltsch's efforts, marked out the area within which Niebuhr accomplished much of his work. The same problem also directed him toward the development of a dialectical way of thinking by which he wove patterns of comprehension from the interplay between rigorous attention to the concrete events of human history and the deliverances of revelation. Hans Frei interprets Niebuhr's encounter with both Barth and Troeltsch as resulting in an effort "to unite a doctrine of radical monotheism and Christocentric revelation with an understanding of our life as responsible persons in an endlessly varied cultural history."[4]

Only brief mention may be made of others who have discernibly influenced Niebuhr. Jonathan Edwards, to whom Niebuhr gave protracted attention, weighed heavily in the formation of his own theories on value as well as in his theological understanding of American culture. Josiah Royce, with his treatment of the themes of loyalty and community, and F. D. Maurice, in whom, said Niebuhr, "the conversionist idea is more clearly expressed than in any other modern Christian thinker and leader," have both dealt with themes near to Niebuhr's paramount concern with culture. Martin Buber's "I-Thou" played an extremely important role in Niebuhr's formulations of the personalistic character of revelation. Indeed, much of Buber's influence on American Protestant thought probably came through Niebuhr's teaching and writings. Although one would have difficulty in tracking down with precision the influence of A. N. Whitehead, it could be maintained with some success that Niebuhr's sensitive concern for nature in the divine economy, his portrayal of the dynamic interrelations of created beings and relativistic interpretation of value, and perhaps certain tendencies to metaphysical formulation owe something to Whitehead's process philosophy.

Yet having said as much as this concerning influences, one realizes that all talk of formative factors comes to an end in the frustration of mere conjecture. The inexplicit influences of home and family, friends, and conversations with colleagues and students—the value of which Niebuhr was ever ready to acknowledge—may weigh as heavily as the formal, academic factors.

MOTIFS IN NIEBUHR'S THEOLOGY

If any one theme can be considered pivotal in Niebuhr's theology, it is his theocentrism. In *Radical Monotheism and*

---

[4] *Faith and Ethics*, p. 64.

Western Culture we have noticed his treatment of the concept in relatively abstract or ontological terms. And in more personalistic terms it forms the burden of the concluding chapter of *The Meaning of Revelation.*

To affirm the pre-eminence of God over life is not to offer for logical or empirical testing a hypothesis about the possible existence or nature of deity. Nor is it to be taken first of all as doctrine to be defended through thick and thin. Rather it is the confession that when a person and a community have been met by the Ultimate One, revealed through Jesus Christ, life moves from a new source of strength and intelligibility for which no other finite, created being can be substituted. The mystery which enfolds the beginnings and endings of life is illuminated by the awareness of One whose knowledge and love meet man's searchings; the chaotic and mutually conflicting ends feverishly sought fall into intelligible focus, and the potential meaninglessness of human existence is subverted by a developing trust in Him who is trustworthy above all others.

There may be other ways in which the question of God's nature and existence may arise, but for Niebuhr the problem was first of all practical, "a problem of human existence and destiny, of the meaning of inner life in general and of the life of self and its community in particular." Therefore his approach to the conception of deity was by way of "the universal experience of faith, of reliance or trust in something," by which men seek to find meaning in life. A study of the manifold faiths to which men pathetically cling shows that polytheism is the common form religious faith takes—a polytheism centered upon the competing gods of success, sex, national honor, class, family, and even religion itself. Yet none of these stands the test of a universal and absolute commitment; none of these objects of adoration sustains the erosive work of time and the destructive power of fierce conflict for supremacy. "The causes for which we live all die." Yet there is that which in Whitehead's terminology meets man as the Void or the Enemy, that implacable reality which is the enemy of all the gods, but which itself is the power by which all things come to be. For the Christian, as Niebuhr understood the matter, the turning point comes when man's faith is attached to the Void or Enemy, who in that faith is found also to be the trustworthy Friend and Sustainer.

In that transition and its continuing impact lies the basis of a life lived not in restful ease but in hope and confidence, ever sensitized by repentance, thereby constituting the permanently revolutionary character of Christian existence. Henceforth in referring to God, implicitly if not explicitly, one confesses that He is "Our Father or Lord," since whatever assertions are made about deity are uttered from the ground of the faith relation itself. Questions about the First Cause, the nature of substance, or the Final Purpose are not to be pursued as though in independence of that relation satisfactory answers to life's meaning could be found. When questions such as these are posed they presuppose doubt about the existence and goodness of deity, which is to say that the questioner, if in earnest, has simply moved to some other faith in which doubt of deity becomes the first principle of inquiry. Or, one is asking a metaphysical type of question to which the proper answer must be given in metaphysical or speculative terms rather than in existential or religious terms. In fact, in these inquiries the term "God" has itself shifted in meaning, from the living God of personal encounter and faith to God conceived as an impersonal explanatory principle behind phenomena. But for Niebuhr conceptions of the latter type were beside the mark. God is not known as He is in Himself (aseity). Rather, "What is known and knowable in theology is God in relation to self and to neighbor, and self and neighbor in relation to God."[5] From within this intense interrelatedness of God and man in which, to be sure, not man but God is always first in a logical and valuational sense, the Christian theologian does his work of clarifying the nature of the relation itself. He does not possess faith without reason, nor reason without faith; he operates, so far as human capacity allows, with faithful reasoning to carry out the explicative and normative task which his vocation as theologian lays upon him. Thus Niebuhr's theocentrism manifests itself at last in dictating the context and mode in which the theologian works.

By saying that God is first, one is also affirming that revelation is first. It is the beginning point of theological reflection. For Niebuhr the term "revelation" did not refer to a method of private access to divine truths. It was not tied to the defensive

[5] *The Purpose of the Church and Its Ministry* (N.Y., Harper, 1956), pp. 112 ff.

strategy of churches who wish to safeguard their authority and influence over society. Nor was it an attempt to stir up the fires of the fruitless ancient controversy of faith versus reason by reversion to the biblical literalism of yesteryear. Rather, in turning to revelation the Christian movement once more seeks to understand its sources of vitality, to chart and correct its course in an era where the presuppositions and points of view with which men evaluate life are of crucial importance in understanding what is valuable and true. The reinvestigation of revelation takes place in a context of thought where men's statements about the universal or absolute are themselves neither universally valid nor absolutely true. And the theologian's problem is set by this realization that the relativity which marks statements made in other areas of thought no less marks statements which he makes. He must work, conscious that theological formulations of the past as well as his own are relativized by the cultural forces in which they arise. He can speak from no pinnacle of observation which is exempt from the cultural stream in which others are also immersed.

However, recognition of this fact does not in Niebuhr's view necessarily lead to skepticism nor to an irrational loss of confidence in reason itself. In the case of theology an adequately critical approach to its task may, within the segment of history for which it assumes responsibility, seek the intelligible patterns of the religious life of the Christian community, without at the same time demanding that its findings be normative for all religious life. Historical reason will know the "length of its tether," but it will not yield to the false notion that a conditioned standpoint must deny the reality of that which is seen from that standpoint. "It is not apparent," as Niebuhr argued, "that one who knows that his concepts are not universal must also doubt that they are concepts of the universal, or that one who understands how all experience is historically mediated must believe that nothing is mediated through history."[6] To be sure, all acceptance of reality is accompanied by some form of faith, but faith also finds justification in ways appropriate to its nature and by its fruits.

[6] *The Meaning of Revelation* (N.Y., Macmillan, 1941), pp. 18–19.

Thus the theologian, although confined "to the knowledge of God which is possible to those who live in Christian history," can think with Christianity about God from the standpoint which that position affords, interpreting, clarifying, and correcting the insights found there. He has no choice but to begin his work from those standpoints which have developed from revelatory events in Christian history. He also has the exacting task of spelling out the contemporary nature and significance of that reality as it continues to disclose itself. "Such a theology of revelation is objectively relativistic, proceeding with confidence in the independent reality of what is seen, though recognizing that its assertions about that reality are meaningful only to those who look upon it from the same standpoint."[7] Its characteristic mode of expression must therefore be confessional and non-defensive.

Niebuhr had many ways of describing revelation. In a general statement he spoke of revelation as an event which occurs in Christian history conditioning all thinking: ". . . through this happening we are enabled to apprehend what we are, what we are suffering and doing and what the potentialities are. What is otherwise arbitrary and dumb fact becomes related, intelligible and eloquent fact through revelatory event."[8] When he interpreted revelation more fully, he referred to it as

the moment in our history through which we know ourselves to be known from beginning to end, in which we are apprehended by the knower; it means the self-disclosing of that eternal knower. . . . Revelation means that we find ourselves to be valued rather than valuing and that all our values are transvaluated by the activity of a universal valuer. . . . When we speak of revelation we mean that moment when we are given a new faith, to cleave to and to betray, and a new standard, to follow and deny.[9]

That event in the internal history of the Christian community which makes sense of human existence in its heights and depths, which itself is intelligible and which, by the decision it calls

[7] *Ibid.*, p. 22.
[8] *Ibid.*, p. 138.
[9] *Ibid.*, pp. 153–4.

forth, sets in motion the unending transformation of mind and life, is revelation.

Although Niebuhr saw the locus of revelation in Jesus Christ, he carefully distinguished the role of Christ from the ultimate object of revelation. Christ does not take God's place. It is one thing to seek the triumph of Christ's cause; it is another matter "to substitute the Lordship of Christ for the Lordship of God," as though Christ's devotion to the will of the Father were a matter of indifference to Christian faith.[10] Christ's fidelity to the Father and his status as Son of the Father indicate that there is One beyond him to whose service he summons men. Even as he lived to God and through him God lived with men, so his followers are called to the double movement in the religio-ethical life; from the world to God and from God back into the cares and concerns of the world.[11] In Christ men may find what Niebuhr called "three notes": "The note that the valuing, saving power in the world is the principle of being itself; that the ultimate principle of being gives and maintains and re-establishes worth; that they [men] have been called upon to make the cause of that God their cause."[12] Thus Jesus Christ is inseparable from revelation, but what is revealed by him is the Ultimate One whom men meet in the personal encounter of the I-Thou relation.

In the outworking of revelation Niebuhr discerned a process which converts men's natural appreciations and evaluations of moral law, attitudes toward nature and science, history and religious knowledge. The moral law is now known as the demand of one from whom there is no escape, "whose seriousness of purpose will not suffer that his work be destroyed by the evasions and transgressions of this pitiful, anarchical creature. . . ."[13] It has universal sway, including in its domain both rational and arational creatures, "good" and "bad" people—as the world judges them. And since men are dealing with a living God, there can be no absolutizing of commandments into specific rules of conduct. "What is commanded by God is commanded anew in

---

[10] *Radical Monotheism*, pp. 59–60.
[11] *Christ and Culture* (N.Y., Harper, 1956), p. 29.
[12] *Radical Monotheism*, p. 43.
[13] *The Meaning of Revelation*, p. 165.

every new moment for that moment" and calls in turn for a resiliency of spirit answerable to a living authority, as well as to the concrete deeds of the situation. Similarly the human provincialisms and pride which infect men's views of nature are brought under judgment by revelation. When one meets the Creator, "it is no longer necessary to defend man's place by a reading of history which establishes his superiority to all other creatures. To be a man does not now mean to be a lord of the beasts but a child of God." Science is free to go about its business without fear of a new theological bondage in the light of a faith "that nothing God has made is mean or unclean," or forbidden to its search.[14] Man's natural knowledge and expectations about God are likewise cast in a transforming light by revelation. In Christ, God meets men "not as the one beyond the many" gods but "as the one who acts in and through all things." His unity of will draws men's disunity into a new integrity of being. His power, displayed in the apparent weakness of the cross, turns out to be a conquering power which makes even death its instrument of hope and salvation. His goodness reverses human expectations for self-centered benefits, and men discover that they "sought a good to love and were found by a good that loved them."[15]

It would be easy to conclude that since revelation takes place in what Niebuhr called internal history, he had lost sight of its relation to external history. Yet the dialectical bent of his mind can be seen in the way in which throughout his analysis of revelation he has also retained a firm grasp upon the realities of external events. He has continued to move between the realm of participative, lived history and the realm of speculative, observed history. Or as he flatly put it, "Internal life does not exist without external embodiment." Therefore the Bible, the traditions, rites, and story of the churches' behavior in history, as well as the events in human culture generally, have their part to play in the way in which the Christian lives his life. The life under revelation does not take place in a vacuum. Revelation cannot be reduced to publicly observed events, but the perspectives and attitudes it creates find expression in the public domain.

[14] *Ibid.*, p. 173.
[15] *Ibid.*, p. 189.

Though we cannot point to what we mean by revelation by directing attention to the historic facts as embodied and as regarded
from without, we can have no continuing inner history through
which to point without embodiment. . . . External history is the
medium in which internal history exists and comes to life.[16]

MOTIFS IN NIEBUHR'S ETHICS

Niebuhr left behind him no final, systematic treatise on Christian ethics. His posthumous volume *The Responsible Self* might
have been the prologue to such a work, but it must now remain
a broken fragment barely pointing directions which he might
have taken had time served him better. For the most part the
book does not introduce unfamiliar motifs of his thought, but
it does indicate his persevering interest in seeking out highly
illuminative symbols and figures in which to express the moral
life and the relevance of Christ to ethics. Here he offered a
phenomenology of the moral life cast in the model of man the
answerer or responder who seeks a fitting response to a situation.
In this analysis he construed the moral situation as such without
particular reference to Christian elements, but in the Appendix
of the volume he turned to the subject of adequate metaphors
and symbols in which to cast the role of Christ in respect to the
moral life. The conception of man the answerer Niebuhr saw
as the image in which ethical decisions in fact take place in any
community, but in the Christian community where his own
thought came to lodge he saw man as the being who is responsible to the dynamic, single God revealed in Jesus Christ. Thus
in this book as in his earlier works his radical monotheism
comes to the foreground as one of the central motifs of his
constructive endeavors.

From his radical monotheism was drawn his insistence upon
the relativity of all created beings, events, and principles. This
meant that one does not expect from Niebuhr the detailed laying
out of certain virtues, rules, or principles which popularly are
thought to constitute Christian ethics. Principles, values, virtues
may have their place within ethical reflection and action, but
Niebuhr would not hear of the absolutizing of any of them, not

[16] *Ibid.*, pp. 89–90.

even that of love. God is the only absolute and universal being; all else has a temporary validity. From the principle of radical monotheism also comes the freedom for the moral agent to take account of the many factors relevant to moral decision in concrete situations. He does not begin with some abstract norm which then is applied to specific cases; he begins rather with the concrete situation as interpreted in the light of what God has done and is doing—sustaining, judging, and redeeming. It is the obligation of the moral agent to reflect into that situation, with all the resources of knowledge and insight at his command, his understanding of the divine will. In general—and therefore in somewhat misleading terms—the Christian's task is to bring to bear, so far as possible, that sensitively unifying relation among beings which he finds disclosed by God in Jesus Christ.

No man's moral actions fulfill perfectly the imperatives of faith, but he stands justified by grace in his shortcomings. He cannot callously hold himself guiltless before men and God; repentant action is still called for. But grace operates redemptively by enabling him to accept himself with his failures and to get on with the job of responsible moral action without the self-concerned introspective scrutiny of motive which halts action. And the Lord of history takes even the misshapen products of human decision and action within the orbit of his grace and power, turning them into the service of his own glory. Man's job is to be a faithful, hopeful, and conscientious respondent to God's claim; it is not that of assuming proprietary obligations and rights over the universe.

Responsible moral action was in Niebuhr's view no simple matter. Faith calls men to know the technical dimensions of the situations wherein they are called to act. The secular world is laid under tribute with its knowledge of psychology, philosophy, sociology, economics, and government, for one does not become a Christian moralist or actor by closeting himself with books on "Christian ethics." As James Gustafson sees it, "Significant meaning and interpretation of life can be derived from disciplines which are not concerned with the ultimate meaning of life, or which even have a clearly inadequate view of life's meaning."[17] The structures of power and authority within which

[17] *Faith and Ethics*, p. 121.

life is lived, as well as the nature of the deeply personal and interpersonal relations by which values come into being, must be understood. If the Christian is to be relevant to his time and place, he must do vastly more than concentrate upon his motivations. Love, justice, and sincerity are no substitutes for knowledge. Neither are abstract speculations about value or ontology replacements for informed policy decisions.

Thus there seem to be several foci to Niebuhr's view of Christian ethics. The first is the revelational foundation which is spelled out in the theological and ethical implications of the permanently revolutionary character of the Christian life. The second is the intensely existential, participative character of ethical reflection, decision, and action. The third is the concern for social relevance and realism. And the fourth is the sense of the dynamic interrelatedness of personal, religious, and social factors in human history within which moral action takes place. The critical understanding of these foci as they continuously interplay within the Christian community and between it and culture generally marks Christian ethics as a field of study.

EVALUATIVE COMMENTS ON NIEBUHR'S THOUGHT

The vigor and persuasive power with which Niebuhr participated in the contemporary theological scene have attracted both negative criticism and enthusiastic respect, often from the same person. The direction taken by this criticism can be indicated by certain types of questions which his position evoked. However, no attempt will be made to reach a final assessment of either Niebuhr or his critics.

Some of the principal questions cluster about two centers in his position: his theological presentation with its emphasis on revelation and radical monotheism and his treatment of ethics as it focuses upon relativism.

Niebuhr speaks of the impossibility of understanding Christian revelation except from the faith posture which revelation itself creates. Does this mean only that one cannot appreciate an experience until one has passed through it for himself? And if so, then is not the participant in the experience cut off from any significant discourse about the experience with those to whom the revelatory event has not occurred? Can he speak to or hope for understanding from only those within the community where revelation has been doing its work? One can talk around revelation, it seems; can speak and act from the ground it affords, but one can never state directly what the content of revelation is without seriously misleading others as to its true nature. Yet if one is to carry on a dialogue with a culture which denies or is unaware of revelation, what possible grounds remain for intelligible discourse? To argue that every person speaks from a faith stance which is ultimately inaccessible to others may be correct as an observation, but since it appears that more people are able to understand each other on these grounds than the proponent of revelation can muster for his position, the argument remains indecisive. There is no universal court of appeals in which the reality of faith postures can be adjudicated. The answer lies in conversion or decision. As Niebuhr saw it, the full intelligibility of human existence swings into view only when man is encountered by the Ultimate One. It is God, not man, that at last is the supreme actor in providing the grounds for communication between the "outsider" and the "insider." Short of that resolution, a gulf stands between Niebuhr and his critic.

In a similar vein the agnostic question is raised as to how one judges among competing "revelations." What criteria can be offered by which to test the validity of revelation? Of course the manner in which this type of question is posed shows that the critic has not grasped Niebuhr's interpretation. That is revelation which itself provides the criteria by which all other options are tested; therefore whatever tests are offered as ultimately decisive are themselves outside the arena of the testable. They provide the grounds for evaluation, but are not themselves being evaluated. But even these, as they are held by finite, fallible humans amid the relativities of historical existence, provide no test for universal and absolute validity. After all, man is not himself a universal spectator of existence; he cannot pretend to possess, as over against the Ultimate Being, a standpoint of evaluation which escapes his finitude and sin. Interpretive presuppositions are inevitable, but they are to be held confessionally, and their validity can be assessed not simply by their initial convincement but by the degree to which, in the presence of an enormously varied human experience, they do justice to the full flavor of existence and bring intelligibility into its confusion.

In respect to Niebuhr's ethic, questions have often centered on his insistence on "relativity." His extreme concern for social relevance and his understanding of the way in which radical monotheism relativizes all finite beings and functions seem to have led him to an extravagant estimate of the role of "relativism." Some critics see this emphasis as derogating from the importance of ethical principle for the sake of expedience, or even threatening to undermine the integrity of the moral agent.

As a way of avoiding the wooden rigidity of much ethical speculation and the inherent difficulty of gearing ethical values into the dynamics of society, Niebuhr's "contextualist" or "situational" ethics acts both as a corrective and as a way of meeting unpredictable moral demands. If Niebuhr had employed the term "relationalism" to describe the ethical situation, possibly the taint of the term "relativism" could be removed and his position would be more adequately represented. It is in relations that values come to be; it is in faithfulness to relations that moral action takes place; it is in relation to God, the self, and one's companions that virtues are to be defined. In any case, what is distinctly inappropriate to Niebuhr's thought is any notion of "relativism" which would conceive good or bad as merely expressions of psychological approval or disapproval.

The questions raised above touch only the more obvious directions which criticism may take. The fertility and subtlety of Niebuhr's thought inevitably provoke questioning, but also prompt reassessment of one's own position. His views on the relation of value and being, his Christology, his dialectical manner of thinking, or any one of a number of issues he treated may at first puzzle, then interest, and finally persuade his listener or reader that he too must bend his mind to a more profound and complex formulation of these issues. So questioning begun in criticism or for information has a way of turning into appreciation, or more importantly, into a renewal of one's own quest for theological understanding.

NIEBUHR THE TEACHER

Niebuhr's influence has been felt as much as a teacher as by the books and articles he has written. In the classroom he lectured

as one who vigorously reconsidered at the time what he is saying, and he thereby exhibited an amazing capacity for involving
his students in the development of his thought. He moved about
and through a subject from many angles, and seldom did one
leave without feeling that he had not only watched a first-class
supple mind at grips with a major issue, but that in some strange
way he had participated in an intellectual exploration of territories scarcely known before.

Even as he demanded much of himself, so his students were
held to the mark of careful preparation and hard thinking. Yet
he did not seek a meek acceptance of his views. It was characteristic of him that he welcomed the challenge and thoughtful
criticism of his students rather than a slavish discipleship. His
was not a system of theology or theological ethics to be learned
by rote or repetition; it was a way in which to walk, a method
which, by opening new viewpoints, might even be turned against
Niebuhr himself.

As a counselor of students of high degree and low, he was
considerate and sensitive. Many a student in personal or vocational perplexity found in him a tactful and intelligent guide,
one whose openness of manner preserved the dignity of the
inquirer, yet in a quite unsentimental way accepted him into the
orbit of his concern. It is no wonder that the high respect in
which he was held usually merged into affection.

Niebuhr's influence continues to be felt in the academic world
through these students, many of whom teach in theological
seminaries, colleges, and universities. His past writings continue
to challenge the attention of both the church and the world, as
their various reprintings show. His writings charted new directions of theological inquiry as his restless, probing mind continued to pioneer on the frontier of human existence where the
spirit of man is searched, wounded, and healed by the Eternal.

Bibliography

H. Richard Niebuhr, *Christ and Culture*, N.Y., Harper, 1956.
(Harper Torchbooks).

Faith and Ethics, Paul Ramsey, ed., N.Y., Harper, 1957.

KARL BARTH

Daniel Jenkins

Karl Barth is considered by many students of theology to be the outstanding Protestant theologian of the twentieth century. As far back as 1937 H. R. Mackintosh, the shrewdest and most balanced of Scottish scholars, declared that in Barth "we have incontestably the greatest figure in Christian theology that has appeared for decades." Others have mentioned him in the same breath with Luther and Calvin. He is credited with having had the decisive influence in the remarkable change which has overtaken theology in the past generation.

To those who know him, Karl Barth is also one of the outstanding persons of our time. He was born in 1886, the son of a Swiss professor, and since his dismissal from his post at the University of Bonn by the Hitler regime he has spent the larger part of his working life as Professor of Theology in his native city of Basel. He is a brisk and vigorous man of bursting eloquence and lively humor, with a face of the greatest authority and distinction. The size and range of his theological output strikes awe into the hearts even of those trained in the remorseless schools of German scholarship, but he is also a lover of Mozart and likes nothing so much, after a day's hard work on his *Church Dogmatics,* as a drink and a smoke and a visit to the cinema. When he visited England in 1956 to receive a *Festschrift* on his seventieth birthday, he completely captivated the journalists of the secular press who interviewed him.

Yet as a theologian he is also much spoken against and the impression given of his teaching in short summaries is often hard to reconcile with the impression he makes as a man. His influence may be widely diffused, but the number of his professed followers, especially in the Anglo-Saxon countries, appears to be quite small. His voluminous works are more often referred to than actually quoted, and his distinctive position in theology is frequently described in singularly unattractive terms.

He is said to have brought original sin back into theology, to have emphasized the greatness of the gulf between God and man, and to have poured scorn on reason and philosophy. In all, he is made to appear like an old-fashioned Evangelical preacher of the type popularly known as "strict Calvinist."

Barth is certainly not that, and the peculiar impact which he has made upon the theological thought of our time is best understood when he is seen against his historical background. Like most of the Protestant students of his generation, he was brought up under the influence of theological liberalism. He spent some time at the feet of Harnack in Berlin and, like Tillich, was influenced by the movement of religious socialism. Then came the catastrophic event of the First World War and, although Barth was a citizen of a neutral country, he found himself questioning radically the assumptions upon which thought and life had been based in church and society. As a young pastor in Safenwil in Switzerland, he discovered that he had nothing to preach when he stood up before his people in the pulpit. In his perplexity he turned to that unfailing source of renewal to the men of the Reformation, the Epistle to the Romans. He did so, as he has said, like a man clutching at a rope when he was falling. When he wrote his commentary on Romans to describe what he had found, he discovered that the rope had rung a bell which could be heard all over Europe. This brilliantly sophisticated young liberal had learned again what the Epistle to the Romans was all about—that God, the living God, had come to deliver perplexed, self-contradictory men like himself from their sins through the power of Jesus Christ.

This was much more startling news in the theological world of 1918 than it would be today. Up to that time there had been two main lines of interest in Protestant theology. One was that of historical criticism of the Bible. This was of great value on its own level, but it often led men to disparage the significance of the testimony of the apostolic community to Jesus as being based not on history but on faith. The picture of the "historical Jesus" which, despite the critical work of Albert Schweitzer and others, still fascinated men, seemed often to owe as much to current notions of ideal manhood as they did to the New Testament. The other interest of many theologians was that of trying to find a justification for religious experience in a universe dominated by ideas, derived from scientific philosophy and other sources, which seemed to leave little room for such experience.

Such theology seemed always to be on the defensive and more anxious to accommodate the Christian faith to other influences in the world around it than to heed what the Bible really says. The result was that when preachers spoke about God they sounded as though they were doing little more than speaking about man in a loud voice. What Barth discovered from the Epistle to the Romans was that this was not the way to speak about God. He had received entry into what he called "the strange new world within the Bible," where God and not man was in the center. The effect of his commentary on Romans, which was a huge, breathless, exciting sermon rather than a commentary in the accepted sense, was to make men aware with new freshness and power that God had really come into the midst of human self-contradiction and despair and that what He thought about men was more important than what they thought about Him. What Kierkegaard had been trying brokenly to express in a largely negative way in Denmark nearly a century earlier was now boldly trumpeted forth.

Perhaps no other book of Barth's has had the same impact as the *Römerbrief,* and even now, after all these years and despite many changes of emphasis in his position, it remains the best introduction to his work. No book expresses his spirit more vividly and dramatically. Since it appeared, however, a vast corpus of literature has poured out from his pen. He must be among the most prolific not merely of theologians but of all writers. Even Erle Stanley Gardner cannot have produced more words than Karl Barth. He has published two sets of expositions of the Apostles' Creed, a series of Gifford Lectures, an outstanding book on Anselm, many pamphlets and occasional papers, and, in a different vein, a large volume of studies of nineteenth-century thought, translated as *From Rousseau to Ritschl.* All these, which would add up to a substantial life's output for an ordinary scholar, are dwarfed, however, by his gigantic *Church Dogmatics.* This remarkable work has developed throughout the years into one of the vastest literary projects ever undertaken by a single individual. Twelve volumes have already appeared, all of them very large and some of them running to nearly a thousand pages, with many long sections in small print—and the end, after over thirty years of work, is still not in sight. It is this great range of Alpine peaks which makes Barth's major contribution to theology and by which he would have his work assessed.

What are the qualities of Barth's work, as exemplified chiefly in the *Dogmatics*, which make intelligible the extent of his reputation and influence? There are at least seven which stand out.

First, his is the most massive and sustained theological enterprise of our time, rivaling the greatest systematic efforts of history. We are so accustomed to hearing of the dethronement of theology from her place as the "Queen of the Sciences" as compared with the "ages of faith" that the very existence of Barth's work is a testimony to the reality of God. Confronted by the long shelf of the *Dogmatics*, one is compelled to say, "Here, at least, is a man who believes in God." This is not, of course, a matter of their bulk alone. It is, as we shall see, a cause for regret that Barth has not found it possible to produce his work in more concentrated form. But he has created a great treasure house of theological truth, where fresh insights into familiar matters and into others which have been long neglected are constantly to be found. Whether one agrees with his general approach or not, no one seriously concerned with theology can read Barth on, say, the Trinity, the nature of religion, the attributes or perfections of God, predestination, angels, the nihil, time, and relations between men and women, or upon the significance of the "deep sleep" into which Adam fell before the birth of Eve or the divine beauty or capital punishment, war and peace, and be the same again. Here indeed is God's plenty. Barth has a great chapter on "sin as sloth" in the *Dogmatics* IV:1. This is a sin from which he himself is peculiarly free and he fills his readers with new zest for the theological task.

Second, this is more than a tour through the wide realm of theology with a guide of genius. It is a tour conducted by a man who knows what he is doing and where he is going, and who chooses his own route. Barth's overriding concern throughout the whole *Dogmatics* is so to state theological truth as to make clear the sovereignty and initiative of God in His revelation.

That he largely succeeds in doing this is his decisive theological achievement. His watchword is the same as that of Luther, "Let God be God." If since Schleiermacher the tendency has been to place man at the center of theology, with God pushed to the periphery, Barth firmly places revelation again at the center. And this God is the God who was in Christ. Barth is the theologian of the sovereignty of God, but because he is that he is no less the most christocentric of theologians. The chief motive lying behind his violent polemics against natural theology and against approaching revelation with inadequately examined philosophical assumptions which are appropriate only in another frame of reference is that he wishes to expose these as threats to the divine initiative and therefore to God's real coming in saving love. To look for God, in the first place, elsewhere than in His revelation in Christ when we have that revelation already before us is to imply that we know better than God who He is. Theology is "the Church's concentrated anxiety and concern about her own most intimate responsibility." That responsibility is to ensure that when the church tries to proclaim the Word of God to man it is, in fact, the Word of God which is being proclaimed, and not a word of man masquerading as a Word of God. This means that the church's proclamation must always be inspired and controlled and checked by reference to God's revelation in Christ as declared in the Bible.

This leads us to consider Barth's third great quality as a theologian. He performs superbly the main function of a theologian concerned to state systematically the Church's fundamental beliefs, which is what a dogmatic theologian is supposed to be. He leads the church back to the Bible as a medium through which God speaks to His people here and now. This is in contrast to a theologian like Paul Tillich. Tillich tries to relate the questions posed by modern man to biblical revelation and in so doing helps many people to see more clearly what biblical revelation is about. But his strength does not lie in his making the ideas of the Bible more luminous; it consists in his conveying meaning through terms which he has invented himself. Barth speaks to modern man by trying to show him that God in His revelation poses more radical questions to all men than any which even the most discerning and critically minded modern man has been able to put to God. He would not make a distinction, as Tillich does, between kerygmatic and apologetic theology, because the kerygma, that which the Bible proclaims, cannot be properly stated or grasped without facing and overcoming its contradiction in the hearts and minds of sinful men.

Whether Barth is an altogether faithful biblical exegete is a matter of dispute. He is certainly not a fundamentalist. He insists that it is essential that the Bible should be open to critical examination from all sides. Otherwise, men try to hinder the freedom of God to vindicate Himself in the truth of His revelation. His whole understanding of the dynamic, existential character of revelation, in which God is never an Object, rules out the possibility that Barth could ever have much real sympathy with fundamentalism. Yet his conviction of the normative character of the Scripture for the Christian life is so strong that he is often tempted to read more into the Bible than most other people can find there, and to treat critical considerations with a certain arbitrariness. One of the most notorious examples of this is his discussion of the relationship between men and women in the form of an exposition of the Creation story in Genesis. There may be some justice in the complaint of those who say that, although Barth himself may not be a fundamentalist, students who follow this procedure without having grasped the vital principle of his theology may easily become indistinguishable from fundamentalists. It is not enough for Barth to deplore the existence of "Barthians"; he has some responsibility for ensuring that his followers do not misunderstand and misapply his teaching.

Yet when all qualifications have been made, it remains one of Barth's greatest contributions that he has made the Scriptures come alive in a new way for many people in many lands who have to preach the Word of God. He of all men has made us see that when the great words of Scripture seem stale and platitudinous, it is not because they are no longer "relevant" but because we ourselves are no longer in the right place for hearing what they have to say. His theology is best described as a theology of the Word of God, and Barth is indeed a true doctor of Holy Scripture.

Fourth, Barth has achieved a notable critical reinterpretation of classical theology. For many Protestants brought up in the liberal tradition he has been a theological mentor who has awakened their interest in great figures of the past to whom otherwise they would have paid little attention. He has introduced many non-Lutherans to Luther. He has revivified the Calvinist tradition, although his freedom in handling Calvin has earned him the displeasure of Calvinist traditionalists, who brand his theology as a "new modernism" (the title of a book attacking Barth by Cornelius Van Til). He breaks boldly with Calvin over predestination and reinterprets him on the Trinity, but it is not simple enthusiasm which makes many believe that if Calvin were alive today he might be more disposed to agree with Barth than with those who stick close to the Calvinist letter. Barth has also uncovered much buried treasure among the Protestant scholastics. He has always been deeply attached to Anselm, and has said that his book on Anselm is the one which gave him most satisfaction to write. In recent years he has shown a growing sympathy with Thomas Aquinas even though he still maintains, against Thomist sympathizers who dispute his interpretation of Thomas, that the Thomist doctrine of the *analogia entis* is the root of a great deal of theological evil. Barth was one of the first writers of any kind to draw inspiration from the works of Kierkegaard, and it is through Barth that many people have approached Kierkegaard. Characteristically, he quickly dissociated himself from Kierkegaard lest he be thought to depend too much on existentialism, and he did not include an essay on Kierkegaard in his series of studies on nineteenth century thought. He always speaks in an illuminating manner of Schleiermacher, whom he greatly admires while he deplores much of his influence. And despite his alleged lack of concern with philosophy, he has much that is original to say about the philosophers of the Enlightenment and about Marx and Feuerbach and Nietzsche and Sartre.

Fifth, Barth has presented a vigorous reinterpretation of the radical Reformed doctrine of the Church. He is a firmly committed member of the Swiss Reformed Church and asserts that dogmatics is a responsible activity of the Church community. But he insists that the Church can never be taken for granted as automatically the possessor of divine grace. The Church has constantly to find her life in the events of proclamation and sacrament; she never simply has it by being there. The theology of Barth and his colleagues in the early days was known as "crisis theology," not in the sense that it was produced in a period of tension in world affairs but in the sense that it laid great emphasis upon the fact that men could not hear the Word of God without being thrust into a situation where the whole basis of their existence was imperiled—where their lives were at a crisis and where they were judged by God—and where their only hope was in the leap of faith. The expression of the idea at the time obviously owed a great deal to existentialist philosophy, but the idea itself is central to the New Testament understanding of faith and to the Reformed approach to the doctrine of the Church. Faith and crisis are inseparable. This is why judgment always has to begin at the household of faith. This, in its turn, is why the way of renewal in the life of the Church is always the way of reformation. Reformation is not something which happens at particular periods in the Church's history, so that after such a period the Church can relax and celebrate its own purity. Reformation must be a persistent activity in the Church's life. There is a sense in which it is true that whenever the Church gathers together out of the world for worship every Sunday it is making an act of reformation.

Barth sees the Church as living between the times of reconciliation and final redemption—he edited a series of pamphlets at one time with the title *Zwischen den Zeiten*—and emphasizes that the Church holds her true life only as she moves toward her coming Lord. She is, in her nature, a pilgrim Church, and once she settles down as an earthly institution she is in danger of being conformed to this world which passes away.

It is this aspect of Barth's teaching which causes greatest resistance among Catholics. They claim that he denies a real coming of God to man and any continuity and dependability in the divine grace. His sacramental teaching, especially about baptism, is certainly "left wing" and in his thinking about the Church in general he has a good deal of affinity with British Congregationalism. His concern, however, here as always, is to assert the Lordship of Christ in His own house. The Church owes her life not to her inherent vitality nor to temporal succession but to her Lord. She has constantly to die that she might live, to know even in her earthly form the fellowship of Christ's sufferings if she is to manifest the power of the resurrection. He emphatically believes in a real coming of God to man, but it is a coming in "the form of a servant." There is continuity in the action of the divine grace and there is dependability; these may have their adumbrations in the life of human institutions, but they are ultimately apprehensible only from the Godward side, in faith. Where men imagine that things are otherwise and that they can produce guarantees of the divine reliability, they are, as he says in his exposition of the Scots Confession of 1560 in his Gifford Lectures, in danger of turning the Church into a "filthy synagogue of Satan."

Barth's attitude to the Church as a human institution is closely connected with his attitude toward religion. No one is more aware of the ambiguity of human religion. It is he who coined the aphorism, "Religion is the enemy of faith." Religion in this sense he defines, in the *Dogmatics* I:2, as man's attempt to enter into communion with God on his own terms. Man must, therefore, transcend his religion if he is to arrive at the real self-giving of faith in which he dies and Christ lives in him. True religion, which issues out of genuine faith, is a real possibility, but a possibility only because revelation has taken place and men can realize that they are able to transcend themselves in faith.

We may reasonably question whether Barth has said all that needs to be said about so complex and many-sided a phenomenon as human religion and yet can recognize that what he is saying is of the profoundest importance for the inner life of the Christian community itself. The lesson of the failure of the old Israel is taken to heart by Barth as by no other theologian. Religion is not good in itself. Like all human activities it needs to be redeemed. It was religion which crucified Christ and, as religion goes, it was good religion. The watchword of the modern ecumenical movement is "Let the Church be the Church." Barth would probably agree with it, but would want to make clear what the conditions are which enable the churches to become truly churches of Jesus Christ.

Sixth, Barth brings wide sympathy and broad humanity into his theological work. This will surprise those who think of him rather as an opinionated and aggressive theologian, and it has to be admitted that he himself must bear a large part of the responsibility for giving this misleading impression. His characteristic method, in the German rather than in the Swiss manner, is to lay down his thesis in thick black type and in its starkest and most uncompromising form at the head of each chapter, as though to challenge anyone to dare deny it. His way of dealing with his critics is to go after them with a hatchet and cut them to pieces, making sure that nothing of them is left after he has finished. His treatment of Emil Brunner over natural theology and of the early Paul Tillich in the very first half-volume of the *Dogmatics* are cases in point. Those brought up according to the gentler conventions of Anglo-Saxon scholarly discourse may reasonably feel that there are more courteous and more constructive ways of conducting theological arguments. At the same time it is fair to say that, as many of those who have studied with him insist, he proceeds upon the assumption that his opponents are as tough as he is, that he expects to be answered in kind and that he retains his good humor.

His method is doubly unfortunate, however, because it serves to conceal the extent to which, as his argument develops, Barth does in fact take account of objections to his thesis and different approaches from his own. It also serves to conceal the extent to which he is sensitively aware to the movements of thought and life around him. We have already referred to his love of Mozart and the cinema. These are only slight indications of his conviction that the theologian is a man among men who must clearly recognize his complete involvement in the human situation with his fellows. In his exposition of the doctrine of man in the *Dogmatics* III:2, he does not directly use Bonhoeffer's ideas of "holy worldliness" and mature manhood but, as Bonhoeffer acknowledged, their ideas are very close to each other. In his comparatively recent paper on "The Humanity of God" (1956) he says that it is this side of the Christian faith which needs particular emphasis today, just as when he started the Otherness of God needed emphasis. Barth the theologian may not always provide us with the best exemplification of what this might mean, although Barth the man would, but even the theologian can give us a great deal of help in trying to work it out.

Seventh, Barth may be claimed as one of the genuinely ecumenical theologians of our time. He himself has taken little direct part in formal conversations sponsored by the World Council of Churches, although he did attend the Amsterdam Assembly and has contributed to various ecumenical symposia. But he is the acknowledged theological mentor of the General Secretary of the World Council and many others who are active in its affairs look to him for leadership. He has disciples in most of the larger churches of Christendom and he is increasingly studied and admired in the more advanced Roman Catholic circles. The reason is that, although he speaks so uncompromisingly out of the Reformed tradition, his purpose is to recall men to those central realities of the Christian faith which provide the most enduring inspiration for the ecumenical movement. The chief cause of the disunity and ineffectiveness of churches is that they do not believe enough in God. We have seen that Barth's greatest contribution to theology is to recall men to what belief in God really means. This makes men critical of their ecclesiastical traditions, in their religious ambiguity, and at the same time reminds them of their solidarity in sin and their participation in a common hope in Christ. This gives them strength to persevere through the disappointments and frustrations of the ecumenical enterprise in the knowledge that the Church belongs not to themselves but to God.

Barth contributes to the ecumenical movement also because his work has an ecumenical sweep and scope. He tries to see Christian truth as a unity and places it firmly in a cosmic setting. He has his blind spots, but there is very little that is sectarian or provincial about Barth's theology. If it is true that the more truly ecumenical Church toward which we all aspire cannot come into being without theology of an ecumenical quality and range, Barth is one of its chief architects.

The seven qualities we have mentioned indicate the greatness of Barth's work, and the impact of his genius is such upon those who have learned to appreciate him that it is often hard for them to become aware of any of his limitations. But if there were none, this would contradict some of Barth's own most characteristic insights. And Barth has given himself to his readers with such prodigal generosity and has been at work for such a long time that some of his weaknesses have become visible even to his admirers.

The first weakness that suggests itself is that Barth does not always escape the danger of placing the theologian on a pedestal, above criticism. This is related to the excessive biblicism which we have already noted, since, if you read more into the Bible than can really be found in it, you are in danger of claiming the authority of Scripture for what are no more than your own opinions. Nothing could be further from Barth's professed intention than this. In the prolegomena to the *Dogmatics,* in the book on Anselm, and in various occasional papers Barth constantly insists that the theologian can only perform his functions of criticism, proclamation, and witness if he himself is constantly brought into the situation of radical self-criticism which confrontation with God's Word produces. But he sometimes leaves his reader wondering whether he has always succeeded in being faithful to his own best principles. He echoes Kierkegaard's famous question, "Can a theologian be saved?" in his commentary on Romans and he would still insist that this is a serious question, but he sometimes gives the impression that it is only the theologian who can be saved. When a theologian is moved to maintain that Jesus Christ is the only source of true revelation and that his method of interpretation of Jesus Christ is the only right one, he must be particularly careful to be humble and generous in his accounts of the positions of theologians who think differently and in his attitude toward other religious and philosophical traditions than his own. Barth succeeds in showing this care more frequently than his critics allow, but he is far from being invariably successful.

The very size of the *Dogmatics* is a partial indication of this. An unsympathetic critic, E. L. Mascall, has said that it takes so much time to read this theologian of the Word that no time is left to read the Word itself. The choice is between Barth and the Bible. This is ungracious, but Barth would perhaps have made us even more grateful than he has if he had given more consideration to how he could have spoken more economically. The words of Scripture, "God is in heaven, thou art on earth; therefore let thy words be few," have a very Barthian ring. It would have been reassuring if more concrete evidence had been provided that this exhortation applied even to Barth. Speaking of the first volume of the *Dogmatics*, he said, "I know where I mean to come out, if the Lord will." At that time he apparently thought of five volumes of five hundred pages each. Perhaps his work would have been even more influential, and his tendency to theologism more firmly checked, if he had managed to keep his work close to those limits.

Barth's second limitation arises from a defect of one of his very greatest qualities. Barth is incomparable at uncovering for us again the peaks of theology in their full majesty. One thinks especially here of the chapters on the Knowledge and the Reality of God in the *Dogmatics* II:1. He is not so good at leading the gentler of his readers over all the confused and broken foothills in which they easily get lost in these days and which they must traverse before they reach the peaks. In general, it can be said that the more fundamental the question is, the surer Barth's touch becomes. For this we cannot be too grateful, but it does appear to be the case that only those who are trained in rigorous theological schools or those with his own kind of imagination can readily keep company with him.

This is partly a matter of his style, which some find vivid and exciting while to others it seems turgid and repetitive. It is also a matter of his method of thinking. He has an unerring instinct for the distinctively theological point in any discussion, but he rarely indicates to the reader how he reaches it and he concentrates most of his energies upon repudiating any argument which seems to threaten his position. In the process he deals with many of the familiar criticisms which are made of him and produces many incidental felicities, but only the patient reader can discover these things and they are not always dealt with in a frame of reference familiar to the reader. Barth operates with a theological bulldozer, moving a vast amount of earth and then proceeding to build, with excellent materials, a great rough tower to the glory of the Lord. But he leaves plenty of mess for others to tidy up and a great deal of work for the builders of approach roads.

A final limitation of Barth as a theologian is his lack of interest in a number of important questions which he might reasonably be expected to be concerned with. For example, he appears singularly uninterested in the relation between Christianity and other faiths. What hints he gives us suggest that his attitude toward them would not necessarily be as unconstructive as most people assume, but it has to be admitted that, in all the wide spaces of the *Dogmatics,* the references to other religions are pitifully few. When Barth has given us so much, it seems unreasonable to ask for more, but the other religions of the world do pose questions of great importance to anyone who is trying to produce a work of systematic theology. Barth needs to define his attitude toward them carefully even if, as he is entitled to, he does not regard it as his function to enter into dialogue with them.

Yet it is doubtful whether this catalogue of limitations does more than underline the fact that Barth is one theologian among others and that other voices need to be heard as well as his. He is such a magnificent solo instrumentalist that it is easy to imagine that he is the whole orchestra. He has called his theology a corrective, and would claim that in the end this is the best that all systems, however elaborate, can hope to be, needing their own correctives in due season. The present writer is a part-time professor of theology, but he also has to preach to a congregation Sunday by Sunday and to spend much of his time alongside busy people much engaged in the day-to-day life of one of the world's great cities. He would like to say that he has found no theologian to be of more practical help than Karl Barth, in leading him and others to the knowledge and service of God revealed in Christ.

Bibliography

Karl Barth, *Church Dogmatics: A Selection,* N.Y., Harper, 1962. (Harper Torchbooks).

Georges Casalis, *Portrait of Karl Barth,* N.Y., Doubleday, 1963.

EMIL BRUNNER

J. Robert Nelson

It is remarkable that the two men who have exercised the greatest influence upon Protestant theology in this century have come from the small land of Switzerland. Emil Brunner of Zurich and Karl Barth of Basel have been the undisputed champions of the theological revival variously known as "dialectical theology," the "theology of crisis," or more generally "neo-orthodoxy." Neither of the two Swiss professors gave these names to his pattern of thought. The content, not the name, is important. Their basic purpose, said Brunner in 1931, was simply "to declare the *Word* of the Bible to the *World*."[1] But herein lay a difference between the two men. Barth addressed himself primarily to the community of faith, Brunner to the dubious or the uninformed both within and outside it.

Despite the fact that their names are often spoken in the same breath, Brunner and Barth in more than forty years of writing and teaching have never been colleagues and, though residents of the same part of Switzerland, have encountered each other on very few occasions. But they are linked together because at about the same time both came to the same conclusion about prevailing Protestant theology, and they prescribed roughly the same kind of antidote for its illness. "The Protestant theology of our day," announced Brunner, "is in a state of rapid dissolution. . . . The substance of Christian theology, the content of Christian faith, is in a stage of complete decomposition. Christianity is either faith in the revelation of God in Jesus Christ, or it is nothing."[2] He was launching a vigorous attack upon the whole body of theological liberalism which derived from Friedrich Schleiermacher, Albrecht Ritschl, and Adolf von Harnack, and which until World War II remained

[1] *The Word and the World* (London, SCM Press, 1931), p. 6.
[2] *The Theology of Crisis* (N.Y., Scribner's, 1930), p. 2.

410

regnant in Great Britain and America. Its most grievous faults were a humanistic picture of Jesus Christ, an optimistic view of man's essential goodness, and a progressive idea of history as inevitably leading to the Kingdom of God.

Brunner has not regarded himself as either a traditionalist or an innovator. He has tried only to be true to the historic faith of the Church as grounded in the Bible, and to make this intelligible and compelling for people of his own time. His so-called neo-orthodoxy did not involve a return to the rigid dogmatic confessions of the Lutheran and Calvinistic orthodoxy of the seventeenth century. Instead he was disposed from the outset to study the Bible with a mind trained in historical criticism (he detested biblicism!) and there to find, and therefrom to expound, the self-revelation and saving work of God in Jesus Christ. The Gospel he found there was not one of general religious and ethical values, as the liberals taught, nor of propositional dogmas, as the Roman Catholics and certain Protestants believed it to be. The foundation of biblical faith is the coming of the infinite God to finite man in the person of Jesus Christ. This is itself a paradox which the human mind can never resolve because of the mind's inherent limitation. The Word of God is like a rod thrust in the water: its shape is broken in contact with the world. Nevertheless, this event is critical for every person; it is literally a "crisis" which demands decision on the part of each man to say Yes or No to God in either faith or revolt.

How did Brunner come to this interpretation of Christian faith, so different from what prevailed in contemporary sermons and theological books? He has himself often indicated those to whom he was most indebted. The first was the south German pastor Christoph Blumhardt (1842–1919), a man of deep spirituality, intense mind, and ethical passion. Still greater was the influence of Hermann Kutter (1863–1931), a disciple of Blumhardt, who perceived how Christian thought was straying and boldly declared to his generation how it should be recalled. Through another dynamic Swiss theologian, Leonhard Ragaz (1868–1945), who was his teacher at Zurich, the young Brunner learned to know the works of Søren Kierkegaard. In many places in his writings Brunner pays special tribute to the brilliant Dane as the most important Christian thinker since Luther. It is significant that none of these mentors of the young Brunner was a powerful exponent of Switzerland's Reformed tradition, either Zwinglian or Calvinistic. But they taught with great force the reality and present relevance of the coming of God in Jesus Christ, with implications for radical change in both individual and society.

From the time of his birth, in 1889, through his university years, Brunner remained in his native land and was nurtured in its rich though limited culture. In 1911 he spent a semester at Berlin, but was not impressed by either Harnack or the great city. He felt greater affinity for Anglo-Saxon culture after his visit to England in 1913–14. Here he began to learn English, which he soon spoke flawlessly. The outbreak of the war necessitated his return to his homeland, where he spent two years in military service, guarding its neutral borders. In 1916 he was appointed pastor of the church at Obstalden, a mountain village in Kanton Glarus. The following year he married Margret Lauterberg, a niece of Hermann Kutter. For more than forty years she has given him much assistance in his literary output. And she raised a family of four sons, for whom Brunner has had the deepest fatherly affection. Much to their parents' grief, two sons died in their maturity, one from an illness and one in an accident. Another is a pastor, and the fourth a businessman.

Through the ecumenical leader Adolf Keller, arrangements were made for Brunner to study in the United States during 1919–20 at Union Theological Seminary. His relationship to America, as to England, grew stronger during the ensuing years. In the twenties he lectured extensively in both lands. He was visiting professor at Princeton 1938–39. And still later he gave major lectureships in these countries, where most of his many books were known through English translation.

The University of Zurich recognized the talent of the scholarly pastor-theologian by calling him to be professor of systematic and practical theology in 1924. While his fame grew as a theologian, few of his readers and admirers outside Zurich realized that Brunner also taught homiletics and pastoral care. He never allowed academic theology to stifle his pastoral calling, and for many years he was a preacher to overflow congregations in the old Fraumünster church.

During the thirties he was drawn into a number of international spheres of activity. Both the Faith and Order and the Life and Work streams of the growing ecumenical movement claimed his participation. The Group Movement, under Frank Buchman's leadership, attracted his interest; it seemed to offer the new life he longed for in the rather moribund Swiss churches. But when the Group Movement was changed into Moral Re-Armament, with the tacit loss of its christological center, it also lost the services of this eminent Christian.

It is notable that Brunner's experience and influence in Germany were never extensive. Hitler is to blame. For even though he has been a most prolific writer in German, Brunner's books were banned by the Nazis and he was not permitted to lecture in the land. The fact that Karl Barth was teaching at Bonn and was expelled by the Nazis after inspiring the rebellious Confessing Church has given this other great Swiss a much stronger role in German theology than Brunner's.

As he approached the age of retirement, a new and exciting chapter of his life opened unexpectedly. On the invitation of John R. Mott, Brunner agreed to be theological advisor to the worldwide Y.M.C.A. In 1949 he traveled through Asia, lecturing, teaching, and learning. His vision of the Church's mission was thereby enlarged. And in 1953 he returned to Japan for a two-year sojourn as professor at International Christian University in Tokyo. Here he found particular satisfaction in discussions with Christian laymen of various occupations, as well as with Buddhists and Shintoists. The coming of so prominent a European theologian had strong effect upon Japanese Christianity; in turn, the experience left an indelible impress on his mind.

It was on the homeward journey from Japan in 1955 that Brunner suffered a stroke, which ever since has hindered his work. In his *Dogmatik* Vol. III (1960) he apologizes to the reader for not having provided all the usual scholarly footnotes and expresses gratification that his health permitted him to finish the book and thus complete the series, which crowns his illustrious career as a theologian.

BRUNNER'S THEOLOGY BRIEFLY SKETCHED

The Doctrine of Jesus Christ

In his criticism of prevailing Protestant thought during the first quarter of this century, the young Brunner discerned its most vulnerable point to be that of Christology. In place of the Lord of the New Testament faith and the Christ whom Christians for centuries had believed and adored as the Son of God made man, many theologians had been describing a Jesus of Nazareth who was no more than a religious genius. Sharp attacks upon this humanistic and essentially unitarian portrayal of Jesus are found in Brunner's books. And it is significant that his first major book on Christian doctrine was precisely on this central issue. In 1927 he published *Der Mittler (The Mediator),* which quickly won recognition in many lands, and which is still one of the best books on Christology. Thanks to the skilled work of translation by Olive Wyon, who thereafter made many of his books available in English, *The Mediator* soon held a commanding place in British and American theology. The importance of this book lies not in its new teaching, for the author expressly disavowed any such novelty. He wanted only to make a fresh restatement of the ancient and indispensable belief of the Church. But the timeliness of the book, as well as its lucidity of style and cogency of assertion, account for its wide effect on the thought of Christians.

Brunner's starting point is the problem of revelation. How does God, the omnipotent Creator and infinite Father, make Himself known? Not through the ideas of general religious principles, which arise in men's minds, nor through occult revelations. For Brunner the avenues to knowledge of God which are followed by both philosophers and mystics are blind alleys. Only upon His own initiative and through Himself does God reveal to man who He is and what His will is. So God chose one person at a particular time in man's history and amongst a particular people to be His self-revelation. The appearance of Jesus Christ was unique and unrepeatable. Comparisons between Jesus and other ancient religious prophets and teachers are interesting but pointless. He is not to be regarded as the first among equals, but as the one and only incarnation of the Word of God. In Jesus Christ "we are confronted with an absolutely incomparable new fact, or rather a new category which transcends history and is thus no longer history at all, the fulfillment of time in the midst of time."[3] Brunner does not simply retreat from the processes of reason by taking refuge in a dogmatic and defiant declaration of God's self-disclosure in Jesus Christ. He shows consistent respect for the uses of the intelligent mind in respect to man's knowledge. But he simply holds that the Christian faith cannot recognize reason alone as the ultimate arbiter of truth.

The Old Testament prophets, as well as other religious teachers, have been heeded as bearers or interpreters of the Word of God. But Jesus Christ was not a mere bearer of the Word: he *was* the Word. The revelation of God is Jesus Christ. Brunner emphasizes strongly the teaching of the Gospel according to John—that whoever has seen or known the Son has thereby known the Father. Such knowledge is mediated to us in the present time by the message of the apostles, the original eyewitnesses; and this message is found first in the New Testament. Therefore, while rejecting a literalistic reading of the Bible as a whole, Brunner stresses the primacy of the biblical witness to the Word of God, who is Jesus Christ.

During the first four centuries of the history of the Church, theologians struggled to find definitive words to speak of the relation between the Father, the Son and the Holy Spirit, and also to indicate how Jesus Christ was at once divine and human. Brunner sees the need for examining the same problems today. Espousing the classic position of Irenaeus and Athanasius, he considers and rejects several theories about the person of Jesus Christ which keep appearing in history. He gives no ground to the idea that Jesus Christ was a mere human being who was "adopted" by God to be the Son, or conversely that he was a nonhuman, phantasmal appearance of the divine, or that he was an angelic being neither really divine nor really human. None of these speculations, either in ancient form or in contemporary dress, can account for the identity of the one whom Christians call Lord and Savior.

[3] *The Mediator* (Philadelphia, Westminster, 1947), p. 86.

Asserting the divinity of Jesus Christ does not, in Brunner's judgment, imply acceptance as literal fact of the traditional idea of the virgin birth of Jesus. Some find it difficult to reconcile Brunner's "high Christology" with his skepticism about the manner of Jesus' birth. But his intellectual sincerity is evident here. He finds the biblical evidence, apart from the romantic stories in the Gospels according to Matthew and Luke, to be too scanty to warrant acceptance. Moreover, he reasons, the great miracle of the incarnation is not enforced but rather minimized by the idea of a supernatural birth without human father. Human paternity and normal birth make the coming of the Word of God into history an even greater wonder, and more important, they leave no room for doubt about the authentic humanity of Jesus Christ.

Defense of Jesus' true humanity is of much import for Christian theology. It keeps the faith from floating above the material realities of history upon a cloud of religious speculation. Some critics of *The Mediator* have charged Brunner with denying to Jesus an authentic humanity, a real personality, in his zeal to teach the divinity of Jesus Christ. But Brunner has disavowed this criticism.[4] He is content to accept the definition of the Council of Chalcedon (451) that Jesus Christ is at once true God and true man. But even this formula has its dangers, he says, if it is unduly intellectualized. The truth about the Lord is discovered not through theorizing on His nature but through personal encounter with Him.

This personal encounter, which for Brunner is a primary category of faith and theology, is possible today because of the resurrection of Jesus Christ. He does not shrink from asserting the reality and indispensability of the resurrection. This is something different from the virgin birth. It is the *risen* Lord whom the apostles witnessed, and to whom they bore witness. It was the assurance of their continued communion with him that gave the apostles something to proclaim to the world. Here is the basis for Christian faith and preaching, and hence for the Church. It is as inexplicable in historical terms as the incarnation itself, but none the less real. Without the resurrection, all

---

[4] *The Christian Doctrine of Creation and Redemption (Dogmatics* II) (Philadelphia, Westminster, 1952), p. 360.

discussion of the mystery of the person and saving work of Jesus Christ—indeed, all claims of the Christian faith—would be without meaning. But they have meaning, because he is risen.

God Known in Personal Encounter

Christians are always prone to falsify the knowledge of God by holding one or the other of two extreme positions. One is a false objectivism. This is exemplified by unquestioning biblical literalism, by the dogmatism inherent in the teaching office of the Roman Catholic Church, and by the confessional orthodoxy of certain Protestant traditions. This objectivism is like a frozen waterfall, giving the appearance of life and movement but actually immobile and lifeless. The other extreme is subjectivism. It is seen in those movements of Christian enthusiasts and mystics, as well as in romantic liberalism, which seek knowledge in experience and feeling. As Brunner declared in a famous series of lectures delivered in Sweden in 1937, both extremes, widespread as they are, are a threat to the integrity of the Christian faith.

As his chosen title asserts, the truth of God is known only in personal encounter—*Wahrheit als Begegnung*, or in English, *The Divine-Human Encounter*. The biblical witness to God shows Him always to be God-approaching-man; man is always man-coming-from-God; and their meeting point is Jesus Christ.[5] Man by his striving and seeking cannot know God. Only God can take the initiative to make Himself and His will known to man. What is known as divine revelation is a two-sided relation in which "God is completely and wholly the Giver, the first, and man is completely and wholly the receiver, the second."[6] But God does not overwhelm His creature; He treats man as the free and responsible being whom He loves, and whose choice is to accept God's grace in faith or to reject it in sin. This is the choice which confronts man when he hears or reads the gospel of Jesus Christ.

If the knowledge of God's truth and saving love comes

[5] *The Divine-Human Encounter* (Philadelphia, Westminster, 1943), p. 46. (New translation, 1963.)
[6] *Ibid.*, p. 69.

through real personal encounter, where does that encounter take place in human experience? Brunner is disposed to recognize several areas of history and experience wherein revelatory encounter occurs. He does not mean to weaken the faith that God reveals Himself as Lord and Savior uniquely and decisively in Jesus Christ. But he willingly admits the reality of God's revelation in the created world in which man lives. He sees the biblical revelation as twofold: the promise given in the Old Covenant between Yahweh and Israel, and the fulfillment of the promise in Jesus Christ. Because Jesus Christ is both true God and true man and is genuinely personal, the revelation in him is final and complete. But the revelatory action does not end with the termination of Jesus' earthly life. It continues in the witness of the Holy Scriptures, in the faith of the Church, and in the personal testimony of the Holy Spirit in the hearts of men. Finally the hope of man lies in the expectation that God will make Himself known in communion with man at "the end," when the consummation of the reign of God shall take place. Since revelation is thus a series of divine actions, God gives meaning to human history. His revelation is neither timeless nor confined to a certain point of time. He keeps encountering man.[7]

These views of Brunner's on revelation brought him into a famous disputation with Karl Barth in 1934—the theological *cause célèbre* of the decade. Unfortunately in the heat of dispute the two Swiss giants not only broke apart their former theological alliance but also allowed their sharp differences to be felt personally. In subsequent books Brunner has made frequent reference to this debate; and more than twenty-five years later referred to Barth's rebuttal entitled *Nein!* as that "terrible book."[8]

Despite mutual misunderstandings in their essays, the main issues between Brunner and Barth emerge as follows: Does God reveal Himself solely and exclusively in Jesus Christ as known in the Scriptures, or does He also use creation and on-going his-

[7] From the long treatise *Revelation and Reason* (Philadelphia, Westminster, 1946), Part I.

[8] *Natural Theology,* comprising "Nature and Grace" by Emil Brunner and the reply *"No!"* by Karl Barth (London, Geoffrey Bles, 1946).

tory as media of revelation? Has the image of God in man been so utterly defaced that man no longer has any capacity to receive God's revelation? Is there to be found in man no "point of contact" for the saving action and revelation of God? Is it legitimate at all for Christian theologians to speak of "natural theology" and "natural law" without capitulating to Roman Catholic doctrine?

Barth accused Brunner of deserting faith in the singularity of Jesus Christ as the revelation of God's saving truth, and thus of reopening the way for the 19th-century Protestant liberalism against which they had both contended. Brunner accused Barth of a christological one-sidedness which made him virtually reject the goodness of creation and the humanity of man. And years later Brunner often maintained that Barth in his huge book on the doctrine of creation had tacitly changed his mind and agreed with him. Undecisive as the argument proved to be, it stimulated extensive discussion of these questions, so vital to theology, and prompted numerous Christian thinkers to reappraise their views of the nature of man and the revelation of God.

The Doctrine of Man: the Creature in Contradiction

In an interview for British television in 1961, Brunner said that he considered his chief contribution to theology the 1937 book *Der Mensch im Widerspruch (Man in Revolt)*. A brilliant statement of the Christian understanding of what it means to be human, its importance is enhanced by the fact that it was published at a time when the Western world was awakening to the terrors of dehumanizing totalitarianism. The deadly trends of fascism and communism in Europe were being abetted by certain schools of psychology, biology, and philosophy which in effect stripped man of his God-given humanity.

In this work Brunner acknowledged his debt to two thinkers only a bit older than himself: Ferdinand Ebner and Martin Buber. They refined and developed the theme of the I-Thou relationship which has been highly influential in much modern theology. In this deep insight into personal communion between individuals and between a man and God, as opposed to the growing impersonalism and collectivism of modern life, Brunner saw the clue to interpreting in the present time the Christian idea of man's nature. Man is made for community with his Creator and his fellows, but this community derives first from his relation to the Creator as *Thou*.

This relationship is determined by man's inherent responsibility to God. Such responsibility is the common property of every man. The believer in God is conscious of it, the unbeliever does not acknowledge it. Yet neither can escape it. Nor does the plenteous grace of God annul it. The human *I* responds to the divine *Thou*; and the nature of that response determines the quality of his life. For Brunner, a Christian, in contrast to Buber, a Jew, this claim of responsibility to the personal, divine Thou is discerned in Jesus Christ, the Word of God. Brunner claims to have been the first Protestant theologian to make use of this I-Thou scheme, having referred to it in an essay in 1912.

There would be no basis for responsibility if man were not created in the image of God. The idea of the divine image in man is fundamental not only for the Christian understanding of man but for the history of Western civilization itself. Confused thinking on the matter has led to three confusing and pernicious lines of thought: (1) a distinction between the *image* of God, as rationality and freedom, which has been retained in man, and the *similitude* of God, as a divine element in human nature, which has been lost; (2) the concept that in the fall of man only a *relic* or vestige of the image remained; and (3) the secularized notion, since the Enlightenment of the 18th century, that the image is a fiction. Against these widespread ideas, Brunner has contended that the *imago Dei* is simply man's personal relation of total responsibility to the holy, loving God. It is this which makes man human.

But man is in contradiction, in revolt against God. This is his predicament. He is irresponsible, and so allows himself to be robbed of true life. It is not enough to say that there is within man something contradictory; rather, the whole man, because of his revolt against God, is against himself. "Sin is defiance, arrogance, the desire to be equal with God, emancipation, a deliberate severance from the hand of God."[9] There is

---

[9] *Man in Revolt* (Philadelphia, Westminster, 1947), p. 129.

no need to take the story of Adam's fall literally nor to posit the existence of a golden age to which man longs to return. The fact that man has contradicted both God and his own nature is self-evident in history, in psychology, and in ethics. Thus every man is Adam. And, to use Pascal's words, each man is aware of his misery only because he knows something of his defaced grandeur.

Of course the whole struggle of man's life is to overcome this contradiction of his nature. And the significance of Jesus Christ is precisely his effective—not merely exemplary—work in enabling persons to find restitution in terms of personal communion with God, moral responsibility to Him, and community with one another.

The Ethics of God's Command and the Earthly Orders

Evident throughout the writings of Brunner is a sustained and intensifying ethical concern which at times is expressed with genuine passion. He has never been an ivory-tower theologian. In accord with the essential genius of the Christian faith, he ponders doctrinal questions in relation to their ethical consequences.

His first effort to set forth a system of ethics for Protestant thought was in *Das Gebot und die Ordnungen* (1932); it appeared in English two years later with the title *The Divine Imperative*. Though Brunner agreed to that title, he later expressed regret that it misses the import of his original subject, "The Command and the Orders," for the book is built on these two concepts.

As a Christian he sees the starting point of ethical judgment and behavior in the relation to God through faith in Jesus Christ. Philosophers brood over the problems of human relations and endeavor to generalize concerning the nature of the Good. But if they follow the Hebraic prophetic tradition and its culmination in Jesus Christ, they will recognize that the Good is not to be defined in abstract theories but rather in terms of the known activity of God. The highest manifestation of God's activity is in the self-giving and crucifixion of Jesus Christ. "Here alone is the meaning of the word 'love' disclosed."[10] In the cross-event is seen the distinct difference between love as self-seeking (eros) and love as self-giving (agape).

Brunner defines Christian ethics as "the science of human conduct as it is determined by Divine conduct."[11] Now the essential character of God's conduct is self-giving love. This is not only taught by but also supremely exemplified in Jesus Christ. The same quality of love is God's primary *command* to mankind. To live in faith, to be fully responsible to God and thus to be completely human means to live in love. It is equally perilous to think of love legalistically as a principle of conduct and to consider it sentimentally as a mere emotion. Brunner shuns both distortions. Love is of the nature of God, and so it is His command to human beings created in His image. From this command are derived the various commandments, which include the tempering influences of righteousness, equity, and mercy. Man's obedience to the command and the commandments should be with singleness of heart, but the manner of obeying is always determined by the particular circumstances which call for decision and action. The countless variations of circumstance require the formulation of ethical laws; but these are derived from and are in consonance with the primary command of love. Moreover, the Christian ethical imperative, in contrast to other types, involves the dimension of time. There is much urgency for every person that he obey God's command *now,* with no excuse for delay. The leisurely approach of the "good pagan" to better patterns of living is not tolerated by the insistent command of God addressed to all men, and heard and heeded by those who have faith in Him.

Even such ethical considerations as these must be seen in relation to the several spheres of man's individual and communal life in which decisions are made and actions taken. Here Brunner adopts the idea of the "orders of creation." These are the five dimensions of human community which are written into the historical existence of mankind. Three of them are clearly outlined in the given nature of life: the male-female community, or family; the community of work, or economics; and the com-

[10] *The Divine Imperative* (Philadelphia, Westminster, 1947), p. 55.
[11] *Ibid.,* p. 86.

munity of law and nation, or the state. The fourth order, still essential, derives from man's intellectual impulses, the community of culture. And the fifth, springing from and embracing the impulses of faith, is the religious community, or Church. Lack of space forbids even an outline of his views on the meaning of each of the five orders; a few words must suffice.

Despite the vigorous tone of his writing, Brunner reveals himself as neither a traditionalist nor a social revolutionary. He is prepared to say that economic capitalism and communism are twin brothers: the extremes of individualism and collectivism meet each other, since both destroy human values. The divine command of love can be better obeyed today in a moderately controlled economy.

The state is ordained by God both to restrain evil and to conserve justice. But it is also susceptible to grossest corruptions, as witnessed in contemporary totalitarianism. Certainly Brunner's own considered loyalty to Swiss democracy has been an ingredient in his view of the state. And throughout the era of German Nazism and Russian communism he has been increasingly polemical in his criticism. He sees in the phenomenon of the *Totalstaat* the very opposite of love and the end of freedom.

Since 1932 Brunner has not felt constrained to write more on ethical problems of marriage and family. But those who know him personally have seen him as a nearly ideal instance of the Christian husband and parent. His example is more significant than his articulated thought on the subject. Also a man of rich cultural appreciation—a devotee of Bach and Rembrandt—with considerable knowledge of the physical sciences, he shared his thoughts on the community of culture in his Gifford Lectures, published as *Christianity and Civilisation* (1948).

The community of faith, the Church—the nature of which he holds to be the "presupposition for Christian Ethics as a whole" —merits more extensive treatment.

The Church—Not Institution but Fellowship

The participation of Brunner in the life of the Church in Zurich as well as in the world at large has been notable. Nevertheless he has been consistently critical of prevailing understandings of the nature of the Church and of practices which he regards as injurious to its proper life. As early as 1932 in *The Divine Imperative* he was developing thoughts on the Church which came to fruition in the fifties with the publication of *The Misunderstanding of the Church* and Volume III of his *Dogmatics*. His oft-repeated thesis is this: the Church as ecclesiastical institution has nothing to do with the Church (Greek: *ekklēsia*) of the New Testament. They are two different and contrary entities.

Brunner sees the New Testament *ekklēsia* as a free fellowship of faithful Christians, united in common life and worship by their faith in Jesus Christ and led in their service and witness by the Holy Spirit. This simple fellowship was truly of both divine and human nature and could rightly be called the Body of Christ, though it was virtually without institutional structure or official ministry. But the process of institutionalization began even in New Testament times. It is seen in the Pastoral Epistles, where frequent reference is made to regular ministry and sound doctrine. Thereafter came the Catholicizing process, the development of new doctrines about the sacraments, and, worst of all, the patronizing adoption of the Church by the Empire under Constantine and Theodosius. The Reformation promised to restore the Church to its character as *ekklēsia*; but the great Reformers acquiesced to a partly Roman Catholic notion of the Church. So Protestant churches, especially those in Europe enjoying particular favor of the state, are criticized by Brunner no less harshly than the Catholic.

To a large extent Brunner has followed, though not uncritically, the thinking of an earlier German scholar, Rudolf Sohm. He regards as wholly inadequate the common conception of the Church as the congregation where the Gospel is preached and the sacraments administered. He is especially distressed by the undisciplined practice of infant baptism. He can see no justification for the prevailing separation between clergy and laity. Even though he has given much time to the ecumenical movement, he sees neither need nor hope for the visible unity of institutional churches. What is deplorable is the lack of spiritual brotherhood in the churches, not their divisions as institutions.

In his own experience Brunner has found the true character

of the *ekklēsia* more often in voluntary associations of Christians than in the churches as such. Thus he gave much attention to the Group Movement until 1938, when it changed into Moral Re-Armament and lost its distinctly Christian character. He has been an ardent supporter of the Y.M.C.A., as well as the movement for laymen's institutes. And most significantly, when he reached Japan he found an indigenous expression of Christianity, the *Mukyokai*, or Non-Church Movement, which embodied his own theories about the New Testament *ekklēsia*. In later years he has done much writing to make the *Mukyokai* known in the West.

One of his reasons for criticizing the institutional churches is their lack of missionary zeal. He believes that the mission of the gospel would be better served if the true *ekklēsia* were more evident. Time and again he has asserted that his theological work is entirely in the service of mission. For years he has stressed the need for what he calls "eristics": a combination of both the apologetic commending of the faith and the polemical defense of it. He has demonstrated "eristics" in his treatment of non-Christian religions and the secular rivals of Christian faith.

BRUNNER'S INFLUENCE ON CHRISTIAN THOUGHT

The widespread effect of Brunner's many books has been evident for years. Several generations of theological students have used them assiduously. Their titles have become meaningful labels for types of theological concern. His published sermons and semipopular books and lectures have helped many people understand the complex questions aroused by Christian faith. Nevertheless he has not been the head of a particular "school" of theology. The adjective "Brunnerian" is seldom seen or heard. This is in accord with his wishes. He has been content to be the protagonist of living, biblical faith and the relentless antagonist of all that is inimical to it.

For exposing the weaknesses of Protestant liberalism and setting theology on a new course in this century Brunner has received much credit. Yet his own mind is literally a liberal one, free and open. And strangely enough, recent critics have described him as only a somewhat reformed liberal in theology.

This is a matter of definition of terms and of critical judgment. Most people still think of him, however, as one of the so-called neo-orthodox theologians.

His great books of Christian doctrine have manifested an unusual staying power. And there are scarcely any important doctrinal issues which he has neglected: God and creation, Christology, anthropology (i.e., man's nature), ethics, the Church, and the end of history and the future life. In the three volumes of his *Dogmatics* he has restated and summed up his thoughts on all these questions.

Brunner's career has been oriented toward both scholarship and teaching on the one hand and interpreting the Christian faith to the modern mind (both Western and Oriental) on the other. A favorite project has been the laymen's academy at Boldern, near Zurich, where he and his friends have tried to make the faith known to persons of many vocations.

Finally, he has over the years been the lucid, cogent, friendly teacher of a great many students from many countries. They remember his opening a 7 A.M. class with a rousing hymn, his orderly lectures delivered at times with passion, his wise counsel in courses on pastoral care, the hospitality of his home and the countless evenings of discussion there. These personal influences—consistent with his fondness for the I-Thou relation and for personal encounter—are as important and lasting as his books.

Bibliography

Emil Brunner, *The Divine Imperative*, Philadelphia, Westminster, 1947.

The *Theology of Emil Brunner*, Charles W. Kegley, ed., N.Y., Macmillan, 1962.

FRIEDRICH GOGARTEN

Theodore Runyon, Jr.

History is one of those all-important—if somewhat mystifying—words in current theological discussion. And no contemporary theologian has devoted himself more persistently to clarifying what we mean when we say "Christian faith is historical" than has Friedrich Gogarten. Gogarten's concern has been twofold: to rethink the traditional doctrines of the church in historical rather than metaphysical categories, and to show the relevance of Christian faith—understood as a kind of history—to a mankind which has become conscious of the overwhelming responsibility it carries for present history.

Born in 1887 in the Ruhr industrial city of Dortmund, Gogarten received his university training in Berlin, Jena, and Heidelberg. After serving as an assistant pastor in Bremen, he took a small country parish in Thuringia, bought himself a complete edition of Luther's works, and began to steep himself in the thought of the Reformer. Up to this point Gogarten had been a rather conventional "liberal" in the tradition of German idealism. His first book was on the religious thought of Fichte. But his absorption in Luther resulted in an abrupt break with the past, a break which first found expression in his sermons. The peasants who dutifully listened to those sermons might not have been aware of an emerging theological position, but students from the university at nearby Jena soon began making pilgrimages to the village church to hear the young pastor and spend the day discussing theology.

"The Crisis of Culture,"[1] an address delivered in 1920, first brought Gogarten to public attention. Spengler's *Decline of the West* was a best seller, and no one in postwar Germany needed to be reminded that civilization was in crisis. Gogarten's task

[1] Reprinted as "Die Krisis unserer Kultur," in *Anfänge der dialektischen Theologie*, Vol. II, Jürgen Moltmann, editor (Munich, 1963), pp. 101–121.

was rather to clarify the relation of religion to the crisis. And here he differed sharply with many of his fellow theologians. The question they faced was this: Can Christianity as a Western religion survive the downfall of Western civilization? Many concluded that while Christianity as a historically conditioned form of religion may not survive, that matters little if the essential religious truths expressed in Christianity are preserved. And this is assured, they reasoned, for Christianity like all religions is an expression of the deep, inner religious consciousness of man. And this consciousness will persist even if Christianity passes away with Western civilization.

Gogarten's response is not so much a defense of Christianity's present forms as an attack on a liberalism which sees the crisis as limited to these forms. Liberalism is not radical enough. It continues to think of the religious consciousness of man as a kind of storm cellar from which he can emerge after the crisis has blown over. But this is hardly the Biblical understanding, which never conceives of crises as simply external, nor as excluding any part of man—least of all his religious consciousness. The real crisis, asserts Gogarten, is not defined by the instability of Western civilization but by that which shakes all foundations: the judgment of God. And the religious consciousness is no place to hide from this judgment, for it begins precisely with man and his religion—with the man who has named the depths of his own spirit "God," and thus completed the circle of reality within himself. For this man, his culture, *and* his religion there is no road to renewal which bypasses death. There are no "good" elements which might be salvaged. For this culture's highest good—the human spirit—is just that which has usurped the place of God. Therefore the death sentence must be pronounced; the *No* must be said. And at the present moment it may have to be said so loudly there seems little room left for a *Yes*. But the *No* of God's judgment is not the *No* of cynicism; it is not ultimately negative. "The death sentence is the entrance into life."[2] It is said in order that the *Yes* might be said, the *Yes* of God's new creation.

This new creation does not signal the end of crisis, however.

²*Ibid.,* p. 111.

If the life of faith means continually receiving oneself from the hand of the Creator, it is a life lived always at the end of human possibilities, never self-sufficient, always dependent for continued existence on help from beyond. Thus the fundamental crisis is permanent, written into the very nature of faith itself.

This awareness of the radical character of the crisis, along with the dialectic of judgment and grace under a sovereign God, made it natural for the young German pastor to join forces with a young Swiss pastor, Karl Barth, who was also disengaging himself from earlier theological idealism and striking out on a new course. In 1922, together with Eduard Thurneysen and Georg Merz (later joined by Rudolf Bultmann and Emil Brunner), they founded a journal which was to provide a forum for this new direction in theology known in Europe as "crisis theology" or "dialectical theology" and in America as "neo-orthodoxy." The journal took its name from the title of one of Gogarten's articles, "Zwischen den Zeiten" (Between the Times).

FAITH AND HISTORICAL RELATIVITY

The book which was to secure Gogarten a permanent place in the theological world, *I Believe in the Triune God,* was published in 1926. Subtitled "An Examination of the Relation between Faith and History," it is a vigorous attack on the historicism tempered with idealism of Troeltsch, Harnack, and Seeberg. Their historical research had forced them to face the *relativity* of Christian ethical and doctrinal positions traditionally considered absolute. They finally had to ask, Is there anything in Christianity which is absolute? Troeltsch's answer is characteristic of the general view: Christianity is "the historical concretion of a universal truth."[3] The historical form, marked as it is by the peculiarities of a particular time and place, is not absolute. It is only the shell within which dwells an essential idea that is timeless. The absoluteness of Christianity is to be found in the universal value of its history-transcending essence.

But this solution does not satisfy Gogarten. Can an approach which grants validity to historical events only as they can be

[3] *Ich glaube an den dreieinigen Gott* (Jena, Diederichs, 1926), p. 96.

reduced to a universal essence unconditioned by time and place do justice to Christian faith? If Christian faith is the product of God's creative activity, and if this activity not only takes place in history but *makes* history, then the "essence" of faith most certainly cannot be nonhistorical. Quite the opposite. *Faith is history.*[4]

This claim is basic to Gogarten's whole approach. But it needs explanation, for certainly he does not mean by *faith* much of what passes under that name. Indeed, he protests those views which have gradually diluted the distinctively Hebrew-Christian understanding of the relation between man and God, substituting for it aesthetic experience, participation in a world spirit, or religious intuition. Nor is Gogarten any more friendly toward a sterile dogmatism which mistakes assent to theological propositions, however important, for faith. All these views are deficient because they fail to see that faith cannot be defined exclusively in terms of man's feelings, intuition, convictions, or ability to assent. Faith is faith only as God himself is actively involved, only as it is happening between God and man. "The final, most profound, yet simplest fact is that you cannot have God without God."[5] Faith in God must be called forth by God himself, the God who communicates to man his trustworthiness and elicits faith and obedience. Faith is therefore an event, a relationship in which the Creator is active with the creature.

It follows that "faith is history" does not mean that faith is simply *past* history. For just as "faith" must be carefully defined, so "history" cannot be understood in the ordinary schoolroom sense. It designates instead the process of interaction in which being and meaning are created ever anew. Therefore faith is present history, history now taking place. And if it is not present history it is nothing.

Gogarten recognized in the I-Thou approach being developed by Grisebach, Buber, Ebner, and Heim an interpretation of history akin to his own. And Bultmann's *Jesus and the Word,* the first edition of which appeared in 1926, applies a similar methodology to New Testament studies. The reality of history is neither the reality of ideas in the mind of the interpreter, who

[4] *Ibid.,* pp. 17 f.
[5] *Anfänge der dialektischen Theologie,* Vol. II, p. 119.

by virtue of these ideas makes the facts fit together in a meaningful pattern (subjectivism and idealism), nor the reality of the "facts" in themselves in their detached isolated state (objectivism and positivism). The truth cannot be known by coming down on one side or the other of a fence between subject and object. It is found instead in the interaction between subject and object—or better, in the case of God and man, between Subject and subject. Reality is an event which happens in the "between," in history.

Thus the problem of relativity as it concerns Christian faith is solved not by escaping from history into a realm of absolute ideals and universals but by living in history the *responsible* life of faith. And faith is itself a kind of relativity, man's relativity to God in every new moment.

In his next major work, *Political Ethics,* Gogarten examines the implications of this view of history for the relationships between men. Here again relativity is the problem. Historical research had mercilessly exposed the relativity of supposedly absolute ethical norms and standards. Seeking to rebuild on the wreckage, Christian ethical theorists were tempted to search for universal principles within Christianity which would be valid beyond the relativities of Christianity as a historical religion, on the assumption that if such universals could be found a system of Christian ethics could be formulated which would have all-embracing validity and lasting authority. From Gogarten's standpoint, however, historical contingency—while undermining an absolutist ethic—is not inimical to ethics as such. Indeed, the fact that history is composed of contingent relationships is what makes it unavoidably ethical. One has his being in creative encounter—being is always being-from-the-other (*Von-dem-Andern-sein*)—and his continuing existence in being-with-another (*Mit-dem-Andern-sein*). These are not secondary modes of existence preceded by a primary mode of being-in-and-for-oneself (*An-und-für-sich-sein*); rather, individuality is secondary and the interpersonal is primary.[6]

Accordingly, ethical decisions and actions are the result not of adhering to abstract, nonhistorical standards of what one does

[6] *Politische Ethik* (Jena, Diederichs, 1932), pp. 26 ff., 173. Thus "thou-I" would be a more appropriate characterization of Gogarten's approach.

or does not do, but of responding to each situation out of the being which one is in the relation to God and neighbor. The Christian life is a life of openness and obedience. The two go together. Obedience is understood not as strict compliance with laws and ideals but as that kind of openness which marks the genuine listener (*obedience* means literally "to hear toward") whose action is a creative response to what he hears. In ethics as elsewhere, therefore, the problem of relativity is overcome not by substituting nonhistorical absolutes for the relativities of history but by facing each situation as a call to responsible action in history out of the being one has in faith. Thus Gogarten provides us with one of the earliest formulations of a "contextual ethic," which has become a hallmark of most contemporary, theologically based ethical thought.

Not content to rest on the level of individual relations, Gogarten pursues the implications of his position for an ethic of the state. Contemporary Western theories of society and the state have their roots in the individualism of rationalism. They are I-oriented. The fundamental mode of existence is understood as "being-in-and-for-oneself." Society and the state are thus secondary, artificial realities created by man for the furtherance of his welfare, goals, and ideals. Over against this Gogarten sets an understanding of the state as a fabric of interresponsibility in which each has his being in his function of being-for-another.[7] The state is given power over the individual member to ensure that the needs of the body politic will be met by forced obedience, if necessary, where the individual is irresponsible regarding his duties. Such obedience is not true obedience in the intended sense, of course, but is necessary to maintain order in at least an external sense even if fallen man does not will it.

Discernible here is the influence of Luther's doctrine of civil authority, which grounds the magistrate's authority and power in the Fall. His Lutheran unwillingness to risk anarchy was to make Gogarten less prone to criticize the state in the first years

---

[7] Thus Gogarten's preference for the title "political ethics" rather than the usual "*social*" ethics." The *polis* is an organic whole, in which each member has his function and duty for the maintenance of the body politic, rather than merely an *association* of individuals. Cf. pp. 115 f., 147 ff.

of the National Socialist regime in Germany than were many of his friends in the circle of dialectical theology. During the same period there was a gradual parting of the ways theologically between Gogarten and Barth, the latter accusing Gogarten, Bultmann, and Brunner of leaving the common ground of the earlier dialectical theology and making theology too dependent upon philosophical presuppositions.[8] This led to the discontinuation of the journal *Zwischen den Zeiten,* as well as the partnership which had created it.

Though continuing to teach (at the University of Breslau, from 1931 to 1935, and at the University of Göttingen, from 1935 until his retirement in 1955), Gogarten published no further major work until after World War II.

FAITH AND SECULARISM

In most of his major postwar works Gogarten continues his interest in history, but whereas his concern earlier had been to overcome idealism and answer the problem of historical relativism, he now turns to what he considers *the* problem confronting a technological age: the relation of Christian faith to secularism. And he does this by developing the implications of a theology of history for the traditional theological questions of Christology and soteriology (in *The Proclamation of Jesus Christ*), law and gospel (in his magnum opus, *Man between God and the World*), faith and works (in *The Fate and Hope of the Modern Era*), and subjectivism versus objectivism (in *The Reality of Faith*).

While the popular attitude toward secularism regards it as the archenemy of the faith, Gogarten asks whether a certain kind of secularization is not implicit in the Christian gospel itself. For example, the secular view sees the world as depopulated of those spirits once thought to have the world's well-being under their control. The task of maintaining the order of the world passes out of the hands of the demons, angels, "principalities and powers" and into the hands of man, who takes over the responsibility of ordering and caring for the world in accordance with his own needs and desires. Such a secularization is, however,

[8] *Zwischen den Zeiten,* Vol. XI (1933), p. 311.

by no means foreign to the Christian faith, in which man is understood as receiving his being from the God whose creative Word calls man not just into existence but into an existence-in-responsibility. The world is directly involved in this responsibility, for the being into which man is called is, in Pauline terminology, the being of a *son* (Galatians 4). A son is distinguished from a child in that, whereas the child is completely dependent upon the parent for his continued existence, the son—who has come of age and received an inheritance which is his to manage—has the ability to stand on his own, to be independent (*selbstständig*), no longer bound to the father by the necessities of his physical survival. The inheritance bestowed upon man is the *world*; he is given dominion over it and charged with the responsibility to "till it and keep it." His position with regard to the world thus frees him for a mature and noncompulsive relationship with the Father, while his filial relation to the Father frees him for a mature and noncompulsive attitude toward the world.[9]

Now we are in a position to understand the context of Gogarten's recurrent insistence that the examination and ordering of the world be delivered to man's reason with no strings attached.[10] His regular conversations with his physicist colleague at Göttingen, C. F. von Weizsäcker, convinced him of the very real necessity of clarifying the relation of formal and technological reason to faith, especially as it bears on the responsibility of the scientist. Again he finds the answer in Luther's understanding of faith and works and the doctrine of the two realms. Faith has no business anxiously hovering over reason lest reason discover something about the world that would undermine faith. A faith which could be so undermined would actually be pre-Christian, i.e., it would in effect assume that the world has a power over one's salvation which the early Christian message specifically denied that the world possesses. In genuine faith man receives the world and his existence as steward of the world

---

[9] Note the similarity between Gogarten's development regarding the nature and place of the world in Christian faith and Dietrich Bonhoeffer's seminal idea of "the world come of age."

[10] E.g., *The Reality of Faith* (Philadelphia, Westminster, 1959), pp. 90 ff.

—but not information about the world. The latter is *his* responsibility and is to be gained through his efforts. Nor need he justify himself before God by piously limiting his reason in the pursuit of this task. He is justified by faith alone, i.e., by the sustaining relationship with the Father, which frees him to explore his world with true "objectivity," unhampered by the subjective necessity of justifying his existence by his works.

However, contends Gogarten, if faith is not present, if man does not continue to receive his existence from the Father, then the crucial balance—reason operating within faith—cannot be maintained. Freedom and openness are destroyed, anxiety sets in, and a now heteronomous "faith" seeks to extend its authority and control over an autonomous "reason," and vice versa, in the anxious effort to re-establish the wholeness and unity of life lost with the death of genuine faith. It matters little which side in this struggle is victorious, for neither is what it was and is meant to be within faith. Both have been fundamentally perverted. Man without faith remains a son, to be sure, but a son who has betrayed the Father. Man without faith retains his mastery over the world, but as a master who is in the ironic position of having to squeeze his meaning and being out of that over which he is lord. Thus the change is not so much the loss of what man previously was as the turning of what he was into its negating opposite.[11] Just as honor betrayed becomes *dis*honor —which is worse than the mere absence of honor—so sonship betrayed becomes worse than the mere absence of relationship; it becomes a corrupted relationship, one of alienation and estrangement.

When this shift comes about and man looks to the world for his being and meaning, the world begins to take on a religious nature. That which was secular now becomes the source of life in a religious sense remarkably parallel to the ancient world, though without benefit of the ancient mythological picture. The reality is the same, however. Man is subject to the powers of the world; they control his meaning or lack of it. Nor are "materialists" the only ones who fall under this subjugation. Indeed, the two classic examples of bondage to the world are religious:

[11] Cf. Romans 1:22-25.

the Greeks' bondage to the cosmos and the Jews' bondage to the law. In both instances one's being was assured only if he adhered rigidly to what was understood as a religious order of things. Absolute conformity brought salvation. Is the picture so different today? Meaning, place, and position are guaranteed if one will conform to a group, class, or national self-image which grants the participant being—but only as long as he continues to conform. Nonconformity results in rejection and threatened loss of being. World views are propounded which promise to reduce the world to a meaningful and manageable whole—but only if one adheres to the assumptions and laws by which their originators seek to introduce order into experience. Stray from the path and chaos reigns again. In this misuse of reason, meaning can be had only at the price of conformity to the law of the world of man's mind. Gogarten's early rejection of idealism was based on the conviction that it was really a form of worldliness; it imposed a subjective scheme of things upon reality and insisted that reality conform to that scheme. A full-scale example of the same phenomenon was National Socialism. Operating on the basis of a quasi-mythological world view, National Socialism methodically destroyed all opposition to its ordering of the world in conformity with its own self-image. All such religio-secularistic attempts are inherently totalitarian. Any opposition calls forth a neurotic response simply because as long as opposition persists the system is in principle undermined, for it has failed to accomplish what it promises: to reduce all of reality to conformity with itself.

Thus the problem of secularism is not its irreligion but its continual tendency to become religious. *It is not secular enough.* Secularism in its various modern forms does not preserve the truly secular nature of the world but tends to give to the world—whether this be the material world, the world of religion, or the world of its own mind—the honor due God alone. Christian faith proposes to keep the world truly secular and thus safeguard man's freedom toward the world through a certain kind of existence, existence as a mature and responsible son under the Creator-Father. Where this existence-in-faith is not present, however, the freedom for which man was created cannot be present. He still remains man, to be sure, and as man he is that being who has his being *in relation,* that creature who must be fulfilled from beyond himself. But this is precisely his difficulty. If not fulfilled through a free relation to his Creator, he will— he *must*—turn to another source of fulfillment; he must enter into a compulsive relation to the world.

In the fateful situation of corrupted sonship God himself acts to restore to man the possibility of authentic sonship. And he does so in and through his own Son.

CHRISTOLOGY AND SOTERIOLOGY

In developing his doctrine of Christ, Gogarten insists that Jesus' divinity must be understood in and through his humanity. Jesus' revelation of God is to be found in his history rather than in a metaphysical nature in which he is consubstantial with the Father. Or, expressed in another way, his history *is* his metaphysical nature through which he reveals the Father to us and brings about reconciliation. In his history the Incarnational event —God assuming our flesh—takes place. What is the nature of this event?

Jesus of Nazareth is fully man, but since he is a man who is completely obedient to the Father, his being is being-from-the-Father. Lived out of the will of the Father, his life is the concrete expression of that will. In the history of Jesus of Nazareth the eternal will of God is enacted. He is that Son who *is* the second person of the Trinity, for in his life the eternal relation between the Father and the Son in the being of God becomes historical.[12] The basic difference, therefore, between ourselves and Jesus is not the difference between natural man and a supernatural being but the difference between sinful history and faithful history, between sonship betrayed and sonship maintained.

But to this must be added that Jesus' relationship is with the Father who wills to restore his estranged sons to fellowship with himself. Consequently, the Son who received his being from the Father reflects in his sonship the concern of the Father for the brothers. He enters into relationship with them and thus also receives his being from their sinful being. Having his being

[12] Cf. "Gottheit und Menschheit Jesu Christi," *Zwischen den Zeiten,* Vol. X (1932), pp. 3 ff.

entirely from God, Jesus turns toward man and, in fulfillment of the second half of the Great Commandment, receives his being *entirely* from man. (This illustrates how "being" as used by Gogarten cannot be understood substantially or quantitatively but as the quality of historical existence.) Thus his full divinity and full humanity are the result of the same divine will and are a description of the same history. He is "made to be sin" (II Cor. 5:21), while at the same time remaining "without sin" (Heb. 4:15) in perfect obedience to the Father. Passages such as these, which for a substantialist approach must remain inexplicable, take on new meaning and relevance when seen as history. The doctrine of the two natures of Christ is meant to be not an unintelligible mystery but an account of Jesus' life with God and man. At the same time, it is an account of the way in which man is restored to that life with God for which he was created, true sonship. Since true sonship is not available apart from faith, the question becomes: How does the action of God in Jesus Christ make faith—and true sonship—possible?

Acting in accordance with the will of the Father, Jesus turns toward the brothers, participating in their being-in-sin through his relationship to them. In so doing, he experiences more radically than can any man the intensity of the alienation between man and God, for he experiences it within his own history. On him the full weight of the curse of this alienation falls, coming to expression in the cry of dereliction. Is it surprising that the cross was interpreted by the early church as judgment, as the place where Christ as the representative of man takes upon himself the judgment which should rightly fall on all men? This is how it looks from man's side. On the cross the man who has received his being from a mankind-against-God is reduced to nothingness. But the cross is not only "the disclosure of the guilt-laden fate of perverted being that lies upon man and his world"; it is also the turning of this fate. It is not only the sign of divine judgment but also "the sign of the salvation brought to man by the crucified One." It is not only the condemnation of man's sin and his reduction to *Nichtigkeit*; also "on the cross the forfeited sonship is bestowed anew."[13] The man-against-God is reduced to nothingness—but in order that he might be raised

[13] *The Reality of Faith*, pp. 123, 125.

a new man by the Creator who re-creates, the God who for-gives and restores, the God who quickens the dead (Rom. 4:17).

Man participates in this history which takes place in Jesus Christ as he encounters the Word directed toward him from the Father, communicated to him through the Son. For the Man who hangs on the cross as the representative of man is also the Son who is the representative of God. In the encounter with the Son, man meets that which both reduces him to nothing and raises him to new life and new sonship. For in the relation with Christ man receives himself and his being from the One who receives his being from the Father and whose being is therefore "historically identical" with that of the Father. In this way man participates in the salvation made available to him in Jesus Christ. But this participation is not metaphysical, nor mystical, nor is it a matter of the moral influence or spiritual interpre-tation of a story, nor any approach which views atonement as taking place exclusively, or even primarily, either in the super-natural world apart from man or within man's mind. It is funda-mentally the reconciliation of persons. It is the event which takes place as man is confronted by the One who in his life, death, and resurrection is God's judgment upon man's life apart from him and is at the same time God's turning toward man in for-giveness and restoration to true sonship.[14]

In this historical event of atonement man is released from his bondage to the world and restored to his intended place over it through the re-establishment of the faith-relation to God. Once again he receives his fundamental meaning and being from the Father and is thus enabled to live in creative freedom toward a world which has been "secularized," stripped of its idolatrous pretentions. (This transformation can be expressed mythologi-cally as the vanquishing of the demonic cosmic powers through the cross of Christ, a victory in which man benefits by virtue of his relation to the Victor. Cf. Rom. 8:38f.; Eph. 1 and 2; Col. 1 and 2.) Thus salvation is at the same time the seculariza-tion of the world, that secularization which, according to Go-garten, is at the heart of Christian faith.

Modern secular*ism,* on the other hand, developing out of the

[14] Cf. *Demythologizing and History* (London, SCM Press, 1955), pp. 68–79.

reorientation which took place in the Renaissance and Enlightenment, has purged the world of gods and devils by splitting all reality into "subject" and "object," the subject—the human mind—taking charge over the world as its object in a way it previously had never dared to do. The world is to be examined in and for itself, disregarding all supernatural associations, in order to define and isolate the intramundane law. The result of this methodology has been a technological advance without parallel. Unfortunately, however, technological control, though it does guarantee the burden of responsibility, does not guarantee meaning. The result is a situation in which man *alone* is responsible for the world—there are no more gods with whom to share the burden—while at the same time the ultimate meaning of this responsibility eludes him. Man feels increasingly victimized by the world about which he is accumulating ever greater amounts of objective information. Yet every attempt to derive meaning from within the world proves finally unsatisfactory. At the end of the subject-object era the *object* has become the real, the vis-à-vis (*Gegenüber*) from which the subject has to receive its being because it is the only reality apart from the subject. As a result, the subject is relativized by that over which it is supposed to exercise dominion. And the values of the subject are now "only relative," "only subjective."

The bankruptcy of the subject-object orientation as an exclusive approach to reality is clear. It has ended in a situation in which man is the victim and captive of that toward which he should—and indeed *must*—be free if he is to carry out his responsibility for the ordering and maintaining of the world under the Creator.

FAITH AND DEMYTHOLOGIZING

It should now be apparent why Gogarten felt called upon to enter the "demythologizing controversy" on the side of Bultmann. The real issue at stake, says Gogarten in *Demythologizing and History,* is the nature of faith and its relation to history.

A charge commonly lodged against Bultmann and his followers is that they have, by the application of rigorously critical methods to the New Testament, reduced the amount of objective, factual material in the gospel records to the point where the bridge between the historical Jesus and the preaching about him has collapsed. If the first Christians were not concerned with reporting the facts objectively in their preaching, but instead made generous use of the language of the then-current world views (*Weltanschauungen*) and of the ancient conception of the physical universe (*Weltbild*) in interpreting and proclaiming what they experienced, we are left with little or no solid ground in reliable fact to which we can point as reinforcing the claim of faith that God has acted decisively in objective history through the life, death, and resurrection of Jesus Christ. And if this be the case, how can we continue to speak of Christianity as a "historical" religion in any more than a strained and indeed mythological sense?

Two assumptions are implicit in this protest which need to be examined. One is that God's action in history is objective; the other, that faith is subjective. The two are, of course, correlated because they are both grounded in the subject-object world view and exemplify the way in which this view must of necessity see faith and history. History is viewed as an independent object which is available to be appropriated by a free and independent subject in an act which is called "faith." The objectivity of that which is espoused keeps faith from being completely subjective. Faith is thus understood in the traditional pattern of *notitia* plus *assensus,* taking notice of an objective fact and also assenting to its validity.[15] Now if there is no independent object toward which Christian faith is directed, but only the subjective faith of the early church, it follows that the believer is set adrift in a sea of subjectivism and relativism. There is no solid historical object in his faith, and the fear that such a faith is "docetic" seems justified.

But Gogarten must question both assumptions: the objectivism of history and the subjectivism of faith. The demythologizers no less than their opponents affirm that "the great acts of God are set before all human existence indestructibly, indissolubly and irremovably."[16] But the reality and permanence of these events, as they are understood in the Bible itself, lie not

[15] *Ibid.,* p. 51.
[16] *Ibid.,* p. 67.

in their independent objectivity but in their being used by God in communicating his intention toward man. This is made especially clear, as we have seen, in the revelation in Jesus Christ. The genuine history of Jesus *includes* his relation with the Father. His very being is being-from-the-Father. Moreover, the being he receives as the Son is God's being-for-man. So that *the history of Jesus is God's turning himself toward man to save!* But obviously neither the relation of Jesus to the Father nor the intention of God toward man enacted through the Son is available through an "objective" approach, not because they are irrecoverable but because both are recoverable only in and through a method appropriate to transmitting the kind of history with which we are here concerned. For this history has a verbal (*worthaft*) character; it intends to communicate. And its reality cannot be grasped apart from a reception of this communication. This is why preaching, far from breaking the connection with the historical Jesus, is actually the conserver and effectuator of the genuine history of Jesus. For he who would understand this history must be involved in it as it becomes the living Word of God to him. This history can be grasped and understood only as its reality becomes present, as it happens here and now. To attempt to reduce this to "objective" history is to engage in a "miserable rationalization of the New Testament history . . . [by which] the New Testament message loses its own historical character."[17]

Likewise, faith for Gogarten cannot be labeled "subjective," for faith is not a subject's affirmation of an object but rather its being confronted by the Word from beyond itself and incorporated into a relationship—into a new history—fundamentally conditioned by the history of Jesus Christ (as that history has just been described). Faith therefore transcends subjectivism by virtue of the fact that it is a historical mode of being, a being-from-the-other and with-the-other. Apart from this "other" and the historical interaction there is no genuine faith.

What happens in revelation and faith thus bursts the bonds of the subject-object approach and simply cannot be comprehended by it. To attempt to do so can lead only to a distortion of the genuine reality involved. The demythologizers recognize

[17] *Ibid.*, p. 76.

this and explicitly operate in a different context in their theological formulations. However, they do continue to use the objective approach where it is appropriate, namely, in historical critical research. The resultant alternation between methods is the source of much confusion to many of their opponents who themselves operate for the most part unconsciously in a subject-object context which is neither so strictly employed in criticism nor so clearly superseded in theological formulation. Thus much of what is said and written in the controversy is unfortunately beside the point. Rather than the destruction of historical truth, the demythologizers see their task as making possible a proper confrontation with a history understood not as a supernatural object but as the divine Word. Their negative contribution is in making it impossible to confuse faith with assent to certain thought forms of the first century. Consequently they have to be critical of the *form* of expression of the first century, but only in order to open up the genuinely historical *content* which was and is being communicated: God's Word to man.

Because of his defense of the existentialist stance in theology, Gogarten's name is today often linked with that of Bultmann, as it once was with Barth. In some respects the present classification is more justified than the earlier one, for Gogarten's Lutheran bias and philosophical interests made him something of an anomaly in dialectical theology. However, it would be a mistake simply to equate Gogarten with Bultmann. For one thing, several of the so-called "post-Bultmannians" are dependent upon Gogarten for their theological orientation, especially Gerhard Ebeling, Brunner's successor at Zurich,[18] and Ernst Fuchs, upon whom the mantle of Bultmann has fallen at Marburg. And Gogarten is credited with anticipating systematically in *The Proclamation of Jesus Christ*[19] many of the conclusions to which these younger critics of Bultmann have since come, on the basis of textual evidence. But perhaps it is his

---

[18] Cf. Ebeling's *The Nature of Faith* (Philadelphia, Muhlenberg, 1961).

[19] *Die Verkündigung Jesu Christi* (Heidelberg, L. Schneider, 1948). For an account of the "post-Bultmannian" development, see James M. Robinson, *A New Quest of the Historical Jesus* (London, SCM Press, 1961).

foremost American admirer, Carl Michalson, who in *The Rationality of Faith*,[20] a programmatic study of faith's relation to history, has given most explicit expression to Gogarten's central concern. For underneath Gogarten's earlier attacks on idealism, as well as his more recent conversations with secularism, lies but one aim: to examine systematically the implications for theology of the fact that reality, in general, and the reality of the Christian faith, in particular, must once again be viewed as it was in the Biblical period—as history.

[20] (N.Y., Scribner's, 1963.)

Bibliography

Friedrich Gogarten, *The Reality of Faith*, Philadelphia, Westminster, 1959.

No detailed study of Gogarten is available in English.

RUDOLF BULTMANN

John Macquarrie

Born at Wiefelstede, Oldenburg, on August 20, 1884, Rudolf Karl Bultmann has spent his entire life in biblical and theological studies. He was a student at the University of Marburg in the years when that center of learning boasted world-famous schools both in philosophy and in theology, and he continued his studies at Tübingen and Berlin. By 1912 he had become a private lecturer at Marburg, and later held academic posts at Breslau and Giessen. In 1921 he returned to Marburg as Professor of New Testament, and remained there until his retirement in 1951. In the meantime he had gained an international reputation as a scholar, and this was recognized by invitations to give the Shaffer Lectures in Yale University in 1951 and the Gifford Lectures in Edinburgh University in 1955.

It was as a radical critic of the New Testament that Bultmann first attracted attention. In an extensive study of the Synoptic Gospels,[1] Bultmann takes up the method of form-criticism which had been adumbrated by Johannes Weiss. On this view, the gospel narrative may be analyzed into units which can then be classified according to their forms, as apothegms, miracle stories, and so on. These units were formulated in the early Christian community to meet its devotional and apologetic needs, and later they were strung together like beads on a thread to make up the Synoptic Gospels. If this point of view is correct, it follows that the Synoptic Gospels give us information about the early Christian community and its beliefs rather than about Jesus himself, and that their value as biographies of Jesus is negligible. Even St. Mark's Gospel, on this view, is a theological document rather than a historical one.

The Fourth Gospel has likewise come under Bultmann's meticulous scrutiny, and he has produced a major commentary

[1] *Geschichte der synoptischen Tradition* (Göttingen, Vandenhoeck & Ruprecht, 1921).

on it.[2] In his view, Gnostic influences have entered very deeply into the thought of the Fourth Gospel, in which the sacrifice of history to theology has been carried to an extreme length.

These theories about the Gospels lead to a profound skepticism with regard to any historical facts they may be supposed to record. This skeptical attitude may be summed up in Bultmann's own statement that "we can now know almost nothing concerning the life and personality of Jesus."[3] We can indeed know something of his teaching, which Bultmann represents as primarily eschatological in character, and as an appeal for decision before the approaching end. But the historical Jesus himself remains in impenetrable shadow, and it is even denied that he ever claimed to be the Messiah. "The historical person of Jesus was very soon turned into a myth in primitive Christianity."[4] It is now impossible to get behind this myth to the historical facts of the matter.

Yet this skepticism about matters of fact has not made Bultmann skeptical about the Christian religion. On the contrary, he combines his negative historical findings not only with Christian faith but with a genuine evangelical concern to win acceptance for the Christian message in the modern secularized world, and he tells us himself that he experiences no discomfort in this combination. For him faith is not dependent on the findings of historical research. Like Karl Barth, Bultmann has reacted strongly against the older liberal school of thought which looked for the "real" historical Jesus, freed from theological interpretations of his person and work. Bultmann agrees with Barth in finding the essence of Christianity in the kerygmatic proclamation of the New Testament—a word of God addressed to man and demanding the response of faith. Some of Bultmann's critics say that he has been driven into this theological orientation because the negative results of his researches have left him with so little in the way of a factual historical foundation for his theology; but other critics allege that he has deliberately stressed the negative findings of historical research in order to make it

---

[2] *Das Evangelium des Johannes* (1941).

[3] *Jesus and the Word* (N.Y., Scribner's, 1934), p. 8.

[4] *Primitive Christianity in Its Contemporary Setting* (N.Y., Meridian, 1956), p. 200.

clear that faith is not at all dependent upon such research. Whatever the truth of the matter, the main theological interest in Bultmann lies in his attempt to interpret Christianity in such a way that one can be radically skeptical about the factual content of the gospel narrative and yet continue to believe in the essential message of the New Testament. Indeed, Bultmann would go further, maintaining that if the essential Christian message is to gain a hearing in the contemporary world, it must be disengaged from the form in which it is presented in the New Testament.

As we have already noted, Bultmann holds that the history of Jesus was speedily transformed into a myth. It is this myth which now confronts us in the pages of the New Testament, and it is futile to try—as Harnack and others did—to get behind it to the facts of the historical Jesus. These facts, whatever they may have been, have undergone an irreversible metamorphosis into the story of a divine pre-existent being who became incarnate and atoned by his blood for the sins of men, who rose from the dead and ascended into heaven, and who, it was believed, would shortly come again on the clouds to bring the present age to a close, to hold judgment upon men, and to establish the new age. This central story is, moreover, embellished and illustrated by all kinds of peripheral legends which tell of miracles and wonders, voices from heaven, victories over demons, and the like. Such a story is called a myth. It belongs to the undifferentiated thinking of a prescientific age, when occult forces, divine or demonic, were supposed to be everywhere active both in human affairs and in nature, and when any unexplained event was assigned to the direct agency of such forces.

Such a mythical way of thinking is impossible for men who live in the twentieth century. They have grown up in a scientific climate of thought, and their understanding of the world is inescapably influenced by it. "It is impossible to use electric light and the wireless and to avail ourselves of modern medical and surgical discoveries," says Bultmann, "and at the same time to believe in the New Testament world of demons and spirits."[5]

---

[5] "New Testament and Mythology," in *Kerygma and Myth*, H. W. Bartsch, ed., (N.Y., Harper, 1961), p. 5.

It is indeed impossible, unless we are to have split minds, with one set of beliefs about the world for religion and another set for our everyday living. If Christianity is inextricably bound up with the outworn mythology and cosmology of the first century of our era, then it would seem that unless we are prepared to make a sacrifice of the intellect, we must reluctantly say good-by to the Christian faith, as so many moderns have felt themselves compelled to do when confronted by the bewildering and unintelligible ideas of the New Testament.

Bultmann himself, however, when confronted with this situation, does not say good-by to Christianity. He believes that hidden in the mythical language of the New Testament lies a supreme truth—nothing less than God's word addressed to man. He is concerned that we in the modern world should hear this word and respond to it. We cannot, it is true, accept the mythical ideas of the New Testament, but these ideas, Bultmann thinks, are not part of the essential message but are simply historical accidents which inevitably attached themselves to the message in the age in which it was formulated. The message itself can be disengaged from its mythical setting. We have already seen that this is not to be done by trying to penetrate behind the myth to some supposed historical substratum. We have to take the myth as it stands and attempt to restate it in a form free from mythical ideas. The task of constructing such a restatement is what Bultmann calls "demythologizing."

Bultmann is therefore engaged in a task of translation. The message of the New Testament is to be translated out of the mythical language in which it has been handed down to us into a language which is intelligible in our times. "Demythologizing," says Bultmann, "is an hermeneutic method, that is to say, a method of interpretation and exegesis."[6] Hermeneutics is the scientific study of the principles of interpretation, and it is a study to which Bultmann has devoted considerable attention.[7] He points out that an interpreter can elucidate the meaning of a document only if he already has some preliminary understanding of the subject matter of the document. For instance, one cannot begin to understand what St. Paul has to say about

[6] *Jesus Christ and Mythology* (N.Y., Scribner's, 1958), p. 45.
[7] See his essay "The Problem of Hermeneutics," in *Essays, Philosophical and Theological* (N.Y., Macmillan, 1955), pp. 234–61.

sin unless one already has from experience some understanding of what sin is. Again, Bultmann claims that the interpreter will be most successful in his task if he approaches the document with the right questions in mind, that is to say, if the interest which guides his questions is sufficiently close to the interest which motivated the author of the document. People go wrong when they ask of the Bible questions which are remote from the interests of the biblical writers—for instance, when they seek information about scientific cosmology from Genesis or when they try to forecast contemporary political happenings from Ezekiel, to mention extreme cases.

Now the key to this hermeneutical problem is found by Bultmann in the concept of human existence. It is as existing, and therefore as already having some understanding of existence, that we are able to have that preliminary understanding which is necessary to us before the biblical writings can mean anything to us at all. And further, it is the question of existence which provides the required community of interest with the biblical writers, and which is therefore the right question to ask of the Bible. This question of existence is one to which each of us is driven by having to decide about his own existence, and the truth concealed under the mythical formulations of the Bible is a true understanding of human existence for which men can decide in the twentieth century just as they did in the first—a new self-understanding, as Bultmann often expresses it. To demythologize is therefore to translate from mythical language into existential language.

The first step in this new orientation is to address to the New Testament existential questions. What does this mean for my existence? What possibilities of existence are disclosed here? Into what understanding of myself does this bring me? But in order that such questions may be asked with the fullest awareness of their implications, we should first of all clarify and analyze that preliminary understanding of existence which we already bring to the task of interpretation. The peculiarity of man, as distinct from any mere inanimate thing, is that he not only exists but always has some understanding of his existence. And while this understanding of existence which is given with human existence may be—and usually is—vague and naïve, it is nevertheless capable of being brought to clarity through philosophical reflection and analysis. The type of philosophy which explicitly applies itself to the task of clarifying the structures of human existence is existentialism, so now we see the reason for the close connection of demythologizing with existentialist philosophy. In particular, Bultmann has found the philosophy of Martin Heidegger very enlightening for his purposes. It would be a mistake to suppose, as some do, that Bultmann has first accepted the philosophical teaching of Heidegger and has then interpreted the New Testament in such a way that it will conform to this secular philosophy. Rather, Bultmann has seen in the categories which Heidegger has forged the very tools which he needs for his own hermeneutical approach to the New Testament. In Heidegger we find an analysis of human existence which enables us to go about the task of existential interpretation with some hope of attaining clarity and precision. As another New Testament scholar, Erich Dinkler, has remarked, "Heidegger's analysis of human existence more than any other modern philosophy offers structures and defines terms fit for theologically clear speaking."[8]

Heidegger thinks that human existence gets misunderstood when we apply to it categories such as substance and accident or cause and effect. These categories are appropriate to objects in the world, but our existence is never such an object. He proposes to find a new set of categories, or "existentials," as he calls them, which will be appropriate for describing human existence, and these existentials will describe not fixed properties but possible ways of being for which man, as an existent, can decide. Heidegger's whole scheme cannot be indicated here, but it will be helpful to consider a few of his more important ideas and show how they provide a framework for Bultmann's exposition of the thought of St. Paul, which ranks among his best exegetical work.[9]

In Heidegger the fundamental possibilities are an authentic existence or an inauthentic existence. In an authentic existence, man lays hold on his potentiality for being and attains the full stature of his selfhood. In an inauthentic existence, his self is

---

[8] "Martin Heidegger," in *Christianity and the Existentialists*, Carl Michalson, ed., (N.Y., Scribner's 1956), p. 120.
[9] See *Theology of the New Testament*, 2 Vols. (N.Y., Scribner's, 1951–55).

scattered in its concern with the world of things, and its decisions are made for it by the collective mass of mankind. In St. Paul we find the corresponding distinction between the spiritual man who has found his true self in a new life and the natural man whose view does not rise above the horizons of the earthly. Heidegger's idea of the collective depersonalized mass of mankind as one of the basic existentials or possible ways of being provides a place in the scheme of existence for the Pauline concept of the "world" which, as Bultmann points out, is an existential rather than a physical concept, and usually designates the whole body of fallen mankind from which the individual can be liberated only by a radical decision of faith. Another of Heidegger's basic existentials is fallenness—the possibility of losing responsible selfhood through submitting to the tyranny of things and of the collective mass. This is alienation from man's true being. Bultmann gives a corresponding interpretation to the Pauline concepts of the "flesh" and "sin." These represent concern with the realm of the earthly, and alienation not only from man's true being but also from God. For Heidegger the way to authentic existence lies through resolvedness. The individual takes on himself responsibility for his existence and projects himself on his own potentiality for being. The Pauline counterpart is "faith," and in his interpretation of this concept we find Bultmann laying stress on the aspects of radical decision and commitment.

From these illustrations we can see how Bultmann uses the conceptual framework provided by Heidegger's existential analytic for an existential interpretation of New Testament ideas. And it can hardly be denied that by taking the idea of existence as his hermeneutical key, Bultmann is able to show the interrelationships subsisting among the various Pauline concepts and is also able to inject fresh meaning into such worn-out terms as "flesh," "world," "sin," "faith."

So far we have considered the application of the method of existential interpretation only to single concepts, but in demythologizing proper a similar approach can be made to whole areas of myth. Let us take as an example the eschatological myth which Bultmann, following Weiss and Schweitzer, regards as a fundamental and pervasive element in New Testament thought. As is well known, the mythology of the last things was taken over by the first Christians from Jewish apocalyptic. According to this myth, the world is viewed as the scene of a cosmic drama. The present age is shortly coming to an end through a supernatural intervention. There will be a final judgment, and men will be assigned to destinies either of bliss or torment. The first disciples' expectation of an imminent end proved to be wrong, and to people nowadays the whole belief, if taken at all literally, must look like an absurd superstition. As Bultmann has expressed it: "History did not come to an end, and, as every schoolboy knows, it will continue to run its course."[10] At least, if history ever did come to an end, it would presumably be halted through some purely physical cause, such as a change in the sun's radiation or a nuclear war on the earth. This is the kind of mythology which makes the New Testament appear so remote and unintelligible to minds that are accustomed to postmythical ways of thought.

But let us now apply the canons of existential interpretation to the eschatological myth, and we discover that we can begin to make sense even of this unpromising material. The ideas of the myth must be related to the here and now of actual individual existence. Every individual stands before the imminent end—his own death. As Heidegger puts it, our human existence is always a "being towards death." Again, in his everyday decisions about the existence for which he is responsible, every individual works out his own judgment. He makes his essence, and here and now either lays hold on his authentic being or loses it. When we understand it in this way, the eschatological teaching of the New Testament ceases to be merely a curious survival from the remote past. When they are transferred to the actual individual existence, the eschatological ideas recover something of their urgency, of the sense of responsibility and of the need for decision before the end. "In every moment," says Bultmann, "slumbers the possibility of being the eschatological moment. You must awaken to it."[11]

[10] *Kerygma and Myth*, p. 5.
[11] *The Presence of Eternity*, p. 155. This is the title given to the American edition of Bultmann's Gifford Lectures (N.Y., Harper, 1957). The original title is *History and Eschatology* (Edinburgh, Univ. Press, 1957).

It must have been the existential significance of the myth—though this had not yet been sorted out from the mythical formulation—that made eschatology so important for the first Christians. If we look at the Fourth Gospel, composed, as is generally believed, around the end of the first century when the hopes of an immediate end were beginning to fade, we do find that the cruder eschatology is beginning to give way to the existential interpretation of it. The writer of the Fourth Gospel no longer thinks of judgment and eternal life as purely future, but brings them into the here and now of Christian existence. Thus Bultmann is able to claim that demythologizing begins in the pages of the New Testament itself.

The kind of approach which has been exemplified in the case of eschatology may be applied to other areas of myth. Myths of creation, for instance, are interpreted not as fanciful accounts of how the world began but as expressions of the finite, creaturely, and dependent status of man's being. Myths of demonic powers which hold the world in subjection are interpreted not as expressions of a dualistic world view—which would in any case be abhorrent to the biblical belief that God is the author of all things—but as representing man's awareness of the tyranny of the world over his life. This tyranny appears to him like that of an alien power, yet it arises from his own decision for the world and against God. In each case the myth is understood as a primitive way of bringing to words some aspect of man's awareness of his own existence. In the myth, this existential awareness has been projected outward upon objects in the world, and the aim of demythologizing is to recapture the existential significance and restate it in a nonmythical form. And if someone asks why we should trouble to do this, Bultmann would reply that these ancient myths often contain important insights which have been lost to more sophisticated and perhaps more shallow generations to whom the myths have become meaningless. In particular, as we have already noted, he thinks that the Christian myth conceals in itself a supreme truth of existence, which is just as relevant to our existence as it was to the existence of men in ancient times.

We have still to consider how Bultmann handles the core of the Christian story—the cross of Christ and his resurrection from the dead. Here we must notice a distinction. The cross can be regarded as a fairly well attested event of history, and is recognized as such by Bultmann. He points out that there is a difference between the story of Christ and a pure myth—such as, let us say, the story of Osiris—in that Christ was a real figure and his death can be dated in world history; he was, as the creed says, "crucified under Pontius Pilate." On the other hand, Bultmann regards the resurrection as a myth and dismisses the stories of the empty tomb as legends. The resurrection simply expresses the significance of the cross. Yet the cross itself has been transposed from the plane of world history onto the level of the mythical cosmic drama. The cross becomes the act of atonement and reconciliation at the very heart of the drama.

"What a primitive mythology it is," says Bultmann, "that a divine being should become incarnate and atone for the sins of men through his own blood!"[12] Yet even this "primitive myth" finds its justification through demythologizing and existential interpretation. Here we must notice briefly the existentialist view of history, which Bultmann has learned from Heidegger and also from the English philosopher, R. G. Collingwood, though the latter could scarcely be called an "existentialist." On this view, the business of the historian is much more than just to discover what happened at a particular time in the past, or to show how particular events were related to other events. His business is conceived to be rather that of exploring the possibilities of human existence which are disclosed in history. This he can do because his own existence is historical and he can, so to speak, re-enact in himself the actions of historical persons. It is when the Christian believer re-enacts the cross in his own existence that he discovers its power as an atonement. To believe in the cross, according to Bultmann, is not to hold some theory of atonement but to make the cross one's own, and so to be reconciled both to one's true being and to God. Acceptance of the cross is the radical decision or commitment of faith. It is the decision to turn from the world to God, to give up self-sufficiency and to live by the grace of the unseen, and so to be at one with one's true self and with God. But this is also experienced as resurrection, the beginning of a new life. By losing his life

12 *Kerygma and Myth*, p. 7.

the believer has found it. He has risen from the death of sin, when his being was scattered and lost in worldly concerns, to an authentic existence.

All this makes sense and enables us to understand the cross as an atonement and the way to wholeness, but so far nothing has been said of the incarnation. For the cross to have its atoning power, is it necessary first to believe that it was the Son of God who died? Bultmann would reply to this question with a counterquestion: "Does he help me because he is God's Son, or is he the Son of God because he helps me?"[13] In other words, we can say that in Bultmann's theology, Christology is subsequent to soteriology. It is because we experience the cross as atonement that we recognize that God was in Christ. Christology also is interpreted existentially. To say that Christ is God is not to make a metaphysical pronouncement about Christ's person, but to declare one's own attitude toward him. Bultmann's Christology is indeed not far removed from that of Albrecht Ritschl, who taught that a christological pronouncement has the status of a value judgment. This way of thinking has a long history in Lutheranism, going back to Melanchthon and Luther himself.

It is then God himself who addresses us through the crucified and risen Christ. It is God's kerygmatic word that lies concealed under the mythological formulations of the New Testament, and this word, Bultmann believes, is still of vital concern and presses us to the point of radical decision. It may seem that in the course of his thinking Bultmann has put aside many things that have been traditionally believed in the Christian Church and many ideas that have been cherished in Christian piety. Yet his motive in doing this has been to set free the essential message of the New Testament from what he regards as the embarrassment of its mythological formulation, and he has done this so that the same message may be heard and awaken the response of faith in our scientific age. The real stumbling block in the way of faith, as Bultmann recognizes, is acceptance of the cross and the surrender of self-sufficiency. Why then, he asks, make things more difficult for the modern man by putting in his way

[13] *Essays*, p. 280.

an additional stumbling block and asking him to swallow a mythology in which he cannot believe any more without destroying his intellectual integrity?

Desperate diseases, we are told, require desperate remedies. No one doubts that our Western civilization today is in the grip of a malaise, as a shallow secularism keeps advancing while religion and spiritual values decline. The Christian message seems to have lost its biting edge. It is not so much rejected as disregarded and dismissed as remote, irrelevant, and unintelligible. Bultmann's demythologizing may turn out to be none too desperate a remedy if Christianity is to count again; and surely Western civilization is unthinkable without a vital Christianity, for it would have ceased to be the Western civilization that we cherish. If demythologizing is not the remedy for Christianity, then something equally drastic is called for. But whether or not we think that demythologizing offers the way forward, we cannot but admire the fearless honesty and integrity with which Bultmann has faced the task—the greatest task now confronting those who still adhere to the Christian religion—of seeking to make Christianity once more a living issue for which men of our time can decide.

The impact made by Bultmann's ideas upon the theological world has been a major one, comparable in its magnitude to the impact made by Barth's theology of crisis a quarter of a century earlier. Since the controversy over Bultmann's views still goes on and shows no sign of abatement, it is impossible to predict what influence he may eventually have on the future course of theology. It can, however, be asserted that he is probably the most discussed theologian at the present time. Since he put forward his program for demythologizing the New Testament, a steady and voluminous stream of books and articles devoted to the subject has been flowing. Contributions have come from theologians of many nations and of many branches of Christendom. Philosophers too have joined in the debate, and this is a particularly interesting and welcome fact, for throughout much of the present century there has been a divorce between philosophy and theology, each regarding the other with indifference or even suspicion. While Bultmann's views have aroused plenty of opposition, something like a Bultmannian school has arisen among some of the younger theologians in Germany, and there are pockets of disciples to be found elsewhere. Although the debate still goes on, the main lines of criticism and of further development have already emerged. For Bultmann's theories, as expounded in the earlier part of this essay, conceal a number of unresolved problems and difficulties, and while his critics have seized upon these, his defenders and he himself have sought to meet the objections. In what follows we shall consider three major problems raised by Bultmann's theology.

The first problem is one which, in various forms, has long vexed the Christian Church—the problem of the relation of philosophy to theology. Bultmann's demythologizing, as we have seen, is closely tied up with existentialist philosophy. Has he had any success in reaching a new *rapprochement* between theology and philosophy? Has he worked out a proper relation between the two disciplines? It must be reported that his attempts to do so seem to have displeased both the theologians and the philosophers, and he has been severely criticized from both sides.

Theologians like Karl Barth are naturally suspicious of the place which Bultmann gives to existentialist philosophy in his exposition of Christianity. Barth himself fought hard to win autonomy for Christian theology and to deliver it from subservience to whatever brand of philosophy might be in fashion at a particular time. In his little book on Bultmann, Barth remarks that for a generation theology had been escaping from what he calls "an Egyptian bondage in which a philosophy lays down what the Holy Spirit is permitted to say."[14] It seems to Barth that Bultmann, by his deference to Heidegger, has initiated a move back to Egypt. For Bultmann has brought Heidegger's existential analytic into his scriptural exegesis, and in Barth's view the truth of Christianity can only be perverted and distorted when an attempt is made to wed it to a secular philosophy. It is not clear, however, that Bultmann does in fact make his exegesis dependent on the demands of a philosophy, and certainly it is not his intention to do so. As has been pointed

[14] *Rudolf Bultmann—ein Versuch ihn zu verstehen* (Zurich, Evangelischer Verlag, 1952), p. 52.

out above, he appropriates Heidegger's existential scheme as a useful tool for his exegetical studies, but he would argue that this tool by no means determines the meaning which he elicits from the biblical text. Its function is only a heuristic one. It opens our eyes to the meaning of the text and helps toward the elucidation of that meaning.

On the other hand, Bultmann finds himself under attack from the philosopher Karl Jaspers.[15] According to Jaspers, Bultmann's apparent interest in philosophy is quite spurious. The essence of philosophy is said to lie in its openness. Bultmann, on the contrary, has shown himself to be exclusive. He has taken one single philosopher—Heidegger—and concentrated on a single work by that philosopher, *Sein und Zeit*. In Jasper's view such a selective procedure is so far from qualifying Bultmann to be heard in philosophical circles that it rather shows him to be entirely lacking in the true philosophical spirit. Moreover Bultmann has used those ideas which he has taken from Heidegger to bolster up a sagging orthodoxy. He is willing to keep company with the philosophers so long as it suits his purpose, but then he appeals to a special divine revelation which, he says, is inaccessible to philosophy. Jaspers may have in mind a passage in which Bultmann himself asks whether a demythologized version of Christianity must not become another philosophy of existence—whether, in fact, Christian theology is not merely the precursor of existentialism and is now to be discarded. But Bultmann goes on to deny that this is the case. Philosophy, he claims, may conceive of an authentic existence, but theology knows of a gracious act which empowers such existence—God's gracious act in Christ, as proclaimed in the kerygmatic word. It is this appeal to a special act of God which annoys Jaspers and leads him to declare that Bultmann's professed interest in philosophy is not genuine. So Bultmann's ventures into philosophical territory are censured as severely by Jaspers as they are by Barth, though for different reasons.

The debates over the relation of theology to philosophy in Bultmann's thought have led to the first major independent development of Bultmann's ideas by one of his disciples—the Swiss theologian Fritz Buri. This younger thinker frankly ac-

[15] See his debate with Bultmann in *Die Frage der Entmythologisierung* (Munich, 1954).

cepts demythologizing and existential interpretation as the most promising way forward for theology in our time, though he looks to Jaspers rather than to Heidegger for his philosophical background. Buri thinks, however, that Bultmann's demythologizing needs to be carried much further. Quite arbitrarily, it seems to Buri, Bultmann has called a halt to demythologizing when he has come to the kerygmatic word which he unwraps from its mythological coverings. But this kerygmatic word, the appeal to which so annoys the philosophers, is itself, says Buri, just a last remnant of mythology. So he asks that we should go beyond Bultmann's demythologizing to what he calls "dekerygmatizing."[16] This would involve the frank recognition that there is in the New Testament no special or unique word of God that is inaccessible to human reflection in general. There is in principle no distinction between Christian theology and philosophies of existence, though there is the difference that theology possesses a wealth of symbolic material for exploration, and its concrete symbols, as Buri recognizes, can be a powerful aid in the quest for an authentic existence.

Buri's radicalizing of Bultmann's theology certainly meets the kind of objections that are put forward by Jaspers, but it may be asked whether it is not Bultmann who does more justice to the experience of Christianity as a religion of grace. The problem of the relation of theology to philosophy in Bultmann's thought turns into the question of whether there is a limit to demythologizing, and if so, why should there be a limit and where does it come? This is one of the major unresolved issues which Bultmann's theology raises, and no doubt it will be the subject of further debate.

A second major problem in Bultmann's thought is the relation of theology to history. Christianity is usually described as a historical religion, because its center is not a code of laws or a world view but an event or series of events focused in Jesus Christ—the "mighty acts" or the "salvation history," to use the terms generally employed by theologians. Now Bultmann, as we have seen, leaves very little in the way of factual objective history to the gospel narrative. What history there was, he tells us, has been transformed into myth, so that we can no longer

[16] See his essay "Entmythologisierung oder Entkerygmatisierung?," in *Kerygma und Mythos,* Band II (Hamburg, 1952), pp. 85–101.

get at the history. He himself transforms the myth into its existential significance and brings the "salvation history" into the present, that is to say, into the historical existence of the believer who here and now dies and rises with Christ. It is true that he can speak of the difference between the story of Christ as a real figure of history and the myths of the Hellenistic cults. It is true also that he can speak of the paradox of the Christ-event, which happened once in the past and which nevertheless happens again and again in every Christian in whose soul Christ is born, suffers, dies, and is raised up. But it seems clear that Bultmann attaches much more importance to what happens now than to anything that may be supposed to have happened long ago—and of course it is obvious that much can be said for this point of view.

Protestant theologians who stress the "once-for-all" character of the Christ-event have been particularly critical of Bultmann's skepticism with regard to the historical events in the gospel narrative. While some of their criticisms are wildly exaggerated, it is a fair question whether Christianity does not need some minimum of factual history to support its message. In one of his early works, R. G. Collingwood remarks that if Jesus was not a real historical person, it might be as futile to exhort men to follow him as it would be to urge an athlete to emulate the feats of Heracles.[17] Such a remark will appeal especially to the empirical temper of the English-speaking peoples. Does the Christian message summon us to a pure speculative possibility of existence, or to a possibility which has been actualized under the real conditions of historical existence? We could have no confidence about embarking on the first of these alternatives. So we come back to the question whether Christianity needs some minimum of factual history, and, if so, how much?

Bultmann's own position on this matter is ambiguous, but again we find that the problem has been taken up by his disciples.[18] Aware of the dangers of being committed to the wor-

---

[17] *Religion and Philosophy* (London, Macmillan, 1916), p. 53.

[18] For an instructive review of recent researches on these lines, see James M. Robinson, *A New Quest of the Historical Jesus* (London, SCM Press, 1961).

ship of a purely mythological Lord, some of the younger German followers of Bultmann are exploring the relation of the Christ of faith to the historical Jesus of Nazareth. One of them, Günther Bornkamm, says that the records which we have do not entitle us to be resigned or skeptical about the historical Jesus, and that "we must look for the history in the kerygma."[19] He and others have proceeded to do this, and so the whole question of history and theology in relation to demythologizing is still an open one.

A third major problem raised by Bultmann's theology is the question of how one is going to talk about God in the context of demythologizing. The Belgian Jesuit scholar Father Malevez criticizes the anthropological bias of Bultmann's approach to the New Testament, which, he says, is primarily concerned to teach us about God. Bultmann's theology, he finds, "is absolutely silent about the God whom it urges us to worship; there is nothing about his nature or attributes."[20] This objection is strongly worded, but there seem to be some grounds for it. Demythologizing, as we have seen, aims at translating mythical language into existential language, that is to say, into statements about possibilities of human existence. If this is carried through consistently, where is there room left to talk about God, or how is he to be brought into the picture?

Yet we do find Bultmann talking about God, and in particular he has much to say about the "acts" of God. Such talk, however, would fall under his own definition of mythology as "the use of imagery to express the otherworldly in terms of this world and the divine in terms of human life,"[21] since, when we speak of an act of God, we are applying the human conception of an "act" to God. But Bultmann's definition of mythology was a bad one, for as many critics have pointed out, it would cover not only myth but all kinds of symbolic and analogical language. Bultmann himself has had second thoughts about his definition, for he now tells us that when he talks of an "act of God," he is using not mythological but analogical language. This is certainly

[19] *Jesus von Nazareth* (Stuttgart, Kohlhammer, 1956), p. 20.
[20] Léopold Malevez, *The Christian Message and Myth* (London, SCM Press, 1958), p. 156.
[21] *Kerygma and Myth*, p. 10, n. 2.

a clarification, but it is at the same time a tacit admission that demythologizing does not succeed in performing the task which it sets out to accomplish. For obviously there is all the difference in the world between an existential statement which refers to human existence, and a statement which, though expressed in terms drawn from human existence, refers analogically to God. We must in fact conclude that when demythologizing has completed its work of translation, we shall have on our hands not only the existential statements which we were promised but also a set of analogical statements of quite another order. It follows that the work of restating the Christian message in a form free of myth is a good deal more complicated than Bultmann originally led us to believe, and up till now he has not carried out a systematic logical analysis of the different kinds of discourse that are involved, nor has he shown how they are related to each other. Of course there is always a drastic alternative to such complications, that is to say, to give up talking about an act of God and to follow Buri along the way of radical dekerygmatizing.

An examination of some of the questions that arise out of Bultmann's theology and of some of the criticisms to which he has been subjected show us that the subject is much more complex than might have been supposed at the end of the straightforward exposition of his ideas which formed the first part of this essay. It is clear that Bultmann leaves us with many unresolved problems and difficulties on our hands. Yet this need not surprise us, for no theology that has ever been constructed is free from difficulties. The test of the worth of a theology is whether it helps to solve some problems, whether it makes a worthwhile contribution to the religious thought of its own day, and whether it offers ground for further advance. Judged by this test, Bultmann's thought must rank high among the theologies of the twentieth century—indeed, the present writer would say that it offers the most promising way forward for Christian theology at the present time. No doubt in the light of further discussion some of Bultmann's positions will call for modification, just as some of his difficulties will be resolved. He has said himself that the task of working out a program of demythologizing would be arduous enough to occupy scholars for a generation.

But leaving aside speculation about the future, we can be grateful for his initiative and for his profound and honest contribution which does so much to keep the Christian faith a living issue in the contemporary world.

Bibliography

Rudolf Bultmann and others, *Kerygma and Myth*, Hans W. Bartsch, ed., N.Y., Harper, 1961. (Harper Torchbooks).

John Macquarrie, *The Scope of Demythologizing: Bultmann and His Critics*, N.Y., Harper, 1961.

DIETRICH BONHOEFFER

Franklin Sherman

Although he met death in a concentration camp before he had attained the age of forty, Dietrich Bonhoeffer during his lifetime had already become well known in Germany for his personal and theological contributions to the church's struggle against Nazism. Since his death in 1945, and largely due to the impact of his posthumously published prison letters and fragmentary *Ethics,* his influence has spread throughout the Christian world.

Born in Breslau on February 4, 1906, Dietrich Bonhoeffer enjoyed the advantages of a highly cultured home. His father was a noted physician who from 1912 onward served as professor of psychiatry at the University of Berlin. Having decided to study theology, Dietrich attended lectures at Tübingen in 1923–24, but then returned to complete his education at Berlin. Here he encountered the liberal heritage of Troeltsch, and himself had the opportunity to study under the aged Harnack; but the young Bonhoeffer felt himself drawn increasingly toward the new "theology of crisis" being set forth elsewhere by Karl Barth.

After a year's internship in a German-speaking congregation in Barcelona, he was appointed a lecturer (*Privatdozent*) in theology at Berlin (1930). Before assuming his duties, however, he undertook a year's further study at Union Theological Seminary in New York. Here he first made the acquaintance of Reinhold Niebuhr and was able to become familiar with American religious life. In Berlin once again, in the fall of 1931, he served both as lecturer at the university and as pastor to students at the School of Technology. During the same period, Bonhoeffer began to take an active part in ecumenical affairs, at first primarily in the World Alliance for Promoting International Friendship through the Churches, which he served as a youth secretary for some years.

An early and outspoken antagonist of the Nazi regime, Bonhoeffer, on February 1, 1933, just two days after Hitler had become chancellor, gave a radio address on "Changes in the Concept of 'Leader' in the Younger Generation" which was cut off the air before completion. Shortly afterwards, in an essay on "The Church and the Jewish Question," Bonhoeffer called on the church vigorously to resist anti-Semitism both in civil society and in its own ranks. By the fall of 1933, however, he was sufficiently discouraged by the victory of the "German Christians" in the church elections to be willing to leave Germany for England, where he became pastor of two small German-speaking congregations in London. During this time there began his lasting friendship with the ecumenical leader G. K. A. Bell, Bishop of Chichester.

In 1935 Bonhoeffer returned to Germany to become leader of a seminary established to train pastors for the Confessing Church, which since the Barmen Synod of 1934 had come to embody the most uncompromising opposition to Nazi efforts to "coordinate" church and state. Although outlawed by the Gestapo two years later, the seminary was continued in a disguised form until 1940. Meanwhile, however, Bonhoeffer had experienced his second "American interlude." In view of the threat of his being drafted into the German army or imprisoned as a conscientious objector, arrangements had been made by Reinhold Niebuhr to secure him a position in the United States. But no sooner had he arrived in New York (June, 1939) than he was conscience-stricken at having forsaken his Christian brethren in Germany, and within a few weeks decided that he must return to share their fate.

Bonhoeffer soon became an especial target of suspicion of the authorities, and was required to report regularly to the police, and was forbidden to speak publicly or to have anything published. Yet at the same time his contacts with leaders of the resistance movement against Hitler (including high officials of the Military Intelligence Service) enabled him to secure credentials for travel on behalf of the resistance. At a fateful meeting with the Bishop of Chichester at Sigtuna, Sweden, in May, 1942, Bonhoeffer presented to the bishop for conveyance to the British government detailed information on the plans for overthrowing the Nazi regime, together with proposals for the subsequent establishment of peace. The proposals reached British foreign secretary Anthony Eden but were summarily rejected; "unconditional surrender" was to be the Allied policy.

The further suspicion that now fell on Bonhoeffer led eventually to his arrest on April 5, 1943. During the eighteen months that he was confined in Tegel Military Prison near Berlin, he was able to keep in touch with family and friends through correspondence (the letters published posthumously). The discovery of his connections with the group responsible for the July 20, 1944, attempt on Hitler's life led to his removal to maximum-security confinement, and finally to his execution at the concentration camp in Flossenberg on April 9, 1945, just a few days before the camp was liberated by the Allied forces.

The dramatic circumstances of Dietrich Bonhoeffer's death undoubtedly contributed to the impact made in English-speaking countries by the first of his books to be translated, *The Cost of Discipleship* (1948). Already when published in Germany in 1937, however, it had won considerable notice, both as a tract for the times and as a work of biblical interpretation. It is in the first chapter of this book that Bonhoeffer makes his famous attack on the "cheap grace" being marketed by the evangelical churches. Under cover of Luther's principle of justification by faith alone, he charges, believers have been relieved of the obligations of discipleship.

> Cheap grace means grace as a doctrine, a principle, a system. It means forgiveness of sins proclaimed as a general truth, the love of God taught as the Christian "conception" of God. . . . The Church which holds the correct doctrine of grace has, it is supposed, *ipso facto* a part in that grace. In such a Church the world finds a cheap covering for its sins; no contrition is required, still less any real desire to be delivered from sin.[1]

Distinguished from this is the "costly grace" that accompanies a life of discipleship. "Such grace is *costly*," writes Bonhoeffer, "because it calls us to follow, and it is *grace* because it calls us to follow Jesus Christ. It is costly because it costs a man his life, and it is grace because it gives a man the only true life."

[1] *The Cost of Discipleship,* 2d ed. (N.Y., Macmillan, 1959), p. 35.

This, he insists, is the grace of which Luther was speaking. For Luther, grace was the answer to an excruciating problem, whereas for his followers it has become an all too readily accepted presupposition. "When he spoke of grace, Luther always implied as a corollary that it cost him his own life."

On the difficult question of the relation between faith and works, Bonhoeffer points out that the standard Protestant formula has been something like this: "Only he who believes is obedient" (i.e., only works done in faith are truly good). Over against this Bonhoeffer places the converse: "Only he who is obedient believes" (only a faith expressed in works is truly faith). He then proceeds to expound, on the basis of relevant passages in the Synoptic Gospels, the notion of "discipleship," which, as he shows, uniquely combines these elements. Discipleship implies *faith* in the Lord one follows, and it implies *obedience* to the will of that same Lord. The Sermon on the Mount, to which Bonhoeffer devotes a good portion of the book, he interprets as a description of the life of discipleship. Jesus is here depicting the new righteousness that is to characterize the new community which he is gathering about himself. But conformity to these new criteria is possible only insofar as the disciples cling to Christ, who alone in his person has "fulfilled" all righteousness.

Bonhoeffer thus offers a christological interpretation of the Sermon: its demands have meaning only as utterances of the One whom the church worships as its Incarnate, Crucified, and Risen Lord. At the same time, he resists all efforts to interpret these demands in anything but their plain, literal sense. The words of Jesus call for "single-minded obedience." Discipleship necessitates a radical "breach with the immediacies of the world."

The concluding chapters of the book are devoted to placing the picture of the life of discipleship as we have it from the Synoptic Gospels into the context of Pauline theology. Bonhoeffer will hear nothing of a supposed conflict between these two parts of the New Testament: "The Jesus of the Synoptists is neither nearer nor further from us than the Christ of St. Paul." The great Pauline equivalent for "discipleship" is "baptism," which like the former involves the death of an old pattern of existence and the initiation of a new one. But baptism means entry into the church, which thus becomes the locus of the contemporary call to discipleship. "If you would hear the call of Jesus you need no personal revelation: all you have to do is to hear the sermon and receive the sacrament."

This emphasis on the communal context of the faith had already been evident in Dietrich Bonhoeffer's first published work, his doctoral dissertation entitled *Sanctorum Communio* ("The Communion of Saints"). The subtitle reveals the character of the project: "A Dogmatical Inquiry into the Sociology of the Church." The contribution of Ernst Troeltsch and his generation had been to focus attention on the sociological forms of the religious life. The Barthians, in contrast, were insisting on a purely theological conception of the church. The young Bonhoeffer now attempts to synthesize these two perspectives. The sociologist, he warns, must be wary of reducing the church to an example of some already established social type, without heeding the testimony of its own self-consciousness; this would be the "historicizing" misunderstanding of the church. But the theologian, for his part, must not overlook the sociological dimension; this would be the "religious" misunderstanding, which would have failed to take seriously "God's will that everything he reveals be revealed hiddenly, clothed in the garments of historical life—as in Christ, so in the church."

Human nature itself, Bonhoeffer reminds us, is inescapably social. It was the merit of the Hegelian philosophy to have made this clear. But Hegelianism tended to lose the concreteness of the individual by stressing the "structural openness" at the expense of the "structural closedness" of personal being. Crucial for the emergence of self-conscious personal life, Bonhoeffer emphasizes, is the encounter with the "limit," whether experienced as the claim of the other person or as the claim of the divine. As a matter of fact, these two claims coincide; for the divine Thou meets us precisely in the human thou. This is what Bonhoeffer calls an "ethical" as opposed to an "epistemological" interpretation of transcendence.

If man's very nature as a created being thus is social, the "fall" is equally communal. The doctrine of original sin implies the solidarity in guilt of the whole human race. Hence man's redemption must be equally corporate in character; and so it is, since it consists precisely in the creation of a community of the redeemed. In Jesus Christ as a "collective person," as "deputy" or "representative" for all mankind, the humanity of Adam is transformed into the humanity of Christ. Through his life, death, and resurrection, the communion of saints is realized. There is thus the closest possible identification between Christ and the church. "The Church," writes Bonhoeffer, "is the presence of Christ, as Christ is the presence of God." Or as he puts it in an adaptation of a phrase from Hegel, the church is "Christ existing as community."[2] Therefore the principle of the church's life can be none other than the same deputyship or vicarious love that was shown forth in Christ's own life. The Christian is dependent on his brother for the word of grace and for the word of counsel. It is in order to make concrete this mutual dependence of the brethren that Bonhoeffer here advocates, as he was to do repeatedly, the restoration of private confession, as well as a greater willingness to heed the ethical consensus of the church.

In his second dissertation (the *Habilitationsschrift* which qualified him to lecture in theology), Bonhoeffer again devotes himself to the doctrine of the church, this time employing it as the resolution of a basic problem in theology that he epitomizes in the title of the dissertation: *Act and Being*. How shall revelation be conceived? Only in terms of a series of discrete "acts" of God, a sequence of revelatory "moments" in which God "touches" man's existence? Or does revelation have a continuity, an historical embodiment of such a character that man's "being in" revelation is conceivable? The former is the viewpoint of Karl Barth—a man with whose theology the young Bonhoeffer, as we have noted, had much sympathy. But with respect to its denial of all "being" categories (i.e., its rejection of ontology), Barth's theology, Bonhoeffer charges, is determined more by Kantian philosophy than by the Bible. For the Bible does know of a continuity of man's being both "in Adam" and "in Christ."

"Being" theologies are those which stress the embodiment of

---

[2] *Christus als Gemeinde existierend.* The word *Gemeinde* has a wide range of meanings, but here it clearly refers to the specifically religious community; the phrase could therefore equally well be rendered "Christ existing as the church."

revelation in some form whereby it is more readily available, whether in the ecclesiastical institution (Roman Catholicism), in "pure doctrine" (Protestant orthodoxy), or in "religious experience" (Protestant liberalism). As against all these, the merit of the Barthian theology, according to Bonhoeffer, is that it has restored the realization that God is not, after all, at man's disposal; the initiative in revelation remains his. But this "act" theology fails to reckon with the fact that God in his mercy has, in another sense, chosen precisely to place himself at man's disposal, in that he has entered into history in Christ and in the church. As Bonhoeffer states in *Act and Being,* in words that were later to be echoed by Karl Barth himself:

> The question after all is not so much the freedom of God beyond his revelation, God's eternal remaining with-himself, his aseity, but rather God's coming forth, his coming out of himself in the revelation, his *given* word, his covenant. . . . God is not free from man, but for man. Christ is the word of the freedom of God. God *is* here, not in eternal non-objectivity, but—let us say it with all due caution—"havable," graspable in his word in his church.[3]

This is what Bonhoeffer calls a "material" as contrasted to a "formalistic" understanding of God's freedom: it is a freedom-in-Christ.

In a further criticism of act-theology as it affects our understanding of the life of faith, Bonhoeffer notes that Rudolf Bultmann, with his interpretation of faith as consisting in repeated acts of "decision," is unable to explain the continuity of the deciding self. Again, for Bonhoeffer, the continuity is to be found in the believer's life within the church. Yet the church itself, as he must emphasize once more against the theologies of being, remains constantly dependent on the "event" of preaching. Thus in the church—which is to say, in Christ-existing-as-community—Bonhoeffer finds the unity of contingency and continuity, of transcendentalism and ontology, of *Akt* and *Sein.*

It was the advent of Hitler's National Socialist regime that gave occasion for Bonhoeffer's doctrine of the church to be put

[3] (N.Y., Harper, 1961), pp. 67 ff.

to an acutely practical test. The Nazi efforts to infiltrate the church with their hypernationalistic ideology had been met with the ringing testimony of the Barmen Declaration (May, 1934) to the sole sovereignty of Jesus Christ, with its concomitant repudiation of the "false teaching that the church can and must recognize yet other happenings and powers, images and truths, as divine revelation alongside this one Word of God." Barmen further had warned against permitting the structure of church government to fall under the state's totalitarian control. It soon became evident, however, that the majority of the church leadership were more disposed to compromise with the proposals of the regime, even including the application of anti-Semitic legislation to converted Jews within the church. Further inroads by the Nazi ideology together with the assumption of arbitrary power by the new Hitler-sponsored "national bishop" Ludwig Mueller caused the Confessing Church group at its second synod (held in Martin Niemöller's church at Dahlem in October, 1934) to declare that the existing church government had in fact divorced itself from the Christian church. In its stead, Dahlem set up a "Provisional Church Government" with a "Council of Brethren" at its head.

Bonhoeffer's assuming the pastorate in London had removed him from the German scene just prior to these fateful meetings, but their decisions clearly represented his own position, and he quickly became one of the staunchest defenders of both the Barmen and the Dahlem declarations. He startled many of the Confessing Church leaders themselves with his readiness to identify these synodical pronouncements with the will of God. The Barmen Declaration he regarded as a genuine "confession" to be considered just as determinative for purity of doctrine as the classic Reformation documents. He prized, too, the unity between Lutheran and Reformed elements that had become visible in the confessing situation, and strongly opposed the later tendency to separate these elements again. Through his contacts in the ecumenical movement, Bonhoeffer agitated continually through the mid-thirties for the recognition of the Confessing Church as the sole body that could legitimately speak for German Protestantism, and to his own countrymen he stated, in an article published in 1936 that gave to the ancient principle *extra ecclesiam nulla salus* a disturbingly specific application: "Whoever knowingly separates himself from the Confessing Church in Germany separates himself from salvation."

This effort to define the limits of the church represented the negative side of Bonhoeffer's concern for the integrity of the community in Christ. The positive side came most fully to expression in his work as director of the seminary of the Confessing Church. Bonhoeffer had long since come to doubt the wisdom of entrusting theological education to the universities. Needed today, he had said, are "monastic-like schools" in which three things are taken seriously: pure doctrine, worship, and the Christian life. Alongside the seminary proper, he now established at Finkenwalde a "Brethren House" in which his long-standing emphasis on the concreteness of the communion of saints could find expression. Each resident pledged himself to share in a common regimen of daily prayer, oral confession of sin, shared livelihood, and readiness to answer any emergency call by the Confessing Church. When the seminary was forced underground in 1937, the Brethren House had to be discontinued. To preserve the fruits of the experiment, Bonhoeffer wrote the little book *Life Together* (published 1939), which had the largest sale of any of his writings during his lifetime, and which has been widely read in connection with the many similar ventures in communal living that have appeared in Protestantism since the end of World War II.

The book demonstrates that Bonhoeffer was well aware of the spiritual dangers attendant on such an enterprise. Its disciplines, he insisted, must be understood solely as means of preparation for effective service in the world, and its benefits received in trust for the whole church. He counseled the avoidance of all wish-dreams about what such life together would be like, and drew a clear distinction between the mutual deputyship of Christians and the merely human psychological phenomena of domination and dependency. "Let him who cannot be alone beware of community," he wrote. But he added, "Let him who is not in community beware of being alone."

Although he laid great emphasis upon the role of prayer in the life of both the individual and the community, Bonhoeffer apparently had little interest in the liturgical movement in a formal sense, and even had some suspicion of it. "Only he who cries out for the Jews dare also sing Gregorian," he once remarked. More important than the restoration of historic forms was learning to pray in one's own words. Similarly with respect to the interpretation of the Scriptures, he felt that the greatest need was not further training in "objective" scholarly research, but a recovery of the capacity to read the Bible as the Word of God, addressed to the community of faith.

We have a number of brief Bible studies from Bonhoeffer's hand, as well as one longer work based on his Berlin lectures and published in 1933 (English translation 1959) under the title *Creation and Fall: A Theological Interpretation of Genesis 1–3*. His interpretation here proves to be not only theological but christological. Genesis 1–3 deals with what is "in the beginning"; but, says Bonhoeffer, we are not "in the beginning" but "in the middle," and we know of the beginning only because the "end" has come upon us. The doctrine of the primeval state is "hope projected backwards." Thus Bonhoeffer's interpretation of the "image of God" in which man is created is christological. It consists in freedom; but this does not mean merely man's freedom from the limitations of the brute creation. Rather, just as God in Christ has shown his freedom to be a freedom not from but for man, so man's true freedom is a freedom for God and for his fellow man. This is the explanation of the *Imago dei* as an "analogy of relationship" that Barth later adopted from Bonhoeffer as a substitute for the Thomistic doctrine of analogy of being.

Creation and Fall is noteworthy for its anticipation of a number of themes that come to light again only in Bonhoeffer's last years. Among these is the insistence that God's presence is to be found not at the periphery of man's existence but at its center. This is the significance that Bonhoeffer sees in the placement of the Tree of Life "in the midst of the garden." Striking also is his interpretation of the creation of the woman to be man's "helper." Her deepest role is to help him not merely with his sundry tasks, but with his fundamental problem of learning to live within the limits of his finitude. "In his unfathomable mercy the Creator knew that this creaturely, free life can only be borne in limitation if it is loved, and out of his mercy he created a companion for man who is to be at once the embodiment of Adam's limit and the object of his love." When the primal pair do nevertheless transgress the limit, God still does not withdraw his mercy. He resolves to preserve even his fallen creatures: this is the significance that Bonhoeffer finds in the report at the close of Genesis 3 that "the Lord God made for Adam and his wife garments of skins, and clothed them." The orders of creation have become "orders of preservation on their way to Christ."

In the semester following his course on "creation and fall" Bonhoeffer devoted his Berlin lectures directly to the topic of Christology. Unfortunately these lectures never saw publication, nor has Bonhoeffer's manuscript for them been found; but his friend and posthumous editor Eberhard Bethge has made available a conflation of students' lecture notes that he believes to be a reasonably close equivalent to the original. This is included in the third volume of Bonhoeffer's *Gesammelte Schriften* (collected shorter writings), published in 1960.

Bonhoeffer divides the topic of Christology into three parts —the contemporary Christ, the historical Christ, the eternal Christ—although he was able to cover only two by the end of the semester. That he begins with the contemporary is significant; again, his stress is on "Christ existing as the church." As he puts it here in analogy to the Lutheran view of the Lord's Supper, the church *is* (not merely signifies) the Body of Christ. But even the historical Christ, he insists, did not exist in and for himself, but as a Christ "for me." This is the "deputyship" that he assumed not only for me but for the whole of nature and of history.

Bonhoeffer lays great stress on the "humiliation" of Christ and the "incognito" that makes him recognizable, whether historically or contemporaneously, only to faith. At the same time, he draws a sharp distinction between this humiliation and the incarnation as such. The humiliation is not God's becoming man (for this in itself is glorious), but the subjection of the Incarnate One to the conditions of existence under sin. Humiliation is concealment, while incarnation as such is revelation. The humiliation pertains to the fallen creation, the incarnation to the primal creation. The humiliation, therefore, is temporary, whereas the incarnation is permanent: with the return of Christ to the Father, humanity has been assumed into the eternal life of God himself.

With Luther, Bonhoeffer objects to any effort even to conceive of Christ's humanity and his divinity as separable entities. If Christ is the Logos (God's creative and communicative Word) made flesh, then, Bonhoeffer insists, everything that is asserted of the Logos can be asserted of the man Christ Jesus. The finite, as he maintains in conscious opposition to the Calvinist tradition, *can* contain the infinite.

The lectures on Christology remained incomplete, but in one of the concluding chapters of *The Cost of Discipleship,* Bonhoeffer further clarified his own position as well as its antecedents when he wrote:

> As they contemplated the miracle of the Incarnation, the early Fathers passionately contended that while it was true to say that God took human nature upon him, it was wrong to say that he chose a perfect individual man and united himself to him. God was made man. This means that he took upon him our entire human nature with all of its infirmity, sinfulness, and corruption, the whole of apostate humanity.[4]

Here Bonhoeffer reveals his dependence on the tradition, particularly strong in Greek theology, whereby the notion of humanity as an entity (rather than merely a plurality of individual men) makes it possible to conceive of the redemption as universal in its scope. As to the character of that redemption, Bonhoeffer describes it here as the restoration of the proper "form" of man as he was originally created in God's image. In Jesus Christ as the Incarnate, Crucified, and Risen One, this true image once again takes form in human history.

It was against such a background of ideas that Bonhoeffer undertook the project that was to occupy him during his final years: the writing of an ethic that should be both firmly grounded in Christology and oriented to man's concrete situation in the present hour. He was unable to complete the project, or even to pursue it very far into specific problems; what we

[4] P. 213.

have in the *Ethics* as published by Bethge in 1949 (English translation 1955) is more nearly a set of alternative beginnings for the book. Yet it has proved extremely influential, not only at the level of theological method but also as the testimony of a sensitive Christian conscience facing the collapse of the whole Western moral heritage in Nazi Germany.

The question of ethics, says Bonhoeffer, is the question of the "formation" of man. For Christians this can mean nothing other than "conformation" with Jesus Christ. To be conformed with the Incarnate One: this means to have the freedom to be the man one really is. While we are engaged in vain attempts to transcend our manhood, God affirms it by becoming man, real man. To be conformed with the Crucified: this means to submit oneself wholly to God's judgment, and thereby to be released from the world's criteria of success. To be conformed with the Risen One: this means to participate, though hiddenly, in the renewed humanity that the Risen Christ bears within himself. In all this, Bonhoeffer emphasizes, it is no alien form into which man is transformed, but rather his own proper form. "Man becomes man because God became man."

A life that is truly ethical, Bonhoeffer suggests, would combine simplicity with wisdom, in accordance with Jesus' counsel to be "wise as serpents and innocent as doves." But simplicity derives from single-hearted concentration upon God, while wisdom requires intimate acquaintance with the world. How are the two combinable? Only by virtue of the reconciliation between God and the world that has occurred in Christ.

> In Christ we are offered the possibility of partaking in the reality of God and in the reality of the world, but not in the one without the other. The reality of God discloses itself only by setting me entirely in the reality of the world, and when I encounter the reality of the world it is always already sustained, accepted and reconciled in the reality of God.[5]

Most ethical systems, Bonhoeffer notes, focus attention on those conflict situations in which life is threatened by some disvalue or by a clash of values. In the New Testament, however,

[5] *Ethics* (London, SCM Press, 1955), p. 61.

precisely because it springs from the reality of reconciliation, "the life and activity of men is not at all problematic or tormented or dark: it is self-evident, joyful, sure and clear." The Christian lives not by lists of prohibitions and requirements, but by God's commandment, which is distinguished from all human laws in that what it commands is freedom. The commandment of God is in fact nothing other than "the permission to live as man before God."

If Christian ethics thus is by nature wholly positive, it is also wholly concrete. The wise man, says Bonhoeffer, will be aware of the limited receptiveness of reality for "principles." The will of God is not a set of rules established in advance, but is "something new and different in each different situation in life." Bonhoeffer thus allies himself with what since has come to be known as "situation ethics" or "contextualism." But he carefully guards against the implication that God's will is therefore to be grasped solely by intuition; quite the contrary, "the whole apparatus of human powers," including the heart, the understanding, observation, and experience, is to be set in motion for the task of "proving" what is the will of God (Romans 12:2). It is in this connection that Bonhoeffer again calls for the restoration of private confession. Roman Catholicism, he says, with its strong emphasis in the training of its clergy on dealing with moral problems as encountered in the confessional, has tended to fall prey to legalistic casuistry. But Protestantism, with its almost exclusive emphasis on public preaching, has rested content with the enunciation of general moral principles that remain purely formal. Only by "rediscovering the divine office of confession," Bonhoeffer asserts, can the Protestant church "find its way back to a concrete ethic such as it possessed at the time of the Reformation."

In further explication of the way in which God's commandment confronts us, Bonhoeffer now introduces the concept of the "divine mandates"—marriage, labor, culture (sometimes listed by him under labor), state, and church. This he intended as a substitute for the traditional notion of the "orders of creation," to which he had long objected on account of its use to provide an unambiguous religious sanction for a given social order, whether the old order or the "new order" of National

Socialism. Already in 1932 he had proposed the substitution of the more functional concept of "orders of preservation," which were to be understood as retaining their legitimacy only so long as they actually served God's purpose to preserve the world for Christ. It was this latter category that Bonhoeffer had used in explanation of the pacifist position that he took during the 1930's. International peace, he had said, is the great "order of preservation" willed by God for our time. But he added the significant proviso that like all such orders it is relative, not absolute, and so can and must be broken when the higher criteria of truth and justice are endangered. Here was a little-noticed clue to Bonhoeffer's later willingness to cast his lot with military men in the resistance movement against Hitler.

By the time of his work on the *Ethics,* however, Bonhoeffer had become disillusioned by the uses to which even the concept of orders of preservation could be put in the defense of Nazism, and so had devised the new term "mandates." These are to be understood not as arising from below (i.e., from history itself) but as imposed from above; they are not earthly powers but divine commissions. True, the mandates do involve relationships of superiority and inferiority (father and child, teacher and learner, ruler and ruled, etc.), but the "superior" is distinctly limited. He is limited from above by the God who has conferred this deputyship upon him; from below by the just rights of the inferior; and laterally by the coexistence of the other mandates. The state thus has no warrant to invade and tyrannize the realm of culture or the family. Nor is the church called to dominate the other mandates; quite the contrary, it is the place where the commandment of Jesus Christ is to be made known as the "word of freedom" that emancipates each of the other mandates for the realization of its own essential character.

Bonhoeffer strenuously opposes what he calls the habit of "thinking in terms of two spheres," which assumes that life is divided into Christian and non-Christian sectors, the problem being somehow to relate the two. Whether it be the scholastic differentiation between nature and grace, the "pseudo-Lutheran" doctrine of two kingdoms, or the sectarian view of the struggle of the elect against a hostile world, the fault, he says, is the same: the assumption that there are realities outside the reality of

Christ. In truth, "there are not two realities, but only one reality, and that is the reality of God, which has become manifest in Christ in the reality of the world." He therefore proposes in place of the spatial concept of two spheres, the qualitative (or more precisely, eschatological) categories of "the ultimate and the penultimate." The ultimate reality of God's grace in Christ does not annihilate the penultimate reality of man's ongoing life in history, but rather validates it, while at the same time limiting it. The penultimate is preserved in order that it may become "the outer covering of the ultimate."

Within this realm of the penultimate, Bonhoeffer felt it crucially important that Christian ethics recover the ability to make distinctions between the relatively better and the relatively worse. In a widely noted section of the *Ethics* calling for a recovery of "the concept of the natural" in Protestant thought, Bonhoeffer points out that the Reformers' emphasis on the all-sufficiency of grace had unintended consequences:

> Before the light of grace everything human and natural sank into the night of sin, and now no one dared to consider the relative differences within the human and the natural, for fear that by their so doing grace as grace might be diminished. . . . The sole antithesis to the natural was the Word of God; the natural was no longer contrasted to the unnatural.[6]

The result was that the Christian conscience was left unassisted in vitally important decisions, while the realm of nature and of civil society was allowed to fall prey to forces of disorder. In a similar vein, Bonhoeffer objects to the church's glossing over of the difference between relatively good and relatively evil people, which has amounted sometimes to an actual preference for the latter (presumably on the grounds that they are more fit subjects for conversion). "Whatever humanity and goodness is found in this fallen world must be on the side of Jesus Christ," he writes. "It is nothing less than a curtailment of the gospel if the nearness of Jesus Christ is proclaimed only to what is broken and evil and if the father's love for the prodigal son is so emphasized as to appear to diminish his love for the son who remained at home."

[6] P. 101

The idea of "the natural" seems to have functioned for Bonhoeffer as still another equivalent for the concept of orders of preservation: it is the tendency toward health that God has implanted in the very structure of existence. "Life is its own physician," he notes, and "so long as life continues, the natural will always reassert itself." Included in the notion are natural rights and duties as well as natural relationships between man and man. In a chapter which was to provide a detailed exposition of these matters, Bonhoeffer begins with "the natural rights of bodily life," defending the legitimacy of bodily pleasures such as those of sex, food, and recreation, and discussing the problems of corporal punishment, torture, euthanasia, murder, suicide, and birth control. He intended to continue with sections on "the natural rights of the life of the mind" and "the natural right to work and property," but the chapter remained unfinished.

In thus setting out to articulate what apparently would have amounted to a full-fledged theory of natural law, Bonhoeffer did not feel that he had swerved from his original aim of founding an ethic wholly on Christology. For it is from Christ as Mediator of creation (i.e., as Logos) that the character of all created things derives. The incarnation only reinforces this relationship. "Just as in Christ the reality of God entered into the reality of the world, so, too, is that which is Christian to be found only in that which is of the world, the 'supernatural' only in the natural, the holy in the profane, and the revelational only in the rational." In fact it is only the Christian believer, Bonhoeffer asserts, who is able to live a truly natural and "worldly" life, since only he is free from the need to deify the world. For the Christian knows that precisely in its secularity, the world has already been accepted by a gracious God.

Bonhoeffer seems to have had a premonition that this work on ethics would be the last book to which he would set his hand. "I often feel as though the best part of my life was already past," he wrote from prison in December, 1943, "and that all I have to do now is to finish my *Ethics*." What he could not foresee was that the letters he was writing to parents and friends during these very months would when published later (in German, 1951; English translation 1953), have an impact equal to or greater than that of any of his other works. In part this is due to the intimate portrait of the man Dietrich Bonhoeffer that they offer, especially of the remarkable intellectual life that he was able to sustain even in prison. He read avidly in everything from Plutarch to the church fathers to nineteenth-century romantic literature. The letters are most notable, however, for the theological discussions with his friend Eberhard Bethge in which he pursues the idea of "Christian worldliness."

The urgency of the theme derives from Bonhoeffer's conviction that we have arrived at the end of the "religious" era in our culture. From the thirteenth century onward, man has been learning how to get along without any hypothesis of "God"; indeed, he has lost practically all awareness of what "God" might mean. This development, which Christian apologists almost universally deplore as "secularization," Bonhoeffer describes simply as the world's arrival at "adulthood" (*Mundigkeit*), its having "come of age." This he regards as an irreversible development. What are its consequences for the Christian faith?

> The thing that keeps coming back to me [he writes in April, 1944] is, what *is* Christianity, and indeed what *is* Christ, for us today? The time when men could be told everything by means of words, whether theological or simply pious, is over, and so is the time of inwardness and conscience, which is to say the time of religion as such. We are proceeding towards a time of no religion at all: men as they are now simply cannot be religious any more. . . . Our whole nineteen-hundred-year-old Christian preaching and theology rests upon the "religious premise" of man. What we call Christianity has always been a pattern—perhaps a true pattern—of religion. But if one day it becomes apparent that this *a priori* "premise" simply does not exist, but was an historical and temporary form of human self-expression . . . what does that mean for Christianity?[7]

In the letters that we have available (others were destroyed when Bethge was arrested), Bonhoeffer is hardly able to begin an answer to his own question, but several things are clear.

---

[7] *Prisoner for God* (N.Y., Macmillan, 1954), p. 122. (British ed. is entitled *Letters and Papers from Prison,* as is 1962 U.S. ed.)

First, a Christianity appropriate to a world come of age would speak of God "not on the borders of life but at its center." Bonhoeffer has no patience with the effort to spy out human weaknesses and drive men to despair before the Gospel can be preached, or with the use of God as a stop-gap for the incompleteness of our scientific knowledge. "We should find God in what we do know, not in what we don't," he writes. "We must not wait until we are at the end of our tether: he must be found at the center of life: in life, and not only in death; in health and vigor, and not only in suffering; in activity, and not only in sin."

Secondly, the church in the new age will have to learn what it means to live in deputyship for man. Bonhoeffer was critical even of the Confessing Church in this respect:

> During these years the church has fought for self-preservation as though it were an end in itself, and has thereby lost its chance to speak a word of reconciliation to mankind and the world at large. So our traditional language must perforce become powerless and remain silent, and our Christianity today will be confined to praying for and doing right by our fellowmen. Christian thinking, speaking, and organization must be reborn out of this praying and this action.[8]

Thirdly, when the church does speak again, a new language will be required. It is in this connection that Bonhoeffer introduces his famous proposal for a "non-religious interpretation of Biblical terminology" (and of theological concepts generally). His remarks on the subject are so tantalizingly brief that in subsequent discussion there has been a natural tendency to identify them with the more fully articulated "demythologizing" program of Bultmann, although Bonhoeffer himself, on the basis of Bultmann's key essay of 1941, explicitly rejected such an identification. "I am of the view," he wrote, "that the full content, including the mythological concepts, must be maintained. The New Testament is not a mythological garbing of the universal truth—this mythology (resurrection and so on) is the thing itself—but the concepts must be interpreted in such a way as not to make religion a pre-condition of faith (cf. circum-

[8] P. 140.

cision in St. Paul)." In the latter respect, Bonhoeffer stated,
Bultmann had not gone far enough. Neither had Karl Barth,
who although he had begun the criticism of religion had lapsed
into a mere "positivism of revelation," a "take it or leave it"
attitude.

In undertaking a nonreligious interpretation of biblical concepts such as he proposes, the church would only be permitting
the Bible to assume its own true character again, Bonhoeffer
is convinced, for the Bible knows nothing of "religion" in the
ordinary sense. "Religion" is concerned with inwardness, the
Bible with the whole man. "Religion" is individualistic, while
the Bible is concerned with corporate existence. "Religion" is
metaphysical, i.e., interested in a world beyond; the Bible is
concerned with the renewal of this world. This nonreligiousness
is clearest in the case of the Old Testament, but it is equally
true of the New Testament, Bonhoeffer asserts, when it is interpreted as it should be, in the light of the Old. "Jesus does not
call men to a new religion, but to life."

In the subsequent discussion of Bonhoeffer's thought, it has
been much debated whether the theme of the "worldliness" of
Christianity as we have it in the letters represents a departure
from Bonhoeffer's earlier theology or is in continuity with it.
Undoubtedly there are grounds for both positions. The letters
do present a contrast with the tendency in *The Cost of Discipl*-
ship to draw a sharp line of demarcation between church and
world; Bonhoeffer himself was quite aware of this contrast (see
his letter of July 21, 1944). But the motif of worldliness can
also be seen as in direct continuity not only with his *Ethics* but
also with his earlier work, especially *Creation and Fall* and the
lectures on Christology. It is in his doctrine of Christ, both as
the Mediator of creation and as the crucified Redeemer, appearing in humiliation to reconcile God and the world, that
Bonhoeffer's theme of "Christian worldliness" is rooted.

Man is challenged to participate in the sufferings of God at
the hands of a godless world. This is the decisive difference between Christianity and all religions. Man's religiosity makes him
look in his distress to the power of God in the world; he uses
God as a *Deus ex machina*. The Bible however directs him to
the powerlessness and suffering of God; only a suffering God

can help. To this extent we may say that the process we have described by which the world came of age was an abandonment of a false conception of God, and a clearing of the decks for the God of the Bible, who conquers power and space in the world by his weakness.[9]

[9] P. 164.

Bibliography

Dietrich Bonhoeffer, *Letters and Papers from Prison*, N.Y., Macmillan, 1962.

John D. Godsey, *The Theology of Dietrich Bonhoeffer*, Philadelphia, Westminster, 1960.

PAUL TILLICH

Walter Leibrecht

Paul Tillich has spoken to modern man with great penetration. It is the honesty with which he approaches reality and the freshness with which he discusses the perplexities and joys of our individual and collective lives that make his writings fascinating.

Tillich is a thinker working on the frontiers of thought. One might call him a philosopher's philosopher, as Einstein was a scientist's scientist. He has influenced many men in the field of philosophy and theology, and mainly through such men made an impact on contemporary thought. He is not one of those who counsels the skeptical modern man to abandon his autonomy as the root of his lostness and to subject himself without questioning to the doctrines and authority of the church. For Tillich, modern man has no possible way back to medieval heteronomy, to a faith understood as intellectual sacrifice. Where faith is possible only by the suppression of doubt, Tillich asserts, it will likely result in fanaticism or cynicism; indeed, it is modern man's doubt that testifies to the intensity of his quest for absolute truth. In his presentation of the Christian faith Tillich does not ignore modern man's intense desire for truth and, sharing this desire himself, he is constantly seeking the meaning of the Christian doctrines.

As there is no truth without doubt, so there is no being without nonbeing. And as truth is present in the moment of doubt, there is for Tillich no realm of life, even life in estrangement, which exists without relation to the ultimate. This, to him, is the very center of Christian faith. Man experiences the presence of the ultimate in the moment of utter estrangement and despair—which signifies that in the moment of separation he may be close to God as the origin of his being. As with Luther, Pascal, and others, it has been Tillich's experience that the way to God—to truth, to ultimate reality—leads through the desert. In the moment of despair, in the moment life is threatened by meaninglessness, man reaches out for meaning—for being. The word "being," which is of central importance in Tillich's vocabulary, is not a static but a dynamic word. Thus he speaks of the "power of being"—that to which I reach out and that by which my whole being can be grasped. Tillich refuses to speculate as a detached observer about being as such. Being itself is the very ground of my being, that by which I live. It is not a physical reality up in the clouds. It can be given expression only through the ultimate character of my faith.

Paul Tillich and Karl Barth offer two great theological alternatives in our generation. Barth's theology tends to be swallowed up in Christology; it rejects the possibility of any natural theology, describes the God-man relationship primarily in terms of sin and forgiveness and sees the human life as being determined by the historical acts of God's salvation. Barth concentrates on the acts of God and is highly dialectical in regard to the question of how these acts actually determine and shape human life.

Tillich starts from the central Christian conviction that the word became flesh—that the Logos entered reality and that reality, individual as well as cultural, is transformed through crisis and renewal by the power of divine grace. Man, by the very fact that he is and not merely by his being baptized, is related to the divine and dependent on it. For Tillich Christianity is the revelation not of new beliefs or doctrine but of a new reality which is at work renewing the old. Tillich deplores the attempts of many of the despisers of religion in our time to cut religion off from life and thus make it meaningless. This is the basic goal of secularism—to claim the world in its material reality for itself and to restrict religion to the realm of fancy and dreams.

Tillich feels that Barthian dialectical theology offers only a wooden sword in the struggle against secularism, since such theology tends to agree with secularism's basic assumption that in its creatureliness the world as such does not reveal its divine origin. Condemning natural theology, the followers of Barth seem not to recognize that life as such is related to its divine originator and is therefore sacred. Tillich is convinced that it is the task of the theologian to witness to the holiness of all being and to proclaim that everything that is, is only through the power and grace of God, and that therefore the profane and the sacred cannot be artificially separated.

Like Barth, Tillich rejects the nineteenth-century culture-Protestantism which tended to adapt religion to the demands of modern civilization to such an extent that civilization itself determined the content of faith. But while Barth repudiates the mediating role of theology, Tillich accepts it as an essential part of theology. In this sense Tillich continues the great nineteenth-century theological tradition of mediation, with its effort to overcome the schizophrenic split between the religious and the scientific consciousness of modern man. However, Tillich approaches the problem from an entirely new angle and does so within the intellectual and cultural situation of the twentieth century. Mediation is for him never an easy or uncritical adaption of religion to modern man's cultural or scientific maxims. He does not seek the absorption of the religious into the secular as present-day secularism demands. Nor does he share the romantic dreams of those who think it possible to return to a medieval order in which the secular is subservient to the ecclesiastical. Opposed both to a secularized culture separated from religious concern and to any sort of ecclesiastical imperialism, Tillich seeks a true reconciliation between the religious and the secular.

Tillich takes seriously the Johannine statement that "God so loved the *world* that he sent his only begotten son." Therefore a purely spiritual or ecclesiastical salvation would not for him be Christian salvation. Salvation—the reality of the "new being" as revealed in Jesus Christ—is always concerned with man and his world; divine grace reuniting and healing man's broken life encompasses the totality of man's world. From this centrally Christian concern for salvation Tillich as theologian and philosopher sets out on his task of mediation. Here is where he breaks with neo-orthodox colleagues who concentrate on theology yet often leave the fallen world to its own devices.

Religion is defined by Tillich as the dimension of depth in all of man's life functions, rather than as a special function of his spiritual life. But, contrary to the charge of some of his critics, he does not thereby reduce religion to a merely human act, for by "dimension of depth" Tillich refers to that which is ultimate, infinite, and unconditional in man's spiritual life. Hence he defines religion or faith as "ultimate concern," as concern directed toward the ultimate. And as ultimate concern religion is at the origin of all cultural expression, giving substance, meaning, judgment, and creative courage to all the functions of the human spirit. Both religion in its forms of expression and culture are grounded in the experience of ultimate concern and therefore belong together. Their separation in contemporary life, Tillich asserts, is artificial and must be overcome if religion is to remain pertinent and our culture creative. Both religion and culture can issue in demonic perversion and destruction wherever a finite entity or ideal rather than the ultimate is the focus of their unconditional concern.

In his basic approach Tillich is a philosopher of religion. The true theologian, he contends, cannot avoid being a philosopher; instead of using philosophical forms in an underhanded or uncritical way the theologian ought to be fully conscious of the philosophical framework within which he operates. Tillich rejects the kind of religious philosophy inherent in the approach of much neo-orthodox theology, according to which the meeting of God and man is merely accidental since God and man do not essentially belong together. Over against this approach Tillich opts for the ontological approach, according to which man discovers himself when he discovers God—discovers something that is identical with himself although it transcends him infinitely, something from which he is estranged but from which he has never been nor can be separated. Tillich is convinced that the ontological method—used, among many others, by Augustine—not only represents the true emphasis of Christian faith but is basic for every genuine philosophy of religion. He is also convinced that only on such a basis can the destructive cleavage between philosophy and theology be overcome and a reconciliation between religion and secular culture achieved. However, having discovered this ontological principle implicit in classic Augustinianism, Tillich sometimes carries his effort to overcome the gap between religion and culture to a point where the offered reconciliation is one of "mere thought." Although Tillich rejects the Hegelian reconciliation by thought and the Barthian reconciliation by faith and demands reconciliation in reality, he is tempted to fall back on a philosophy of consciousness whenever he moves from basic Christian existential experience into ontological analysis, applying the Hegelian maxim that everything that is real is also rational—a maxim which hardly seems commensurate with the words of the Creator in Genesis: ". . . and God saw that it was good."

Nonetheless Tillich the Christian existentialist keeps Tillich the ontologist from giving way to the notion of a philosophical salvation. Like Kierkegaard, he believes that the ultimate discloses itself only to the "passionate" man, the man who allows himself to be "grasped by the ultimate." As an adherent of the passionate approach Tillich holds that faith can be expressed not in terms of objective experience but only through symbols and myth—a problem he discusses in his many writings on the nature of symbol, myth, and religious language. But whereas Kierkegaard was satisfied with direct existential expressions of an existential religious attitude, Tillich attempts to translate this attitude into philosophic expressions and concepts.

Clearly recognizing the inner limitations of existentialism and existentialist psychoanalysis, Tillich nevertheless feels that these two movements have bestowed a "tremendous gift" on modern theology in terms of understanding the human situation. He interprets both existentialism and depth psychology as modern expressions of the age-old protest against philosophies of consciousness. In his view existentialism's emphasis on the unconscious and the irrational will and its analysis of human predicament and estrangement were transformed by Freud into a methodological scientific language. Existentialism and depth psychology are thus for him inseparable. Though their great significance lies in their detailed descriptions of man's existential predicament and estrangement, they are also significant insofar as they point at least indirectly to man's teleological nature. Existentialism and depth psychology are, however, both unable and unwilling to define this true nature of man; though they raise the ultimate questions of life in a profound way, they cannot answer the questions they ask. Neither do they in themselves have the capacity to heal the disruption they have discovered. In Tillich's opinion the psychologist may be able to treat a person's pathological symptoms, but he cannot deal with the basic existential estrangement that made escape into neurosis or psychosis desirable or necessary in the first place. States Tillich: "Neither existentialist analysis nor psychological methods can overcome the existential negativity, meaninglessness and guilt which not only the sick person, but man universally carries." This existential estrangement which cannot be healed by the most refined therapeutic techniques is, as Tillich puts it, "the object of salvation." In this regard Tillich has been instrumental in suggesting ways in which the psychologist and theologian can work together. He indicates how the theologian can benefit from the psychologist, but he also shows how the psychologist needs grace—the power to heal—in order really to address himself meaningfully to man's root problem and thus do more than merely relieve the patient's symptoms of his deeper suffering.

Parallel to his relating of religion and depth psychology, Tillich deals in ever new and fresh approaches with the basic relatedness of the center of our faith to the various secular spheres. The special merit of Tillich's many writings on theology vis-à-vis culture, science, and politics consists in their combination of profound thought penetrating into the very structure of reality and seeking the basic relatedness of religion to the field in question, and practical down-to-earth advice directed not only to ministers but to doctors, artists, educators, and others concerning the achievement of the kind of cooperation in creative tension through which reconciliation can be realized.

The key term in Tillich's understanding of religion and culture and their mutual relatedness is "ultimate concern." Faith as ultimate concern signifies first of all that it is an act of one's whole being and not only his mind. It also signifies that only that concern which is directed to the ultimate as such deserves to be called faith. Tillich has noted man's inclination to be idolatrous, to make something in the finite world his ultimate concern, and that wherever man focuses his ultimate loyalty on something which is not ultimate he brings destruction upon himself. The most ideal-sounding goal will corrupt us if we confuse the finite with the infinite. Whether it be the ideal of national honor as in fascism or the socialist state of communism, as soon as it is declared absolute all else is sacrificed to its achievement, and incalculable suffering follows for those who do not adhere to it. Likewise, if modern man makes success, ambition, happiness or honor his ultimate concern, it brings suffering upon himself and others and he becomes impervious to all the other concerns of life. Only the ultimate itself deserves ultimate concern. This does not mean, in Tillich's view, that we should withdraw from the world into some vague mysticism, shunning all involvement and practical action. On the contrary, if we are ultimately concerned, our inner being will not be dominated by one concern; rather, it will express itself in new integration and wholeness. If we are ultimately concerned, all our finite concerns will be informed by ultimate concern, becoming the media and expression of ultimacy itself.

The great painter, Tillich writes, is not a man who falls in love with the aesthetic effects of his painting, but one who creates a great work because he is ultimately concerned. The mark of the true genius is that he is dissatisfied with himself and ceaselessly tries to express something ultimate. A culture without ultimate concern, Tillich is convinced, will lose its creative power. He points to the loss of ultimate concern—of any sense for transcendent reality—in the civilization of the second half of the nineteenth century. He is merciless in his attack on the spirit of placid finitude which he sees expressed in the artistic, political, cultural, and even ecclesiastical world of the late nineteenth and early twentieth centuries. In his eyes Western bourgeois society and its civilization are doomed to destruction not from without but from within. Accordingly, his method has become radical analysis, attacking the "self-complacency and self-sufficiency" inherent in our culture.

The total world view of nineteenth-century man was shaped by his utter confidence in inevitable progress—progress defined by ever-increasing material wealth and opportunities. But World War I broke his world to pieces. He discovered that science, his precious instrument for mastering the world, had turned against him by becoming a means of mass destruction. When Tillich returned from that war, a social revolution was afoot in his native Germany. The question in his mind was, What is the task of the postwar generation? Was it the demand of the hour to mend the broken house of the nineteenth century—to join the ranks of the conservatives and nationalists, as most of Germany's educated people thought, particularly those active in the churches? Or was the world of the past beyond repair, making a new structure necessary? Tillich felt that after the revolution a new kind of civilization should be introduced. The immediate task for the intellectual, as he understood it, was to identify himself with the rebelling proletariat. The fact that the proletariat fought for the socialist cause and that socialism seemed to reject religion did not disturb him fundamentally. He felt that there was promise in the irreligious character of the rising proletariat, since it challenged hypocritical and smug middle-class religiosity. Tillich believed that among the frustrated unemployed and those of the working class who had been deprived of all opportunity creatively to express their true humanity he would find a deep desire for true self-realization. These men, he thought, could become the bearers of a new culture in which man could freely realize his own potential.

Together with some friends, Tillich founded a movement for religious socialism in Germany. They hoped to lead the proletariat to a new and deeper understanding of their goal, to interpret its deeper meaning to its followers. The principle out of which this new society was to grow was "theonomy." Theonomy as a divine demand Tillich set in opposition to modern man's oscillation between empty individualistic autonomy and imposed totalitarian heteronomy. Theonomy, he said, is not a divine law over and against man that demands his total subjection, nor is it a disguised form of heteronomy; it is a form of culture in which all concerns of life are informed by ultimate concern. Theonomy does not impose on man's reason beliefs which are strange to man's rational nature; rather, it is "autonomous reason united with its own depth."

Religion is here understood by Tillich as the root of culture— culture as the efflorescence of religion. Accordingly he is concerned to show what he feels is the essential relatedness of each cultural expression to its religious ground. Theonomy also, Tillich believes, creates a basis for a truly ecumenical encounter between Protestantism and Catholicism. Theonomy includes the

Protestant principle of protest against any form of idolatry, but unites Protestant prophetism with priestly sacramentalism by the awareness of the holiness of all being and the awareness that the presence of being, of God, always is dynamic, overcoming and renewing all that is old. The prophet speaking the word of crisis becomes the priest healing that which is broken.

But Tillich's hope for the realization of religious socialism informed by theonomy never came true. The dehumanized and dishonored proletariat felt its needs more directly expressed by a man like Hitler, who promised them bread and work, an automobile and security. Both politically and theologically, it was heteronomy and its accompanying totalitarianism which became the dominant trend in the Germany of the late 1920s.

A few weeks before the Nazis' rise to power, Tillich published a book in which he warned his countrymen against Nazism and its demand for ultimate loyalty to something which was not ultimate. The rise of the Führer was, for Tillich, a truly demonic development which could lead only to destruction. Along with Thomas Mann, Albert Einstein, and others, he had to leave his country in 1933, emigrating to the United States at the age of forty-seven though he had no knowledge of the English language. The fact that he has since become one of America's leading spirits is a compliment both to the man and his rare intellectual power and to the country ready to receive him as one of her own and to listen to him. Whereas in Germany Tillich was chiefly a philosopher, he has primarily been a theologian during his years in the United States.

Although religious socialism did not find its actualization in history, it did contribute importantly to modern thought. In particular it articulated new truth and insight about man's nature and the meaning of history. Tillich had spoken of the *kairos* of religious socialism. *Kairos* means the fulfilled time—the right moment to act in a given situation. Every kairos situation expresses its own inner demand. Kairos is the moment when time is invaded by eternity. In the kairos situation the restoring power of being is present—the power which transforms man and society and which fulfills what is potential in history and nature.

The concept of kairos informs Tillich's whole approach to

ethics. He is concerned not so much with the eternal law written down once and for all as with the ethical demand of a given situation. While he finds the material for his ethics in an ontological analysis of love, power, and justice, he rejects any casuistics and emphasizes the need for a new decision or act which will do justice to a situation's inner demand. Thus careful analysis is the precondition for ethical decision.

Kairos, eternity in time, becomes also the key for a new interpretation of history. Contrary to what some of the late romantics thought, history knows no static, timeless togetherness of the infinite and the finite; for Tillich history is a process of moving from one transition to the next—a process of eternal crisis and renewal. This is the way in which the power of being is present in history—not as a superhistorical reality but as the ultimate ground and power of every historical situation. Hence historical interpretation cannot rest content with the compilation of historical data but must grasp the depths of reality in which its divine foundation and meaning become visible. "Historical realism" reaches the ultimate ground of meaning of a historical situation and, through it, of being itself. Tillich shows that the historian must write as a man who participates in history—a man involved in the contemporary struggle. The historian has a kind of prophetic responsibility: he must be able to understand the structural necessities of the present and derive from such analysis a direction for action. Freedom to act is possible only by means of a thorough analysis of the given situation; man has the power to transform history only if he knows what is involved. Thus an understanding of kairos in history has profound ethical consequences. In every crisis situation man is confronted with a new creative possibility. Every historical situation has an aspect of destiny, but man can make a decision and, if it is based on a thorough understanding of what is given, he can act freely. This freedom is never infinite, however. Tillich's awareness that human freedom is always limited and finite leads him to emphasize the tragic element in human existence. With Kierkegaard and Heidegger he can say that "man is finite freedom," which means that while man cannot be man without actualizing his freedom, through the act of self-actualization he estranges himself from his original union with being, from his state of "dreaming innocence." Here we see the strong influence of Schelling in Tillich's thought.

Even ethical action cannot lead to reunion with God. It is not the awareness of the radical character of depravity which leads Tillich to the assumption that a mere ethical reconciliation is impossible, but his idealist notion that man, originally in paradisic unity with being and thus in a state of dreaming innocence, separates himself from the divine by exercising his freedom—i.e., by any act in which he realizes his freedom in a finite world. Once separation has taken place, once dreaming innocence is lost, it is impossible for man to achieve by his own efforts a reunion with God, with the ground of being. Thus we are estranged, and action leads only to further estrangement. Reunion with being—the overcoming of estrangement—is possible only when man's heart lets itself be grasped by the divine spirit, only when being itself, entering man, overcomes and conquers the resistance of estrangement and despair.

In his emphasis on the power of reconciliation which is necessary to reunite the separated one with the ground of being Tillich often seems closer to the Greek tradition than to biblical thought. In the Old Testament it is man's disobedience, his use of his freedom against the will of God, which estranges him from God, rather than his use of freedom as such. The Greek concept of freedom evokes a tragic connotation insofar as freedom is viewed both as the means by which man realizes his true being and as the means by which he separates himself from the grace of the gods. For the biblical writers man is constantly abusing his freedom by making himself the end of all things. But they do not look upon freedom as such as a destructive element; for the most part they praise it highly. Even Paul, in his interpretation of Adam's fall as having become the destiny of mankind, does not necessarily identify estrangement with man's self-actualization as such. Tillich tends to combine Greek and Christian insights concerning estrangement in his statement of the fundamental predicament of human existence. But in his thought the feeling of tragic inevitability is united with an overpowering feeling of guilt, revealing his deep kinship to Kierkegaard.

As a philosopher Tillich has asked unceasingly the question

of man's being, has relentlessly sought the meaning of man's life. The analysis of man's estranged situation is the center of Tillich's philosophical effort. It is the philosopher's task to analyze the human situation and to invite man to a radical act of self-knowledge. But knowledge cannot effect reconciliation. Only a new reality can do this, and it is the theologian's task to proclaim and open up this new reality. Thus it became a necessity for Tillich to be not only a philosopher but also a theologian. Tillich has a place in the great tradition of Christian mysticism; in his writing traditional theology is not simply recapitulated in orthodox fashion but becomes instrumental in the expression of his own encounter with the divine. He is a theologian as one who is "ultimately concerned."

At the same time, like many of the great mystics, Tillich has no intention of abandoning classic Christian doctrines. What he does is to show their true and deeper meaning by interpreting them symbolically. Symbol and myth are two of the most important categories in Tillich's thought. He rejects all literalistic interpretation of the biblical witness. The ultimate cannot be expressed directly, Tillich emphasizes, because the infinite is beyond the finite, and every finite picture we use to point to the infinite can be employed only analogically and symbolically. But he also rejects any reference to a particular Christian doctrine as "only a symbol." Symbol and myth are the highest forms of religious speech, and a true symbol participates in the reality which it symbolizes. As such, a symbol becomes a bearer of revelation, a self-manifestation of the ultimate.

It is not, Tillich insists, the task of the theologian to create new symbols; in fact symbols cannot be created: they grow and die. If we are fully conscious of the intellectual and spiritual atmosphere of our time we will know which symbols have the power to manifest the ultimate for our time. There are certain symbols, Tillich feels, which in the Middle Ages or the Reformation period were extremely powerful but which do not convey reality to the man of the twentieth century. He maintains, for instance, that just as the powerful symbol of the Virgin Birth lost significance in the piety of the Reformers, the symbol of God as the father often evokes the wrong connotations in modern man. No doubt Tillich has done great service to modern theology in showing that many biblical expressions are used symbolically rather than literally; he thereby has made many Christian teachings newly acceptable to modern men. However, his preoccupation with symbol, and particularly with the central symbol of the Christian faith, Jesus as the Christ, has often led him to lose interest in the historical aspect of the event symbolically interpreted.

Led by his awareness of the kairos situation in history—in which something new appears, creating a crisis for the old—Tillich finds a new interest in Christology, which for him becomes central to any serious effort of Christian thought. Since the presence of the new in our lives and in history is not static but is a "breaking into existence," the New Being which appears in Jesus as the Christ is to be understood as the breaking into existence of the power of the New Being. When Tillich's terms such as "kairos situation" and "the demand of the hour" were misused by adherents of Nazism and applied to their movement and leader, he had to make unmistakably clear what the ultimate criterion of every kairos situation is.

This criterion is the "logos," the New Being which appeared in Jesus, the Christ. Christ as Jesus, as the bearer of the New Being, surrenders his finitude and thus becomes completely transparent to the ultimate he reveals. Tillich says that Jesus is the Christ through his sacrificing that which is Jesus to that which is Christ. Since Jesus is able to do this without losing himself, he must first completely possess himself. This means that Jesus as the Christ is truly united with the ground of being and thus can be called the "true man." In him essential manhood is revealed. This and not any of his personal finite characteristics is what makes him the Christ. His personality, teachings, and acts are not the cause but the expression of his being the Christ. In Tillich's view any attempt to make the finite self of Jesus the object of religious devotion is to be rejected as idolatry. Neither Jesus himself nor the church but only that to which he witnesses is final. This does not mean that Tillich takes the biblical picture of Jesus lightly. In fact he continually uses the episodes, parables, and teachings of Jesus as the basis of his sermons. But through the presentation of these the ultimate itself becomes manifest. The New Being which is in Christ is for Tillich the creative power which is active in all history.

For Tillich the Christ-event is the key to the very structure of the universe; it is the revelation of the ultimate relationship of the divine and the human. It leads Tillich to the ontological statement that the holy and the profane cannot be separated, and to the insight that ultimate reality or the power of being is the power of history itself and cannot be understood in a supernaturalistic sense. It is the power of history constantly overcoming that which is old and reconciling that which is separated. This is the power of the New Being.

Tillich's emphasis on the universal meaning of that which was revealed in the Christ-event was a needed balance in contemporary theology. Nonetheless the question remains whether the revelation of God through Christ gives way for Tillich to some form of higher gnosis—to an ontology which perhaps makes faith unnecessary. Tillich deals with this problem himself in his book *Dynamics of Faith*. While faith always leads to gnosis, gnosis cannot, he says, substitute for faith. Faith is always conquering doubt and as long as we remain human, faith involves risk. Tillich's theology of the New Being finds powerful expression also in his volume of sermons titled *The New Being,* and more thorough expression in his *Systematic Theology.*

Tillich's emphasis on the healing function of the New Being has led him to a rediscovery of the original meaning of the word "salvation"—namely, healing, making whole that which is broken. It is this latter emphasis which has drawn him into vital discussions with men in the healing professions. Only the reality of the New Being of grace can heal that basic estrangement of man from his true self—from the ground of his being.

The power of the New Being, says Tillich, is expressed in love which overcomes all separations. If I am driven by love, I participate in the power of love and therefore in the power of being. Tillich's analysis of the nature of love is one of the deepest reflections of his philosophical mind. In his volume *Love, Power and Justice* he discusses libido, eros, philia, and agape not as different types of love but as aspects of the one true love, as forms of man's self-realization. Tillich confronts the self-realization through freedom which leads to estrangement with the self-realization through love, finding in the actualization of ourselves in and through love a way of fulfillment in which separation is overcome. Love does not always lead to freedom, but freedom can be truly experienced only through love. He further points out that there is no such thing as true love in which one does not do justice to and respect the freedom of the other person; both justice and freedom need love to remain just and free. Love makes us whole again, makes us real by making each of us a self-related being able to resist dissolving into something else.

If one embraces this reality of love, having recognized its truly healing function, must one, in Tillich's view, go back to the Christian faith to find its original source? In making self-realization the ultimate criterion of religion and love and by defining love as the power toward self-realization, does not Tillich elevate the eros concept of love over others? Is not his view tempered by Plato's concept of eros seeking fulfillment through self-realization of the individual and by the romantic ideal of the individual personality? Tillich united the basic insights of Greek thought and classic Christian theology in a form in which both become newly relevant to modern man. There are, however, tremendous inner tensions in his thought which cannot easily be overcome by the rationality of his system. His work does not present us with ready answers, but it does offer us new questions—questions which will stimulate the discussion of a whole generation of theologians.

Theologians in all ages have felt the urge to bless or accept the cultural status quo of their time. Even Karl Barth, after all the judgment he has pronounced over this fallen world, has, like Bonhoeffer, discovered great "promise" in the secularity of secularism. Both Barth and Bonhoeffer have created a theological vogue of talking about *Weltlichkeit* (secularity), which among their disciples often amounts to mere world acceptance with no attempt to inform the secular world and its culture with truly Christian meaning. Reinhold Niebuhr, after writing much on "crisis and renewal," has in recent years reached the conclusion that the kind of sober pragmatism according to which the best among the children of this world handle their affairs is, after all, the best way in which to act; Christian faith simply adds a sobriety, through its awareness of human sinfulness, and a dash of mercy. Although none of the neo-orthodox thinkers mentioned here can be accused of disinterestedness in the affairs of this world, their recent positions do not suggest themselves as a basis for a deeper renewal of our cultural life by the reality of Christ.

Tillich alone among the great Protestant thinkers of our time still strongly believes that the Gospel is of such nature and power that it transforms the whole of life. He believes that this Gospel is the power of reconciliation and renewal in this world and for this world in its totality. He alone really dares to spell out the forms and structures not only of crisis but of renewal and the ways in which reconcilation in reality is achieved. He dares to have a vision of what man essentially is, and of what culture essentially is in its God-given structure and purpose. Even if one cannot follow Tillich in some of his detailed conclusions and ontological analyses, one must admire him for the tremendous power of his faith and intellect in resolutely linking the center of our faith to all the realms of God's and man's world. He does so as a theologian who takes seriously the profound consequences of the Christian doctrine of creation and redemption for both our individual and our cultural life.

Bibliography

Paul Tillich, *The Courage to Be*, New Haven, Yale, 1959.

The Theology of Paul Tillich, Charles W. Kegley and Robert W. Bretall, eds., N.Y., Macmillan, 1952.

Notes on Contributors

NOTES ON CONTRIBUTORS

SYDNEY E. AHLSTROM is Professor of American History and Modern Church History at Yale University, where he teaches in the Divinity School, the History Department, and the American Studies Program. He contributed to *The Harvard Divinity School,* edited by George H. Williams, and to *The Shaping of American Religion,* edited by James Ward Smith and A. Leland Jamison.

ROBERT McAFEE BROWN, former Auburn Professor of Systematic Theology at Union Theological Seminary in New York City, is presently Professor of Religion at Stanford University. Among his books: *P. T. Forsyth: Prophet for Today, The Significance of the Church, The Spirit of Protestantism,* and *Observer in Rome.* The last is a report on the second session of Vatican Council II, which Dr. Brown attended as an official observer for the World Alliance of Reformed and Presbyterian Churches.

FRITZ BURI, who teaches at the University of Basel, is the author of *Die Reformation geht weiter, Theologie der Existenz,* and *Dogmatik als Selbstverständnis des christlichen Glaubens.*

GEORGE B. CAIRD, Lecturer and Tutor at Mansfield College, Oxford, is the author of *The Truth of the Gospel, The Apostolic Age,* and *Principalities and Powers.*

JOSEPH FLETCHER, since 1944 Robert Treat Paine Professor of Christian Ethics at Episcopal Theological School, Cambridge, Massachusetts, has written *Church and Industry, Christianity and Property, Morals and Medicine,* and *William Temple: Twentieth Century Christian.*

A. DURWOOD FOSTER is Associate Professor of Christian Theology at the Pacific School of Religion, Berkeley, California.

S. C. GUTHRIE, JR., presently Associate Professor of Theology at Columbia Theological Seminary, Decatur, Georgia, helped translate Oscar Cullmann's *The Christology of the New Testament.*

ROBERT T. HANDY, Professor of Church History at Union Theological Seminary, New York City, is the author of *We Witness Together* and *Members One of Another.*

MARTIN J. HEINECKEN, Professor of Systematic Theology at Lutheran Theological Seminary in Philadelphia since 1945, is the author of *Basic Christian Teachings, The Meaning of the Cross, Beginning and End of the World, God and the Space Age,* and *The Moment Before God: An Interpretation of Kierkegaard.*

HANS HOFMANN, formerly a Professor of Theology at Harvard Divinity School and Director of the Harvard University Project on Religion and Mental Health, is now Executive Director of the Center for the Study of Personality and Culture, Inc. He is author of *The Theology of Reinhold Niebuhr* and author-editor of *Religion and Mental Health* and *Making the Ministry Relevant.*

CLYDE A. HOLBROOK, Danforth Professor of Religion and Chairman of the Department of Religion at Oberlin College, has written *Faith and Community* and *Religion, a Humanistic Field.*

DANIEL JENKINS, presently Chaplain at the University of Sussex, is a Congregational minister. His books include *Beyond Religion, The Strangeness of the Church,* and *Equality and Excellence.*

WALTER LEIBRECHT, who has taught at Harvard Divinity School, Garrett Theological Seminary, and the University of Chicago Divinity School and has headed Chicago's Ecumenical Institute, is presently director of Schiller College, a new residential college for international students in Marburg, Germany. He is the author of *Being a Christian in Today's World* and the editor of *Religion and Culture: Essays in honor of Paul Tillich.*

JOHN MACQUARRIE, former Professor of Systematic Theology at Glasgow University, now holds the same post at Union Theological Seminary, New York City. He is co-translator of Martin Heidegger's *Being and Time* and author of *An Existential Theology, The Scope of Demythologizing,* and *Twentieth-Century Religious Thought.*

BERNARD E. MELAND, Professor of Systematic Theology at the University of Chicago from 1945 to 1964, has written such books as *Seeds of Redemption, The Reawakening of Christian Faith, Higher Education and the Human Spirit, Faith and Culture* and, most recently, *The Realities of Faith.*

CARL MICHALSON, Professor of Systematic Theology at Drew University, is the author of *The Hinge of History: An Existential Approach to the Christian Faith, Faith for Personal Crises, Japanese Contributions to Christian Theology,* and *The Rationality of Faith.*

J. ROBERT NELSON, former Fairchild Professor of Systematic Theology in Oberlin College's Graduate School of Theology, is now Professor of Systematic Theology at the Boston University School of Theology. His most recent book is *Criterion for the Church.*

RICHARD R. NIEBUHR, Lamont Professor of Divinity at Harvard Divinity School, is the author of *Resurrection and Historical Reason: A Study of Theological Method* and *Schleiermacher on Christ and Religion.*

WILHELM PAUCK, Charles A. Briggs Graduate Professor of Church History at Union Theological Seminary, New York City, is the author of *The Heritage of the Reformation* and the editor of Martin Luther's *Lectures on Romans.*

WARREN A. QUANBECK, Professor of Systematic Theology at Luther Theological Seminary in St. Paul, Minnesota, is the editor of *God and Caesar* and one of the four editors of *Christian Faith and the Liberal Arts.*

HERBERT R. REINELT is Assistant Professor of Philosophy at the University of the Pacific in Stockton, California.

THEODORE RUNYON, JR., is Associate Professor of Systematic Theology at Emory University's Candler School of Theology, Atlanta, Georgia. A former student of Friedrich Gogarten at the University of Göttingen, he assisted in the translation of Gogarten's *The Reality of Faith.*

FRANKLIN SHERMAN, Lutheran Tutor at Oxford University, is the author of *The Courage to Care: A Study in Christian Social Responsibility.*

MATTHEW SPINKA, Waldo Professor Emeritus of Church History at the Hartford Seminary Foundation, has written such books as *The Quest for Church Unity, The Church in Soviet Russia, Christian Thought from Erasmus to Berdyaev,* and *Nicholas Berdyaev: Captive of Freedom.*

GUSTAF WINGREN, Professor of Systematic Theology at the University of Lund in Sweden, is the author of *Creation and Law, Man and the Incarnation, The Living Word, Luther on Vocation,* and *Theology in Conflict.*

WILLIAM JOHN WOLF, Howard Chandler Robbins Professor of Theology at the Episcopal Theological School, Cambridge, Massachusetts, is the author of *Man's Knowledge of God, No Cross, No Crown: A Study of the Atonement,* and *The Religion of Abraham Lincoln.*